Crisis of the State

CRISIS OF THE STATE

War and Social Upheaval

Edited by

Bruce Kapferer

and

Bjørn Enge Bertelsen

Berghahn Books
NEW YORK · OXFORD

Published in 2009 by

Berghahn Books

www.berghahnbooks.com

©2009, 2012 Bruce Kapferer and Bjørn Enge Bertelsen
First paperback edition published in 2012

All rights reserved. Except for the quotation of short passages for the purposes of criticism and review, no part of this book may be reproduced in any form or by any means, electronic or mechanical, including photocopying, recording, or any information storage and retrieval system now known or to be invented, without written permission of the publisher.

Library of Congress Cataloging-in-Publication Data

Crisis of the state : war and social upheaval / edited by Bruce Kapferer and Bjørn Enge Bertelsen.
   p. cm.
   Includes bibliographical references and index.
   ISBN 978-1-84545-583-5 (hbk.) -- ISBN 978-0-85745-653-3 (pbk.)
   1. Political violence. 2. State-sponsored terrorism. 3. Civil-military relations. 4. War and society. I. Kapferer, Bruce. II. Bertelsen, Bjørn Enge.

JC328.6.C75 2009
303.6'2--dc22

2008053965

British Library Cataloguing in Publication Data

A catalogue record for this book is available from the British Library

Printed in the United States on acid-free paper

ISBN 978-0-85745-653-3 (paperback)   ISBN 978-0-85745-654-0 (ebook)

Contents

List of Tables and Figures ... vii

Acknowledgements ... viii

Introduction: The Crisis of Power and Reformations of
the State in Globalizing Realities ... 1
Bruce Kapferer and Bjørn Enge Bertelsen

Section I. Transformations of Sovereignty, Empire, State

1. The Military-Industrial Complex and the Crisis of U.S. Capital ... 29
June Nash

2. Post-Soviet Formation of the Russian State and the War
in Chechnya: Exploring the Chaotic Form of Sovereignty ... 53
Jakob Rigi

3. Market Forces, Political Violence, and War: The End of
Nation-States, the Rise of Ethnic and Global Sovereignties? ... 83
Caroline Ifeka

Section II. War Zone

4. Rebel Ravages in Bundibugyo, Uganda's Forgotten District ... 97
Kirsten Alnaes

5. Fear of the Midnight Knock: State Sovereignty and
Internal Enemies in Uganda ... 124
Sverker Finnström

6. The Shepherd's Staff and the AK-47: Pastoralism and
   Handguns in Karamoja, Uganda   143
   Frode Storaas

Section III. Sovereign Logics

7. The Sovereign as Savage: The Pathos of Ethno-Nationalist
   Passion   163
   Christopher Taylor

8. The Paramilitary Function of Transparency: Guatemala
   and Colombia   187
   Staffan Löfving

9. Sorcery and Death Squads: Transformations of State,
   Sovereignty, and Violence in Postcolonial Mozambique   210
   Bjørn Enge Bertelsen

10. Collective Violence and Counter-State Building:
    Algeria 1954-62   241
    Rasmus Alenius Boserup

11. Malignant Organisms: Continuities of State-Run Violence
    in Rural Liberia   265
    Mats Utas

12. Israel's Wall and the Logic of Encystation: Sovereign
    Exception or Wild Sovereignty?   292
    Glenn Bowman

Contributors   305

Index   309

TABLES AND FIGURES

Table 1. Amount Spent on U.S. Private Security Contracts   42

Table 2. Typology of Forms of Violence   257

Figure 1. Tutsi ingratitude.   173

Figure 2. The assassination of Ndadaye.   178

Figure 3. "The politics of the cattle thieves causes problems" cartoon from *Umurangi,* no. 14, 10 December 1992.   180

Figure 4. Palestinian graffiti.   293

Acknowledgements

This volume is the fruit of the first seminar in the Vital Matters seminar series held at the University of Bergen from 2004 onwards. The format of the Vital Matters series was inclusive and it gathered scholars from various backgrounds and disciplines and provided a forum for scholarly debate relating to a wide variety of human problems addressed by the physical and biological sciences, social sciences and humanities. A grant from The Bergen University Foundation was instrumental in funding the Vital Matters seminar series and equally important was Ove Stoknes at what is now UNIFOB Global in administratively supporting the project. We are grateful for both the funding received, and we extend our thanks to Stoknes for his efforts and enthusiasm regarding Vital Matters. The Department of Social Anthropology through both its academic and administrative staff has also supported the project greatly and contributed to its success. At Berghahn Books, the support, the insights and the enthusiasm for the project by Marion Berghahn is greatly appreciated as is the able way in which Ann Przyzycki and Melissa Spinelli at the New York office have patiently steered us through the different phases of production. The editors' thanks are extended to all of the above.

Introduction

THE CRISIS OF POWER AND REFORMATIONS OF THE STATE IN GLOBALIZING REALITIES

Bruce Kapferer and Bjørn Enge Bertelsen

The essays in this volume explore situations of civil strife, violent resistance and war in the circumstances of shifts in the organization of state power and the emergence of new forms of sovereignty. The specific empirical contexts analyzed are those in which the agents and organs of state power are effectively at war with the populations over whom they claim control. In these situations the character of particular state orders, the nature of sovereignty and the manner of their legitimacy are thrown into relief. These are major concerns of the arguments presented here which are alive to the fact that the state, real or imagined, is neither monolithic nor universal in form but has taken shape in often very different historical circumstances. The authors in the main concentrate on civil strife and war at the colonial or postcolonial peripheries of dominant state-metropolitan centers. However, the extent to which the state circumstances of these contexts are linked with larger metropolitan-centered processes is of major concern in this volume. As the contributions argue, war and civil violence within specific states has much to do with the dynamics of such linkages. That is, many of the dimensions of intra-state conflict and war are not a function of particular state orders alone but of the larger arenas of political and economic action in which they are set often involving relations of contest with other states and/or consequences not apparently related to particular state practice. Thus, Max Gluckman 1963 [1956] dem-

---

Notes for this section are located on page 21.

onstrated that the internal violence of the Zulu state associated with the rise of Shaka Zulu was connected with European colonial expansion into southern Africa which at that time was not part of the consciousness of the Zulu. Eric Wolf, in *Europe and the People Without History* (1982), makes the point strongly demonstrating how events taking place apparently well-beyond the horizons of particular states are vital in the often highly destructive processes that took place within them. It is well-known that the rise of Fascist states in various parts of the world in the last century was precipitated by the crisis of global capital in the Great Depression. Contemporary civil disturbance within and between states (as well as the violent effects of state regulatory practice e.g. in relation to immigration) is undoubtedly connected to processes just as much external to state order as those internal to it. Thus, the political and economic flows within the complex transnational assemblages of ethnicity, of business and industry, of crime and so on that are discussed through concepts such as globalization are forces that can not only escape state control but exacerbate violent state repression. However, these obvious points should not overlook other cultural and social forces that are constitutive of state processes (e.g., the various institutions of state nationalism), as well as those relatively independent of state practice that are part of the terrain of the state. These relate to the crisis of power that is integral to all kinds of state formation—potentially also, inherent to their destructive dynamic.

In the analyses presented here, the state is *not* the abstract phenomenon of political philosophy but is rather embedded in lived realities both as part of the cultural imaginaries of populations and as a presence implicated, if not always explicitly, in the formation of ongoing social realities. How this is so and the way the agents, agencies and institutions of state power engage with the specific local forces whom they seek to control or with whom they may vie, is the chief concern of the discussions.

The central aim of these introductory remarks is to explore some of the dynamics or processes of modern states that are implicated in the production of violence and war. We concentrate specifically on those kinds of violence and war that are organic or systematic with particular kinds of state dynamic or ordering. Our argument is not that the state essentially or necessarily is the cause of war and violence (and there are many excellent approaches that assert this) but that the kinds of violence and war that takes place in its environment gathers a particular dimension at least partly through the socio-political and ideological dynamics and organization of state power. To put it another way, the very methods and procedures whereby states achieve and legitimate the domains of their control and power are integral to the kind of violence the particular state formations are likely to perpetrate.

In our usage, the state is a political order or politics machine that is distinguished by a *totalizing* dynamic whereby it (its agents, agencies and institutions) creates or shapes relations and processes to the terms of its dynamic in the sociocultural fields into which state orders intrude and/or from which they emerge.[1] We broadly regard the dynamics of the state to be one that is oriented to achieving an exclusive and overarching determining potency in the fields of social relations in which it is situated and which state or state-related practice attempts to define. State agents and agencies achieve this through a diversity of procedures among them being the incorporation and regulation or else the exclusion, marginalization, or suppression of communities, organizations or other forms of sociopolitical orders (including competing state entities) that may be present in their environment. Some of the typical political techniques of the state, its agents, and agencies, in achieving these effects are *territorialization* (not just geographical but the bounding and controlling of regions or spaces of interest), including the *coding* or *definition and differentiation* of socioeconomic life (usually of a bureaucratic kind), and control of *subjectivities*, as well as their production, relative to the hegemonic interest of those in command of state agencies.[2]

We follow Gilles Deleuze and Félix Guattari (2002 [1980]; 2004 [1972]) who suggest that such dynamics are intrinsic to all social and political formations regardless of whether an actual state order exists or not. They conceive this state dynamic to be counteracted by that of the "war machine"—each dynamic being bound to and implicit in the other, the kind of violence that may be expressed being thrown up in the specificities of their folding of relation. Altogether different in principle, the war machine dynamic is *rhizomic* in practice and open-ended, a relational and structuring process that spreads out laterally in all directions. Both dynamics are apparent in most social processes, although they will manifest in particular ways relative to the manifold historical, cultural and other contingencies of context or situation. These kinds of dynamic draw their distinction through contrast. Thus, the state dynamic is hierarchical (an apical treelike process), vertical, and bounding (territorializing), whereas the war machine is thoroughly ahierarchical (radiating across a number of nodal points, often unconnected). It is acentered and relatively unsystemic or counter systemic. The relations and structuring of the war machine create and generate the flow of their socially forming energy along spreading networks, blurring or overrunning bounded, territorialized, or categorical entities. The war machine is a deterritorializing dynamic when brought into relation with state, tree-like processes.[3]

In the Deleuze and Guattari approach, these dynamics perduringly coexist and are intertwined.[4] They are so not in a dialectical sense of either a Hegelian or Marxian kind, perspectives that Deleuze and Guattari seek to avoid. Thus, the two dynamics are irreducible to each other. Neither are they dissolvable or capable of being synthesized into a third term that is either their singular base or ultimate resolution. One of their central arguments is that these processes are potentially mutually annihilating and in their full emergence in the context of each other, realize thoroughgoing destruction. This clash is of the nature of the cancelling out effected through the coming together of two positive forces (see Kapferer 1997b for an empirical example of insurrection in Sri Lanka).

What Deleuze and Guattari conceptualize as "state" and "war machine" dynamics we regard as comprising key aspects of the structuring logics involved in contemporary empirical contexts of globalizing and state processes. The dynamics, of course, assume particular accent and significance in the cultural and social constructions and situational contingencies that comprise the flux of history, and it is our concern here to outline dimensions of the logics of state and war machine as these may be contemporarily apparent.

Before proceeding, it is crucial to stress that modern states and processes that are apparently antagonistic or subversive of them do not fall neatly into the dynamic categories of state and war machine. Both the political and economic orders of actual states and the processes that are contestant or resistant of these states usually comprise a mix of such dynamics, often in tension but frequently in complementary coordination. Actual states may give greater prominence to the dynamics of the war machine (and not just in military enterprise or in processes of conquest) at particular moments of (re)formation or at particular sites of their extension. Examples from the past might be Ottoman Turkey or China pursuant on the Mongol invasions. Contemporary states in processes of reformation in relation to dominant corporate interest—what we will refer to as *corporate states*—and especially in the context of what are discussed as neoliberal or neoconservative policies, express major aspects of the war machine.

Overall our approach is not one that asserts that the phenomenon of the state is either at the root of violence and war or is necessary for the production of peace. Neither is our argument directed to ascertaining some kind of idealistic hierarchy of sociopolitical forms defined in terms of their propensity to inflict the suffering and devastations of violence and war. Undoubtedly, in our opinion, dictatorships are likely to engender more harm than democracies though this is by no means certain. Democratic populisms are vulnerable to sliding into autocracies—as de Tocqueville (1969 [1840]) has extensively argued with respect to North America. The totalitarianism of socialist and populist states in Europe in the last century achieved the peak so far of human devastation. The colonial states and the violence with which they subdued the majority of their subjects are also stark examples of this human destructive potential. Athenian democracy wrought extreme destructions upon the states and societies in its environment, a factor which Thucydides observed at the time. Machiavelli (1970 [1531]) addresses the failure of democratic systems in the ancient Mediterranean world with reference to his contemporary Renaissance realities setting out principles against their subversion either by populist or oligarchic interests. Marshall Sahlins (2004), in a recent analysis of the forces leading to the defeat of the Athenian democracy in the Peloponnesian wars, offers an ironic commentary on the current democracy-inspired adventure of the United States and Britain in Iraq. John Gray (2007) most recently has attacked utopian idealisms of human liberation and peace mainly of the doctrinal sort as in themselves covering or leading to annihilating consequences, a view also expressed by Theodor Adorno (1973) regarding idealisms in general, although in our opinion Russell Jacoby (1999) offers some important modification. It is not idealism per se that should be challenged (as Jacoby stresses Nazism is not an idealism in his terms) but the social and political processes that may throw up certain kinds of idealistic discourse that may then set the conditions for human destruction. This was so, as Karl Polanyi (1957) argues for the Europe of the last century, where ideologies of peace seemed to be connected to processes of financial deregulation that laid the ground for the human annihilations of Fascism. Karl Polanyi deserves reconsideration in the current global climate of financial crisis and the proliferation of what Alain Joxe (2002) describes as "dirty little wars." In our perspective and as also reflected in the works cited above, what is conceived as the state has innumerable potentialities, their realization for the benefit or destruction of human populations being empirically contingent.

The Crisis of the State and Aporia of Power

The state, as any social or political assemblage, is in a continual process of formation. This is so simply because the state, its structures and practices, is a social fact created in social processes and constantly subject to them. Forces within the domains of state sovereignty as well as external to them demand that state orders, in the disparate contexts of their practice, must constantly be adjusting to shifting circumstances, events and situations. That the state is in constant formation is exacerbated by what, by and large, defines it: that is, an assemblage given to power and intrinsically oriented to its monopolization and/or regulation.[5] Such monopolization is distilled in the idea of the state's capacity to command the greatest violence—the principal condition of state sovereignty, as Thomas Hobbes made clear (1991 [1651]). Power, no less a social fact than the state and continually created in social processes and always in excess of that which the state can command or control, is potentially challenging of state monopoly and potentially resistant or subversive of state containment, control or regulation.[6] This is at the foundation of the enduring crisis of modern states, specifically the contemporary and still dominant nation-state form. The crisis is of an enduring and specifically aporetic, irresolute nature because the social forces (in which alternative sources of power and assertions of interests arise) can never be totally commanded.

The state as a focus of constant crisis, virtually the specter or imaginary of crisis, even where the state is non-existent, is evident across time and space (see Pierre Clastres 1998 [1974]). This is unavoidable in so far as it is the crucible of power in all its disguises (see John Gledhill 2000 [1994]). But the crisis of the state achieves a particular intensity in modernity and especially in revolutionary and post-revolutionary Europe and the Americas. Therein emerged an intense questioning of the legitimacy of sovereign power and a heightened consciousness of the connection of state orders with the production of human misery and oppression, often on a massive scale. Current debates about the state (and political orders generally) echo many ancient debates but achieve new significance in modern processes of secularism fueled in the energies of religious reformation, the Enlightenment argument, the development of scientific rationalism, and industrialization and urbanization.

What may be typified as the modern state emerged from the challenges to the various formations of the state especially in Europe but also in the United States. In the reconfiguration of state orders that ensued, the state was effectively recentered as thoroughly an assemblage oriented to the production of society.

Thus, the modernist state in Europe and in America was oriented to the production of society as the *society of the state*. This was evident in ideological representations of the state such as those that declared the order of society as being dependent on the power of the state. Hobbes's *Leviathan* (1991 [1651]) ideally depicts the state as the condition for the existence of a harmonious society whereby the state orders the conflicting and fractious elements of society that are otherwise essential to it. Written at the time of the English Revolution, and still a major reference in discussions concerning the architecture of the state, *Leviathan* expresses what most modern states claim to be their central function as both ordering and protective of the social.[7] The nation-state, still the globally dominant form, marked common identity or the creation of a person/individual similarly oriented to the production of a common community—even despite surface differences—as the cohering principle of its society of the state.

Foucault's work, devoted to comprehending the modern state, demonstrates how much of its institutional practice had the effect of habituating the state in the person and routine social practices.[8] In effect, Foucault's argument might be seen as also theorizing how the interests of ruling groups largely in control of state apparatuses are met through processes not immediately associated with state power.[9] The general point is that in modernity the state became not merely a transcendent entity but one submerged in the ordinary activities of everyday life which reproduced the order of the state. We stress two points.

First, the modern state, its agents, and its institutions, became consciously oriented to the creation or production of the very society in which its sovereignty was defined and, furthermore, engaged the citizenry to this task in a variety of discursive practices. Power and control became an effect of social production in line with state interest. This is so as much for democracies as for dictatorships. In other words, the activity of the agents and agencies of the state in social production and the creation of its moral order, and in varying degrees the involvement of the citizenry, can be seen as a major strategy for addressing forces that may challenge or resist the state.

Second, and arising from the first, the violent power that is at the heart of the authority of the state was distributed through a variety of state and non-state disciplinary practices involving education, the family, and work among others. Not only are such practices supported by the ultimately violent power of the state but also these reinforced the overall authority of the state, further facilitating the state as the central force in the production of the social and of society. The very notion of the social contract between state and society, so vital to legitimating state power, is further grounded in such processes and itself is a major ideological instrument for the production of the society of the state whereby the crisis of power at the heart of the state may be averted.

It should be noted that while the physical violent power at the center of the state is covered or suppressed in other, less violent practice, it is an ever-present capacity underpinning state order and far from being a practice of last resort. What Pierre Bourdieu calls *symbolic violence* (1992 [1977]:190–197) operates in the context of the violent power of the state which yields to a great variety of acts potency that does not inhere in the acts or assertions as such or in themselves, as performatives (Austin 1962 [1955]), but in the backing in the order and organization of agencies and institutions in which the violence of the state is latent. Giorgio Agamben recently has argued for the centrality of the *state of exception* in analyzing the nature and practice of state power, the state of exception marking "... a threshold at which logic and praxis blur with each other and pure violence without *logos* claims to realize an enunciation without any real reference" (2005:40). In so far as many modern states do constitute states of exception, as in the current *War against Terror,* the violence, both symbolic and other, that guarantees them is more overtly on display as are the Others more directly identified and targeted (see also Burke 2007).

Modern nation-states have commanded and directed social production through bureaucratic institutions and related practices of cultural (re)invention. The modern state largely took its current form through the development of a rational bureaucratic system. Its logic—what Don Handelman describes as a bureaucratic logic (2004)—involves a process of coding or recoding populations largely according to the way personal attributes fit with predetermined categories relevant to the bureaucratically defined problem at hand. In this process, for example, dimensions of the person that are constituted in the fluidity of social action and often are situationally relative become assigned to the more fixed categories of a bureaucratic order (see Kapferer 1997a [1988]). The nature of their everyday social production is interrupted or subverted in state-authorized bureaucratic processes. In the recoding of the state dynamic, abstracted bureaucratic categories may then be regrounded through a variety of institutional practices (educational, medical, varieties of planning, etc.) often assuming a factuality that they did not previously have. In other words, state-bureaucratic processes are engaged in redrawing social realities in such a way that they may generate a relatively original habitus, or what we have referred to as the society of the state.

The authoritarian, oppressive, rigid and dehumanizing—indeed violent potentialities—of state bureaucratic practices have been widely discussed (see, e.g., Bauman 1989; Scott 1998). The Holocaust, the Stalinist pogroms, or the Pol Pot massacres demonstrate the extremes of human annihilation that state-bureaucratic machineries have facilitated. But we stress that modern state-bureaucratic processes, as a particular exemplar of a state dynamic, have impetus in creating the conditions for human destruction. A factor, of course, as Hannah Arendt (2004; 2006) and others have stressed, is the abstract, rule-governed rationalism of bureaucratic processes that can appear to have an energy of their own, often anti-humanitarian within which human agents can avoid responsibility for their action. However, we focus upon the logic of inclusion/exclusion of bureaucratic processes and their fixing of relatively unambiguous boundaries in order to produce a legible, ordered, and striated space. Added to this is the tendency of bureaucratic processes to classify into discrete categories that can assume a purity of type such that they become not merely categories but rather indicators for action oblivious to situated complexities. Moreover, bureaucratically established types have ideal or stereotypical properties that, supported by the power of the state, have constitutive potency. The social terrain so mapped can force *the ideal as the real*, creating social communities of the category effectively and systematically recoding the complexity of processes engaged in social (and identity) formation. This forcing of the ideal as real can generate a resistance that itself frequently engages the same categorical logic of the imposed bureaucratic dynamics. Broadly, the kind of bureaucratic dynamic outlined not only operates a symbolic violence, a violence of the category, but can be a critical factor in the generation of actual physical destruction, even imparting a particular shape to the violence.

Much ethnic violence and racism in contemporary nation-states provides support for this argument. British colonial bureaucratic coding of India laid some of the groundwork for the shape of the communalism that burst out so destructively at the time of Partition. Undoubtedly, political and religious passions drove the violence, but these were distilled in bureaucratic categories instituted by the power of the colonial state exacerbated by hastily drawn-up and bureaucratically decided territorial assignments. The bureaucratic categories of the current Indian state concerning backward and scheduled castes and tribes involving various entitlements, is a filter for current violence both in resistance and reaction relating to Dalit and Adivasi movements. In regard to these, one among many paradoxes is that bureaucratically realized categories permit the recognition of disadvantage and inequality but simultaneously create new categories for their identification (usually giving them new essential significance) and regrounding them in the modernist stratified hierarchies of the state, which creates new circumstances for the continuation of disadvantage and prejudice.

The ethnic civil war in Sri Lanka owes some of its direction to the bureaucratic coding of the colonial period and its postcolonial extensions. British rule was facilitated through the bureaucratic designation of distinct cultural communities and social-political regions that were, in varying ways, given degrees of autonomy within the colonial state. The colonial process was one that sought control by capturing within the colonial order a variety of cultural/historical processes and subduing them to the hegemonic interests of the colonial state. In so doing the colonial authorities accentuated earlier divisions, giving them new significance in the colonial order and effectively politicizing dimensions that previously did not have this import. Religion was politicized both in its capacity to organize resistance to colonial power and also as a consequence of the rationalist orientation of the colonial order.[10] The colonial society of the state also intentionally suppressed class forces (which were resistant of the colonial order) (Guha 1982). These became part of the potency of an increasingly violent communalism, which also engaged the passions of religious ideas and practice (see Kapferer 1997a [1988]). In the postcolonial years, the bureaucratic logic of the state dynamic was further engaged to the construction, this time, of the independent society of the state. The communalist direction already implicated in the colonial state was pursued further and in a nationalist interest to assert Sinhala hegemony over Tamils. Much of this was and is oriented to the reproduction of the class power of communally-supported elites and has gathered increased force in the reactivation of the government war, after a brief interlude of relative peace. The state dynamic, strongly bureaucratic, has effectively been instrumental in the creation of a society of the state in which Tamils are by and large excluded, unless they accept, in effect, an inferior position in realities subordinated to Sinhala hegemony.

Numerous other examples can be given of the role of bureaucratic processes in modern nation-states in establishing the ground upon which war and other forms of human suffering build. Gérard Prunier (1995) has demonstrated how the comparatively recent ethnic extermination in Rwanda took its direction through a colonial bureaucratic fixing and hierarchializing of ethnic difference (see also Taylor's contribution in this volume). The case of apartheid in South Africa is well known.

Bureaucratic processes that assume particular force in the socially formational and regulative dynamics of modern states—and that, indeed, may inhabit the conventional thought processes of citizenry (a thinking as much as a "seeing" like a state)—can give form to state violence. In Sri Lanka, government forces concerned to root out insurgents against the government used the logic of bureaucratic categories or social indicators (e.g., age, caste, village) to identify potential threats. This magnified the extent of the human destruction and defined the nature of state terror. The bodies of victims were often thrown to the margins of human habitation, an action that simultaneously symbolized their exclusion from the social order commanded by the state (and indicating their threat to it) as well as indicative of the reterritorializing discourse of state violence (see Kapferer 1997b). Variations on this Sri Lanka example are common worldwide.

While the efforts of modernist states and especially nation-states can be conceived of as oriented to overcoming the crisis of power by constituting the social order upon which their power is founded, this is an impossibility. The aporia of this in itself is provocative of violence, as varieties of totalitarian dictatorship demonstrate. No amount of bureaucratic overcoding or recoding, for example, of social identities and relations into the order of the state, engagement of institutional agencies (e.g., educational, religious, penal) for the capture, production, or confinement of citizens, can yield those who control the state the capacity to encompass totally forces of social formation or to completely submit the social to the political. The dynamics of social formation are such as always to escape controlling institutions of state power and to be capable of establishing potentially rival centers. Modernist states, as other state formations throughout history, are always vulnerable to such internal crisis. This is so as a consequence of their own structuring dynamics as also other dynamics that are already internal to them, most especially the dynamic that Deleuze and Guattari describe as that of the war machine (2002 [1980]). In their understanding this is ultimately antithetical to state processes, even though this might be captured into the impetus of state forces.

The rhizomic nomadic force of the war machine often complements the destructive potency of modern states, which engage it to their own deterritorializing and reterritorializing interests. Forces that arrange themselves against modern states repeatedly take a rhizomic form, deliberately refusing the spatializing, territorially containing aspects of state dynamics. Paramilitary organizations often promoted by states to counteract resistant movements regularly assume rhizomic tactics mirroring those of the organizations they oppose (see also Löfving this volume). Beyond the extreme destruction wrought on the heavily populated areas of Gaza by the use of conventional military techniques and weaponry—a violence unfolding as this introduction is written in early 2009—the Israeli army operating in Gaza has in fact also engaged Deleuze and Guattari virtually as a training manual for the IDF (see Weizman 2007). The IDF adaptation of the rhizomic dynamic of the war machine involves military units smashing through walls of houses, suddenly breaking into living areas, and then breaking through walls again into adjacent living spaces of neighboring families. Given the housing arrangements in which the dwellings of lineage members are closely abutting, the Israeli military units in their movements parallel the rhizomic patterns of Palestinian kinship. Effectively a state terror courses along the lines of relatedness invading the very social dynamics of everyday support and security of Palestinians, which is likely too to be the basis of Palestinian resistance. In Israeli use, the state terror of the military—already organized in terms of a bureaucratic logic—amplifies its own deterritorializing potential when used against Palestinians by combining it with the deterritorializing potency of the rhizome (on the rhizomatic nature of the war machine, see also Bertelsen's contribution this volume). We note that this may be even more destructive than the conventional Israeli method of simply bulldozing and clearing away space, a tactic relevant to a state dynamic. This is so, for in the Israeli instance the use of the war machine strategy attacks the very process of Palestinian social and political formation, the dynamics of relatedness themselves. As Bowman demonstrates (this volume), such radical rhizomic deterritorialization is combined in the building of the wall sealing off Palestinian settlements with a reterritorrialization and intensification of Israel's bureaucratic coding processes.

As the foregoing exemplifies, state and war machine dynamics can coexist and generally do so in state systems. The rhizomic dimensions of kinship, of lineage, can bolster elite control operating independently of bureaucratic or state dynamics; indeed, they can be the force for capturing state power as is clear in so many contemporary and historical contexts, and be vital in directing the violent force of the state. But these can also undermine the authority of those in control of state apparatuses, especially in modernist contexts of bureaucratic rationality where rhetorics of corruption (which we note is thoroughly a state discourse) render such states vulnerable.

The political economy of many past and above all contemporary states is rhizomic, especially where trade assumes predominance over production. This is all the more so where production itself is decentered, as in the cyber-mediated forms of industrial production dislocated from state-regulated territories, or, as Hardt and Negri, building on Deleuze and Guattari, put it: "The transcendence of modern sovereignty thus conflicts with the immanence of capital" (2000:327). The nesting of rhizomic processes within state processes and their frequent synchrony masks the potential of a mutual negativity, indeed a destructive conjunction, that is the enduring crisis of the state.

Globalization and the Intensification of the Aporia of the State

What is generally glossed as globalization, both past and present, has distinct rhizomic war machine properties. As widely discussed, it is marked both in its social formations and political and economic dimensions by a breaking down or transgression of the territorial and regulative limitations of nation-states.[11] It has intensified the crisis of power at the center of nation-states. Their capacity to control the circumstances of the reproduction of their power has been considerably reduced. A major factor was the expansion of fiscal processes well beyond the control of individual states. This has undermined the bureaucratic orders of many states that have depended on state fiscal controls. Furthermore, the development of cyberspace is an important factor in not only loosening the regulative capacities of nation-states but also in breaking the preeminent position of many states in controlling the reproduction of social value and the institutional orders in which such value could be established.

Social communities (as well as communities of more narrow interest) can be created through cyberspace or given more intensified connectivity. This is especially so in the case of diasporized communities that often are largely produced through colonial or imperial-motivated political and economic conditions rooted in previous centuries, impelled by contemporary often violent forces fueling the exodus of refugees, and motivated in continuing demands for labor, now frequently of a high-skilled kind. Through cyberspace, such communities are enabled to generate not only an expanded and perhaps more intense sense of identity consciousness but also to realize bonds that transcend national boundaries. These can become an important source of support and pressure against national governments for overcoming political and social disadvantages. For example, diverse indigenous "tribal" minorities have been able to forge transnational links to some advantage of their particular causes. Currently, the Indian Dalit movement has benefited through the extension of its support through cyberspace.

What is described as the development of global cyber or virtual communities are implicated in the maintenance of intranational state and anti-nation-state violence and war. In Sri Lanka, the nationalist ethnic Sinhala/Tamil war has drawn much of its energy from diasporized members of the ethnic categories. Much of this diasporization has its roots in the imperialism of the past to which current forces of globalization have given added impetus.[12] This does not rule out the diasporizing effects, especially for Tamils, of the war itself. Cyberspace is a new factor in uniting widely distributed members of the ethnic categories living outside Sri Lanka territory in ideological and material support of the war. In a sense, the dynamics of the war is conditioned by this and other extra-state territorial factors. A major effect of the United States' *War against Terror* related to the way state processes were able to intervene against the rhizomic dimensions of Tamil state resistance facilitated by larger global forces. The Tamil rhizome was effectively counteracted by a variety of state processes (themselves assuming certain rhizomic capacity) that are achieving success against Tamil resistance.

Rhizomic dynamics are not limited only to the creation of new cyber realms of community and diaspora transcending physical space—or to the virtual extensions of such in cyberspace. Several recent conflicts evidence a cyberspace war fought alongside the physical battlefield in which hackers and other so-called *cyberwarriors* are involved. A case in point is the second Intifada in 2000, where pro-Israeli hackers shut down Hezbollah's website while pro-Palestinian hackers took down both the main Israeli government website as well as that of the Israeli Foreign Ministry. All in all over one hundred websites were manipulated or else shut down (Denning 2001).[13] In mimicking the physical non-cyberspace battlefield, the virtual attacks and battles within cyberspace are seemingly propelled by the rhizomic logic of a destabilizing war machine. As such, it seems to represent a formation of non-territorial communities and a corresponding non-territorial form of warfare. However, by aligning itself with, or being aligned by or being directed from nascent or actual state formations, the transcending (and, some would still argue, emancipatory potential) of much of the type of cyberwarfare seems to be only partly rhizomic. Moreover, the massive employment of digital warfare or information warfare (Mandel 2007), the alignment of the bloggosphere with formal political entities (Williams, et al. 2005), and the increasing presence and control of cyberspace according to state and corporate interests (see, e.g., Google's deal with China to censor the software and application of its search engines [Healy 2007] or the government of Burma's 2007 shutdown of internet access in a time of crisis to quell opposition [BBC News 2007]) suggest that, in a Deleuze and Guattarian sense, the encroaching state presence also must be seen as one striating the smooth cyberspace—also in the context of cyberwars and political conflict.[14] In other words, in contemporary processes rhizomic and state dynamics are being brought into greater complementarity.

As we have already indicated, the current *War against Terror* and the heightening of state security concerns, arising from conceptions concerning the dangers of globalization from the perspective of state orders, indicate the development of new forms of violence and war (Kapferer 2004b, also Nash's analysis of the United States' military-industrial complex in this volume). However, the direction of the argument that we present here is that the forces of globalization are enmeshed with and integral to reconfigurations of contemporary state orders.

In regions where particular nation-states are already in a dependent relation to global political and economic powers, usually as part of the postcolonial condition, global forces have weakened their autonomy further and exacerbated preexisting tensions toward internal fracture. In some situations, this drives tendencies toward dictatorial and totalitarian rule in efforts to overcome the crisis of power that the fracture causes nation-states. This is impelled further by a mythos concerning their independence and totalizing autonomy. Such is vitally embedded in nationalism, which in postcolonial contexts is linked to continuing imperial global hegemonies.

The Corporatization of States and Globalization

But globalizing forces such as we have described have influenced diverse shifts in state orders from that of the nation-state to that of a more corporate state or oligarchic kind (see Kapferer 2005). It is far too glib to speak of this as a shift of states from a political-economic to an economic-political form. But this draws attention to processes that indicate that state orders are being reconfigured after the ideals of contemporary business and industrial corporations. Thus, there is a move away from the impersonal rationalist, equalizing, bureaucratic schemes that dominated ruling governing institutions of nation-states to managerial, person-centered, even autocratic and hierarchical orders, that espouse ideologies of flexibility, individual-responsible or accountable decision-making, and transparency. This transformation of the whole field of bureaucratic ordering within the neoliberal framework—as in the ideology of New Public Management (Strathern 2000)—has often profoundly altered the dynamics, scope and logic of territorial nation-states. Moreover, through neoliberal policies corporate organizations are given more explicit governing functions (see also Kapferer 2005; Strange 2004).

The major change that we underline in the discussion of *the corporate state form* is an abandonment of the social project of the nation-state—that is, the concern to meet the crisis of power at the center of the state by commanding the institutions for the reproduction of the social. At this point, we must stress that our use of the term *corporate* (or *oligarchic*) state does not indicate that it is necessarily the next stage in state formation—a formation that we regard as inherently multidirectional and nonlinear. We also insist that in our usage of the term *corporate* we do not adopt what might be conceived as an economistic argument (hence our avoidance of a possible concept such as "market state"). Our orientation is explicitly social, and the usage of corporate is to indicate a particular imaginary and style of social ordering and structuring.[15]

What we describe as a corporate state form is already well established in the United States, which in many ways has become a model for the corporate state globally, wherein the state by and large retreats from the social project, which is presented as a voluntary space: the ideologically laden domain of freedom. The formation of the social in this domain has largely been dominated by corporate or corporate-style forces. We note that these are not business or industrial forces alone but include powerful nongovernmental groups, often of a major charitable kind (but which are cross-linked into business and industrial interests), as well as ethnic and religious communities (which adopt corporate styles of action) (Comaroff and Comaroff 2009). These various groups are frequently in contest over social value but patterns of conformity nonetheless develop mediated by what might be regarded as market forces, in which state machineries continue to play a regulative hand (machineries within which corporate interests are inevitably bound).

Perhaps a clear example of what we call the corporate (or corporatizing) state, and its effects, is the current global financial crisis which can be described as a further transmutation of the state into a corporate form. The pattern of extraordinary financial bailouts in the United States, England and in the European Community, is not only an instance of the state operating primarily in oligarchic fashion (a feature of state action throughout history) but also a further development of the corporate formation of the contemporary or post-modern state. The financial bailouts of 2008 and 2009 have in England and also the United Stated been presented ideologically as an attempt to restore state regulation as if the state is still largely an independent apparatus. This masks the fact that the state has become a subordinate functionary of corporate economic power, the enormous financial bailouts using taxpayers' money being the illustration. In this process, there is conspicuously little Hobbesian mediation between corporate interests and those of the general population, for example. The Social Contract has largely been abandoned by state agents having little choice other than bow to corporate demand and further realize the state as a corporate order in the effort to sustain oligarchic interests that otherwise threaten social chaos. In other words, the state is held ransom to an ideology of its own legitimation as the ultimate institution of the social good which is now grasped as the corporate good.

Further, advertising and patterns of consumption in corporate states or rapidly corporatizing states become vital hegemonizing instruments no less than those adopted by nation-states. Social and political rhetoric and discursive practice is being increasingly reframed in the social and motivating terms of business and corporate logic. Human beings are reconstituted as consumers/stakeholders in dominant discourses that also provide and distribute often highly commodified pragmatic solutions tailored to individual rather than social needs and political emancipatory and encompassing social programs involving the restructuring of social orders. If these advertising and consumption patterns continue they assume a highly moral form that is both universalist in nature and markedly lacking in specific content. Perhaps paradoxically, they are anti-differentiating by building on a singular and relatively uncomplicated view of the human being. One aspect of this is a playing on erstwhile class and status distinctions involving a commodified expansion of their symbolic dimensions often visible in service and consumer-oriented categories. For example, Virgin Atlantic advertises its first class air travel as Upper Class!

Through such commodification, populations vicariously participate in the symbolic worlds (virtual realities) of the class, status, and power orders that dominate them. In this, class forces are in a way domesticated, made friendly, as it were, and their political potential to threaten state orders is reduced. Through a symbolic participation in the play of class and status, people enter into effectively illusory worlds in which they are members although actually excluded. The contemporary cultures of celebrity would appear to work this way. In a sense class and status are virtualized, dislocated from specific contexts of interest and trans-socialized or transnationalized and globalized. A consciousness of class and its connection to the oppressive dynamics of those who control power is reduced, and the polarities threatening to the machineries of power are denied or otherwise rendered irrelevant. The corporatizing process is directed at the defusing or obfuscation of the significance of class forces.

Of course in contemporary contexts nation-state orders often operate in concert with corporatizing processes. There are widespread efforts to get the public to participate in corporate-like practice, indeed to mimetically participate in what seems to be identical action—playing the market, investing pensions and becoming "stakeholders." Indeed, conversely the rhetorics of individual liberation from the oppressive shackles of the nation-state are often employed in this process.

In countries where poverty is of considerable issue (and always potentially subversive of ruling groups and state power) there are antipoverty programs that, quite aside from their potential benefits, constitute a new kind of disciplining—a regimen of support for the corporatizing state. An example is micro-credit. Targeting particularly women—who in certain regions as Southern Africa are disadvantaged by the long-term migration of men to regional centers, cities, and overseas in search of work (see Wolpe 1972)—common practices involve the "schooling" of participants in activities of investment, the taking of loans, and the calculation of interest. There is the production of an illusion both in rich and also in impoverished countries of participation in practices that, as a cruel paradox, are involved in the reproduction of disadvantage (see Lazar 2004).

The corporate or corporatizing state is—as Rigi (in this volume) notes for Central Asia and Russia (especially when moving out of erstwhile extreme forms of state control)—renders vulnerable that notion of the state as founded in the monopolization of violence. Such monopolization of violence—underpinning state claims to sovereignty and being ideologically integral to the authority of nation-states—is threatened in processes of corporatization. This is all the more so in global discourses concerning human rights which, quite aside from their ethical significance, function to temper the abuse by states of sovereign power and also, if not intentionally, to subvert it and open states further to corporatization by privileging individual civic and political rights (e.g. the current rhetoric of citizenship) rather than basic economic and social rights (see also Englund 2006 for an exploration of a Malawian case). What we stress is that the formation of corporate states and the dynamics of corporatization expand forms of violence already apparent in nation-states. The corporatization of states can further extend oppressive potentials sometimes paradoxically in a discourse that claims to overcome it.

In this volume, Rigi uses the term *chaotic form of sovereignty* to describe the situation in Russia and Central Asia where corporatization opens up a political arena given over to intense contest over sovereignty. A situation of what Kapferer has called "wild sovereignty" (Kapferer 2004a) can develop in which the extreme annihilating violence that rests as the ultimate sanction behind most forms of state or statelike political sovereign power comes into the open in the rivalry over sovereign claims that may develop.

Civil war is both an increased potential of corporate or corporatizing states and changes its pattern. No longer vertical in structure (aimed at the control of the institutions of the state as being at the apex of a hierarchical order), civil war becomes intensely horizontal—concerned with the delineation of autonomous domains and endemically standing against the formation of hierarchies of power that appropriate all sovereignty.

A major feature of the formation of corporate states, as we have already indicated, is a break with (or at least a modification of) the Hobbesian or Rousseauian notion of the state as bound by a social contract with its population. That is, in the corporate state there is a shift away from the state as being in a mediating society-producing relation to its population (which assumes increasingly its policing of its own moral orders) to a focus on controlling, surveillance, and security functions. Iraq is a clear instance of such a shift wherein the corporate takeover of vital state functions is integral to the rise of private military and security services, thus challenging the Westphalian order of the nation-state (see, e.g., Schreier and Caparini 2005).[16] The conduct and practices of private military firms in Iraq—especially Blackwater (Scahill 2005; 2007)—constitute the externalization of the violence of the corporate state: Protecting enterprises in the process of neoliberal re-formation of the Iraqi state, firms like Blackwater police and punish violations and threats against these interests in a rhetoric of security and development (see also Ifeka's exploration of a Nigerian case in this volume).[17] Thus, rather than seeing the violence of the Iraqi war as transitional, it may also be understood as a violence that is constitutive of what we describe as the corporate state form.

State and private agents become concerned not so much to protect the society of the state as before but rather to protect the agents and agencies of power from the orders or societies of the population the state contains. The recent APEC meeting of state leaders in Sydney, Australia, was an outstanding example of a security operation whereby state agents were cocooned from the population at large (in the manner of the buildings of business or industrial corporations that closely monitor and restrict public entry). Other examples abound—from WTO and G8 meetings to major national political meetings—where the practice of cordoning off or orchestrating popular presence is policed by corporate or state security entities.[18] The corporate state evinces a new turn in the violent relation of the state to society and the people. Indeed, the current security consciousness of states in the context of the *War against Terror* is impelled not only by this event but by the very corporatization processes—linked, as they are, to globalization—that are among the critical conditions underlying that particular crisis.

A final suggestion. We began this introductory essay with a reference to concepts of state and war machine as articulated by Deleuze and Guattari. In their analysis, these ordering dynamics engage entirely distinct and irreducible processes. Yet, they are in numerous empirical contexts co-present, in intimacy with one another, each being—or rather becoming—the annihilating potential of the other. In centralized state orders such as nation-states, the war machine often works at the periphery of the state order, frequently in a covert way, and accordingly it supports the state in a particular circumstance of crisis. The corporate state involves a radical bringing together of the two processes. Rhizomic process might be said to come more openly into the center of state operations, realizing intensely a mutually decentering potential that may fuel violent processes at the heart of power giving force to new violent shapes of the state.

The Chapters

All the contributions to this volume address these issues of the changing relations between state, society, and people as these are manifest in particular contexts of violence and war. The essays explore both historical contexts, often at the height of nation-state formation in modernity involving genocide and struggles against colonial rule, and contemporary situations of violent civil war.

The first section, Transformations of Sovereignty, Empire, State, includes essays that are concerned directly with the relation between dimensions of the corporate or corporatizing state and formations of war and violence. Thus, June Nash in her chapter addresses the U.S. military-industrial complex historically tracing militarization and in the process exploring the contradictions and transformations of the American imperial formation. Nash's discussion is thoroughly based in her fieldwork in Pittsfield, a location at the heart of the United States' military-industrial and imperial interests. Jakob Rigi's chapter is concerned with the war in Chechnya and how this provides a prism for understanding the transformation of the state in post-Soviet Russia. Rigi argues for the emergence of a more general chaotic form of domination that is organic, in our view, with the emerging corporatizing form of the state that we have discussed. Caroline Ifeka analyzes the Nigerian situation, and her text highlights more generally how market forces, the military and violent conflict increasingly are entangled with the global production of new non-nation state sovereignties.

The essays in the next section, War Zone, shift away from a concern with the larger structural contexts in which war and violence are produced to a consideration of the concrete experiences of the human beings who are caught within and must live the effects of these processes. Building on decades of fieldwork and knowledge of the area, Kirsten Alnaes discusses the situation in the Bundibugyo district of Uganda, an area bordering on the Democratic Republic of the Congo. She presents the terrifying realities of victims in worlds far away from the nerve centers of states but who must experience the savagery born of the effects of their crisis and disruption. Sverker Finnström focuses on Acholiland in a different part of Uganda. Finnström depicts and analyses the violence as exercised by both state and guerrilla as this is experienced by its inhabitants, and also points out significant connections to larger national, global and imperial forces of domination and inequality. Finally, Frode Storaas traces the effects of the introduction of modern firearms among the Turkana and Karamajong pastoralists in northeastern Uganda and how this has dramatically intensified violence, transforming the retributive dynamics of ongoing sociopolitical relations.

The final section, Sovereign Logics, examines shifts in the organization of state sovereignty, concentrating on processes where the state is either threatened in its sovereignty (e.g., where its monopolization of violence is contested) or where the state's sovereignty has been parceled out to other parties. Empirically, the essays in this section are concerned with guerrilla movements, paramilitaries, death squads and other modalities of state, non-state and anti-state terror. In his text, Christopher Taylor explores the forms and meanings of violence relating to power and authority in the context of the 1994 Rwandan genocide. Analyzing Colombia, in particular, but also extending his argument to other Latin American countries, Staffan Löfving takes his cue from the long-standing practices of paramilitary violence seeing its use as being systemically related to the perpetuation of U.S. global hegemony. Bjørn Enge Bertelsen's chapter focuses on the civil war in Mozambique and the emergence of death squads. He analyzes these processes in the context of postwar transformations of the state whereby many of its erstwhile domains of control are distributed among ostensibly non-state or "undercover" state functionaries. Rasmus Boserup's essay investigates the collective violence orchestrated by the Algerian state and the guerrilla FLN movement in the period 1954–62, showing how the FLN's use of violence was instrumental in the formation of a counterstate. Similar aspects underpin Glenn Bowman's chapter, which examines the continuing logic of formation of the state of Israel through its particular violence of self-containment (encystation) and exclusion epitomized by the reterritorializing dynamic of its building of an "anti-terrorist fence" or wall. Bowman demonstrates a process of sovereign expansion that may fit with our notion of the corporatization of state processes. The process can be conceived as a continuation of the territorializing, bordering, dynamic of a highly modernist state. However, there are corporatizing dimensions—declarations of domains of interest that as yet are not in reality borders but rather a kind of moving front of monopolization. Finally, Mats Utas' essay explores the historical continuity of both formations of violence and the exploitative and disciplining state formation particular to the Liberian context in the context of the Liberian civil war in the 1990s.

All the chapters argue for an historically informed analysis of sociopolitical state formations. Not only do they empirically ground our very general formulations present in this Introduction, but the essays also express the great diversity and, indeed, specificity of situations of violence and war in the continuing circumstances and redirections of particular contexts of the state.

Notes

1. The arguments of the state as characterized by a totalizing dynamic is, of course, a main prong in the classic critiques of the state by Pierre Clastres (1994 [1980]; 1998 [1974]).
2. An important argument for a *territorializing dynamic* being crucial to the state is made by Scott (1998) in his analysis of modernist state planning schemes and its effects in countries as diverse as Russia, Brazil, and Tanzania. As a central element of organizing, disciplining, and surveillance, *social redifferentiation* by bureaucratic means was central to and evident in the establishment of the colonial state (see, e.g., Anderson 1991; Appadurai 1996). The formation and production of *subjectivities* is also a central dynamic in a Foucauldian vision of power, state, and its workings. He, for instance, argues that in an

analysis of domination and power one should be "… showing how actual relations of subjugation manufacture subjects" (Foucault 2003 [1997]:45).
3. The concept of "war machine" explicitly indicates that it is a dynamic oriented to war. This is not what Deleuze and Guattari or we intend. War machine or, perhaps less ambiguously, rhizomic dynamics assume warlike, annihilating properties, in their relation with state dynamics. The destructive potential of rhizomic dynamics are realized when they are confronted by the bounding, categorizing, spatializing forces of state-like dynamics. There is no essential or inherent warlike orientations of rhizomic dynamics.
4. Examples and imagery of the nomad and the state is used extensively to analyze the dynamics of war machine and state. The directionality of the war machine in its nomad form against the state is central: "The was machine is that nomad invention that in fact has war not as its primary object but as its second order, supplementary or synthetic objective, in the sense that it is determined in such a way as to destroy the State-form and city-form with which it collides" (Deleuze and Guattari 2002 [1980]:418).
5. The directionality or *telos* of the state toward oneness and against multiplicity, concentration of power, and verticality has been consistently argued by Pierre Clastres—both in terms of state and non-state societies and in the relations between ethnocide and the state (1974:105; see also 1998 [1974]).
6. Numerous works within different disciplines testify to power's excess, the phenomenon giving rise to resistant or subversive practices (Kapferer 1997b; Keesing 1992), practices and cosmologies in which people collude and play with (excess) state power (Mbembe 2001), or where excess power and state power is enacted and appropriated (Taussig 1997).
7. For two recent contributions discussing *Leviathan*, see Joxe (2002) and Hansen and Stepputat (2005).
8. See, e.g., Foucault (1991). However, in other works, especially the 1977–78 lectures contained in *Security, territory, population* (2007 [2004]), Foucault expands his work on government to also encompass the political techniques and workings of the state in more detail.
9. For António Gramsci (1996 [1973]:52ff), the unity of the ruling groups within the context of the state, the state's organic relations to wider societal and political institutions and arrangements, and the corresponding non-unity of what he terms the subaltern classes are central elements in understanding how elite/class interests, the state and wider society are interwoven.
10. One feature of the rationalism of British colonial policy was the equalization of religions. All religions were given equality of status before the colonial government. Effectively this reduced the taken-for-granted position of Buddhism among the Sinhalese population and made it a focus of intensified consciousness. This was all the more so because colonial policy functioned to give greater status to Christianity, the religion that had political support as an effect of colonial rule.
11. For some critical works on the transformative powers of globalization, see Friedman (2003), Joxe (2002), Ong (2006), Sassen (1995), and Strange (2004).
12. The class force of contemporary elites owes much to the British colonial period, when powerful families were able to build the political and economic power by establishing themselves in imperial metropolitan centers (such as London, Paris, and New York). The building of local power was expanded through their multiple locations in foreign parts. Globalization is continuing and expanding this process.
13. This manipulation of websites is often called *web defacement* and is a growing trend in both international political conflicts and among activists critical to for example globalization and the expansion of capitalism in what is often called *cyberconflicts* (Karatzogianni 2004).
14. For an incisive critique of the information age's relations to war and American dominance, cf. Paul Virilio (2000; 2002).

15. Here we would like to distinguish the kind of stance we are taking from that of the very interesting and important arguments of commentators such as Arrighi (1994) and Harvey (2006). For all their crucial insights, they are marked by a reductionist economic determinism that neglects, in our opinion, the prior force of the social in which the economic is always embedded.
16. The situation in Iraq is not unprecedented historically, and the increasing importance globally of so-called "corporate warriors" were in the early part of 2001 expected to have a turnover of USD 100 billion (Singer 2003:78), and the turnover of the private military industry globally in 2010 is estimated at USD 202 billion (Schreier and Caparini 2005:2). These estimates were made prior to the Iraq war—a war in which the number of the so-called privatized military firms (PMFs) swelled considerably—some alleging their numbers in Iraq being between 20,000 and 45,000 in 2005 (Schreier and Caparini 2005) while others estimate that by late 2006 there were 100,000 operating (Merle 2006). A PMF like Blackwater naturally recruits both former soldiers and military professionals from the formal military system. But Blackwater also, interestingly enough, recruits heavily from former imperial ventures like non-U.S. mercenaries, commandos and death squads trained at the U.S. Army School of the Americas, contributing to Chilean commandos making up a large part of Blackwater's troops in Iraq (Scahill 2007:182ff). On the global reach of recruitment to the private military and security operations in Iraq, see also Maclellan's (2007) account of how the recruitment practices drawing Fijians to Iraq mirror those of recruitment to imperial and colonial companies and armies.
17. In the United States, former Defense Secretary Donald Rumsfeld is central to formulating the shift toward the private sector in military matters, famously stating in 2002 that there is a need to transform both the armed forces and also the Defense Department: "We must promote a more entrepreneurial approach: one that encourages people to be proactive, not reactive, and to behave less like bureaucrats and more like venture capitalists; one that does not wait for threats to emerge and be 'validated' but rather anticipates them before they appear and develops new capabilities to dissuade and deter them" (Rumsfeld 2002:29). However, it seems the "entrepreneurial approach" and "venture capitalist" behavior commended by Rumsfeld and which Blackwater has capitalized on, has since been tentatively curbed by the Pentagon (see Schmitt and Shanker 2007).
18. For an activist's insider's account of the confrontations between state agents and demonstrators, a contribution detailing the Genoa demonstrations in 2001 is illuminating (*On Fire* 2001).

Bibliography

Adorno, Theodor W. 1973. *Negative Dialectics*. London: Routledge and Kegal Paul.
Agamben, Giorgio. 2005. *State of Exception*. Chicago and London: University of Chicago Press.
Anderson, Benedict. 1991. *Imagined Communities: Reflections on the Origin and Spread of Nationalism*. London: Verso.
Appadurai, Arjun. 1996. *Modernity at Large: Cultural Dimensions of Globalization*. Minneapolis, MI and London: University of Minnesota Press.
Arrighi, Giovanni. 1994. *The Long Twentieth Century: Money, Power, and the Origins of Our Times*. London: Verso.
Arendt, Hannah. 2004. *The Origins of Totalitarianism*. New York: Schocken Books.

———. 2006. *Eichman and the Holocaust*. London: Penguin.
Austin, J. L. 1962 [1955]. *How to Do Things with Words: The William James Lectures Delivered at Harvard University in 1955*. Cambridge, MA: Harvard University Press.
Bauman, Zygmunt. 1989. *Modernity and the Holocaust*. Cambridge: Polity Press.
Bourdieu, Pierre. 1992 [1977]. *Outline of a Theory of Practice*. Cambridge: Cambridge University Press.
Burke, Anthony. 2007. *Beyond Security, Ethics and Violence: War against the Other*. London and New York: Routledge.
Clastres, Pierre. 1974. "De l'Ethnocide," *L'Homme* XIV(3–4):101–110.
———. 1994 [1980]. *Archeology of Violence*. New York: Semiotext(e)/MIT Press.
———. 1998 [1974]. *Society against the State: Essays in Political Anthropology*. New York: Zone Books.
Comaroff, John L. and Jean Comaroff. 2009. *Ethnicity, Inc*. Chicago: Chicago University Press.
Deleuze, Gilles and Félix Guattari. 2002 [1980]. *A Thousand Plateaus: Capitalism and Schizophrenia*. London and New York: Continuum.
———. 2004 [1972]. *Anti-Oedipus: Capitalism and Schizophrenia*. London and New York: Continuum.
Denning, Dorothy. 2001. "Cyberwarriors: Activists and Terrorists Turn to Cyberspace." *Harvard International Review*, 23(2):70–75.
Englund, Harri. 2006. *Prisoners of Freedom: Human Rights and the African Poor*. Berkeley and Los Angeles, CA: University of California Press.
Foucault, Michel. 1991. "Governmentality," in G. Burchett (ed.), *The Foucault Effect: Studies in Governmentality*. London: Harvester Press, pp. 87–104.
———. 2003 [1997]. *"Society Must Be Defended." Lectures at Collège du France, 1975–1976*. New York: Picador.
———. 2007 [2004]. *Security, Territory, Population: Lectures at the Collège de France, 1977–78*. Basingstoke and New York: Palgrave Macmillan.
Friedman, Jonathan (ed.). 2003. *Globalization, the State, and Violence*. Walnut Creek, CA: Altamira Press.
Gledhill, John. 2000 [1994]. *Power and Its Disguises: Anthropological Perspectives on Politics*. London and Ann Arbor, MI: Pluto Press.
Gluckman, Max. 1963 [1956]. *Custom and Conflict in Africa*. Oxford: Basil Blackwell.
Gramsci, Antonio. 1996 [1973]. *Selections from the Prison Notebooks of Antonio Gramsci*. London: Lawrence and Wishart.
Gray, John. 2007. *Black Mass: Apocalyptic Religion and the Death of Utopia*. Farrar, Straus and Giroux: New York.
Guha, Ranajit (ed.). 1982. *Subaltern studies. Writings on South Asian History and Society*. Vol. 1. Delhi: Oxford University Press.
Handelman, Don. 2004. *Nationalism and the Israeli State: Bureaucratic Logic in Public Events*. Oxford: Berg.
Hansen, Thomas Blom and Finn Stepputat (eds). 2005. *Sovereign Bodies: Citizens, Migrants and States in the Postcolonial World*. Princeton, NJ: Princeton University Press.
Hardt, Michael and Antonio Negri. 2000. *Empire*. Cambridge, MS and London: Harvard University Press.
Harvey, David. 2006. *Spaces of Global Capitalism*. London: Verso.
Healy, Shawn. 2007. "The Great Firewall of China." *Social education* 71(3):158–163.
Hobbes, Thomas. 1991 [1651]. *Leviathan*. Cambridge: Cambridge University Press.
"How governments censor the web." 2007. *BBC News*, 22 March 2007. Retrieved 15 October 2007 from http://news.bbc.co.uk/go/pr/fr/-/2/hi/technology/6475911.stm.
Jacoby, Russell. 1999. *The End of Utopia: Politics and Culture in an Age of Apathy*. New York: Basic Books.
Joxe, Alain. 2002. *Empire of Disorder*. Los Angeles and New York: Semiotext(e) / MIT Press.

Kapferer, Bruce. 1997a [1988]. *Legends of People, Myths of State*. Washington and New York: Smithsonian and Berghahn.
———. 1997b. *The Feast of the Sorcerer: Practices of Consciousness and Power*. Chicago: University of Chicago Press.
———. 2004a. "Democracy, Wild Sovereignties and the New Leviathan," *Bulletin of the Royal Institute for Inter-Faith Studies* 6(2):23–38.
———. 2004b. "Old Permutations, New Formations? War, State, and Global Transgression," in B. Kapferer (ed.), *State, Sovereignty, War*. New York and Oxford: Berghahn Books, pp. 1–15.
Kapferer, Bruce (ed.). 2005. *Oligarchs and Oligopolies. New Formations of Global Power*. New York and Oxford: Berghahn Books.
Karatzogianni, Athina. 2004. "The Politics of 'Cyberconflict.'" *Politics* 24(1):46–55.
Keesing, Roger M. 1992. *Custom and Confrontation: The Kwaio Struggle for Cultural Autonomy*. Chicago: University of Chicago Press.
Lazar, Sian. 2004. "Education for Credit. Development as Citizenship Project in Bolivia," *Critique of anthropology* 24(3):235–255.
Machiavelli, Niccolò. 1970 [1531]. *The Discourses on the First Ten Books of Titus Livy*. London: Penguin Books.
Maclellan, Nic. 2007. "Fiji, Iraq and Pacific Island Security," *Race and Class* 48(3):47–62.
Mandel, Robert. 2007. "Reassessing Victory in Warfare," *Armed Forces and Society* 33(4): 461–495.
Mbembe, Achille. 2001. *On the Postcolony*. Berkeley, CA: University of California Press.
Merle, Renae. 2006. "Census Counts 100,000 Contractors in Iraq. Civilian Number, Duties Are Issues," *Washington Post*, 5 December, D01.
On fire: The Battle of Genoa and the Anti-capitalist Movement. 2001. Edinburgh and Oakland, CA: One off press.
Ong, Aihwa. 2006. *Neoliberalism as Exception: Mutations in Citizenship and Sovereignty*. Durham and London: Duke University Press.
Polanyi, Karl. 1957. *The Great Transformation*. Boston: Beacon Press.
Prunier, Gérard. 1995. *The Rwanda Crisis 1959–1994: History of a Genocide*. London: Hurst.
Rumsfeld, Donald H. 2002. "Transforming the Military," *Foreign Affairs* 81(3):20–32.
Sahlins, Marshall. 2004. *Apologies to Thucydides: Understanding History as Culture and Vice Versa*. Chicago and London: University of Chicago Press.
Sassen, Saskia. 1995. *Losing control? Sovereignty in an age of globalization*. New York: Columbia University Press.
Scahill, Jeremy. 2005. "Blackwater Down," *The Nation*, 10 October, 1–4.
———. 2007. *Blackwater: The Rise of the World's Most Powerful Mercenary Army*. New York: Nation Books.
Schmitt, Eric and Tom Shanker. 2007. "Pentagon Sees One Authority over Contractors," *New York Times*, 17 October.
Schreier, Fred and Marina Caparini. 2005. *Privatising Security: Law, Practice and Governance of Private Military and Security Companies*. Geneva: Geneva Centre for the Democratic Control of Armed Forces (DCAF).
Scott, James C. 1998. *Seeing Like a State: How Certain Schemes to Improve the Human Condition Have Failed*. New Haven and London: Yale University Press.
Singer, P.W. 2003. *Corporate Warriors: The Rise of the Privatized Military Industry*. Ithaca and London: Cornell University Press.
Strange, Susan. 2004. *The Retreat of the State: The Diffusion of Power in the World Economy*. Cambridge: Cambridge University Press.
Strathern, Marilyn (ed.). 2000. *Audit Cultures: Anthropological Studies in Accountability, Ethics and the Academy*. Cambridge: Cambridge University Press.
Taussig, Michael. 1997. *The Magic of the State*. New York and London: Routledge.
de Tocqueville, Alexis. 1969 [1840]. *Democracy in America*. Garden City, NY: Anchor Books.

Virilio, Paul. 2000. *The Information Bomb*. London: Verso.
———. 2002. *Desert Screen: War at the Speed of Light*. London: Continuum.
Weizman, Eyal. 2007. *Hollow Land. Israel's Architecture of Occupation*. London: Verso.
Williams, Andrew Paul, et al. 2005. "Blogging and Hyperlinking: Use of the Web to Enhance Viability During the 2004 US Campaign," *Journalism Studies* 6(2):177–186.
Wolf, Eric. 1982. *Europe and the People Without History*. Berkeley, CA: University of California Press.
Wolpe, Harold. 1972. "Capitalism and Cheap Labour-Power in South Africa. From Segregation to Apartheid," *Economy and Society* 1(4):425–456.

Section I

TRANSFORMATIONS OF SOVEREIGNTY, EMPIRE, STATE

Chapter One

THE MILITARY-INDUSTRIAL COMPLEX AND THE CRISIS OF U.S. CAPITAL

June Nash

The U.S. launching of a preemptive strike against Iraq has revitalized the military-industrial complex during the presidency of George W. Bush. The privatization of services, including military combat in a continuing war against terrorism throughout the world, now threatens the hegemonic accord among communities, corporations, and the military. Rising military costs and spiraling fees for private armed contractors serving military, diplomatic, and development programs compete with shrinking budgets for social welfare within the United States, where outsourcing of jobs has severely weakened the domestic economy. The collapse of financial markets in October 2008 has precipitated a decline in commodity market, investments and precipitated unemployment levels to those of the 1980s crisis. With the election of a new president, Barack Obama, the trend toward empire that has precipitated the crisis may yet be reversed. But in order to recover consumer confidence, the lost reputation in world affairs, the revival of industrial production levels will require years of recovery. Living within twenty miles of my fieldwork site in Pittsfield, Massachusetts, where the General Electric plant was a center for the military-industrial complex put in place during the Reagan presidency in the l980s, I continue to raise questions about the impact at home of military production and intervention as I did in my earlier study and now do in Iraq (Nash 1989).

I argue that the militarization of society breaks down the social fabric of communities that are host to the armaments industry, distorting economic

---

Notes for this chapter are located on page 49.

priorities and threatening the very values for which the administration pretends to be fighting. The growing dependence on ordinance production of military orders distorted economic priorities in the 1980s, leaving Pittsfield a brownfield area when General Electric closed the plant at the end of the decade. The incipient critique of imperialist wars by Vietnam veterans was, for some silenced as they became incorporated as patriots more than a decade after their return. Others remain bitter about the recourse to war by those "who push the buttons" and send others out to fight. The transition in the United States from a military-industrial complex that recognized distinct spheres of policy related to government, the military, and business, to a fusion of private corporations and contractors, Pentagon, with U.S. government command structures in the Iraq War, erases the line between civilian and military life. During the Bush regime, Washington has taken as its governing model privatized corporate capitalism now outsourcing the jobs in industry, diplomacy, and development that once insured the prosperity that strengthened hegemonic control. With the newly elected President Barack Obama about to take office, we pose some of the dangers the new administration faces as they attempt to reverse a process that has brought about a crisis in the nation and the world.

The military-industrial complex about which President Dwight Eisenhower warned the American people upon leaving office in 1961 renewed its control over the domestic economy in the emerging American empire. As Commander of the Allied Forces in Europe during World War II, Eisenhower saw the intimate relations generated between armaments manufacturing corporations and military political agencies. This was an extension of the close relationships between major corporations such as General Electric and the U.S. government that grew in World War I and persisted throughout World War II, the Vietnam and Korean wars, and the Cold War in the 1980s. Since the attack on the World Trade Center on September 11, 2001, Washington has become the control center of a "War on Terrorism" modeled on private corporate capitalism where the divisions between industry and government are erased and national and international rules are ignored. As former Secretary of Defense Donald Rumsfeld anticipated in a speech delivered the day before the September 11 attacks, "We must promote a more entrepreneurial approach, one that encourages people to be proactive, not reactive, and to behave less like bureaucrats and more like venture capitalists" (cited in Scahill 2007:iv). The attacks on the World Trade Towers and Pentagon provided him with the rationale for pursuing what is now called "the Rumsfeld Doctrine." His overhaul of the Pentagon called for a greater use of the private sector to wage American wars, emphasizing covert actions, sophisticated weapons systems, and greater use of special forces and contractors. Even after his resignation, the costs of a privatized war continue to shock the sensibilities of a society that claims democratic values.

The militarization of society brings home to the United States the violations of human rights that were an export to the Asian perimeter during the Korean and Vietnam wars, and to Central America during Regan's presidency. As Catherine Lutz and Donald Nonini argue (2003:73), the use of violence reinforces the political economy of the state with its own institutional force. The priority given to war as a means of countering terrorism serves to advance the growing imperial power of the United States while threatening the domestic polity and society. The "contradictory fusion," as David Harvey (2003:26) calls it, of a politics based on national territorial identity and the commitment of its population to defend capitalist accumulation occurring worldwide threatens both national and imperial integrity.

I shall argue that the Bush strategy in waging war and reconstructing Iraq has exacerbated distortions in the domestic political economy as a result of the fusion of corporate, Pentagon, and U.S. government command structures. Privatization of the war in accord with the dominant corporate model has further alienated the American citizenry already distanced from the political process by the violence committed in their name during the Vietnam War. Unconscionable disregard for the safety of American troops who were put in harm's way on the basis of mendacious claims of an Iraqi threat to national security, is now compounded with the corruption of major corporations claiming to serve the troops for super-inflated profits. At the same time that President Bush claimed to be waging war for liberty and democracy in the Middle East, he deprived immigrants and citizens of their constitutional rights, holding them as terrorist suspects in Guantánamo, and negating the Geneva conventions of war regarding captives held in the Iraqi prison Abu Ghraib. These practices are institutionalized through the Patriot Act in a flagrant denial of the government's claims to be fighting the war to bring democracy to the Middle East. The privatization of the American economy and polity is creating a permanent underclass that has little opportunity or even hope for realizing the American dream.

I shall explore the impact of militarization in the city of Pittsfield, where I studied the buildup of the military industrial complex in the 1980s, and relate this to current trends in the Iraq War. Interviews I conducted in 1983 with veterans who fought in World War II and the Korean and Vietnam wars, and return visits to question veterans about the present conflict in Iraq, provide a context for analyzing the contradictions in the growing fusion of militarism and the state. The generation forced to fight the Vietnam War questions the validity of military action in Iraq but differ in the course that they would take to redeem the political process. Since the General Electric Company abandoned the production of power transformers in 1987, closed down military production of Ordnance Systems by 1990 and sold its plastic division to a Saudi Arabian firm in 2007, Pittsfield was stigmatized as a brownfields area, contaminated by the PCBs dumped in the Housatonic River from the 1930s until the l980s.

With the military orders generated by Bush's "war on terrorism," economic growth reverted to military production. General Dynamics Advanced Information Systems, a Pittsfield company that picked up military contracts when GE closed its ordnance division, is increasing its workforce from 600 to 800 people to produce programs for submarines that fire Trident ballistic missiles and those that launch Tomahawk cruise missiles (*The Berkshire Eagle*, 4 July 2004:D1,3). The Pentagon awarded another contract to a Pittsfield firm, Protech Armored Products, which has grown substantially to employ 139 workers making protective armor plates used by soldiers in combat. When the Pentagon awarded a $40-million contract for body armor to Pittsfield Protech Armored Products, Massachusetts Senator Edward M. Kennedy, a leading opponent of the war in Iraq, was there to laud the "company that is in the vanguard of leading this nation in terms of this new technology ... so that our servicemen and women are better protected." He received the dog tags of a Massachusetts soldier killed in Iraq whose parents promoted the equipment in memory of their son (*The Berkshire Eagle*, 19 June 2004:A1, A4). The hundreds of new jobs "created" by the naval signal systems in General Dynamics may also revitalize the military-industrial complex.

Yet, in comparison with over seven thousand employees in the General Electric ordnance division during the 1980s, few opportunities for high-wage employment exist for Pittsfield High School graduates, who were enlisting in greater numbers in the military (*The Berkshire Eagle*, 13 June 2004:A1,A5). Some efforts to attract tourism and revitalize the downtown area have stimulated commercial activity on North Street, but these hardly compensate for the steady year-round jobs once ensured by a stable industrial base. Pittsfield is again tying its future to the military-industrial complex.

Pittsfield buildup of the infrastructure for capitalist imperialism during the 1970s and 1980s illustrates how the application of information technology to defense technology fostered the merging of the domestic and military command structures. The decline of peacetime production in the transformation to high-tech defense industries for super profits created distortions in the domestic political economy that played out in Pittsfield and other U.S. cities during the Cold War. The fusion of corporate, Pentagon, and U.S. government command structures in the current War on

Terrorism marks the end of stable jobs covered by union contracts once provided by companies like General Electric. Structural violence within the nation, caused by the diversion of public funds from health care, education, and local police and fire services, increasingly alienates a population called upon to fight on foreign soil. Pittsfield teachers, firemen, and police read of the billions of dollars going to pay for private contract services in Baghdad and express their outrage in letters to the local press. The privatization of not only the economy but also the polity is creating a permanent underclass that has little opportunity or even hope of realizing the American dream.

Formation of the Military-Industrial Complex: A Case Study

I chose Pittsfield, Massachusetts, as the site for my study of the impact of a multinational corporation on community in the 1980s. I soon learned the significance of military production on industrial growth. Pittsfield's first industrial production of textiles and weapons began in the War of 1812 with England, when mercantile interests on the New England coast and southern cotton plantation owners rejected the revolutionary government's declaration of war. Pittsfield's mills and forges provided uniforms and rifles for U.S. soldiers and sailors. Following the war, and especially after the Tariff Act of 1824, the "infant industries" that helped supply the federal army developed into major textile industries. Tanneries, textiles, and iron forges grew with the military needs of the nation for uniforms, blankets, and weapons during the Civil War.

The transition from textile production to electrical power transmissions occurred in 1883, when the Stanley Electrical Manufacturing Company began producing alternating current power transmission. The incorporation of the company with J. P. Morgan financiers in 1891 allowed the company to expand capital investment and the workforce a hundredfold. This attracted the attention of General Electric Co., which bought the firm in 1903 when there were 1,700 employees working in a plant valued at $4 million (Boltwood 1916). The workforce again expanded from 1,700 to 6,000 workers during World War I. The rise in demand for electrical machinery throughout the nation generated more growth in the interwar years.

The emergent corporate philosophy drawing on the social-Darwinian struggle for survival of the fittest and unconstrained competition helped coalesce corporate hegemony during the first half century of its growth from the 1880s to 1930s. But the failure to provide even a modicum of security or redistribution of the rising fortunes led to labor unrest. Employees in Pittsfield's GE plant joined workers throughout the nation in 1916 as they carried out strikes for shorter hours, higher wages, and other security benefits. The Great Depression of 1929 catapulted the leaders of industry and the government of Franklyn D. Roosevelt to take action. Gerard Swope, who was president of General Electric during this period, also served along with chief executive officers of General Motors and the Ford Company as an advisor to the President developing the "welfare capital" strategy of secure employment for skilled workers. John D. Rockefeller and Walter Teagle of Standard Oil accepted the Wagner National Labor Relations Board and Social Security acts that were drafted and legislated during Roosevelt's administration (Nash 1989). In return, these big and growing industries were ensured of free trade for their intensified export business (James 2002:134). The decisions were made not out of the beneficence of leading industrialists but because of the constant pressure from labor organizations that hastened the implementation of social welfare policies for the predominantly male white workforce in well-paid, stable employment.

The other side of corporate hegemony was forged by the labor movement that enlisted Roosevelt and his cabinet in crafting New Deal policies that rescued working families during the depths of the Great Depression. It was not until World War II, however, that employment opportunities improved and working families were able to look forward to the mobility of their children by providing a college education and advanced professional training. The workforce in the Pittsfield GE plant doubled during the war, with over 13,000 workers producing automated panel controls for battleships and airplanes, communication instruments, and other high technology. Patriotism was at a high level, making the no-strike clause in the labor contract, with wages geared to cost-of-living increases, more acceptable.

In the postwar period, delayed demand for consumer products and domestic power generators kept up production for two decades. Flexible production was a stated aim of the General Electric corporation from the l950s (General Electric Professional Management Vol.I:43). Each division was to be judged in terms of its own record of profit and investment, giving power to headquarters to deploy investments, with the accounting department the whip in the operation. This new accounting strategy provided the rationale for relocating low-profit production units like the small appliance division to nonunion sites in the U.S. South and later overseas, while large-scale power transformer production and the more lucrative cost-plus military contracts paying higher wages were awarded to the northern plants during the Korean War.

This trend became pronounced in the 1970s and 1980s when production in General Electric's Pittsfield plant shifted to cost-plus contracts for Army

Ordnance systems during the Cold War years of the Reagan administration in the 1980s. These contracts included the antiballistic missiles Polaris and Trident, and the gearshift for the Bradley fighting vehicle. Because government contracts required strict compliance with affirmative action in employment, the ordnance department began to employ women and minorities in high-level jobs, often for the first time.[1]

Just as private industries began to employ women and minorities after civil rights were enforced in the workforce, so too did a similar shift in gender and skin color occur in the volunteer army that was being recruited for the Cold War arms competition. In order to avoid using the draft in an unpopular war fighting revolutionaries in Central America, Reagan outsourced army recruits, hiring Honduran freelance soldiers called *contras* to fight the Sandinistas in Nicaragua. When Congress cut off much of the funding at the end of his second term, Reagan's team engineered a deal with the Israelis to sell arms to Iran to raise the extra cash needed for the mercenaries. An impeachment charge threatened, but did not succeed, in undermining the whole operation.

These priorities of the Reagan Cold War of the 1980s are reflected in the employment in the three divisions. Power Transformer, which once employed 5,000 workers, was down to 900 employees in 1988, while Ordnance had grown from a few hundred following the Korean War to 5,000. This was virtually a complete reversal of the proportion of those in civilian and war production at the end of the 1960s. Plastics Research and Development was expected to position Pittsfield as part of a tripartite global enterprise with plants in Bergen Op Zoom and Australia. But because of the growing threats to petroleum resources needed for this fledgling industry, the headquarters (built on what was once called Canoe Meadows when Mohegans gathered to negotiate and trade in the eighteenth century) never expanded beyond 750 employees. In May 2007 the Plastics Division was sold to Saudi Basic Industries Corp., or Sabic, for $11.6 billion. "With an assured supply of polymers," a Sabic company spokesman stated, "the strategy is for our company to be a global leader and to add specialty businesses to our portfolio. ... We'll integrate some of our operations in the Kingdom [of Saudi Arabia] into supply chains and utilize technologies of GE Plastics into other areas that we have there" (*Berkshire Eagle* 22 May 2007:A1, A4).

Resistance to War and Peace Alternatives

Alternatives to defense production were supported nationally by some of the clothing and textile unions, and the public employees' unions. Though the electric workers' unions occasionally hosted delegations of their European counterparts who favored conversion to peace production, they were well aware that it was only in defense-related production that Pittsfield had recovered from the 1982 recession. Trade union issues prevailed over political concerns about the war. The Pittsfield local International Union of Electrical Employees (IUE) did not support John Kerry's bid for the Senate in October 1984 because of his opposition to the Bradley Fighting Vehicle, the Trident 1, and the Trident 2—all made in Pittsfield (*Berkshire Eagle*, 3 November 1984).

Although there was no collective protest against military production by the Pittsfield IUE, individual workers chose to work in Power Transformer rather than take higher-paying jobs in Ordnance because they opposed making weapons of destruction. Pittsfield citizens who carried out a silent vigil in Park Square each year on Hiroshima Day were primarily women and adolescents, some of whom defied parents who were managers in GE Ordnance Systems. Community activities were influenced by the leadership roles undertaken by GE managers. For example, when the Berkshire League of Women Voters was denied the use of the school auditorium for a talk on the proliferation of nuclear weapons, people guessed that it was because four of the five school committee members who voted against it were employed at GE Ordnance Systems.

The military-industrial complex thus achieved hegemonic consent in Pittsfield from World War II through the U.S. intervention in the Far East until the Vietnam War. For American workers and their sons, and increasingly their daughters, who fought the wars, military service was still considered an episode in which peace remained the objective. The army did not lack volunteers, and few objected to the draft until the Vietnam War.

Workers engaged in defense production disliked what they were engaged in but feared the loss of other jobs contingent on an arms buildup. In the 1980s I found the most consistent sentiments against military solutions to international problems among veterans of Pittsfield (Nash 1989:233–44). Although I had anticipated this from members of the Vietnam Veterans of America who were conscripted to fight an unpopular war, I also heard strong ambivalence about resorting to war among Korean and World War II veterans (Nash 1989:233–44).

In the early 1980s, particularly following the hostage crisis when President Reagan welcomed home the Americans held as hostages in Iran, Pittsfield's Vietnam veterans began to organize themselves. In 1983 I interviewed Larry Caperer, who had joined with a few other Vietnam veterans to start the Pittsfield chapter of the Vietnam Veterans in 1982. They intended to gain the benefits that World War II and Korean War veterans had received: college tuition, health benefits for the service-related illnesses, and psychological counseling. He told me that upon their return, the Vietnam veterans seeking help for problems related to chemical exposure had to prove that they were in areas that were sprayed with Agent Orange. This was a defoliant that the army used but for years refused to admit caused any damage until the correlation with cancer and genetic breakdown in reproduction became incontrovertible (Nash 1989:249).

Larry's statement, made back in 1983 when I first talked with the veterans' groups, sums up the shock of returning home to find themselves greeted not as heroes, as other veterans had been, but as pariahs.

> I think that what has happened with the Vietnam veterans is that we were under a lot of pressure in a very jungle-like environment. We had people who were not distinguished as enemies. We've seen kids with grenades on their bodies—little kids that you would like to go up to and say 'hi' to. The main thing about unconventional warfare, you think of wading through jungles with rice paddies and shells going off and trip wires, and you become very paranoid. Now one day you're in the jungle, and the next day you're in the streets of Pittsfield (Nash 1989:249).

That same sense of alienation was expressed by Jim Calahan in December 2003, when I returned to Pittsfield to talk with the Vietnam veterans. I wanted to get a sense of what they felt about the current Iraq war. Jim was waiting in the storefront office of the Vietnam Veterans Association on North Street, along with two other veterans who were active in the organization. Jim reflected on his mustering out days thirty years before:

> I first tried to join the Veterans of Foreign War[s]. They refused because they told me, I wasn't a veteran. Honest to God, they said that! Because they considered the Vietnam War was a mistake because we lost the war. And I didn't try again for a long, long time. I think it was 1984 when I joined here. When I just got back from 'Nam, I just forgot all about everything. I forgot anything about being a veteran. It took me a long time before I got over that.

The desperately needed psychological counseling was not forthcoming from a government that washed its hands of the obligations accorded to veterans in the past. Even when the government finally allowed medical compensations to veterans affected by Agent Orange, there was no punitive action against the chemical companies or the government that had released these toxic substances in the war. Larry told me back in l983:

> It was a compassionate settlement to the Vietnam Veterans, not a settlement of guilt. It didn't really help. I kind of look at it personally—like Richard Nixon. He never admitted he was guilty, but he resigned from office. And I think the chemical companies did the same thing ... The cash settlement, I think, shows that they feel they were guilty. A lot of Vietnam veterans wanted to see them go into court because of the press it would get ...

The settlement did not satisfy the veterans' claims for justice, when the complicity of the military-industrial complex was made public. In 1982 Vietnam veterans marched in the Memorial Day parade for the first time, dressed in battle gear in contrast with the dress uniform of the American Legion and Veterans of Foreign Wars. Congress members such as Silvio Conti picked up on the fact that veterans were becoming a political force, but they limited their support to finding the soldiers missing in action rather than addressing the structural violence to which they had been subjected in wartime exposure to Agent Orange. The desire to "get to the men who press the buttons" in order to influence the government's decisions against waging war were ignored. As August Carbonella (2003) reflects on his and other Vietnam veterans' experience, the "liberationist and anti-imperialist sentiments and politics of the radical U.S. soldiers were often silenced."

In 1987 while I was finishing my book on the construction of the military industrial society, the Pittsfield Ordnance Systems was the most important division. That year General Electric closed the Power Transformer division, joining Westinghouse to produce large transformers in Canada. The reason given was "cost control." I shall never forget the voice of a Lynn GE worker who was an IUE delegate at meetings held in Pittsfield at the time the announcement was made. He protested the move, exclaiming, "GE is climbing into bed with the competition and leaving us bare-assed out here in the cold!" Not only did Pittsfield have a reputation as a militant union town, but also GE could cut costs in Canada where medical insurance was supplied by the host country. By the end of the decade, Pittsfield was left with nothing more than the industrial wastes that had accumulated in Silver Lake and the Housatonic River.

The Decline of Corporate Hegemony

Today, Pittsfield is a shadow of its former presence in Berkshire County. It has lost over ten thousand residents in the prime productive age group, declining from 56,874 in the 1960s to 43,860 in 2005, with most of the decline occurring in the 1990s and 2000s. It has a high crime rate, with eight murders committed in 2003, and a rise in violent crimes from 167 per 100,000 in 2001 to 797 per 100,000 in 2005. The prevalence of single mothers attempting to make a living on their own or with welfare has loomed into a national problem, as Joanna Lipper demonstrates in her 2003 best seller, *Growing up Fast*. The author attributes the plight of six teenage mothers in Pittsfield to economic decline, and there is abundant evidence for this. The rising incidence of crime and drug abuse is a condition often related to unemployment. However, what is happening in Pittsfield is more systemic. It involves the loss of a collective ethic, a fragmentation of the social fabric that leads to drugs, crime, and a boom-and-bust war economy that causes the breakup of neighborhoods and families. The apolitical stance of many of Pittsfield's citizens stem from the injustices inflicted in overseas military adventures and the growing inequalities in a globalized world.

The Pittsfield story is not unusual in the annals of U.S. industrial history. The movement of industrial domestic production to the South and overseas broke the hegemonic compact related to capital accumulation and accepted by workers in exchange for stable, well-paid jobs. Similar instances can be found in Schenectady when it lost the Singer plant that had stabilized production (Newman 1988), and in the flatlands of upstate New York (Doukas 2003), where Remington, the dominant employer, lost out to overseas competition.

The particular distortions related to militarization that we find in Pittsfield are often ignored in the narratives of transformation from a "Fordist regime" ensuring the general welfare of the economy to "flexible production." The Reagan-Bush regimes perfected a formula of military production for a Cold War with deficit spending and cost-plus contracts that could appease American workers' desire for stable, well-paid employment. Demand was infinite, since "the enemy" was unseen and omnipresent given the assumption that the U.S.S.R. was "spreading Communism" throughout the world. The Central American "revolutions," believed to be Communist-inspired, added a stimulus to deficit spending for "pork-barrel" requisitions approved by Congress for the "dirty wars" in Salvador and Nicaragua. And with deficit spending, the budget seemed unlimited. General Electric was a willing partner, so long as it was able to get cost-plus contracts for ordnance production.

But when the Congress began to exercise control over the burgeoning armaments budget toward the end of Reagan's term, the party was over, as it were. Pittsfield and other cities experiencing a decline in armaments production suddenly lost the companies that seemed to ensure their future since there were no alternative production divisions left. Workers realized their worst fears that military production was tied to a boom-and-bust economy, and that its future was jeopardized by the debt incurred in the production process itself.

The American Experience in Wars

Spending in warfare reveals the crucial link between the government and the military industrial complex. Pittsfield's General Electric Workers told me that what got them and other Americans out of the Great Depression was not Roosevelt's welfare policies or the Works Progress (renamed Projects in 1939) Administration—but rather the war economy that promoted factory production even before the United States declared war in 1941. During World War II, 39 percent of the workforce was employed in the defense industry. These workers were released for "peacetime" production of consumer goods until the advent of the Korean and Vietnam wars, when defense production rose to 9.8 percent of the labor force. With its present employment of 627,000 civilians, the U.S. military industry is rebuilding to Cold War levels of 5.7 percent of the labor force, and the defense industry as a whole now employs 3 million, comprising 3.5 percent of the labor force (Hedges 2003:1–5).

In World War II the U.S. government spent $3 trillion, and from the post–World War II period to the end of the millennium another $1 trillion was expended on the Korean War, the Vietnam War, and the first Gulf War (Hedges 2003:1–5). As for the cost of the present war, there have been few comprehensive assessments since April 16, 2003, when Defense Comptroller Dov Zakheir briefed the press on the Pentagon's estimates. To that date, the war had cost $10–12 billion in military operations plus $9 billion in the first three and a half weeks of conflict. In July 2003, Rumsfeld testified before the Senate Armed Services that the war was costing $3.9 billion a month. A year later that estimated expenditure rose to $5 billion a month. In the first year of the war, a total of at least $135 billion was spent.

Because these expenditures were based on deficit spending, people did not feel the pinch when they went to the polls that fall and returned Bush to the presidency. As we approached the 2008 elections, the national debt of over $12 trillion contributed to the financial crisis of October 2008. Stiglitz, former head of the World Bank, estimated over $3 trillion of the debt was a result of the failed war and the end is not, at the time of writing, yet in sight (Stiglitz 2008). Expenditures on the military once promoted dependency of the domestic population on the military for jobs and profits generated by the war reinforcing, as Berthold Brecht captured in his play "Mother Courage," the commitment of noncombatants to the military presence. But with the outsourcing of services to private contractors, the domestic economy has not benefited.

The Iraq War exceeds past wars in the privatization of many service-related functions in supply, engineering, and maintenance, allowing multinational firms based in the United States such as Halliburton, Bechtel, Blackwater, and their subsidiaries to expand their operations with the expectations of huge profits in the Middle East. Fearing the political impact of compulsory conscription, the universal draft was ended after the Vietnam War, and the army itself has become privatized with volunteers drawn into the service by the promise of education or citizenship or for the money. The first Gulf War launched by Bush senior in 1991 was a preview to the new mode of high-technology warfare with low military and high civilian casualties. It allowed the army to test in action the antiballistic missiles and other technology developed during the preceding decade.[2]

Under Bush junior's leadership, the military-industrial complex is more closely wedded to government than ever before, with political functionaries moving from command positions in the corporate hierarchy to serve these same interests as defense specialists and security advisors or from the military to civilian posts in Bush's cabinet. Vice President Cheney is only one of the former executives who left his lucrative post in Halliburton to join the Bush war team, and Colin Powell changed his hat from that of a retired general to secretary of state. The reconstruction of Iraq extends the functions of the national security forces, including the army and National Guard, to defend the operation of private corporations making extraordinary profits. Although the justification for profits used to be cast as the price for taking risk, in this war U.S. AID provides insurance against takeovers to private investors in a turbulent political domain that private insurance operators refuse to enter.

Former Defense Secretary Rumsfeld, who served in Bush senior's administration and was forced to resign in 2007 after many criticisms of his supervision of the war, ran the war on strict corporate principles—a precedent that continues. He has prioritized privatization of the contracts regulating army supplies and deployment, and created a mercenary army recruited on market principles of wages and benefits for soldiers engaged in military action. Like corporations, the army emphasizes technological over human intervention in the deployment of force and prefers outsourcing of ancillary operations. This latter strategy allows multinational firms based in the U.S. such as Halliburton, Bechtel, and their subsidiaries to expand their operations with contract employees for construction and maintenance work. More sensitive employment, such as security forces and prison interrogators hired by the firms Titan and CACTI, commands as much as $1,500 a day. These strategies, however, have reduced the ability of the army to recruit soldiers into the new volunteer service, since it has an annual base pay of a mere $13,000. Even with perks amounting to $24,000 and lures of education, travel, and health benefits, army service is not competitive.

In addition to U.S. mercenaries, the U.S. Army sends military instructors to the trouble spots of the world to train foreign troops in advanced methods of counterinsurgency. Chalmers Johnson estimates (2003:55) that each year the military trains one hundred thousand foreign soldiers in satellites and dependencies throughout the world. This is, he remarks, "a little like a corporation turning to one of its subsidiaries to fulfil its labor requirements." It has the added advantage of maintaining a low profile for high-casualty operations, since "The death of foreign soldiers does not make news." Johnson details the following outsources (2003:56): DynCorp, which operated in Bosnia; Science Applications International Corporation of San Diego; BDM International of Fairfax, Va.; Armor Holdings Inc. of Jacksonville, Fla; Cubic Applications Inc. of Lacey, Wash.; DFI International of Washington, D.C,; and International Charter Inc. of Oregon—which collectively employ thousands of engineers and managers earning high salaries. In Iraq, DynCorp will provide personal protection for President Hamid Karzai of Afghanistan and will take over the training of the national army when the U.S. Green Berets leave. The sales of these companies, linked in their own trade group, the International Peace Operations Associations, are expected to reach $202 billion by 2010 (Johnson 2003:56).

Table 1 shows the rise in foreign contracts made by the Department of Defense, the Department of State, and the Department of Homeland Security in North America, excluding the United States, South America, Africa, Europe, Australia and Pacific zone, and Asia (*New York Times*, 6 October 2007:A25).

Table 1. Amount spent on U.S. private security contracts

Year	2000	2001	2002	2003	2004	2005
Dollars spent ($billions)	219.35	235.21	275.91	326.35	357.74	389.62

The Pentagon, like major corporations, now follows the corporate model of "do only what you do best" and leave the rest to subcontractors.[3] The U.S. troops are serviced by private contractors that provide meals, laundry, and other maintenance services—a precedent that continued throughout the Bush presidency. Among the most privileged suppliers are Kellogg Brown and Root (KBR), which has a ten-year, multibillion-dollar contract to provide the military with "logistical support." Peter Singer of the Brookings Institute estimates there is one private contractor for every ten foreign soldiers in Iraq, ten times the private ratios in the Gulf War (*The Berkshire Eagle*, 30 October 2003:A1, A4). During combat, these privately employed workers have on occasion refused to carry out their duties even though they receive almost two times the compensation of the soldiers. Soldiers complain about the tasteless food and inadequate water—they get only 1.5 liters of water a day—that lowers morale and may contribute to the high noncombat death-rate among U.S. troops. At least one soldier died of heat exhaustion (Paul Krugman, *Berkshire Eagle*, 13 August 2003:A7).

The privatization of the war according to the corporate model of organizational hierarchy and behavior plays out in distinct ways for different sectors of the U.S. population.

First, ethnic discrimination enters into the allocation of soldiers in the war zone in a similar way to the allocation of workers in the employment hierarchy. Just as Puerto Ricans felt that they were preferentially selected for frontline combat in the Vietnam War, Mexican Americans perceive themselves to outnumber all ethnic groups in the advance troops entering Baghdad. The Mexican press's *La Reforma* picked up the story of the first soldier killed in the advance on Baghdad, a Mexican American who joined so that he could get an education and become a citizen. His mother was quoted as deploring the high numbers of very young Mexicans in the first military engagement in Iraq, when the army did not yet know whether they would be met by chemical or germ weapons of mass destruction.

One of the strongest incentives for immigrants to enlist is the promise of citizenship. More than 37,000 noncitizens serve in the U.S. military, many of them deployed abroad. But many of these soldiers cannot manage to fulfil the bureaucratic obligations to complete the extensive process of application for citizenship, missing deadlines and failing to maintain the paper trail. As Tina Susman, *Newsday* correspondent, reported, "The only surefire path to citizenship is getting killed in action" (*Miami Herald*, int. ed, 1 February 2004:5A).

Secondly, just as in corporations, the army's implementation of affirmative action in the armed forces opens opportunities for women's advancement, allowing women to run the same risk of dying in battle as men. American women have participated more extensively in combat in Iraq than in any previous war in U.S. history. Women constitute 15 percent of active troops and 17 percent of reserves, which are now being called to the front at a greater rate than ever before (*The Berkshire Eagle*, 16 December 2003:A1, A4). Bush's team includes a race and color spectrum that is almost like a Bennetton advertisement, with Colin Powell during his first four year term followed by Condoleezza Rice proving the pluricultural democracy they preach.

Thirdly, the reconstruction process is attempting to recreate an Iraqi privatized economy modeled on the U.S. economy. Former Defense Secretary Donald H. Rumsfeld made this explicit, stating that, "Market systems will be favored, not Stalinist command systems" (*New York Times*, 10 January 2004:B9). Even before the much-touted democratic constitution for Iraq had been written, the Coalition Provisional Authority ended restrictions on foreigners owning property and investing in Iraqi businesses. Nor do the investors have to reinvest profits back into the country. Their plans include selling 150 of the 200 state-owned enterprises, even including the Iraqi national airlines. According to *The New York Times* report (10 January 2004:1), this may violate international laws governing military occupation. The United Nations Security Council states that the occupying forces should follow the Hague Regulations and the Geneva Convention, but adds that the coalition "should play an active role in administration and reconstruction" (10 January 2004:B11). This contradiction is yet to be settled.

If one of the vaunted values of privatization is to incur efficiencies, the benefits of the corporate model are hard to see in Iraq. By November 2003 mainstream news journals featured stories about the companies operating in Iraq, noting that the largest contractors, Bechtel and Halliburton, acquired their contracts on a no-bid or limited-bid basis, bypassing Iraqi enterprises and dispensing with accountability to congress (*Newsweek*, 3 November 2003:26).[4] When Bechtel was faced with unexplained financial charges in 2005, the corporation picked up its stakes in the United States and relocated to Dubai. Blackwater USA, which recruits its security forces from a wide array of dissidents from the swamplands of North Carolina to the Middle East to act as security guards for American personnel, is in far deeper legal troubles since 16 September 2007, when its hired guns opened fire and killed seventeen civilians and wounded twenty-four in a crowded Baghdad square. The investigation of the incident in which they were charged with wonton abuse of military force against Iraqi civilians reveals the wide latitude of military behavior allowed in the privatized forces. Regulations in their use of force are ill-defined and non-regulated, and state Department officials complain that there are far too few overseers to manage the 1,200 private soldiers who guard American personnel. Since the only competitor in the business is DynCorp, that the laxity in management persists is, according to State Department officials, understandable (*New York Times*, 24 October 2007:A1, A8). Secretary of State Condoleezza Rice admitted that there was "a hole" in the U.S. law shielding contractors. Blackwater USA responded to the growing critique with a mass mailing, noting that the company is saving taxpayers millions of dollars by providing temporary workers to take the place of full-time government military employees (*New York Times*, 26 October 2007). But by October 30, State Department officials offered immunity to Blackwater guards for their shooting.

The fact that U.S. occupation forces are now subsidizing more than 90 percent of oil in Iraq, a country with the second largest oil reserves in the world, confirms the severe breakdown in the delivery of this prize resource by these private companies in charge of the Iraq occupation (*America's Future Action*/333.our future.org, 3 November 2003).[5] Since global insurance corporations have rejected the attempts by private corporations to insure themselves against takeovers by nationals in the countries in which they operate, the U.S. Agency for International Aid (USAID) is assuming that function at taxpayers' expense (*New York Times*, 10 January 2004).

The central advantage for the government in maintaining a high percentage of privatized functions in these foreign military adventures is that secrecy can be assured. When the resistance movement of the Iraqi's increased in the early part of April 2004, reporters could not find out what the "maintenance" workers hired by a private company were doing. Their actions are not scrutinized by Congress, and their dead do not add to the casualty lists that lead to public outcries. It was not until some of the photographs of Abu Ghraib prisoners in the process of being tortured were leaked to a reporter that the obscene violations of human rights were revealed.

In their quest to maximize U.S. corporate gains in controlling the future of Iraq, President Bush and his administration have committed an egregious diplomatic error in barring France, Germany, Russia, and other nations from the $18.6 billion U.S.-financed privatized reconstruction projects. Since these were among the countries that the administration was asking to assist in paying for the reconstruction, it seriously damaged old alliances and alienated new ones (*The Berkshire Eagle*, 13 December 2003:1–4). As the editor of the local newspaper, *The Berkshire Eagle* opined, "War is hell, business is business" (13 December 2003:1–4). Business is gaining momentum as the peace process plunders on.

No matter how successfully these stories are presented, they are surface expressions of the fundamentally flawed reconstruction process being played out in Iraq. The privatization of the war and the reconstruction has failed to respond to the vaunted efficiencies of free enterprise. When L. Paul Bremer III was appointed the top U.S. manager of the allied occupational forces—or proconsul, as some commentators called him—in May 2003, shortly after the invasion of Falujah, he proceeded to put Rumsfeld's entrepreneurial policies into practice, drawing heavily on Blackwater USA contractors. His experience as an insurance writer for international businesses to cover all their risks against terrorism in the new business climate following the September 11, 2001 attacks gave him the credentials to be appointed proconsul of the American occupation of Iraq. The economic plan for reconstruction of Iraq that he drafted evoked James Galbraith's comment (*U.S. Newsday*, 4 November 2003) that it "looks disastrous: a Morgenthau Plan to deindustrialize Iraq masquerading as a Marshall Plan to rebuild it." He added that "the kind of "Republican Party policy hacks [that] have been dumped on Iraq, unsupervised … are making economic decisions with reckless disregard for local sentiment."

The general weakening of the U.S. economy with prolonged low interest rates, high debt, and low increments of employment even with the third quarter "recuperation" led to Gailbraith's prediction in November 2003 that the United States' commitment to the reconstruction of Iraq was drastically overextending the national resources. Military experts already see a drastic overstretching of U.S. troops.[6] The cost of the war in Iraq must be measured not only in the hundreds of billions of dollars spent there, or the lives being lost every day, but also in the discrediting of the United States reconstruction effort in Iraq and the debilitating effect of psychological impairment. The impunity with which Blackwater USA mercenary forces contractors operated added to the dishonor of the United States missions throughout the world.

Iraq is proving that the high-technology warfare achieved by privatized capitalism might win a war but it cannot reconstruct a nation. Like Humpty Dumpty, the breaking of civil society cannot be easily repaired once it has been pushed off the wall. The war continues unabated after President Bush's premature declaration of peace in May 2003, when he appeared in paratrooper's uniform on an aircraft carrier to announce the return of freedom to Iraq. The low point of the postwar "peace process" came in late October 2004, when repeated attacks on foreign missions and allied troops exposed the administration's attempts to downplay reports of its failure. The deadly attack on the Red Cross headquarters in central Baghdad on 27 October 2004, convinced many countries to stay out of Iraq. It was at this point that President Bush was quoted as declaring that the attacks against U.S.-held sites that were coordinated across Baghdad on the first day of Ramadan should be understood thus: "The more successful we are on the ground the more these killers will react." Long after Saddam Hussein was flushed out of a spider hole in December 2003, the Bush peace process still claims the lives of U.S. soldiers and Iraqi civilians. Long after Iraq regained its sovereignty and the U.S. Congress was urging a withdrawal of troops, the surge demanded by the administration renewed the presence of overextended troop forces.

Conclusions

Pittsfield is a case study in how the process of privatized militarization intensifies the contradictions in capitalist America. During the wars of the twentieth century, industrialists were able to play on patriotism to induce the workforce to work overtime, often with little or no additional compensation, and to recruit volunteer armies during wartime. The public funds that fostered the growth of private capitalist ventures during wartime were revamped as risk capital to justify super profits made at taxpayers' expense. The billions of dollars pumped into the economy during the Cold

War of the 1980s left little heritage for subsequent generations. Few new industries were cultivated as had occurred in the preceding century. In Pittsfield, the memory of its industrial past is stored in the contaminated water and land where waste products were dumped. The vaunted educational system and social services of Pittsfield, though still in place, are starved for funds that have been diverted to the Bush war effort. The people rage at the billions siphoned off from public funds for the reconstruction of Iraq when the city is forced to lay off police, firemen, and teachers.

The future for the population of the city and for the nation is jeopardized most of all because of the way the corporations, and their allies in government, have squandered the patriotism and commitment of the workers and soldiers who served their communities and their nation. This is most apparent in the case of veterans who bore the brunt of the imperialist wars that were fought to control the world, first in the Far East and now in the Middle East. The contradictions that the Vietnam veterans lived as they were censured for doing what was required of them and what conformed to their own sense of patriotic duty, caused some to turn against the political process itself. Jim Callahan told me during our interview in December 2003:

> When Desert war started, I was going back in. I actually started to go back in as a combat medic, but then the war ended. I did want to go back in. I felt I didn't save enough lives, I wanted to save more. I'm not saying I believe in our politics. Politics of Vietnam was stupid, wrong. We didn't need to go to war to lose money and to lose lives. Big business made money. General Electric. Anyone who made weapons made money. The poor guy who graduated from high school anytime from '65 to '69 went into the service and he was scared about it. I took care of the guys who cared about it. And they just pushed us out there and didn't care about us. And I don't want politicians; I detest politicians with a passion.

While Jim's commitment to fellow soldiers made him want to return to battle, it was not in support of the war. It was to help save more lives put into harms way by politicians. Bill, on the other hand, supported the first Gulf War and defended the Iraq War as a job that had to be done quickly or else abandoned: "I don't have a problem going back there and doing what we're doing. I think it's the right thing to do. There's no more massacres, there's no more torture chambers." He believes in letting them "take back their own government, and get the hell out of there. If we have to go back there again, we should pave it over and make it into a parking lot."

I asked Larry if he felt the same, and he said, looking uncomfortable, "Well I'm a liberal." Later, he added, "Well, I just don't believe in the war, and I don't think it should have been started. That's my own opinion." Bill interjected, saying "We will find the WMD's," but Larry rejoined, "Your definition of mass destruction and mine might be different. Anyway, I wouldn't have started the war, and I wouldn't walk across the street for George Bush."

Vietnam veterans were forced to bear the burden of an unpopular war themselves. Too young to vote or even to order a drink at a bar, they fought a war that made little sense to them and that earned them the epithet "baby killers." Some, like Jim, have turned against the political process itself, rejecting the politicians who seemed to them responsible. Others, like Bill, take on war as a necessary job that should be carried out as quickly as possible or "pave it over and make a parking lot out of it," as Bill concludes. Larry urges negotiation and diplomacy through the United Nations.

The lessons of the Vietnam War are not forgotten, but though they live in the tortured memories of those who fought it, they yield unexpected perspectives on the war in Iraq. Candidates for public office can now play up their combat medals in that disastrous war and criticize those like Bush and Cheney who shirked their duty. But some veterans criticize John Kerry, the 2004 Democratic candidate for president, for having criticized the Vietnam war upon his return in 1973; others faulted his failure to vote for armament production during the Cold War.[7] Given the lack of civilian employment opportunities, Pittsfield high school graduates respond favorably to recruiters urging them to enlist in the armed services "to seek training and new challenges" (*The Berkshire Eagle,* 13 June 2004).

Like the last major imperialist war fought by Americans in Vietnam, the preemptive invasion of Iraq contradicts the claims of U.S. foreign policies to be directed toward strengthening democracy throughout the world. Young Americans are still prompted to join the armed services by patriotism, and their expectations that it will provide opportunities for travel, a college education, and greater benefits. But the increasingly privatized military operations and reconstruction in the Iraqi war, with an army made up of volunteers recruited from among the poor and recent immigrants, and with recourse to private, for-profit companies handling everything but the gunning down of the enemy, contradicts the appeal to patriotism. Soldiers may be court-martialed for carrying out orders of their superiors at the same time that security guards hired by private corporations such as CACI and Titan, which provided the private interrogation teams in Abu Ghraib, are unlikely to suffer any punishment.

The recourse to military force by the U.S. government contradicts the claims of U.S. foreign policies to be directed toward strengthening democracy throughout the world. The privatization of the Iraq War with an army made up of volunteers recruited from among the poor and recent immigrants, has thus far enabled the Bush administration to evade the public outcry. So too has the reconstruction of the country by private contractors handling everything but the gunning down of the enemy. Privatization avoids congressional oversight of these operations; when employees of these private corporations are killed, there is no public outrage, nor does it add to the accountability of the regime in charge. But the $8 billion no-bid contract awarded to Halliburton excited some criticism of Bush's running mate, Vice President Dick Cheney, a former Chief Executive Officer of the firm, as the election contest warmed up in July 2004. The indictment of Blackwater security guards' use of unwarranted force in the shootings of civilians in September 2007 may yet become the Armageddon of Bush's war.

The evasion of public responsibility in the face of the many contradictions posed by privatization in the conduct of war for profit is a denial of the democratic process, which threatens not only the national polity but also the nascent global economy. The culture of violence spawned by the U.S. military occupation in Iraq has taken on its own dynamic as the temporal and spatial boundaries between peace and war, military and civilian, and government and commerce have become blurred. This contradiction is at the root of Pittsfield veterans' reaction to the war in Iraq and its precursor in Vietnam. The war has left the country bankrupt at home, and a pariah in the world. It will require a reversal of the trend to reckless imperialist ventures for the Barack Obama administration to mend the damage and set a new course for the country.

Notes

1. Despite the benefits that Pittsfield derived from war production in the 1980s, the billions of dollars in government funds did little to stimulate employment levels nationally. Fewer jobs are created for each billion dollars spent on military investment compared with education or public transportation (Degrasse 1984), and high bids with cost overruns became the norm (Melman 1983). Accounts of fraud, waste, and corruption by military contractors further distorted the economy throughout the Reagan regime. Linked to the shift to high-tech defense production in the 1980s was a corresponding change in the workforce from blue collar workers to "steel-collar robots," the famous automated production related to intensive production (SEC K10 Report Monthly Labor Review, September 1982, cited in Nash 1989).
2. When I watched the Gulf War on television in Mexico City, the footage of antiballistic missiles rising in a perfect arch and always intercepting the enemy missiles, I felt I was back in Pittsfield's ordnance systems division watching the videos of Trident and Polaris on family day, videos used to promote sales to the Pentagon. No guts were spilled, nor were there any offensive photos of prisoner abuse during that showing.
3. Chalmers Johnson details how these operations protect "our" interests and those of our allies while expanding armaments sales (2003:55). The Vinnell Corporation, made up

of retired American military officers, has since 1975 been licensed by the government to train the Saudi National Guard to protect the monarchy. These corporations can be relied upon to train officers in foreign countries in using U.S. technology, thus expanding the market for such weapons and providing a corps of sales agents to carry out the foreign military sales program supervised by the Department of Defense. Jim Krause, Associated Press correspondent, summarizes the many private contractors operating throughout the world in order to free up U.S. troops to fight (*The Berkshire Eagle*, 30 October 2003:A1, A4). These forms of outsourcing mimic the tactics of corporations in evading the regulations on employment and taxation that once ensured responsibility in U.S. society. (See also James Surowiecki, *The New Yorker*, 12 January 2004).

4. *The Wall Street Journal* (10 October 2003:B4) noted that despite Halliburton's gains of $2 billion in revenue and an increase of 12 to 13 cents per share in profit from business in Iraq, the company is still mired in asbestos litigation and troubles in its Brazil operations.

5. Kellogg, Brown and Root, a former subsidiary of Halliburton, one of the largest private enterprises operating in Iraq and one in which Vice President Cheney occupied a leading position before becoming vice president, has been caught overcharging the U.S. government for fuel that it imported for the army from Kuwait, although the company disputes the charges, claiming that it saved taxpayers $164 million (Matt Kelley, *The Berkshire Eagle*, 12 December 2003; Jackie Spinner, *The Berkshire Eagle*, 18 December 2003).

6. The 8,000 troops from two Hawaii-based brigades of the 25th Infantry Division are being sent to Iraq and Afghanistan at a time when Bush's aggressive attacks have renewed hostilities in North Korea. Based on these forebodings, Daniel Sneider (*Miami Herald International Edition*, 28 January 2004:11A).

7. See particularly Jason Zengerle's assessment of "The Vet Wars" (*The New York Times Magazine*, 23 May 2004, Section 6, 30–35A). As the three diverse positions taken by Pittsfield's Vietnam veterans indicate, no blanket assessment of their political interpretation can be made.

Bibliography

Boltwood, E. 1916. *The History of Pittsfield, Massachusetts from the Year 1876 to the Year 1916.* Pittsfield: Pittsfield Eagle Company.
Boot, Max. 2003. "The New American Way of War," *Foreign Affairs* 82:41–58.
DeGrasse, Robert M., Jr. 1984. *The Military Is Shortchanging the Economy.* Washington D.C.: Council on Economic Priorities.
Doukas, Dimitra. 2003. *Worked Over: The Corporate Sabotage of an American Community.* Ithaca and London: Cornell University Press.
General Electric Company. 1953. "Professional management in General Electric," *General Electric Company* (New York) I:43.
General Electric. 1979. *General Electric Pittsfield News.* 15 September 1979.
Harvey, David. 2003. *The New Imperialism.* Oxford and New York: Oxford University Press.
Hedges, Chris. 2003. *What Every Person Should Know about War.* New York: Free Press.
James, Harold. 2001. *The End of Globalization: Lessons from the Great Depression.* Cambridge: Harvard University Press.
Johnson, Chalmers. 2003. "The War Business. Squeezing a Profit from the Wreckage in Iraq," *Harpers* (307)1842:538.
Lutz, Catherine. 2000. "Making War at Home in the U.S.," *Public Affairs* 104(3).

Lutz, Catherine and Donald Nonini. 2003. "The Economies of Violence and the Violence of Economies," in Henrietta L. Moore (ed.), *Anthropological theory today*. Oxford and Malden, MA: Blackwell.
Melman, Seymore. 1983. "Inflation and the Pentagon's Budget," *America* 140(30 June): 532–4.
Nash, June. 1989. *From Tank Town to High Tech: The Clash of Community and Industrial Cycles*. Albany: SUNY Press
Newman, Katherine S. 1988. *Falling from Grace: The Meaning of Downward Mobility in American Culture*. New York: Free Press.
Scahill, Jeremy. 2007. *Blackwater: The Rise of the World's Most Powerful Mercenary Army*. New York: Avalun.
Sheppard, Simon. 1998. "Foot Soldiers of the New World Order: The Rise of the Corporate Military," *New Left Review* 228:128–133.
Stiglitz, Joseph. 2008. *The Three Trillion Dollar War: The True Cost of the Iraq Conflict*. New York: Norton.

Newspaper and magazine articles

Berkshire Eagle. 1985. Reprint of Thomas B. Edsall report in *The Washington Post*, 8 June.
———. 2003. Paul Krugman Column, 13 August, A7.
———. 2003. Jim Krane, Associated Press, "In Iraq, and Around the World, U.S. Counts on Private Armies," 30 October, A1, A4.
———. 2003. Matt Kelley, "Halliburton Tied to Overcharging," Associated Press in *The Berkshire Eagle*, 12 December, A3.
———. 2003. "Editorial," 13 December, A4.
———. 2003. Associated Press Matt Kelley, "Iraq a Proving Ground as Women Fight, Die," 13 December, A1, 4.
———. 2003. Jackie Spinner, "Halliburton Subsidiary Defends Iraq Work," *Washington Post* article reprinted in *The Berkshire Eagle*, 18 December.
———. 2004. "Privatization Follies," 9 May, A8.
———. 2004. Barry Renfrew, Associated Press, "Al-Qaida Growing, Fed by Iraq War, Think Tank Warns," 27 May, A2.
———. 2004. John J. Lumpkin, Associated Press, "Troops Bound for Iraq, Afghanistan Get Tours Extended," 13 June, A1, A5.
———. 2004. Maura Reynolds, reprinted from *Los Angeles Times*, "On Eve of Trip, Bush Likens Terror Fight to World War II," 3 June, A1, A4.
———. 2004. Bill Carey, Berkshire Eagle Staff, "Quietly Growing: General Dynamics Ramps up for New Contracts," 25 July D1, D8.
———. 2007. Scott Stafford, "GE Division Sold for $11.6 Billion; A Plastics Wrap." 22 May, 1A, 4A.
International Miami Herald. 2004. Daniel Sneider, "Iraq, Afghanistan Stretching U.S. Troops," 28 January, 11A.
———. 2004. Tina Susman, "Red Tape Snares Noncitizen Soldiers Deployed Overseas," 1 February, 5A.
Miami Herald International. 2004. Hannah Allam, "Ethnic Tensions Threaten Postwar Oil," 25 January, 6A.
The New Yorker. 2004. Seymour M. Hersch, "Torture at Abu Ghraib," 10 May, 42–47.
———. 2004. James Surowiecki, "The Financial Page: Army, Inc.," 12 January, 27.
Newsweek. 2003. Rod Nordland and Michael Hirsh, "The $87 Billion Money Pit," 3 November, 26.
———. 2003. Michael Hirsch and John Barry, "What Will It Take? Casualties of War," 13 November, 22–27.
The New York Times. 2003. Elizabeth Bumiller, "Bush Defends Policy on Contract," 13 December, A1, 4.

———. 2004. Daphne Evitar, "Free-Market Iraq? Not So Fast," 10 January, B9:1,11.

———. 2004. Frank Rich, "Saving Private England: Sequel to a Hit," 16 May, Arts and Leisure section, 1, 8.

———. 2007. New York Times, 6 October: A25.

———. 2007. John W. Broder and David Rohdie, "State Department Use of Contractors Leaps in 4 Years," 24 October, A1, A8.

The New York Times Magazine. 2004. Jason Zengerle, "The Vet Wars," 23 May, Section 6, 30–35A.

U.S. Newsday. 2003. Kenneth Gailbraith column, 4 November.

The Wall Street Journal. 2004. Susan Warren and Alexei Barrionuevo, "Despite Iraq, Halliburton Profit Falls Short," 10 October, B4.

Chapter Two

POST-SOVIET FORMATION OF THE RUSSIAN STATE AND THE WAR IN CHECHNYA
Exploring the Chaotic Form of Sovereignty

Jakob Rigi

In this chapter I will analyze the relationship between state and war in Chechnya.[1] The relation between the Chechen war and state is a complex one. Three major aspects of such a relation are to be noted. First, the formation of the Soviet multinational state and its nationality policy and the place of Chechnya in the topography of the Soviet state, the particular experience of Chechen nationality, and the late Soviet crisis of the state constitute the historical context, if not the immediate causes, of the Chechen war. Second, one of the major factors that contributed to the outbreak of the war was the desire of a considerable part of Chechen political forces for independent statehood. Third, the war in Chechnya played a significant role in the formation and the transformation of the post-Soviet Russian state. In this chapter I focus on the third aspect, and deal with the first and second aspects to the extent they have influenced the third.

In the summer of 2006 I discussed the war with a Chechen who was running his own NGO focused on human rights. He explained the war by means of a conspiracy theory, condemning both Ramzan Kadyrov[2] and the Chechen fighters for their abuse of the citizens. He claimed that both Chechen fighters and Kadyrov were on the payroll of non-Chechens, mostly Jews and those Russian oligarchs who worked with the Jews. He noted, further, that the Russian government was itself controlled by

---

Notes for this chapter are located on page 77.

Jews. Then he proceeded to argue that the kidnapping of journalists, aid workers, and Australian workers that occurred during 1996–98 was on the order of Boris Berezovsky[3] and the FSB, the Russian domestic security service. He claimed that they paid Chechen warlords to kidnap and behead Australians in order to present Chechens to the world as savage people. He also contended that the Chechen separatist leader Shamil Basayev was paid to invade Daghistan (see below) in order to give the Russian army a legitimate excuse for invading Chechnya. Suggesting that Russian generals and Chechen rebels planned the war together in order to make money, he recounted stories about the cooperation between rebels and the Russian generals on the illegal sale of weapons, oil, and drugs. While some of these stories were plausible, others were contradictory and flew in the face of well-known facts.

I was not puzzled hearing my interlocutor, a learned man, explaining the war as the result of a conspiracy, as such theories are the most common interpretation of the war among Chechens, other Muslims, and Russians. A recurrent theme of these theories is that "Russia was governed by Jews, and that the Jews had created the war in order to divide Russians and Muslims and rule the country diverting the attention of people from the fact they were plundering Russia." To be sure, people who used conspiracy theories also often had additional explanations for the war. Muslims often believed that a major cause was the desire of the Russian ruling class to remain the master (*khozin*) of Muslims, and in this respect they recounted the history of Russian imperial policies and the Chechen deportation during the Stalin era. It is important to note that for these people their anticolonial narrative did not exclude the explanatory value of the conspiracy theory. On the contrary, conspiracy narratives were complementary to the anticolonial ones. To use an Althusserian term, war, in their understanding, was overdetermined by a host of factors, Russian colonial policies being one among many. Conspiracy theories were invoked to explain other, murkier causes of the war.

After visiting Russia in 1995–96 I did not return until the summer of 2003. Russian attitudes toward the conflict, as I will discuss below, had now changed radically compared with those of 1995–96. In discussions I have had with Russians since the summer of 2003, I found that they related to the war mostly in the following two ways.

1) In my experience,[4] a majority of them used various theories of conspiracy in order to explain the war. Some described it as a conspiracy by Islamists against Russia, who used the Chechen fighters as a proxy force. Others depicted it as a conspiracy by Americans and Jews who wanted to dissolve the Russian state, take over its territory, and enslave its people. The third group blamed the Kremlin for both wars but suggested that the

Kremlin was controlled by Jews. Jews had launched the war in order to divide and rule. In all of these theories, Chechens were blamed also for siding with the enemies of Russia. Chechens, it was suggested, did so because of their bigotry, ignorance, and predilection for violence.

2) There was a minority of leftists and liberals who claimed that Russia was a colonial power and that the Chechens were fighting for independence.

Conspiracy theories have changed since 1995–96. In the earlier period, such theories were either less common or were targeted at only the elite. Ordinary Chechens and Russians did not accuse each other of warmongering. On the contrary, they conceived of each other as belonging to one people who were divided and victimized by the ruling elites in Moscow and those who had been ousted from Grozny by the Russian army. While blaming both sides, they maintained that it was mainly Boris Yeltsin who was responsible for the war (Rigi 2007). More striking was the absence of any enthusiasm for the war among the majority of Russians. The "chauvinists" were a considerable minority, and most Russians opposed the war, considering it to be a domestic tragedy that had been triggered by the opportunistic policies of Yeltsin. Journalists, who at that time could still report freely on the events in Chechnya, harshly criticized the incumbent government (Gall and De Waal 1997).

During 1995–96, and as the war continued, I also met Chechen refugees in Almaty who had come to work there. While most of them supported Dzhokhar Dudaev against Yeltsin, they also believed him to be good for nothing on account of his warmongering and his provocation of the Russian military.[5] They blamed Dudaev for destroying the Chechen economy and society, while expressing strong nostalgia for the Soviet era. Although they hated Yeltsin for invading Chechnya, they still considered the Russians and themselves as belonging to the same Soviet people. In their stories, they spoke of Russians and Chechens as having been good neighbors and comrades working together in *kalkhozes* (collective farms) and factories. The war was not with the Russian people but with Yeltsin and his gang. Similar attitudes were prevalent among Kazakhs and other peoples of the former Soviet Union. This common belief in the shared Soviet identity of Chechens and Russians, and their opposition to what they saw as a mafia war, stood in stark contrast to the view prevalent in the West, where the war was believed to be the result of the clash between the Chechens' drive for independence and Russian imperial rule.

In the intervening years—in which I had not been in Russia—obviously a major development had been the rise of Russian chauvinism and the growth of a sharp mutual mistrust between Russians and Muslims. This mistrust blurred the previous line of demarcation between elites and ordinary people. Now, in conspiracy narratives all Russians, or Chechens or Muslims, are implicated as warmongers. In all versions of conspiracy theories, war is depicted as something evil and its agents as aliens. The aliens are the enemy of the "imagined community" (Anderson 1991) of the narrator, and depending on the narrator, this imagined community can be the Chechen nation, the Muslim community, or the Russian people. The war is one of their plots against such an imagined community. While the Jew is the master plotter and leader—and almost always present—there are also other culprits. Again depending on the narrator, these culprits can be the Russian government, the generals, the FSB, the Russians, the oligarchs, the Americans, NATO, Chechens, Muslims, Wahabists, terrorists, Saudis, etc. In terms of style the conspiracy theories borrow from both mythology and scholarly genres of narrative. The narrators combine citations of statistics and scholarly references with all kinds of fabricated legends. In the same vein, they interweave real and publicly known individuals and events with individual and events of their own surroundings, but they embellish these with events and individuals that are the creations of their own fantasies.

Sanders and West (2003) have suggested that conspiracy theories constitute a particular form of knowledge and should be interpreted in terms of their own epistemologies. Boyer (2006) describes how such theories can work as therapeutic devices. In my earlier work (Nazpary 2002: chapt. 6) I argued that conspiracy theories in the context of Kazakhstan constituted a form of consciousness among the dispossessed of the conditions of their own dispossession (cf. Briggs 2004).[6] In Russia today, while the dispossessed still use conspiracy theories, such claims are no longer exclusively focused on narratives of dispossession. First, as mentioned, speakers blur the lines of demarcation between the dispossessed and the dispossessor by establishing new dividing lines on the basis of identities such as Russians, Chechens, Muslims, and Christians. Second, the Russian ruling elite propagate by various means conspiracy theories in order to cultivate Russian nationalism and bolster their own power.

However, in spite of these differences, there are lines of continuity between the theories of conspiracy of these two periods in terms of tropes and content. "The alien" is still the master signifier and the content of conspiracy is the alleged "hidden transcripts" (Scott 1992) of the alien. While in 1995–96 the category of alien consisted of the ruling elites and their alleged American backers (Nazpary 2002: chapt. 6), today the alien, as described above, has become a much more fluid and complex figure.

In Russia, the conspiracy theories of and on war are parts of larger theories of conspiracy about power. These theories are mythologizing metaphors for the logic of power relations, though they may describe inaccurately the actual events and give misleading perceptions of the relation of forces. These metaphors mythologize three major aspects of contemporary mechanisms of power in Russia: 1) the extreme arbitrariness of games of power (Ledeneva 2006; Nazpary 2002; Volkov 2002; Wilson 2005); 2) the instrumentalization of these games for personal gain through patronage (Afanas'ev 2000); and 3) the centrality of plots in these games (Ledeneva 2006; Wilson 2005). Wilson (2005) and Ledeneva (2006) demonstrate that plots not only play a central role in appropriating and holding power but also are instrumental in misrepresenting power through the staging of spectacles. They show that the trope of plot connects conspiracy to spectacle, which is a major lever of power. In a metaphorical sense, conspiracy is "the hidden transcript," while the spectacle is the "public transcript" of the elite.

Chechen war, conspiracy, and spectacle are elements of a particular form of state power that elsewhere I have called the chaotic mode of domination (Nazpary 2002; Rigi 2007). I contend that the Chechen wars are the major outcomes of such a mode of domination in Russia and Chechnya. In the remainder of this chapter, I aim to accomplish the following: 1) theorize the chaotic mode of domination; 2) situate the wars in the actual processes of such domination; 3) describe briefly the ways in which the two Chechen wars contributed to the rise of the Russian nationalism. I conclude the chapter with some remarks on the relationship between war, the chaotic mode of domination, spectacle, and conspiracy.

The Chaotic Mode of Domination

The chaotic mode of domination was a state form that emerged as the response of the ruling elite to the late Soviet "crisis of hegemony" (Gramsci 1971; Nazpary 2002; Rigi 2004, 2007). For Gramsci, a crisis of hegemony is an exceptional situation in which the old ideological and legal paradigms lose legitimacy and fail to function properly. Poulantzas (1983) argued that in response to such crises the ruling classes form exceptional states in which power is exercised mostly through coercive and extralegal methods. He distinguished empirically three forms of such states: Fascism, Bonapartism, and Dictatorship. I have added to this list "the chaotic mode of domination" (Nazpary 2002; Rigi 2004, 2007), which emerged as a response to the crisis of hegemony in the post-Soviet republics and elsewhere in the former Soviet block.

In the late 1980s, the communist elite, failing to unite around a common platform, fractured along several lines. Two centers of power were created: one around Mikhail Gorbachev as the leader of the Communist Party of the USSR and president of the USSR; the other around Boris Yeltsin, president of the Russian Federation and the Russian Supreme Soviet.[7] As the Russian population and territory constituted the bulk of the territory and population of the USSR, Yeltsin became a viable challenger to Gorbachev. The intensification of the conflict between Gorbachev and Yeltsin over who had supreme authority regarding the affairs of the Russian Federation led to the collapse of the power of the center over the periphery. This collapse was accelerated by an increasing split between conservatives and reformists in Gorbachev's camp on the one hand and between center and periphery on the other. While both conservatives and reformists agreed on a transition to a market economy, they differed with respect to the pace deemed appropriate for such a transition. The conflict between center and periphery acquired primarily an ethnic character. Indeed, these two conflicts were locked into each other, as conservatives resisted the demands of the periphery for more autonomy while reformists, through opposing secessionist tendencies, agreed to concede a higher degree of autonomy to the periphery. The intensification of these conflicts led to the failed coup in August 1991 and the subsequent dissolution of the USSR in December of that same year by Yeltsin and the leaders of Ukraine and Belarus.

The chaotic mode of domination went through three phases: 1) the phase of disintegration of the central state, from 1989–92; 2) the phase of plunder, from 1992–99; and 3) the phase of the rise of authoritarian rule, from 1999 onward. In the first stage, the regional elites reorganized themselves into multiple networks of influence, which acted independently of the center (Nazpary 2002; Humphrey 1991). These networks, enjoying enormous illegal and quasi-criminal power, divided the former Soviet territory and its property into overlapping spheres. The political and managerial elite, the informal bourgeoisie, and the newly emerged mafia were key actors in creating these networks.

The second phase has been marked by the emergence of post-Soviet governmental institutions in the Russian Federation and the forging of a new balance of power between the holders of high offices in government institutions on the one hand and members of the networks of influence on the other. The reinforcement of state institutions subordinated the networks of influence to state officials, but did not eliminate them. State officials became supervisors/arbiters vis-à-vis these networks. From this point on the chaotic mode of dominance was characterized by the intertwined overcentralized arbitrariness of the state officials on the one hand and a centrifugal and anarchic arbitrariness of the members of different informal networks of influence on the other. The ways that these two levels of arbitrariness were imposed on the population and articulated with and adjusted to each other—and also the tensions between them—were significant elements of the chaotic mode of domination. A main feature of this mode of domination was the personalization of power, and presidential rule provided the general background for the arbitrariness of state officials. While various networks were plundering the country, Yeltsin's network—dubbed "the Family"—pulled the main strings. In addition to the president himself and his daughter, a handful of oligarchs, a group of pundits, bureaucrats, and politicians were part of this network.

This situation, which was a result of the confluence of the disintegration of the Soviet state and the implementation of neoliberalism, was both an instrument and consequence of the newly emerged predatory rule. Now, not only was state property stolen but the state itself was privatized. The privatization of the state occurred on two fronts: firstly, the state institutions and their resources were used for private ends; and, secondly, certain part of the erstwhile state functions, such as policing cities and taxation (now called "protection fees"), were transferred to informal networks of mafia and private security agencies (racketeers) that were closely related to the police. Although the racketeers and the private security forces are not formal governmental organizations, in practice they are part of the state coercive apparatus in its broad sense. Gramsci (1971), Poulantzas (1983), and Althusser (1994), dealing with the ideological and hegemonic aspects of state, suggested that the hegemony of ruling classes is secured through interlinked practices that permeate both governmental and nongovernmental institutions. Althusser (1994) discussed the network of such institutions.[8] In the same vein, I suggest that in the chaotic mode of domination the coercive apparatus of state permeates the legal and illegal, the formal and informal, the legitimate and illegitimate practices of the governmental institutions and networks of influence. Stated briefly, such an apparatus includes both governmental and nongovernmental organizations and practices.

The chaotic mode of domination is a globally emerging form of sovereignty outside the north as a response to the current global hegemonic crisis (Arrighi et al. 1999). It represents a significant shift in the forms of state. The state cannot anymore be sufficiently defined in a Weberian fashion as the legitimate monopolist of the means of violence, for the simple reason that the formal institutions of government have lost their monopoly over the means of violence. Informal organizations such as mafia or various ethnic gangs also have access to means of violence, and there is a huge market for such means. In the chaotic mode of domination, the coercive power of the state operates alongside complex networks of governmental institutions, private businesses, multinational businesses, and NGOs. Hardt and Negri (2001), following Deleuze and Guattari (1987), have identified a more or less similar form of sovereignty. However, from this they mistakenly concluded that the significance of the state has diminished, and that sovereignty is not territorially anchored anymore. These authors establish a false dichotomy between state and network, considering the former merely a top-down centralized bureaucracy according to its bourgeois mythology (Marx 1973 [1858]; Corrigan and Sayer 1985). By contrast, I suggest that the coercive informal network is part of the state apparatus to the extent that it *and* the state contribute to domination of the subaltern by the ruling classes.

As noted, the practice of coercion by governmental organizations and nongovernmental networks, linked to each other in a random and chaotic manner, represents a major shift in state form. But another significant change is that of the commodification of coercion. Coercion is not only an instrument of enforcing political power, it is also a direct means for the accumulation of wealth. Nongovernmental coercive organizations (mafia, ethnic gangs, and private security firms), alongside the formal institutions of the state, are the main levers of predation by dominant elites. The random and chaotic articulations of and tensions between the overcentralized arbitrariness of top governmental officials—epitomized by presidential rule—and the centrifugal arbitrariness of various networks of influence, result in the chaotic mode of domination. The basic rule of predation is the exchangeability of money, violence, and contacts. The partial privatization of the coercive apparatus and the concomitant commodification of coercion, represent radical transformations of the political and economic systems. That is, although the commodified coercion is a market element (by virtue of being a commodity), it plays a regulatory role vis-à-vis the market (Volkov 2002). Volkov (2002) describes the early predatory rule in Russia as the resurfacing of "the state of nature" in the Hobbesian sense. In other words, while political power has been the midwife of the post-Soviet market economy—and controls, to a great extent, economic transactions—power itself has become a commodity. This is an important feature of the chaotic mode of domination, as politics and economy have become indistinguishable, each essentially a branch of the other.

Bare Life

Sovereign is the one who is authorized by the law to suspend the law in name of "the state of exception," which he alone has the authority to declare (Agamben 1998). This approach might be blind to the fact that power creates the law, not the other way around (Comaroff and Comaroff 2004). Moreover, the power of the sovereign does not originate from law but is a vector of social power, of which law is just one element. However, it has the merit to expose the arbitrary nature of sovereignty and law. Foucault (1978) questioned the idea that sovereignty was an appropriate concept for understanding the nature of power in modern societies. He argued that modern power worked through a mode of production of desire that he called bio-politics. Hardt and Negri (2001), following Deleuze and Guattari (1987), suggest that bio-power is the basis of postmodern empire, a phenomenon that is making the nation-state obsolete. Agamben (1998), while crediting Foucault's concept of bio-power, questions the whole dichotomy between the top-down sovereignty and bio-politics that runs from Foucault, through Deleuze and Guattari, to Hardt and Negri. Following Arendt (1979), Agamben suggests that, besides bio-politics, totalitarian tendencies are important aspects of modernity. Thus, for him the laboratory of modern power is the concentration camp, not the hospital, school, and asylum (as Foucault would have it). Modern power works through the production of "bare life," not life in general. "Bare life" is life that is subjected to the violence of law without enjoying its protection. Bare life and the sovereign are structurally homologous, by virtue of being at the same time excluded and included in law, though in different ways. The increasing global integration of the rich and the marginalization and ghettoization of the poor by neoliberalism (Castells 1998; Nazpary 2002; Friedman 2005), and the cultural segregation by identity politics (Friedman 2005), are major mechanisms of the production of bare life.

Spectacle

Agamben's concept of bare life is very useful for the understanding of the chaotic mode of domination since it rests, on the one hand, on the use of naked force and, on the other, on bio-power. Paradoxically, the more bio-politics penetrates the social, the more it necessitates violence and coercion. However, Agamben's concept of bare life remains legalistic in the sense that it is defined with reference to law. I argue that under late capitalism, bare life is not only deprived of the protection of law but also is dispossessed from property and meaning. It is dispossessed from property through neoliberal reforms, and dispossessed from meaning through what Guy Debord called "the society of spectacle" (Debord 1995). Bare life is primarily a product of the society of spectacle, that is, the production and consumption of self-referential commodity images (Baudrillard; 1994; Jameson 1992). Bio-politics is nothing but the commodification of life under a neoliberal regime. The more capitalism colonizes everyday life, the more the sovereign becomes arbitrary. Therefore, the hidden side of this spectacle is the despair, fear, break-up, and fragmentation of society and humanity. In the West, the consumption of images was accompanied by an increase in the consumption of material goods. In Russia and other post-Soviet countries, where material consumption has decreased dramatically for the majority, material poverty is compensated for through the consumption of empty images. Images thus become the real opium of the masses, unique from the opiate of religion in that religious notions were invested with meaning while the images of post-Soviet spectacle are completely empty and devoid of any meaning. Lack of meaning in social life takes the form of a general chaos. Therefore, the chaotic mode of domination refers not only to social disorder but also to lack of meaning. Just as meaning mediates between contingency and necessity, ethics and person, morality and community, law and citizen, so the lack of meaning results in a complete arbitrariness of social relations and persons beyond personal networks. Other networks viewed from the vantage of a particular network appear to behave in fully unpredictable ways unbound to ethics, law, or morality. Cynicism and chicanery are the order of the day; anyone who is not part of one's network can be cheated and violated. A Russian friend told me, "we have no society in Russia but thousands of islands each with its own rules." This is illustrated by the contemporary ethical relativism in Russia (Shlapentokh 2004).

Competing elite networks for images (money, fame, and objects of desire) constitute a new form of sovereignty in which the leader of the most powerful network—namely, the Russian president—wields enormous power vis-à-vis the members of other networks and the population in general. He is a kind of sovereign who can make decisions about the life and death of his subjects. However, in spite of his enormous power, he has no control over chaos, and his arbitrary rule is nothing but an expression of the arbitrariness of the chaotic mode of domination.

Fight for Territory

Although the notion of deterritorialization has become an article of faith in contemporary social theory, it has been powerfully challenged by some thinkers (Harvey 2003; Wood 2003). There is much ground to argue that the territorial state still plays a significant role in relation to the reproduction of capital. Kaldor (1999), taking contemporary conflicts in Caucasus and the Balkans as her empirical ground, argues that today's wars are fought not for territory but for resources. Reno (1998), in the same vein, has argued that the main purpose of political power has become control of commerce rather than territory. However, such approaches question neither the role of the state nor the idea that the state is territorially anchored.

As I have argued earlier, wars in the Caucasus were influenced by dimensions of the chaotic mode of domination. I also contend that force plays the final role in such a mode of domination. And although the means of violence are dispersed among various networks, the networks of the state officials have the final say. Moreover, while the informal networks have transnational links and are involved in transnational transactions, connections with state institutions that are based in the territory are indispensable. The reason is that the legitimacy of these institutions is recognized internationally, though questioned nationally (cf. Reno 1998). Indeed, this provides state officials with the power to include or exclude, arbitrarily, a particular network or business partner in the plunder of the national economy. In brief, while in the chaotic mode of domination there is a sovereign who represents the state and its territory and enjoys enormous power over the inhabitants of that territory, the centralized bureaucratic state exists only as an image. The state is nothing but the sum of networks, a kind of re-feudalization of power mechanisms. Under this condition, contrary to the perceived wisdom, territorialization is a major aspect of the chaotic mode of domination promoted by globalizing processes that allegedly undermine territoriality. Indeed, the war in Chechnya is nothing but the struggle between Moscow and Chechen ruling networks for the control of the territory of Chechnya, which has considerable oil resources and pipeline routes and is located in a geo-strategically significant place. As we will see, the war became nationalized for both Chechens and Russians not because people supported their own leader's war efforts, but because the combatants indiscriminately violated the civil population of the other side.

The First War (2004–06)

The Chechen war had a host of causes (Derluguian 1999; Evangelista 2002), including the Chechens' historical memory of conflict with and repression by the Tsarist and Soviet states (Dunlop 1998).[9] Although Chechnya was not an ASSR[10] republic (Autonomous Socialist Soviet Republic), it was part of the Autonomous Republic of Chechnya-Inguesh, within the Russian Federation. With the demise of the USSR, it declared its independence. Yeltsin, the president of the Russian Federation, dismissed the Chechens' declaration of independence and vowed to keep the republic within the Russian Federation by all means, including the use of force. This led to the wars of 1994–96 and 1999-onward.[11]

Chechnya had significant peculiarities compared with most other Soviet nationalities. First, Chechens had fresh memories of their en masse deportation to Kazakhstan during the Second World War. Second, most Chechens lived in the countryside and preserved their language and traditions, particularly clan structures and solidarities called *taeipeh*. Third, Chechnya was relatively homogenous ethnically. While in many other parts of the Soviet Union, where often people with numerous ethnic backgrounds lived, Chechnya was mainly populated by Chechens and Russians, with Chechens being the majority. With the introduction of *glasnost* ("openness"), competing social movements emerged in Chechnya, some nationalist in nature and others environmentalist. In 1989 Doka Zavgaev, an ethnic Chechen and the general secretary of the Communist Party in Chechnya, tried to obtain concessions from Moscow. Radical Chechen nationalists were unhappy about his moderate approach toward Moscow, and so they formed the Vainakh (a reference to Chechens and Ingush) party and invited Dzhokhar Dudaev to lead their movement. As Zagaev failed to oppose the coup against Gorbachev, in August 1991 he abdicated office as the Chechen Supreme Soviet dissolved itself. This opened a space for Dudaev's forces to seize the government's buildings and confiscate weapons. As Dudaev became the ruler of Chechnya, he expanded his rhetoric on independence. In response to this, Yeltsin, the Russian president, wrote on 19 October to the Chechen National Congress demanding that Dudaev's forces leave the occupied buildings, return their weapons, disband their military organization, and hold elections on 17 November (Evangelista 2002; Gall and De Waal 1998). Outmaneuvring Yeltsin, Dudaev held elections on 27 October, as a result of which he was elected president. The members of a Chechen parliament were also elected. The Russian parliament declared the Chechen election illegal, and on 2 November Yeltsin dispatched 2,500 troops to take control of Chechnya. Declaring martial law, Dudaev mobilized Chechens against the invasion. All competing functions rallied behind Dudaev with arms. The Russians retreated, which led to a dramatic increase in Dudaev's popularity.

In December 1991, Yeltsin and the incumbent leaders of Ukraine and Belarus disbanded the USSR. Dudaev used this opportunity to declare Chechnya an independent state and to expand his armed forces. Chechnya under Dudaev became a prime example of the chaotic mode of domination. It was anything but a state in the conventional sense. Various armed gangs, independent of each other, roamed around, with Dudaev's armed gangs having the upper hand. It was a criminal place, and all kinds of black markets were booming, including a huge weapons market. The republic had become a center for the operation of the Chechen Mafia as well as for the Russian Mafia and oligarchs. It became an important place for the transfer of illegal money, contract killings, and the smuggling of gold, weapons, oil, and other goods on a vast scale. The Dudaev government had an administrative apparatus in name only. While Dudaev kept himself busy by giving interviews to various journalists, the rest of his crew was idle (Gall and De Waal 1998:104–105). The salaries of the state employees had not been paid for months, and in the harsh winter many households and workplaces were deprived of fuel supplies. The fabric of society had disintegrated and "the civic life had collapsed" (Gall and De Waal 1998:103). Moreover, the economy had collapsed; the production of oil, the major source of income, had fallen dramatically and unemployment was rampant. Corruption was growing fast. Although Dudaev himself was not interested in accumulating private wealth, those around him used all methods to get rich (Gall and De Waal 1998:108). A striking contrast between wealth and poverty was evident. While the newly rich semimafia elite were driving their Mercedes and building their villas in the suburbs of Grozny, the majority of people lived hand to mouth and could barely heat their homes in the harsh winters. As a result, the popularity of Dudaev declined and people started protesting against his regime.

More moderate and politically capable Chechen leaders, most notably Ruslan Khasbulatov, wanted to negotiate a special status, similar to one that Tatarstan had achieved earlier,[12] for Chechnya within the Russian federation. Dudaev and his supporters, however, depicted these moderates as traitors. The opposition launched demonstrations against Dudaev and the Chechen parliament opposed his rule. Dudaev resorted to despotic methods: he disbanded the parliament in April 1993 (Evangelista 2002:29) and banned demonstrations against his government. Dudaev was also extremely simple-minded and inflexible with respect to Russia and aptly played into the hands of hawks in Moscow. He knew only two alternatives: full independence or war, though some commentators (Evangelista 2002) have claimed that if he had been treated with respect by Yeltsin, he might have shown more flexibility toward Russia.

Such was the situation in Chechnya when Yeltsin needed "a small victorious war" in order to boost his popularity in 1994. Yeltsin was the most apt character for the late and post-Soviet politics of spectacle. A cynical populist, he styled himself as the spontaneous and emotional Russian *Mushik* ("real man"). His network of policy advisors, generals, and businessmen were a group of equally cynical people who considered the whole former Soviet territory their private fiefdom. Establishing a chaotic mode of domination, they plundered the resources of the Russian Federation and were involved in extortion in the Caucasus and Central Asia. Yeltsin bombarded the Russian Supreme Soviet in 1993, and through the spectacle of the referendum increased his personal legal authority. His neoliberal regime ruined Russia. Millions became unemployed and the payment of dramatically reduced wages and pensions were delayed for months. While health care had collapsed, suicide and alcoholism were on the rise. Groups of oligarchs and Mafia networks were dividing the country using contacts, bribery, and violence. Most Russian cities had become battlefields for various Mafia groups linked to the ruling elite (Volkov 2002). In the midst of all of this, Yeltsin's popularity was on the decline and his advisors thought that the spectacle of short victories might boost it (Gall and De Waal 1998). Therefore, Yeltsin's side did whatever it could to provoke Dudaev into war (Evangelista 2002).

The majority of both Russians and Chechens were opposed to the war (Gall and De Waal 1998; Evangelista 2002). I spent time during the war in Moscow and St. Petersburg, and I could not help but admire the antiwar attitudes of Russians. Journalists, politicians, human rights campaigners, political parties, soldiers' mothers, and ordinary people all opposed the war.[13]

I spent one and a half years in Kazakhstan doing anthropological fieldwork during the period of war, when there was an influx of refugees, mainly women and children from Chechnya. I had an opportunity to talk with many of them. None of them were hostile to the Russian people; on the contrary, they considered themselves and Russians to belong to the same Soviet people (*Sovietskii Narod*). They would tell me that they and the Russians had worked as good comrades in *kalkhozes* and factories side by side, lived peacefully in the same neighborhoods, celebrated various occasions together, and invited each other to their homes and shared food and drink. They understood the conflict as Yeltsin's war. While they criticized Dudaev for not having done anything good for Chechnya, they supported him unanimously against Yeltsin. They thought that Yeltsin had planned the total destruction of the Chechen people. As other scholars have commented (Evangelista 2002; Gall and De Waal 1998), this was also true of most Chechen political groups who opposed Dudaev. After the Russian invasion, they put aside their differences and rallied behind Dudaev. In this way, Yeltsin nationalized the war for Chechens. Yet for the majority of Russians the war remained the war of Yeltsin. It took five years' worth of national and international catastrophic events, most of them unrelated to Chechnya, to turn the second Chechen war, which started 1999, into a national war for Russians.[14]

On New Year's Eve, a battalion of Russian tanks invaded Grozny. The Chechens, who were well prepared, destroyed most of the tanks and in the course of a few days killed thousands of Russian soldiers and captured hundreds of them.[15] Humiliated by the Chechen's fierce resistance, the Russian army bombarded Grozny savagely and indiscriminately by air and land. After resisting for a month, the Chechen rebels left for the mountains.

The Commodification of War and the Spectacle of Terrorism

The war became a kind of business: the Chechens bought their weapons from the Russian army officers, using dollars they earned through drug trafficking or other illegal means. Ordinary conscripts who had been forced to go to the war sold their weapons in order to get food and money. The Russian invasion increased the number of illegal economic dealings in Chechnya. Networks of rebel leaders, the Russian army, and various elite gangs in Moscow, taking advantage of the war, used Chechnya for their illegal dealings. The Russian army was in shambles; soldiers did not have enough food or suitable dress, and their superiors treated them savagely.

The war also led to terrorism. In June 1995, Shamil Basayev with a group of Chechen fighters invaded the Russian city of Budennovosk and took a few thousand people hostage in a hospital. Initially, the Russian forces attacked the hospital and as a result a number of Russians were killed. But as this embarrassed the regime, Basayev successfully negotiated a deal with Viktor Chernomyrdin (then prime minister) to get a safe corridor for the Chechen fighters to retreat. This was a propaganda coup for the Chechens, because the whole process was covered by Russian television. The Chechens started to stage their own counter-spectacles. In January 1996 Salman Raduyev, another Chechen warlord, occupied the Russian city of Kizliar and again thousands of innocent citizens were taken hostage. Raduyev tried to negotiate a similar deal with the Russian government but the Russians refused Raduyev's request. The Chechens retreated to Chechnya, taking hostages with them. Russian forces attacked the convoy and killed some of the hostages.

The war, which dragged on until 1996, became extremely unpopular. Chechens were killing Russian soldiers on a daily basis. On the other hand, a Russian army in disarray killed and harassed civilians. Soldiers' mothers, peace activists, journalists, and many others opposed the war. As the presidential election was approaching, Yeltsin needed a peace deal in order to boost his candidacy. He appointed Alexander Lebed, a retired army general, to negotiate a peace deal with the Chechens. But the Russians, playing a double game, negotiated peace while attacking the Chechens militarily. They assassinated Dudaev on 21 April. Chechens, responding to the Russians (or, in fact, using the same tactic) stormed Grozny and recaptured it. This was a notable feat in the war of spectacles. Subsequently, a peace deal was signed and the Russian forces withdrew from Chechnya. The Chechens would run the republic independently until 2001, in which the final status of Chechnya would be decided by a referendum.

Chechnya became de facto independent once again. Presidential and parliamentary elections were held, which international observers described as free and fair. Basayev, who flirted with Islamists, Zelimkhan Iandarbaev, an extreme nationalist, and Aslan Maskhadov, a secular and also moderate in his policies vis-à-vis Russia, competed for the presidency. Maskhadov got the majority of votes. By voting for Maskhadov, the Chechen people had voted for secularism and had made a conciliatory gesture toward Russia.

The Second Chechen War and Russia's Transition to the Third Phase of the Chaotic Mode of Domination

In the period between the two wars, the chaotic mode of domination was exacerbated in both Chechnya and Russia. The events that led to the second war and the agents of these events were also significant actors in the chaotic mode of domination. Maskhadov's efforts at establishing a working secular government failed. Maskhadov blamed both Moscow and the Chechen Islamists and extremists. Fragmentation, which had been overcome temporarily in the face of a common enemy, resurfaced more powerfully in Chechnya. The notoriety that the field commanders such as Basayev and Raduyev gained during the military campaign against Russia made it possible for them to question Maskhadov's authority and run their own independent military gangs. The result was total chaos in Chechnya. Raduyev started kidnapping Russians and Europeans in order to extract ransom money. The notorious oligarch Berezovsky, paying him huge amounts of money, negotiated with him for the release of several Russian and foreign hostages.[16] Basayev, now joined by the notorious Ibn al-Khattab, had started an Islamic movement, and his military gangs, not obeying Maskhadov, had carved a sphere of influence for themselves. Lesser warlords were also involved in kidnappings, robberies, smuggling, and various other criminal activities.[17] Maskhadov did not succeed in establishing a unified Chechen government authority that would rule according to law. Chechnya was much closer to what Hobbes called "a state of nature" (Hobbes 1991). Everyone fought against everyone else. Maskhadov probably lacked both the will and the means to discipline warlords. The Chechen fighters were fragmented along the patronage networks of various warlords, and Maskhadov lacked a force that could bring recalcitrant warlords to the law. He particularly avoided disciplining Basayev, though publicly he criticized him. He also gave in to the Islamists, and under pressure from the Sharia court disbanded the Chechen parliament.

The situation was such in Chechnya that in the first days of August 1999, Basayev and Khattab—along with a large number of Chechen fighters accompanied by Islamists from Daghistan and other parts of Central Asia and the Middle East—invaded Daghistan, formally a part of the Russian Federation, in order to help the local Islamists who had rebelled against the Daghistani government. This invasion was not an isolated event but rather one in line with Basayev's and Khattab's strategy to create a unified Islamic state in the Caucasus. Although Basayev and Khattab were forced to retreat to Chechnya under pressure from the local Daghistanis aligned against them, the invasion gave the Russians the pretext to start the second war. The forces of the Federal Interior Ministry arrived in the areas of Tsumadin and Boltikh, the invaded areas, on 4 August.

The second war inaugurated the third phase of the chaotic of mode of domination, coinciding with the rise of and consolidation of Putin's power. A major aspect of this phase is the spectacle of order. One must emphasize the *spectacle* of order because, in spite of the increase in Putin's power, chaos and corruption did then and continue now to exist (Shlapentokh 2003). This third phase was simultaneously an outgrowth of and reaction to the second phase. During the second phase, the vast Russian territory and its disintegrating federal structure underscored the enormous scope of post-Soviet chaos. Uncertainty, fear, rage, despair, and disorientation had become the main features of Russian mass psychology (Colton and McFaul 2003). By this time, the majority of Russians had become disillusioned with the West as well. While in the late 1980s and the early 1990s most Russians in the large cities considered the West to be both a role model and a friend, during the late 1990s they considered it to be a threat. The effects of the neoliberal reforms, peaking during the financial crash of 1998 that ruined most Russians economically, were instrumental in invoking widespread anti-Western sentiments. The expansion of NATO eastward, and the war in Yugoslavia, also contributed to the growth of anti-Western attitudes among Russians. The latter felt that the West had reduced them to a second- or third-rate nation. These negative feelings were reinforced by Western depictions of Russia as backward, corrupt, and despotic: a Russia that not only could not be included in the West but also remained a constant threat, either by being strong or by being weak. When strong, it was (and is) considered to be a threat to the Poles, the Czechs, and other outpost of Western civilization; when weak, it might produce organized crime and spread weapons of mass destruction. Some of these descriptions may point to empirical realities; the West, however, tends to use them often in an Orientalist and cynical manner and denies its own responsibility for contributing to the chaotic mode of domination. Russians are painfully aware of these derogatory and hypocritical attitudes, and after being seduced by the West in the late Soviet and early post-Soviet era, they feel they have been used, cheated, and betrayed. After a decade of neoliberal looting and political chaos, people were (and are) exhausted and deeply disillusioned with what they felt to be the unrealized promises of liberal democracy.[18]

Therefore, the image of a strong man—a great "bully"—who could bring the small bullies under centralized rule and thereby restore a minimal level of order had become popular among Russians by 1998. In 1999, the chaotic mode of domination was at its peak. The two main networks of power in Moscow, "the Family" (headed by Yeltsin) and those who were headed by Yuri Luzhkov, waged a dirty media war for power. They were competing for the forthcoming parliamentary and presidential elections. Besides these two networks, the Communist Party was a considerable contender for power. The main slogan of all parties was "law and order" (Kagarlitsky 2002; Colton and McFaul 2003), a slogan that had a strong populist resonance.

By this time "the Family" and its head had been brought to disrepute through the resurfacing of a series of allegations of corruption in the Western and Russian press. Ironically, the candidate of the family won the presidential election. The reason was the political spectacle that the family, using modern technology, staged. And the war in Chechnya was a main part of this spectacle.[19] The main tropes of the war drama were nation and state, and its main personage was Vladimir Putin, with armies of military, secret police, and troops from the Interior Ministry in the background.

Chechnya was a good site for the staging of the drama. It had become the symbol of the threat that Russians felt. First, in the two years of its de facto independence Chechnya had been the most chaotic place in the Russian Federation. Islamism, warlord-led anarchy, and kidnappings had outraged Russians and spoiled the previous goodwill of the majority of Russians for peace. Even Roy Medvedev supported the new war against Chechnya. Second, Chechens, by defeating the Russian army and demanding their independence, were signifying the perceived threat of the disintegration of the Russian federation. The invasion of Daghistan by Basayev and Khattab poured petrol on the already burning feelings of fear and uncertainty.

Another type of phenomenon, which laid the psychological ground for war, was a range of bombings in Russia. On 4 September 1999, the day before the invasion of Daghistan by Basayev, a bomb exploded in an apartment block, in Buinaksk, Daghistan, killing sixty-four people and injuring hundreds. On 9 and 13 September, respectively, two bombs destroyed two apartment blocks in Moscow. Three days later, a truck bomb exploded near an apartment block in Volgodonsk in Rostov oblast (Evangelista 2002:67; Kagarlitsky 2002). The bombings killed from three hundred (Evangelista

2002:67) to a thousand (Kagarlitsky 2002) and injured more than a thousand others. Evangelista (2002:67) is correct to argue that the bombings created the same panic, confusion, and fear among Russians that the 9/11 attacks created among Americans.

And "the Family" used this mass psychology of panic and confusion to stir up Russian chauvinism and mobilize public opinion for a new war in Chechnya. While these bombings were blamed on Chechens, the Chechens denied responsibility. Many have speculated that the Russian FSB was involved in the bombings in order to create a sense of panic to legitimize the new campaign against the Chechens. The so-called Riazan event is cited as an evidence for such speculations.

On the night of 22 September 1999, the few residents of a working class neighborhood in Riazan observed suspicious activities of three strangers around an apartment block. They called the local police, who arrested the suspects and found a huge amount of explosives on them. The suspects told the local police that they were FSB officers from Moscow and urged them to contact their superiors in Moscow. FSB headquarters in Moscow confirmed that the suspects were officers on a particular mission to Riazan and that they had pretended to plant material in the building in order to test the readiness of the population against a possible terrorist threat. Then the three FSB officers were transferred to Moscow. Later, FSB authorities in Moscow denied that the material was at all explosive and insisted that it was merely sugar, while the local police, journalists, and other authorities insisted that the material was explosive.

Amid chaos and feelings of deep insecurity, "The Family" camp—which had monopoly control over the state-run television service—staged Putin as the champion of law and order, and Putin played his role promptly by taking charge of the war in Chechnya.[20] He flew to Daghistan and took charge personally of the campaign. Then Putin gave an ultimatum to Maskhadov, demanding that he must arrest and hand over to Moscow "the bandits," meaning Basayev and Khattab, within a short period of time or face a Russian invasion. Then Russian forces crossed the Chechen border and began bombarding villages and towns. Later, Putin declared Maskhadov's government illegitimate. This was a completely arbitrary declaration. Notwithstanding his weakness, Maskhadov had come to power in an election in which the majority of Chechens took part and which, according to foreign observers, was fair. Once again, different Chechen groups put aside their differences and united against Russian forces. The Russian army subjected the Chechens en masse to the most brutal treatment (Human Rights Watch 2000).[21] Later, the Chechens resorted to suicide bombing tactics. Though in military terms this war has no winner, both Chechen warlords and Russian networks of influence make money out of it (Politkovskaya 2001) while the mutual destruction of Chechen and Russian civilian communities continues.

The Rise of Russian Imperial Nationalism

The war has also poisoned Russian society with nationalism. I returned to Russia in the summer of 2003 and stayed in St. Petersburg, my favourite city, for three months. I found that things had changed dramatically, as the characteristically generous Russian spirit had, if not vanished, become enfeebled. Various corners of society had been flooded by chauvinism. This chauvinism targeted not only Chechens but all non-Russian or even all nonwhite people.[22] Chechens and Muslims from the Caucasus were particularly subjected to harassment and extortion by the Russian police.

The following story is telling: Mohamed was a Talesh, a small ethnic group living in northern Iran and the post-Soviet republic of Azerbaijan. When I met Mohamed he had already lived in St. Petersburg for ten years, married a Russian woman, fathered a couple of kids, and had otherwise become well integrated into and loved by his wife's family. While his wife and her family were Orthodox Christians, Mohamed remained a Muslim. Giving me a ride one day Mohamed asked me, "Are you a Muslim, Jakob?" I answered, no. "What is your religion, then?" asked Mohamed. "I have got none," I replied. "Are your parents Muslim?" he asked. "Yes they are," I replied. "Then, why aren't you a Muslim?" he asked. "Because, I don't believe that God exists," I answered. "Yes, he exists," Mohamed retorted. "Prove it," I teased him. "I will prove it," he said, adding:

> You know, whenever I am in a difficult situation God helps me. A few months ago the police officers stopped me on the street; you see I am Caucasian. I look like a Muslim, and police officers often stop Muslims in order to extract money from them. They checked the car everywhere but couldn't find anything wrong. Then they searched me, and one of the officers searching my pockets showed me a lump of hash and said, "Aha, you are a drug dealer." I protested that it wasn't my hash, but they arrested me anyway and took me to the police station. The police (*menti*) do this always; they plant drugs in the cars or pockets of people from [the] Caucasus or Central Asia and then the relatives and friends must collect money and offer it to the police in order to free the arrested person.[23] They demanded two thousands dollars from me. I told them that I had no relative in Russia and I myself had no money. They told me if we put you in jail you will find both relatives and the money. While I was sitting sad and desperate there, suddenly, an officer, emerging from another room, shouted "What are you doing here, Mohammad?" I told him the story; he talked with them and they let me go. I had given this officer a ride a while ago and on the path to his destination we spoke and I did not charge him. You see this was a

work of God that I met this officer in the first place and also the work of God that he was in there that night.

Then Mohamed continued to tell me several other stories about chance encounters he had with influential Russian authorities who had handed their cards to him and promised to protect him against the police. God had put all these nice Russians in his path in order to protect him against the police. Mohamed was a real *homo sacer*, and his life a "bare life" subjected to violence of the state without any protection.

Now, let us leave St. Petersburg and go to Moscow and visit another *homo sacer*. His name is Arslan, a Chechen, who lived in Moscow, and had a Russian fiancée.[24] He had lived in Moscow for eight years, had made his military service in the Russian army, and worked in Moscow. On 18 September he went with his fiancée to register following the mayor of Moscow Yuri Luzhkov's order that those who were not the permanent residents of Moscow should re-register. He was arrested and separated from his fiancée, and transported to another police station where there were many other Chechens and Inguishes. There they got some addict to plant heroin in Arslan pockets and wanted Arslan to sign the papers confessing to heroin possession. Arslan refused and instead asked for a lawyer. Meanwhile his fiancée's meeting with the head of the Vykhino[25] police department and district prosecutor succeeded in bailing out Arslan. The police, upset by the fact that Arslan was bailed out, threw him out without documents. Outside the station a crafty man tied his hands and took him back into the prison. Now he was accused of attacking and insulting someone.

These types of attitudes were not limited to the police but rather were widespread among Russians. Let me quote a young woman.

> Caucasians come here in groups, trade here in our soul, threaten and violate Russians. We are from the West and they are from the East. Therefore we have completely different mentalities. Chechens are a violent race and they should not be included in the Russian society. Caucasians should be kept out from the mainland Russia; but Russia has the right to keep Caucasus by force, part of its territory.

She added that she was not a racist, but when she sees terrorist actions she wants to become a racist. She was referring to a suicide bombing that had occurred in Moscow in the previous week. I tried to explain to her the roots of the problem and she was seemingly convinced, but suddenly she said, "if they kill someone I love, then I will say 'fuck these arguments' and I will kill them."

Although the attitude expressed here belongs to a young person and is stated strongly and straightforwardly, it is shared, in a much more subtle and sinister form, by a broad range of the population. What is striking in the above quote is the explicit imperial nature of the young woman's nationalism. She argues that Russia should have the right to rule over the Caucasus while Caucasians have no right to live in St. Petersburg. Implicit in this rhetoric is the legitimacy of the use of force against the Caucasus for keeping intact the Russian Empire.[26] Such attitudes are widely shared among various strata within Russian society, including the intelligentsia. In the summer of 2004, every night I visited a club where a young St. Petersburg intelligentsia of both genders gathered. I stayed the whole night there and spoke with various individuals. To be fair, they were by no means racist and were very generous and friendly to me (I am not "white"). However, in discussions about the Caucasus imperial attitudes and emotions often, if not always, surfaced. The following example is suggestive.

It was the middle of the night, and the club and the part of the street where it is located were fully packed. I was sitting on the pavement drinking beer and talking to Lena, an extremely intelligent hairdresser. A young man whom I knew approached me and said, "We have a discussion and need your help." When I joined them, there were a group of five men and two women. They were discussing whether it was ethically and politically advisable to join Abkhazians[27] in the case of Georgian invasion. Actually, Georgia had threatened a few days before that it might use force against "Abkhazian separatists." They all had been to Abkhazia.[28] The young man told me that Abkhazians were a toiling people and had been repressed by both Georgians and Russians under the Soviet regime. After independence,[29] their living standards improved and Georgia had colonial ambitions toward the Abkhazians. These young people had friends in Abkhazia and therefore felt morally obliged to fight alongside Abkhazia if Georgia attacked. I told them that their intensions were noble, but I had heard many people depicting the conflict between the Chechens and Russia in the same terms. Suddenly, every one became silent and disconcerted. My question had disrupted their discussion and perhaps reminded them that they were not the generous idealists that they thought themselves to be. The implicit undertone of the question, though I did not spell it out, was this: if you genuinely care about the freedom of oppressed people, then you should be concerned with the repression of Chechens by your own government. Otherwise, your benign attitudes on Abkhazia may be an expression of your desire to remain the masters of the Caucasus. This was a learned crowd and therefore they could not fail to understand what my question was hinting at. The man who had invited me broke the silence. He answered that Russian policies in Chechnya are not imperialist but defensive. He went on to say that the West wants to disintegrate Russia, and the Americans to have military bases in Georgia and Azerbaijan. Chechens, he continued, are the puppets of the West. What I did not expect from an enlightened person like him was his attitude toward Chechens. He described the latter as violent, uncivilized bigots. Moreover, these bad characteristics, he claimed, sprang inevitability from the essence of Chechen bad "ethnos."[30] Therefore, the Chechens did not understand any language except that of force. Most Russians hold Chechens in a similar light. Even journalists and academics who claimed to be liberal, espoused similar attitudes or evaded the question altogether whenever I brought up the question of Chechnya. This represented a sharp contrast to 1995–96, when most people were against the war.

Conclusions: Conspiracy, Spectacle, Bare Life, and Violence

Whether the invasion and the subsequent war were planned or occurred in an ad hoc way remains unclear. "The Family," however, used the conflict skilfully to boost Putin's popularity. When Yeltsin appointed him prime minister, declaring that Putin should replace him as president, the latter was a nonentity. At that time his popularity rate was 12 percent, but after the war had proceeded for a couple of months his popularity rate soared to 70 percent. Although the Russian media, which were manipulated by "the Family," exaggerated Putin's popularity (this was an election tactic [Kagarlitsky 2002; Colton and McFaul 2003]), the war turned Putin overnight from a nobody into a national hero.

The invasion, the bombings in Moscow and elsewhere, and the onslaught of the Russian army on Chechnya were spectacles of force. Basayev and Khattab staged the first one, the directors and players of the second one are still unknown, and the third one was orchestrated by Yeltsin's network for cynical purposes. The two first spectacles contributed to the preparation of the psychological ground for the successful staging of the third one. On the basis of such a structural correlation, conspiracy theories have become popularized suggesting that Yeltsin's network was involved in encouraging both the invasion and the bombings. The alleged meeting between Basayev and Alexander Voloshin—Yeltsin's chief of staff—is mentioned as evidence for such a conspiracy. This theory and the purported evidence have neither been refuted nor proved convincingly. However, the conspiracy theory points to an elementary structural logic in the chaotic mode of domination. The extra-legal nature of such domination, and the fact that it is a form of network-based state, makes social and political events extremely contingent and arbitrary. Those who occupy particular nodal points in the networks enjoy enormous arbitrary power over the life and death of others. Their decisions and actions, which constitute the state of exception, are hidden from the rest of the population by staging spectacles. In other words: the chaotic mode of domination is a spectacular/conspiratorial form of sovereignty. Spectacles compensate the lack of transparency in power mechanisms.

What facilitates the marriage between spectacle and conspiracy is that spectacle, like conspiracy, is based on a plot and is equally arbitrary. While spectacle becomes the appearance of conspiracy, it is staged to hide the real content of conspiracy.[31] Now, it might be a far-fetched speculation to suggest that Chechen rebels and the Russian army—or, to take other examples, Ariel Sharon and Hamas, or Osama bin Laden and officials in the U.S. government—coordinate their activities to create chaos and mayhem in order to benefit from it. However, structurally this does happen as the mutual hostilities create a structure in which one party legitimizes its strategies on the basis of the allegedly evil nature of its enemy, the latter being a necessary signifier of legitimacy. Indeed, there is a kind of "structural conspiracy" that coordinates the activities of foes in a way that the actions of one provoke and justify those of the other, though spectacularized for different constituencies. Baudrillard (2002) has described the current situation as the system at war with itself. This is nothing but chaos, however, the system only survives through such chaos. Herein lies the logic of the structural conspiracy. While antagonists fight with hatred against each other, they obey and contribute to the same economy of spectacle; they are the agents of a common universal alienation. They perpetuate and reproduce global capitalism.

Let me elaborate: the era that was inaugurated by the Enlightenment and the French Revolution—that is, the era of capitalism—is in definite crisis. This is a civilizational crisis, meaning one that is at the same time ethical, intellectual (Lyotard 1984), political, and economic.[32] On the ethical level any commitment to emancipation from repression and exploitation is mocked; nothing matters, except cynical pleasure. On the intellectual level, the simulacrum has replaced the truth. These two taken together constitute, as Angela Carter (1984) would have it, the logic of the brothel. And what is contemporary capitalism, if not a global brothel. On the political level, crisis expresses itself on two levels: 1) An international hegemonic crisis (Arrighi et al. 1999); and 2) the emergence of a chaotic mode of domination nationally. These two taken together (again) subject humanity to enormous destruction and violence, which are also the means of restructuring capital. The immediate expression of economic crisis is the slow growth of the economy of advanced industrialized regions of the world since 1970 (Brenner 1999) and the economic destruction of the most of the rest of world (Castells 1998; Nazpary 2002)—with their enormous social effects in term of unemployment and poverty. In response to this crisis the ruling classes launched their neoliberal economic policies, which not only escalated an ongoing dispossession of the masses (Harvey 2003; Nazpary 2002) but also subjected life and nature to the logic of capital: namely, the making of profits. Water, air, plants, human bodies, genes, organs of the body, sperms and eggs have become commodified, a situation that has wrought huge destruction of both nature and life, bringing the capitalist mode of production to its ultimate limits. As nature and life are preconditions to any production, so the mode of production that destroys them questions not only the preconditions of its own existence but any and all production in general—and thereby threatens the very existence of the human race. And such crises impoverish human life materially and spiritually and subject them to violence; they produce bare life.

New imperial policies, various fundamentalisms (be they Muslim, Hindu, Christian, or Jewish), and all kinds of ethnic nationalism, whether in dominant or subordinated nations, are responses to this situation. All of these are the forces of fragmentation, division, and separation that scavenge the boneyards of history to find specious relics and apotheosize them as banners of hatred and violence. The mutual antagonism is a sign of the fact that capitalist civilization is not a horizon (a hegemony) anymore but just a barbaric chaos. And this antagonism is a constituent element of the chaos, a chaotic mechanism through which the capitalist system is reproduced. Herein lies the logic of structural conspiracy.

Is there any hope out of this situation? There undoubtedly is, but it requires a historically unprecedented heroic effort. Humanity needs to invent a new horizon of emancipation, one based not on individualism and commodity fetishism; rather, a horizon that replaces pornographic pleasure with the happiness of love and simulacrum with truth and reinstates the value of revolution. And for all of these we need unwavering and burning commitments, commitment to a lover, to truth, and to revolution (Badiou 2001). From this perspective the main evil is late capitalist cynicism with all kinds of fundamentalisms and ethnicisms being its offshoots.

Notes

1. This chapter is based on fieldwork in Russia 1995–96, 2003, 2004, 2005–06, and 2007.
2. The current president of Chechnya (and son of assassinated former president, Akhmad Kadyrov), allied with the Kremlin, who was then prime minister.
3. A Russian former oligarch of Jewish origin who amassed great wealth and political influence under President Boris Yeltsin. President Vladimir Putin forced him into exile, and he now is living in London.

4. I did not conduct a survey or rely on any previous survey; rather, this judgment is based on personal experience. But in the course of five years I have discussed this topic with numerous Russians, ranging from waitresses to businessmen to intellectuals.
5. Dudaev (1944–1996) was the Chechen president in the period 1991–1996.
6. I published *Post-Soviet Chaos. Violence and dispossession* under the name Joma Nazpary (see references).
7. The conflict between Gorbachev and Yeltsin dates back to the late 1980s. Then Yeltsin, as a member of politburo of the Communist Party, publicly criticized the slow speed of reforms. For this, Gorbachev sacked him from the politburo of the Communist Party. As an outspoken politician, Yeltsin gained popularity among the democrats and other groups who radically opposed the old regime. As a result, he was elected to the Russian Supreme Soviet and became its president.
8. Political parties, family, church, media, and what in bourgeoisie ideology is depicted as civil society are various elements of such an apparatus.
9. During the frequently brutal expansion of the Russian empire into the Caucasus, Chechens offered the staunchest resistance to the Russian armies and were most harshly repressed by Russians. In the eighteenth century, Chechens resisted with arms the Russian intrusion into their territory under the leadership of Sikh Mansur, a religious and military leader. In the early nineteenth century, Russians renewed their attempt to colonize Chechnya. The notorious general Aleksei Ermolov, who led the Russian campaign against Chechnya, destroyed villages and brutally punished anyone whom he suspected of resisting the Russian incursion. Chechens in their turn staged a fierce armed resistance led by leaders such as Kazi Mullah and Shamil. During the civil war, Chechens sided with Bolsheviks against the whites. And the Bolsheviks established the Chechen-Ingush autonomous republic within the Russian Federation. During the Second World War, the whole Chechen population was sent into exile to Kazakhstan by Stalin's secret police, leading to the death of many children, women, and elderly people. After the death of Stalin, Chechens were rehabilitated by Khrushchev and were allowed to return to Chechnya; yet discrimination against them persisted. Chechnya was one of the poorest regions of the former USSR (Evangelista 2002), and it remains the poorest in post-Soviet Russia.
10. The Soviet Union consisted of fifteen such republics.
11. The USSR was an affirmative empire with regard to ethnicity (Nazpary 2002; Brubaker 1994; Martin 2001). And the rise of ethnic nationalism was a byproduct of the late Soviet crisis rather than being a cause of it, though it played a significant role in the demise of the USSR. The Soviet state was a multinational state, organized around the principle of nationality. Its fifteen republics were national republics in which the native elite were the main power wielders. Moreover, those nationalities that lived in compact areas but did not possess ASSR status, had autonomous republics within each ASSR, such as Chechen-Ingush Autonomous Republic, or autonomous regions (*oblast*), or even smaller units (*krai*). Overall, notwithstanding the occasional repression of this or that particular elite group or in some cases the repression of a whole ethnic group, the Soviet state from the beginning to the end promoted the growth and consolidation of various ethnic elites, their languages and cultures. Given the vastness of the Soviet territory, the vast number of the constituent ethnicities and differences in their historical and cultural backgrounds, the processes of ethnic consolidation were uneven and heterogeneous.
12. Tatars, who initially demanded secession from the Russian Federation, decided to stay within it and negotiated considerable concessions from Moscow.
13. Then the media could freely report on the war and criticize the government policies openly (see also Gall and De Waal 1998).
14. Of course, the war was a national concern for Russians as more and more Russian soldiers were killed in Chechnya as the money needed for health care and education was squandered on war, and as the destruction of neighborhoods and villages and the

slaughter of innocent civilians (both Russians and Chechen) proceeded. But most Russians did not consider the war necessary for defending Russian national interests.
15. These events have been vividly described by the journalists Carlotta Gall and Thomas De Waal (1998: chapt. 9).
16. Berezovsky, as noted (n.4), is a businessman who collected his legendary wealth through his connections with Yeltsin. He has been accused of being involved with the Chechen mafia and with providing support to Raduyev. Berezovsky himself claims that he mediated in resolving various kidnapping problems in his capacity as secretary of CIAS's security affairs.
17. They even kidnapped Chechens and Ingushes and sold people into slavery. The following heart-rending story is typical. Mogmat Tsaroyev, an Ingush aged 14, was trained to handle weapons at Khattab's camp near Zherzen-Yourt close to Grozny. During his break he went back home, bringing a friend from the camp with him. But he was kidnapped by four young men who had got the information from his friend that the family was well-off. He was kept in a basement, burned, knifed, and beaten. Then they contacted the family and demanded USD 1,000,000, and later reduced the sum to USD 200,000. The youth's family reported this to all authorities but to no avail. Then the "Shariat Security Forces" told the family that either the family should pay them or another gang to free their son. And this would cost less than the ransom that the kidnapper had demanded. The family sold their house for USD 17,000 and paid the force. Incidentally, the force was cooperating with the kidnapper, and when they realized that the family had no more money to pay they sold Mogmat. He was sold five more times before he succeeded in fleeing (Polittkovskaya 2001:237–243).
18. This disillusionment has deepened under Putin's rule. The failure of the liberal parties to get any seats in the last parliamentary election (January 2004) is an indication of this.
19. The formal politics in post-Soviet era has been a politics of spectacle. The ruling elite using the modern media stage political dramas in which politicians act as actors. Guy Debord (1995) was the first who defined the contours of the society of spectacle, yet the operation of spectacle in the political arena remains to be studied carefully.
20. No doubt Putin used the war and the general psychological atmosphere in order to get elected as a president. But he was also genuinely concerned about the future of the Russian state. He wanted to restore the authority of the state in the center and bring the regional networks under the control of Moscow.
21. This shocking report reminds one of the worse brutalities of repressive regimes in Asia, Africa, and Latin America. Chechen detainees who arrived at Russian Chernokozovo "filtration" camp in January 2000 would be greeted by the ominous "Welcome to Hell" and then would be forced to walk through a human corridor of baton-wielding guards. This was only the beginning of a ghastly cycle of abuse for most detainees in early 2000, who suffered systematic beatings, rape, and other forms of torture. Most were released only after families managed to pay large sums to Russian officials (Human Rights Watch 2000). General Kvashinin the commander of Russian forces declared that any Chechen male 10–60 years old should be treated as a suspect. This led to the arbitrary detentions, abuse, rape and torture. According, to Human Rights Watch there were two major methods of arresting people: First in the extended network of checkpoints which were established by various Russian forces inside the borders of Chechnya; second through systematic raids into Chechen villages and neighborhoods. People were arrested for spurious reasons such as having incomplete documents, having a surname similar to a fighter, being in a place outside their residential area, or because they were assumed to be a fighter or a relative of a fighter. Their detention was not acknowledged, they were taken to unknown places and the authorities refused to inform relatives about the whereabouts of detainees. Verbal and physical abuse of detainees was a common practice in the point of arrests. Detainees were subjected to the harshest form

of abuse and torture during the detention period. The most notorious detention center was Chernokozovo. The detainees were often savagely beaten and injured during transport to this center. Then were forced to pass through corridors guards who beat the prisoners up from both sides. And at least one person was killed during such a beating. Then the detainees were thrown into cells, some of them stripped of their cloths, and were beaten again the cells to point that some of them became unconsciousness several times. The abuse was never ending. The detainees were made to stand naked and usually kicked them in their genitals. There were cases in which guards had raped both men and women, though Human Rights watch estimated that the number of rapes were under-reported because of notion of honor and shame among the Chechens. The detainees were forced to stand in the sells for more than 24 hours. During the interrogation the guards forced the detainees to crawl from their cells to the room where the interrogator was waiting for them, while the guards were beating them.

Jambekov, a Chechen detainee described this as follows. "The would make us say 'Comrade Colonel, let me crawl to you' but he wasn't a colonel, that was just his dream. After they beat us, they made us say 'thank you,' and if couldn't stand then they would still make you say 'thank you' and crawl away" (quoted in pages 33–34). During the interrogation two guards were standing behind the detainee and would beat him in case he would refuse to sign documents or deny that he was a fighter. Then they were forced to crawl back to their cells and were beaten again.

The process of release was one of extortion and bribery. As no lists of the detainees were published and as their whereabouts were unknown relatives had to pay bribes in order to find the place where their loved ones were kept. Secondly, they had to pay money in order to get them released. This happened through Chechen intermediaries who had contacts with those Russians who were in charge of detention centers. The Russian authorities demanded either money or guns or both. The amount of money demanded varied from 2000 roubles to 5000 USD. In a way, arrests were a means of extortion, in some cases the negotiation for release starting immediately after the arrest. And in some cases proven fighters were bought free from prison. After the release the detainees were at risk and in continuous fear of being arrested again.

22. Russians widely use the negative stereotype *chernye* ("blacks") to designate people from Caucasus and Central Asia as a different race. Here black refers to the color of hair and not that of skin. The stereotype for black African is *neger* which means black is linguistically a neutral word, i.e. has no negative connotations. However, this does not mean that Russians treat black Africans more favorably than Central Asians or Caucasians. On the contrary, Africans have been subjected to the worst kind of racism in Russia.
23. This is a story that I heard from many other people, even a Russian businessman told me, if the police wanted to arrest him, they could plant drugs in his car and arrest him.
24. This story is taken from Anna Ploikovskaya's book *A Dirty War*, pp. 52–56. She paid with her life for reporting on such stories. She was gunned down 6 October 2006.
25. A district in Moscow.
26. The present Russian Federation by recent territorial drawing and infringements over other nationalities rights within Russian Federations become more and more like an empire.
27. A territory that broke away from Georgia in a civil war and is de facto independent, but not recognized as an independent state by any state. Georgia claims sovereignty over it.
28. Located beside the Black sea, Abkhazia has become a tourist destination for Russians.
29. Then Abkhazia was de facto independent. It still enjoys this status.
30. Primordialist theories of ethnic identity popularized by the Soviet and Russian ethnographers are used to give a quasi-scientific guise to these racist attitudes (for an example, see Gumilev 1990).

31. The most notable example of conspiracy/spectacle politics is the way that the Bush administration used the events of 9/11 to launch the war in Iraq.
32. In this context the term *civilization* refers not to any particular culture but rather to the capitalist values of individualism, self-interest, contract, exchange, utilitarianism, law, bureaucracy, and property.

Bibliography

Abrams, Philip. 1988. "Notes on the Difficulty of Studying the State," *Journal of Historical Sociology* 1(1):58–89.
Afanas'ev, M.N. 2000. *Klientelism i Rossiikaya Gosudarstvennost'* [Clientelism and Russian Statehood]. Moscow: Moskovskii Nauchnyi Fond.
Agamben, Giorgio. 1998. *Homo Sacer: Sovereign Power and Bare Life*. Stanford: Stanford University Press.
Althusser, L. 1994. "Ideology and Ideological State Apparatus," in S. Žižek (ed.), *Mapping the Ideology*. London: Verso, pp. 100–140.
Anderson, Benedict. 1991. *Imagined Communities: Reflections on the Origin and Spread of Nationalism*. London: Verso.
Arendt, Hannah. 1979. *The Origins of Totalitarianism*. New York: Harcourt Brace Jovanovich.
Arrighi, Giovanni, Beverly J. Silver and Iftikhar Ahmad. 1999. *Chaos and Governance in the World System*. Minneapolis and London: Minnesota University Press.
Badiou, Alain. 2001. *Ethics*. London: Verso.
Baudrillard, Jean. 1994. *Simulacra and Simulation*. Ann Arbor: University of Michigan Press.
———. 2002. *The Sprit of Terrorism*. London: Verso.
Boyer, Dominic. 2006. "Conspiracy, History and Therapy at a Berlin Stammtisch," *American Ethnologist* 33(3): 327–339.
Brenner, R. 1998. "The Economics of Global Turbulence," *New Left Review* 299 (special issue).
Briggs, Charles. 2004. "Theorizing Modernity Conspiratorially: Science, Scale, and the Political Economy Public Discourse in Explanation of a Cholera Epidemic," *American Ethnologist* 31(2):164–187.
Brubaker, Roger. 1994. "Nationhood and National Question in the Soviet Union and Post-Soviet Eurasia. An Institutional Account," *Theory and Society* 23(1):47–78.
Carter, Angela. 1984. *Nights at the Circus*. London: Vintage.
Castells, M. 1998. *The End of Millennium*. Oxford: Blackwell.
Chossudovsky, M. 1998. *Globalisation of Poverty*. London: Zed Books.
Colton, Timothy J. and Michael McFaul. 2003. *Popular Choice and Managed Democracy: The Russian Elections of 1999 and 2000*. Washington, D.C.: Brookings Institution Press.
Comaroff, John and Jean Comarroff. 2004. "Criminal Justice, Cultural Justice," *American Ethnologist* 31(2):188–204.
Corrigan, Philip and Derek Sayer. 1985. *The Great Arch*. Oxford: Basil Blackwell.
Deleuze Gilles and Felix Guattari. 1987. *A Thousand Plateaus*. Minneapolis: University of Minnesota Press.
Evangelista, Mathew. 2002. *The Chechen Wars: Will Russia Go the Way of the Soviet Union?* Washington, D.C.: Brookings Institution Press.
Debord, Guy. 1995. *The Society of Spectacle*. New York: Zone Books.
Derluguian, Georgi M. 1999. "Che Guvaras in Turban," *New Left Review* 237: 3–27.
Dunlop, John B. 1998. *Russia Confronts Chechnya: Routs of a Separatist Conflict*. Cambridge: Cambridge University Press.

Foucault, M. 1978. *The History of Sexuality.* Vol. 1. New York: Random House.
Friedman, Jonathan. 2005. "The Relocation of the Social and the Retrenchment of the Elites," in B. Kapferer (ed.), *The Retreat of the Social: The Rise and Rise of Reductionism.* New York: Berghahn Books, pp. 19–29.
Gall, Carlotta and Thomas De Waal. 1998. *Chechnya: Calamity in the Caucasus.* New York and London: New York University Press.
Gramsci, A. 1971. *Selections of the Prison Notebooks.* London: Lawrence and Wishart.
Gumilev. L. N. 1990. *Etnogenez i Biosfera Zemli.* Gindrometoizdat: Leningrad.
Handelman, S. 1995. *Comrade Criminal.* New Haven: Yale University Press.
Harvey, David. 2003. *The New Imperialism.* Oxford: Oxford University Press.
Hayenes, M. and P. Glatter. 1998. "The Russian Catastrophe," *International Socialism* 31.
Hobbes, Thomas. 1991. *Leviathan.* Cambridge: Cambridge University.
Human Rights Watch. 2000. *"Welcome to Hell": Arbitrary Detention, Torture, and Extortion in Chechnya.* New York and London: Human Right Watch.
Humphrey, Caroline. 1991. "'Icebergs' Barter and Mafia in Provincial Russia," *Anthropology Today* 7(2): 8–13.
Jameson, Fredrick. 1991. *Post-modernism, or the Cultural Logic of Late Capitalism.* London: Verso.
Kagarlitsky, Boris. 2002. *Russia under Yetlsin and Putin.* London: Pluto Press.
Kaldor, Mary. 1999. *New and Old Wars.* Stanford: Stanford University Press.
Ledeneva, Alena. 2006. *How Russia Really Works.* Ithaca and London: Cornell University Press.
Lyotard, Jean-François. 1984. *The Post-Modern Condition.* Minneapolis: University of Minnesota Press.
Martin, Terry. 2001. *Affirmative Action Empire: Nations and Nationalism in the Soviet Union, 1923–1939.* Ithaca: Cornell University Press.
Marx, K. 1973 [1858]. *Grundrisse.* London: Penguin Books.
Nazpary, Joma. 2002. *Post-Soviet Chaos: Violence and Dispossession in Kazakhstan.* London: Pluto Press.
Politkovskaya, Anna. 2001. *A Dirty War.* London: the Harvill Press.
Poulantzas, Nicos. 1973. *Political Power and Social Classes.* London: New Left Books.
———. 1983. *Fascism and Dictatorship.* Tehran: Pezhvak.
Reno, William. 1998. *World Politics and African States.* Boulder, Colo.: Lynne Reiner Publishers.
Rigi, Jakob. 2004. "Chaos, Conspiracy and Spectacle: The Russian War against Chechnya," *Social Analysis* 41(1): 143–148.
———. 2007. "The War in Chechnya: The Chaotic Mode of Domination, Violence and Bare Life in the Post-Soviet Context," *Critique of Anthropology* 27(1): 37–62.
Scott, James. 1992. *Domination and the Art of Resistance: The Hidden Transcripts.* New Haven: Yale University Press.
Shlapentokh, Vladmir. 2003. "Russia's Acquiescence to Corruption Makes State Machine Inept," *Communist and Post-communist Studies* 36(2):151–161.
Turner, Terence. 2003. "Class Projects Social Consciousness and the Contradictions of Globalization," Jonathan Friedman (ed.), *Globalization, the State and Violence.* Walnut Creek, Calif.: Alta Mira Press.
Volkov, Vadim. 2002. *Violent Entrepreneurs.* Ithaca: Cornell University Press.
West, Harry and Todd Sanders (eds). 2003. *Transparency and Conspiracy in the New World Order.* Durham: Duke University Press.
Wilson, Andrew. 2005. *Virtual Politics.* New Haven: Yale University Press.
Wood, Ellen M. 2003. *The Capitalist Empire.* London: Verso.

Chapter Three

MARKET FORCES, POLITICAL VIOLENCE, AND WAR
The End of Nation-States, the Rise of Ethnic and Global Sovereignties?

Caroline Ifeka

In the post–Cold War era, political violence associated with wars of gain is key to economic and political transformations across nation states.[1] Under the "Pax Americana," multinational corporations interacting in "old boy" networks of the global capitalist class control armaments, oil production, and cyberspace. Industrial and military multinationals, as well as global financial institutions, are extending their decision-making structures while becoming more concentrated[2]; there is a "hyper concentration" of (unregulated) economic and military power, predominantly Euro-American (Virilio and Lotringer 1997:99). Global militarization legitimized in discourses of "protecting freedom" secures world oil and gas resources for Euro-American and Sinic industrial use, promotes corporate profits, and supports the post-2000 Pax Americana. The Pax's "command and control" system seeks to checkmate Muslim control of 60 percent of world crude oil supplies by destroying "rogue" regimes and investing in multinational corporations exploiting oil, diamonds, coltan (*Columbite Tantalite*), and other (finite) industrial resources in non-Muslim controlled African states (Meacher 2003). Preparation for total war is economic war.

The capitalist class's facilitation of wars in the European, African, South American, and Asian semi-peripheries has the potential to end all history, especially now that this class includes large Asian multinational corporations acquiring the capacity to compete with the American industrial-mili-

---

Notes for this chapter are located on page 92.

tary complex—on earth and in cyberspace (Joxe 2002; Sklair 2002). Political violence and endemic "small, cruel wars" help sustain, and are sustained, by 1) authoritarian political systems masquerading as "democracies"[3]; and 2) socioeconomic inequalities, and widening poverty whose wounds global "development" agencies soothe in discourses and practices of "participatory" or "community development."[4] Yet the political violence, suffering, and decay of nation-state capacity to protect what Hobbes calls every man's "natural right of self preservation" (Tuck 1988:68–9) and to deliver minimal justice and equitable assistance grows—and grows.

Cascading violence is especially visible at intersections of the global and local, where the disordering impact of industrial market forces is breaking down "law and order" so people feel insecure, and withdraw their consent to the colonial-derived nation-state in favor of the protection they believe their ethnic "nationality" offers them. New ethnic formations are emerging, battling for sovereign (nation-state) jurisdiction over their ancestral resources, terrains, kith and kin, seeking rights in international law to deal with global oil sovereigns.

The implications for nation-states of these market-driven economic and military forces receive little attention from the social sciences, including anthropology. Notable exceptions are the exciting theoretical contributions of a few philosophers, political scientists, and military strategists based in France and America, a handful of anthropological analyses of civil wars and regimes of terror (Kapferer 1988; Nordstrom 1992); equally important are the very detailed empirical reports by advocacy NGOs such as Human Rights Watch, the Centre for Public Integrity, CorpWatch, and radical international relations researchers on political violence integral to multinational and American involvement in economic wars.[5]

I outline below elements of a new framework for exploring, critically, discourses and practices of political violence and state re-formation in geopolitical locations dominated by extractive industries.[6] In what follows I focus on a major philosophical, anthropological, and political issue—the origins of violence, its relationship to power and economy, and its contribution to the contemporary formation of new states—in the context of struggles between multinational corporations, communities, and nation-states for control over oil at the point of intersection of the global and the local in the Niger Delta and southern Sudan.

Power, Violence, and Fundamentalism

Arendt (1970) and Girard (1972) stand out among scholars for their nonconventional, almost antithetical, interpretations of the role of violence in social formations. On the one hand, Arendt (1970:45–9) argues that in functional Euro-American states institutionalized power appears in the guise of authority demanding obedience and respect—this is the outward manifestation of society's inner consent—with limited reliance on physically violent (legitimate) means of coercion.[7] Power is "the human ability not just to act but to act in concert" with others, so power belongs to a group as long as the group keeps together; in its pure consensual condition, power is an end in itself and therefore does not require coercion or other violent means of control. Violence, though, is instrumental. It is a means to publicly legitimized ends and requires justification through the end it pursues; it is very different from (consensual) power. Thus, Arendt (1970:56) argues of totalitarian regimes "violence appears where power is in jeopardy, but left to its own course it ends in power's disappearance." However, she admits that power and violence are often used in combination, as when the nation-state sends out its armed forces to protect citizens against foreign invasion or internal saboteurs. On the other hand, Girard (1972, 1987; Mack 1987) contends that culture commences in an act of collective murder; the violence enacted in sacrifice is key to the human condition; rivalry and competition between groups contribute to exclusionary practices, scapegoating, and the (murderous) sacrifice of surrogate victims. Girard argues that revenge-killing cycles can end in one "final" killing that authorizes new social formations. Applying his argument to economic wars articulating the intersection of the global and local, is it that many ethnic players interpret violence as the basis of a new consensus (power) that legitimates their transformation into sovereignties with independent jurisdiction over their own peoples, terrains, and natural resources? I note that other theorists query violence's putative social creativity, arguing, with Baudrillard (2002:8,17–19), for its power to destroy all lives and systems.

So, on the one hand, (pure consensual) power is portrayed as the origin of sociopolitical organization, while on the other violence is represented as socially creative force as well as the war to end all wars. The latter view is echoed in local politico-economic fundamentalist discourses authorizing the violent practices of multinational corporations, nationstates, and ethnic communities in their oil wars.[8] I shall argue that many features of religious fundamentalism also pertain to organizations engaging in economic wars at the intersection of the global and the local. Consider, for example, the group's insistence on strict adherence to basic principles of behavior that it believes distinguish it from others competing for followers/markets, the group's preoccupation with boundary maintenance in competition/rivalry with other faiths/groups, its emphasis on member's adherence to basic principles (Ali 2002; Boyer 2002), and of course its capacity for violence—even mass killings of internal dissenters and external opponents, as in the Albigensian crusade and the Spanish civil war (Oldenbourg 2000; Borkenau 2000).

The inner violence of rivalry, I suggest, is an essential element in the structuring of religious fundamentalism as well as its politico-economic variants in the industrial arena. Rivalrous violence is a key component of the industrial-military complex manifesting at the local in the guise of corporations, sometimes backed by national armed forces and/or private military firms: impelled by the pursuit of profit in very competitive markets, oil companies do abandon peaceful for forceful tactics in the pursuit of profit—when they think that they can—so as to conquer rival companies and coerce communities to accept. The latter often claim the rights of traditional owners over terrains now producing oil as well as the right to resist oil spillages and forcible displacement by companies building roads and pipelines across their lands (HRW 1999:56–70; 2003:355).

Consider another aspect of economic fundamentalism structuring violence in relations between corporations, communities, and nation-state. Competition for oil and revenues seems to impel the nation-state in the Niger Delta and southern Sudan to use physical force against civilians, killing innocents and burning settlements, to highlight the military's/state's perception of its absolute rectitude. Corporations, at times, and community activists, also pick up on this violence, reiterating in their domain that they too possess the absolute truth that can legitimize violent action against rival companies or communities—with consequences terrifyingly documented.[9]

(a) Companies: we seek only to "do business in a peaceful environment" by peaceful means, it is others (i.e., the communities) who are violent; we struggle daily against global competitors for "market survival" and have to somehow "maintain our competitive edge" (Ifeka 2001a).

(b) Communities: our brothers have joined the militants/swamp guerrillas to protect our collective ancestral heritage, we are the legitimate owners of all oil lying under our soil, creeks, and offshore ocean, and have been cheated of our rights all these years, we love our youth for their bravery in protecting us against enemies by standing up to companies and government forces; our boys give their lives for us to be free from suffering (Ifeka 2001b, 2002, 2006).

(c) Central government: we are protecting the country's financial "life blood." In the Niger Delta, as in southern Sudan, corporations, community guerrillas, and state rulers interact through unending political violence— the Khartoum government hires mercenaries to destroy and displace thousands of nomads from their homelands (HRW 2003a:67–9)—but each type of organization also engages in more peace-loving activities, some as hired

clients (informers) of company and government who seek to penetrate the "enemy" to weaken their campaigns. The oil majors publish "diplomatic" annual reports on monies expended on community development to bring peace; ethnic nationalities make self-valedictory statements to the press regarding their (peaceful) commitment to full sovereignty and resource control; government stooges hire praise singers to eulogize the president's commitment to "peace" and "economic development" (HRW 2003a:81ff; Ifeka 2002).

These discourses justify actions that solicit, respectively, oil company workers, guerrilla brothers/liberation army, and the nation-state to approve and participate in the violence: each party strengthens its organizational boundaries with laudable logos at once "fraternal" and tacitly threatening; each legitimizes recourse to violence by blaming (scapegoating) the other for nefarious deeds (Kemedi 2003). Each party to these three cornered economic wars identifies strongly with their group's beliefs—perceptibly unchanging sacred tenets are rigidly endorsed by all members, and workers and militants urge one another to protect their group against defectors and betrayal in war—while each group prepares its members to defend their beliefs and identities. At times, when fundamentalist interactions are climaxing, each party adopts the structure's preordained asymmetrical roles of (subordinate) victim or (superordinate) killer: the killer seeks to justify the violence of genocide and executions by invoking the enemy's sins. And so with each violent exchange the victim-killer structure is perpetuated and political conflict diffuses everywhere.

Thus, corporate fundamentalisms of the global, and ethno-religious fundamentalisms of the local, embed in market-driven networks in swamp, ocean, and mine, where low-priced natural resources are extracted (violently) in exchange for high-priced manufactured goods. Popular support for nation-state personages and policies declines as absolutist values flow forth into an increasingly unitary global circulation system: the political violence of impoverished peoples resisting oppression grows—and grows—as states crumble and ethnic nationalities claim the sovereignty of statehood.

Toward a New Framework: Structure

Making inductive inferences based on my fieldwork in Nigerian oil-producing communities, I propose three sets of elements for an analysis of processes structuring discourses and practices of violence in extractive-industry locations.

(1) Divisions, intolerance and double-dealing. Fundamentalist discourse in contemporary multinationals, ethnic community organizations, and nation-state political regimes feeds on divisions, making ethnic or religio-cultural difference the basis of political reordering through bloodshed, which nourishes more intolerance to which increasing numbers consent (Apter 1997:4–5). So, contrary to Arendt, in these economic wars in less mature states than the European regimes with which Arendt was familiar, violence transforms into consensual power—through sacrificial killings?—apparently supporting Girard's theory of the capacity of violence to create/regenerate social formations.[10] Engagement in violence, however, does not exclude participation in "law and order" activities of the nation-state. As indicated above, companies, communities, and nation-states discourse daily (with passion) on their peace-loving credentials while simultaneously practising violence; governments and companies recruit (for pay) clients in the communities who play double roles—now part of a community guerrilla group or liberation army, now a community representative in peace talks with the government or a company—so situations at the intersection point of the global and the local seem very confusing, lacking consistent patterns with apparent disorder. At the same time, Pentagon and UK government contracts enable armament companies to chalk up remarkable growth in annual turnover as they supply arms traffickers with relatively cheap weapons to be sold, in turn, to nation-states, community guerrillas, and, at times in the past, to some oil companies (ICIJ 2003:10–21; Okonta 2003:137).

(2) Violence and sacrifice. Each party to the three-cornered struggle legitimizes violence so that, at times, dominant organizations (nation-state and multinational) feel free to seek surrogates to be sacrificed (killed), ostensibly to knock out rebellion in the communities but, actually, to vent their hatred of ethnicities continuing for decades to rebel against lack of rights to ancestral terrain and resources. Anecdotal evidence suggests that sections of communities in the pay of national government and/or multinational companies are also complicit in selecting victims for a "final" act of sacrificial killing. The selected victim must be recognized as a surrogate for the guilty party (or parties), be vulnerable, be unable to retaliate, and be seen as lacking champions who will have the courage and commitment to continue the vengeful violence (cf. Mack 1987:8). The Nigerian government's execution of the Ogoni leader, Ken Saro Wiwa, and his eight comrades in 1995 fulfilled most of these criteria, but it also flagged additional elements of "final" sacrificial killings that rather than end actually reproduced the structural relationship between victim and killer and thus ensured, contrary to Girard (1987), that the cycle of violence would continue.[11] For

example, sections of the Ogoni oil-producing community in government pay and engaging in violent infighting with their principal leader (Saro Wiwa) ensured, through their fratricide and documented connivance of Shell and Chevron corporations, that Saro Wiwa was "selected" as the sacrificial offering to end the killing—once and for all (Okonta and Douglas 2003:157ff). Shell held a "watching brief" at the "trial" of the Ogoni Eight and Saro Wiwa, while the Abacha dictatorship watched and videoed the executions (Olorode 1999:277, 398, 400ff). In this, and in similar cases in which security forces supplied by the state are complicit with oil multinationals, as in the southern Sudan, in attacking and uprooting communities that "block the path" where oil pipelines must be laid—there being no alternative route—the state and the company reveal a capacity for the kinds of absolutist thinking that creates and legitimizes discourses and practices of political violence (HRW 1999:77–82; HRW 2003:182–3,191–209).

A sacrificial killing is expected to end the violence (Mack 1987:9), but in the struggles examined here such killings failed to check the violence.[12] Rather, political violence emanating from Ogoniland in the mid-1990s has extended to the residents' Ijaw kith and kin. In 2001–03 eight million Ijaw-speaking people occupying three states in the Niger Delta strengthened the Ijaw National Congress into a quasi-national assembly, nominated a governor general, and, it appears, began in some cases to think of those guerrilla groups that hi-jack oil personnel and occupy terminals as the Ijaw nation's own armed forces. In Ijawland today, political violence solicits widespread consent, making it is difficult to say where violence ends and pure (consensual) power begins.

(3) Power and violence as ends in themselves. Each party to these three-cornered battles claims that their organization's continued existence, well being, and progress constitute an end in itself; implicitly they maintain that power is their organization's essence, not violence. They "only" resort to violence from necessity to achieve their objectives. Arendt supports this popular belief in her contention that violence is instrumental and requires justification through the political end it pursues (Arendt 1970:49). Thus, she argues, power is primary in sustaining social formations, violence is secondary. Yet, in these oil wars, each of the three parties is experiencing violence as primary; as argued by Apter, Virilio and Lotringer, and Baudrillard, many people on all sides now feel that violence is becoming an end in itself as principle and interest reinforce each other, feeding a fundamentalist belief that God-given (absolute) ethno-religious difference sanctifies sovereignties, whether ethnic or theocratic.

And that is why nation-states are decaying and new ethnic sovereignties are emerging, empowered to tackle corporate global sovereigns.

Toward a New Framework: Process

My Nigerian fieldwork data suggest four or five historical phases in the waning of colonial-derived nation-states and the waxing of ethnic state power. Each phase reflects a progressive expansion in the consensual basis of violence, and in the community case suggests also its much demanded transformation into (consensual) power currently legitimizing as the ethnic state. When a group/citizenry identifies with perceived past frustrations, exploitation, and impoverishment, they move from an original phase of 1) innocent acceptance of domination by corporation and obedience to the nation-state; and in so doing create 2) a transitional political opening within the state: they call themselves marginalized, excluded, the poor majority, ordinary people resisting oppression, displacement, and even genocide by engaging in open (peaceful) protest. Then, after months or years, they move into a third phase, that of 3) questioning rulers' credentials (authority), declining to accept subjugation, and commencing rebellion by engaging in armed combat with government and multinational corporation security that in theory could proceed to 4) revolution. Then, the power that should be at the state's core is no more; the nation-state collapses, and 5) a large space of consensual power opens up wherein triumphant rebels assume control: then "the people's" rightful political representatives of ethnic states legitimized as sovereign over the ethnicity's terrains, arms, resources, and economy promise a wonderful new order of peace, law and order, and economic development for everyone.

Transforming themselves from ethnicity to nationality, the emerging state claims a jurisdictional power equivalent to the global sovereignty exercised de facto by unregulated global multinationals.

Conclusion

Preparation for total war, argues Virilio and Lotringer (1997:160), is economic war. Indeed, my analysis has identified several elements for a new analysis of violent structures and processes in African locales, where oil multinationals articulate market forces in interaction with ethno-religious fractures and colonial-derived nation-states at the point of intersection between the global and the local.

To summarize key elements in our conceptual framework for explaining the unending expansion of violence at the intersection point of the global and the local:

(a) Sacrificial killing is the most emotional of "proofs" that enemy organizations are "killers," the most arousing of passions in "victim" communities supplying the sacrificial offering; I have argued it is the primary process at work in the depths of social interaction, structuring relations between companies, communities, and the nation-state in violence.
(b) Governments' and companies' use of "divide and rule" to keep communities fractured on ethnic, religious, and class lines so as to bring double dealing, dishonesty, and lack of trust in Phases 2 or 3 to its culmination in sacrificial killings, ensures that all parties rely on violent means of seeking control of oil resources.
(c) Similarly a key is the transformation of violence into consensual power, as in Phases 3 or 4 of economic wars, when popular discourses of company, community, and state legitimize violence as pure (consensual) power.
(d) And then there is the arrival of the "revolutionary moment," when company managers or state soldiers no longer obey commands, making the means of violence of no use. Arendt (1970:49) argues that victory depends in the longer term on superior (consensual) organization of power, not superior means of coercion—for "Everything depends on the power behind the violence." Here, Arendt abandons her position that power and violence are diametrically opposed, implying that violence, too, can be creative; and so she moves closer to Cabral (1980:257), Girard (1987), and Fanon (1967), who believe, passionately, in the revolutionary capacity of armed struggles against oppressive regimes to cleanse society when the vast majority of "our people" support the armed liberation struggle, their consent transforming violence into (consensual) power.

Kapferer (1997:164) concludes his analysis of political violence in Sri Lanka by arguing that discursive practices are indeed constitutive. My analysis, too, has identified processes that structure the fundamentalist (killing) beliefs of global and emerging ethnic sovereignties multiplying as the nation-state decays within. I have shown how economic wars articulate the conflictful insertion of global market forces in the local—violent encounters that nourish corporate and ethno-religious fundamentalisms whose rigidities of thought and action structure the principal parties in the asymmetrical roles of victim and killer. Indeed, as Kapferer and Bertelsen argue in this volume, these painful and dynamic processes constitute a "corporate" state, a "radical bringing together of war machine and state order" (2008:13).

Effectively, companies, communities, and nation-states are complicit in reproducing cycles of war on the periphery that serve the financial, military, and profit-centered interests of the global capitalist class and perpetuate America's "Empire of Disorder" (Joxe 2002:189).

Notes

1. By *violence* I mean the exercise of physical, mental, or emotional force to effect harm, injuries, and destruction on others. By *war* I mean armed conflict between two or more opponents, nations, or states in which both seek to kill the other, destroy their assets, and reduce them to rubble.
2. Some multinational corporations generate annual revenues of over $250 billion from operations in more than 150 nation-states, are unregulated in the bulk of their activities, dictate their terms of operation to governments, and speak to the chief executive of the global hegemon (America) as equals (ICIJ 2003; Litvin 2003). On the UK-based armaments giant BAE, see Lilley (2003) and other CorpWatch reports.
3. By *authoritarian* I mean government by a small elite with wide (despotic, dictatorial, domineering) powers.
4. "Development" agencies and personnel include those with a social conscience whose work in difficult and often dangerous conditions (e.g., Medecins sans Frontieres) ameliorates but, under present global conditions, cannot cure.
5. See works cited in the bibliography, e.g. Joxe 2002, Virilio and Lotringer 1997, Baudrillard 2002, Apter 1997, Peluso and Watts 2001. See also the very detailed empirical reports on human rights abuses of oil companies by Human Rights Watch, the independent Centre for Public Integrity's detailed documentation of linkages between financial, military and industrial companies engaged in "the business of war," the UK advocacy NGO Cornerhouse Briefings, etc. Stiglitz, a former World Bank manager, has written an "insider" study of the "management" of globalization from the very top down (2002).
6. Certain scholars argue, somewhat obscurely, for a "political ecology of violence" (Peluso and Watts 2001:26–28). Applying their argument, I find no significant association of type of discourses and practices of political violence with environmental context—e.g., that there is more sacrificial killing, divide and rule, and fundamentalism in the open lands of the Sudan compared to the more cramped terrain of the Niger Delta. Or that there are more revenge killings, more extreme and continuing forms of violence in the Sudan compared to the Delta. On the contrary, my analysis shows that, notwithstanding religio-cultural and historical differences, basically similar structures and processes of political violence are at work in the two oil-extracting locations.
7. Violence is often combined with power, but for Arendt the two are dissimilar. Power belongs to the state as long as opinion supports the decisions of officeholders; when lost, as in Africa's crumbling regimes lacking authority (respect given without resort to coercion or suasion), the ruler's strength or independence of public opinion wanes, so the nation-state's capacity to impose even minimal "law and order" vanishes (cf. Arendt 1970:45).
8. Fundamentalism, in the sense of strict adherence to the basic principles of the belief system that leaders impose by peaceful and violent means with group consent (power), is more usually analysed in relation to religious movements intending to purify societies of evil and devil worship, as in contemporary Islam and Christianity (cf. Ifeka 2002; Boyer 2002).
9. In the 1990s, under the Nigerian military, some oil companies allegedly hired their own

armed security forces, but they upheld their company's peaceful policies and insisted they took "many risks," relying largely on paid mobile police, guards, and armed contingents deployed by the federal government to protect company installations (HRW 1999:115–6,123ff). In Sudan, in the late 1990s, the Khartoum government sought to impose "peace" by carrying out massive destroy-and-displace raids against civilians as well as by sending in troops to strengthen company security men around oil wells (HRW 2003:244–70).

10. But note how in regimes of terror that grip mature totalitarian states, violence is destructive, engulfing all (Sudrez-Orozco 1992).

11. In the late 1980s Ken Saro Wiwa founded with colleagues the Ogoni-based Movement for the Survival of the Ogoni Peoples (MOSOP) that challenged Shell, the operator of many oil wells in Ogoniland, to cease oil pollution and gas flaring, to deal respectfully with the Ogoni people as the customary owners of the land and oil, and to recognize the Ogoni people's right to determine whether Shell extracts oil or not from Ogoniland. Shell and the Nigerian military saw Saro Wiwa as a threat to "peace in the Niger Delta," a leader who must be stopped in his tracks before the Delta rebelled and seceded from the Nigerian federation (Olorode et al. 1999). The regime may have remembered Isaac Boro, who proclaimed the independent Niger Delta People's Republic in 1962. See also a large literature on the Internet: viz. Two Day National Conference of Eminent Persons Meeting under the Ijaw National Congress, November 27–28, 2003. http://www.niperdeltacongress.com/iarticles/iiaws%2Ospout%20fire.htm.

12. Other sacrificial killings in the Niger Delta include those suffered by the Ijaw people, as the Twon Brass Three in May 2000, when three youths at the head of a large following insisted that they enter the Agip oil terminal—despite company warnings to desist and warnings from some sections of the Brass community—and were shot dead by troops. Genocide—mass massacres in 1999 by the Federal Nigerian Army of three thousand inhabitants of the village of Odi, Bayelsa state. Similar massacres of many civilians by government troops are documented in the southern Sudan in the mid- to late 1990s (HRW 2003).

Bibliography

Ali, T. 2002. *The Clash of Fundamentalisms: Crusades, Jihads and Modernity.* London: Verso.

Apter, D.E. 1997. "Political Violence in Analytical Perspective," in D.E. Apter (ed.), *The Legitimization of Violence.* Basingstoke: Macmillan, pp. 1–32.

Arendt, H. 1970. *On Violence.* San Diego: Harcourt Brace and Co.

Baudrillard, J. 2002. *The Spirit of Terrorism.* London and New York: Verso.

Borkenau, F. 2000. *The Spanish Cockpit: An Eyewitness Account of the Spanish Civil War.* London: Phoenix Press.

Boyer, P. 2002. *Religion Explained: The Human Instincts That Fashion Gods, Spirits and Ancestors.* London: Vintage Books.

Cabral, A. 1980. *Unity and Struggle: Speeches and Writings.* London: Heinemann.

Eshiet, I.U., O. Okome and Felix Akpan. n.d. *Ken Saro-Wiwa and the Discourse of Ethnic Minority in Nigeria.* Calabar: University of Calabar Press.

Fanon, F. 1967. *The Wretched of the Earth.* Harmondsworth: Penguin.

Girard, R. 1972. *La Violence et le Sacré.* Paris: Grasset.

———. 1987. "Generative Scapegoating," in R.G. Hamerton-Kelly (ed.), *Violent origins: Walter Burkert, Rene Girard and Jonathan Z. Smith on ritual killings and cultural formation.* Stanford: Stanford University Press, pp. 73–145.

Human Rights Watch. 1999. *The Price of Oil: Corporate Responsibility and Human Rights Violations in Nigeria's Oil Producing Communities.* New York: Human Rights Watch.

———. 2003a. *Sudan, Oil and Human Rights*. Brussels: Human Rights Watch.

———. 2003b. *The War Crisis. Fueling Violence*. New York: Human Rights Watch.

Ifeka, C. 2000. "Ethnic 'Nationalities,' God and the State. Whither the Federal Republic of Nigeria?" *Review of African Political Economy* 27(85): 450–459.

———. 2001a. "Field notes on the killing of three Twon Brass youth on May 29, 2000, in the Agip Oil Terminal," pp. 21–22.

———. 2001b. "Oil, NGOs and Youth: Resource Control Struggles in the Niger Delta," *Review of African Political Economy* 28(87): 99–105.

———. 2002. "Field Notes on Oil Producing Communities, Akwa Ibom."

———. 2006. "Youth Cultures and the Fetishisation of Violence in Nigeria," *Review of African Political Economy* 33(110): 721–736.

International Consortium of Investigative Journalists (ICIJ). 2003. *Making a Killing. The Business of War*. Washington DC: Center for Public Integrity.

Joxe, A. 2002. *Empire of Disorder*. Los Angeles and New York: Semiotext(e) Active Agent Series.

Kapferer, B. 1988. *Legends of People. Myths of State. Violence, Intolerance, and Political Culture in Sri Lanka and Australia*. Washington: Smithsonian Institution Press.

———. 1997. "State and Insurrectionary Violence: Sri Lanka," in D.E. Apter (ed.), *The Legitimization of Violence*. Basingstoke: Macmillan, pp. 159–188.

Kemedi, D.V. 2003. *Community Conflicts in the Niger Delta: Petro-weapon or Policy Failure?* Berkeley: University of California Institute of International Studies. Berkeley Workshop on Environmental Politics. Working Papers 03–12.

Lilley, Sasha. 2003. "BAE System's Dirty Dealings." CorpWatch Report available at http://www.corpwatch.org/article.php?id=9008, retrieved 11 November 2008.

Litvin, Daniel. 2003. *Empire of Profit: Commerce, Conquest, and Corporate Responsibility*. New York and London: Texere.

Mack, B. 1987. "Introduction," in R.G. Hamerton-Kelly (ed.), *Violent Origins. Walter Burkert, Rene Girard and Jonathan Z. Smith on Ritual Killings and Cultural Formation*. Palo Alto: Stanford University Press, pp. 1–70.

Meacher, M. 2003. "This War on Terrorism Is Bogus," *The Guardian*. 6 September 2003, retrieved 15 November 2007 from htttp://www.guardian.co.uk/comment/story/0,,1036571,00.html.

Nordstrom C. and JoAnn Martin. 1992. "The Culture of Conflict. Field Reality and Theory," in C. Nordstrom and JoAnn Martin (eds), *The Paths to Domination, Resistance and Terror*. Berkeley: University of California Press, pp. 3–17.

Oldenbourg, Z. 2000. *Massacre at Montsegur. A History of the Albigensian crusade*. London: Phoenix Press.

Okonta, I. and O. Douglas. 2003. *Where Vultures Feast. Shell, Human Rights and Oil*. London: Verso.

Olorode, O., W. Raji, J. Ogunye and Tunde Oladunjoye (eds). 1999. *Ken Saro Wiwa and the Crises of the Nigerian State*. Lagos: A Committee for the Defence of Human Rights Special Publication.

Orwell, G. 1990. *Nineteen Eighty-Four*. London: Penguin Books.

Peluso, N.L. and Michael Watts. 2001. "Violent Environments," in N.L. Peluso and Michael Watts (eds), *Violent Environments*. Ithaca: Cornell University Press, pp. 3–38.

Sklair, L. and P. Robbins. 2002. "Global Capitalism and Major Corporations from the Third World," *Third World Quarterly* 23(1): 81–100.

Stiglitz, Joseph F. 2002. *Globalization and Its Discontents*. New York: W.W. Norton and Co.

Sudrez-Orozco, M. 1992. "A Grammar of Terror. Psychocultural Responses to State Terrorism in Dirty War and Post-Dirty War Argentina," in C. Nordstrom and JoAnn Martin (eds), *The Paths to Domination, Resistance and Terror*. Berkeley: University of California Press, pp. 219–259.

Tuck, R. 1989. *Hobbes: A very short introduction*. Oxford: Oxford University Press.

Virilio, Paul and Sylvére Lotringer. 1997. *Pure War*. Malden, MA: Semiotext(e) and MIT Press.

Section II

WAR ZONE

Chapter Four

REBEL RAVAGES IN BUNDIBUGYO, UGANDA'S FORGOTTEN DISTRICT

Kirsten Alnaes

When two elephants fight, it is the grass that suffers.

African proverb

Armed with their implements of death
They kill by the roadside
They kill in valleys
They kill in hilltop villages ...

Raymond Ntalindwa: Scalpels of Memory

Preamble

On 13 November 1996 rebels belonging to ADF (Allied Democratic Forces) entered Uganda from then Zaire[1] and attacked Mpondwe and Karambi in Kasese district at the southern end of the Rwenzori massif in western Uganda. The attack was unexpected, including for the military platoon stationed there. An unequal battle ensued that ended with deaths in the UPDF (Uganda Peoples Defence Force), the population, and among the rebels. After a while, however, the rebels who had not been captured or killed were believed to have withdrawn into the Rwenzori mountains. At the time I was staying in Bundibugyo at the northern end of the massif. Although the rebels did not reach Bundibugyo until June 1997 (when I was back in London), I experienced the icy fear that descended upon every-

---

Notes for this chapter are located on page 119.

body, the many frightening rumors, and the threat of the rebels who were said to be hiding in the uninhabitable parts of the mountains.

The attack on Bundibugyo took place on 16 June 1997. Until then, Bundibugyo had seemingly been left in peace. While I was still there, I was told by an old friend, now a local government official, that "according to our intelligence, there are rebels here but we don't see them because they look like anyone else. But *we* are also among *them*. They plan to occupy Bundibugyo and use it as a spring-board to the rest of Uganda." I must confess that I thought the plan was pretty daft, with only an exceedingly bad road or an arduous walk across the mountains to get to the rest of Uganda. As it was, it did not work out quite like that, but Bundibugyo *did* become the stamping ground of the ADF in the years that followed, and the district, especially Bwamba county, was horribly ravaged. The cruelties and stark brutality of these "democratic" rebels are beyond any imagination. After the rebels' withdrawal, the traumatized population had an uphill task of reestablishing some sort of order in their new and chaotic world.

Here I discuss a situation of violence in an area I have known and been in contact with through letters and occasional telephone calls (after 1996) since my first fieldwork there in the late 1950s. The war situation I deal with extended from June 1997 to the end of 2000, although there were sporadic attacks well into 2001. The news that came out of Bundibugyo was perhaps not, in general terms, any different from that of many other war-torn areas on the African continent at the time, but for me, with my direct access to people's experiences, it was an opportunity to get behind streamlined newscasts and newspaper articles and, through the people of Bundibugyo, come close to what was also happening to millions of people elsewhere in Africa. I have therefore kept the expressions people used when I was told about the many atrocities they had experienced, the details they emphasized, and their descriptions of their fears and horrors.

There are times when a part of a country seems to be "forgotten" by its government. Bundibugyo is one of these. Although a war raged there for several years, and was followed by a long period of distress and utter poverty (the one partly dependent upon the other), the population felt that the Uganda government did not really care about what was happening to them. Only when a particularly dreadful assault on innocent people took place would journalists try to get to the scene and report the carnage. This would be followed by promises of help by the authorities, but the help that arrived was mainly more troops. There was a sprinkling of NGOs (nongovernmental organizations) in the area before the ADF onslaught. During the ADF siege MSF (Médicins sans Frontières) and WFP (the World Food Program) came to the area, but every time the situation was seen as being too dangerous all NGOs were withdrawn.

Bundibugyo

Bundibugyo district is an appendix on Uganda. It is situated three English miles (as the crow flies) from the border to Congo on the northwestern side of the Rwenzori mountains, and divided into two counties: *Bwamba*, which stretches southward along the mountainside and includes the last vestiges of the Ituri forest; and *Ntoroko*, which continues northward to Lake Albert and eastward to Kabarole district on the eastern side of the Rwenzori. At the time of the ADF incursion, its only link with the rest of Uganda was one badly maintained road to Fort Portal, the main town in Kabarole. Especially during the rainy season the road used to deteriorate rapidly, becoming almost impassable for anything but four-wheel-drive vehicles and astute local drivers. Most of the areas I refer to are situated within the county of Bwamba.

Bundibugyo is one of the poorest districts in Uganda and populated by BaKonzo, BaAmba, and a small number of people from other parts of Uganda.[2] In addition, people from the Congo side of the border will flee to Bundibugyo when armed local conflicts develop in their area.[3] In Bundibugyo we find some of Uganda's highest infant- and under-five mortality rates; the educational facilities are extremely poor, and while the population has more than doubled since I first lived there in the late 1950s and 1960s, access to land has diminished drastically.[4]

A Short Political History of Bundibugyo

The British included the areas of the BaKonzo and the BaAmba in the Toro area already in 1900, but it was only in 1924 that the Kingdom authorities became fully responsible for the administration of the Toro district. From then on they had the role as "indirect rulers" on behalf of the British Protectorate authorities. Inherent in the "indirect-rule situation" was a negative form of hierarchy where the members of the ruling elite were regarded (*and* experienced) as ruthless oppressors who did what they could to cheat their lesser subjects. This way of seeing the situation was still evident when I first came to Bundibugyo in the late 1950s.

Underneath a seemingly quiet surface there were active resentments and oppositions to the authorities. Already in 1919 the BaKonzo rose against the colonial powers. The uprising lasted for more than a year and, in 1921, ended with the execution by hanging of the three leaders.[5] Although there were no further expressions of direct resistance after the first uprising, resentment continued to simmer, a resentment that was, on a general level, expressed toward the authorities in terms of a series of grievances. One of these was education. The medium of teaching was LhuToro. This meant that a small child, coming to school for the first time, had not only to adjust to the new situation but also to try and understand what was said by the teachers. It took some time before the children were able to read and write, and this, again, was used by the Toro administration to "prove" that BaKonzo and BaAmba children were "backward." Medical services were rudimentary, and neither BaKonzo nor BaAmba had their own chiefs except on the lowest administrative levels. In order to demonstrate that they were equal to the BaToro, some young Konzo and Amba men who had obtained education beyond primary school did their best to emulate Toro ways of being and to use LhuToro as their main language.[6]

In the late 1940s chiefly figures began to write down the history of the BaKonzo, and in the middle 1950s, the history society, "The Bakonjo Life History Research Rwenzori," was formed by the young teacher Isaya Mukirania. The history society, with its detailed and structured constitution, rapidly spread from Bwamba to the entire Konzo/Amba area and was, in practice—and, I reckon, by intent—the forerunner for the Rwenzururu rebellion that erupted in 1962, only a couple of months before Uganda's independence (Alnaes 1969:246–50). This was not, however, the only "face" of the Rwenzururu movement. In what is now Kasese district another branch of the movement was formed at the end of 1960. It favored nonviolent means of resistance and was not accepted by Mukirania. In the following years members of this branch actively stuck to their Rwenzururu nationalism but did not take to arms (Bwambale and Kyaminyawandi 2000:4ff.).

The Rwenzururu rebellion had begun as a joint venture by the BaKonzo and the BaAmba. Their initial demand to the authorities was a modest wish for a separate district independent of Toro authorities. The Toro authorities refused it, and in August 1962 a wave of violence swept the Konzo and Amba areas. This was followed by a declaration of secession from Toro rule by the BaAmba and BaKonzo along with the establishment of a rebel headquarters, and subsequently a kingdom, in the Rwenzori mountains with Mukirania as the king. From then on the BaKonzo took a leading role in the rebellion in the Bundibugyo area.

In 1966 Mukirania died and his young son, Charles Wesley Mumbere with the honorary title Irema Ngoma, was installed as his successor. The kingdom in the mountains lasted until 1982, when Irema Ngoma and his followers "came down from the mountains." A section of the Rwenzururu rebel movement stayed on, however, and would occasionally remind people of their presence by carrying out raids on the general population.

In the late 1980s the National Army for the Liberation of Uganda (NALU) was formed in Congo by two ex-UPC (Uganda People's Congress) Members of Uganda Parliament. Their aim was to unseat President Yoweri Museveni. Soldiers from the Rwenzururu Freedom Movement—an offshoot of the original Rwenzururu movement—became part of their outfit, and President Mobutu Sese Seko of Congo (then Zaire) provided them with training camps in the easternmost part of the country. Apart from infrequent raids, NALU did not make a substantial impact.

In addition to local disturbances, people in the area suffered from the general political situation in Uganda after President Idi Amin's coup in 1971. Being situated in the far west, on the border to Congo, and with difficult access to and from the rest of Uganda, the area did not experience the same extensive devastation under Amin[7] and, after Amin's fall, Obote II[8] as Ugandans did who lived closer to the political center. Nevertheless, the horror was strongly felt, and people were always afraid that they could, at any time, suffer the same fate as relatives and acquaintances elsewhere did. In 1996 people told me how they had always feared informers, and how they never dared to speak freely except in very small family groups whom they trusted. Any outsider was a threat.

The Wider Political Context

ADF's attacks on Bundibugyo and Kasese did not take place in a political vacuum. In November 1996 it was less than two and a half years since the Rwanda genocide had ended. The genocide caused a fall-out of refugees and militias that fled north- and westward, especially to Congo. Not only are Rwanda and Congo Uganda's close neighbors, but they also share aspects of their history with that of Uganda. Here I emphasize events in Rwanda, as these seem to have had an important effect on developments in Bundibugyo.

Rwanda

Already before the borders between Uganda, Congo, and Rwanda were established in 1910, Rwandans lived in what subsequently became Uganda. Later, mainly during the colonial period, labor migrants from Rwanda settled in Uganda. After the independence of Rwanda and the political turmoil that followed, refugees flooded into Uganda. In his discussion of this situation, Mamdani categorizes the Rwandans in Uganda as follows: *Nationals* are those Rwandans whose forebears were settled in Uganda before 1910 and who mainly live in Bufumbira county in Kabale district (Mamdani 2002:162). *Migrants* constitute the labor migrants who moved into Uganda from the mid-1920s. The majority were Hutu agriculturalists, but there were also *petits* Tutsi who worked as cattle keepers in the south as well as in northern and eastern Uganda (Mamdani 2002:162). *Refugees* consisted mainly of Tutsi who fled to Uganda between 1959 and 1964 (Mamdani 2002:164–66). Being categorized as *refugees* by the authorities, their lives were markedly different from those of earlier immigrants. Living in camps meant that their circumstances "clearly divided them from the host society" (Mamdani 2002:164–66).[9]

The Rwandan refugees had a hard time in Uganda. Milton Obote's government saw them as threats to his political power because they were Catholics and believed to support the opposition party, the catholic Democratic Party (DP). During Amin's presidency the refugees were not under the same pressures, but with the return of Obote in 1979 the pressures continued with a vengeance.[10]

From 1981 Museveni conducted the liberation struggle of Uganda with a steadily increasing number of freedom fighters. Among these were a considerable number of Rwandans who had entered Uganda as young refugees in the early 1960s. When Museveni, with his victorious National Resistance Army (NRA), marched into Kampala in January 1986, "roughly a quarter of their ranks of 16,000 were composed of Banyarwanda" (Mamdani 2002:170).[11] Initially, a number of Rwandans were included in Museveni's government, such as, for instance, Paul Kagame, who became the acting chief of military intelligence of the NRA (Mamdani 2002:173). This was possible because the refugees' civil status had changed: Already in July 1986 President Museveni announced that people from Rwanda who had been resident in Uganda for more than ten years would automatically be entitled to Ugandan citizenship (Mamdani 2002:174).

As Museveni was now not only a military but also a political leader, he no longer had the decision-making powers of a supreme military leader. The result was a very short honeymoon period for the Rwandans. Soon they were under pressure again both in civil society and in the military. Within a year of the liberation, many Rwandans had already been evicted from their settlements at the behest of local authorities. Mamdani mentions, for instance, the forced eviction from Teso in 1986 (Mamdani 2002:174). Although the NRA had many soldiers who were seasoned from the liberation struggle, the ratio of Rwandans in the army declined generally in the next few years although the veteran leaders formed a "rapidly expanding core in the officer corps" (Mamdani 2002:174). Soon the safety of the principle of "residence for more than ten years" was abandoned and descent became the overarching criterion for promotions. The Rwandans saw this as a betrayal, and in 1987 the Rwanda Patriotic Front (RPF) was formed.

On 1 October 1990 the RPF invaded Rwanda. The reasons for the invasions were complex. One of the causes that obviously weighed heavily was the abandonment of the Rwandans' right to residence in Uganda and their return to being *refugees* without settlement rights. A couple of particularly painful events, such as the Magwolola uprising in Ankole,[12] seem to have been determining factors. On the day of the RPF invasion, the Uganda government declared that "all Rwandese who had left the NRA to attack Rwanda would be considered deserters under the army's Operational Code of Conduct." This meant that, in case of a court martial, they could be given a death sentence (Mamdani 2002:183).

The RPF invasion of Rwanda could be seen as one of the triggers of the genocide in 1994. Although the RPF were not initially successful in their campaign, their invasion rekindled Hutu attitudes toward the Tutsi such as they had been when the Tutsi were in important power positions before the 1959 revolution, and it created a deep fear in the Hutu population. Ironically, President Juvénal Habyarimana's government had at this point moved toward a new era of ethnic conciliation. If his intentions had succeeded, it could have been perceived as a way of diminishing the Tutsi position of power in Rwandan society, and to establish a more egalitarian attitude to ethnic relations. Instead, the RPF invasion caused a hardening attitude in the organization "Hutu Power" whose goal was exactly what their name implied.[13]

This is not the place to discuss details of the genocide that started on 6 April 1994 and lasted until 14 June. Its unbelievable horror and inhumanity are described and analyzed elsewhere.[14] What is relevant in this context is the fall-out from the genocide in terms of the Rwandans who managed to flee to Congo and establish themselves there.

Congo

From its independence in 1960 Congo was a cauldron of intrigues, uprisings, and militias. The murder of President Patrice Lumumba created a plethora of opposing factions and guerrilla movements that unsettled the population, turned many into refugees, and sowed the seeds of later disturbances. The Rwandan genocide forced all those who were able, to flee to Congo and Tanzania where many of the refugee camps and settlements became political hotbeds (de Heusch 1995:7). In the camps, Hutu Power and the Interahamwe[15] began early to plan how to continue the struggle against the Tutsi. As Mamdani puts it: "Conventional wisdom in Goma and Bukavu has it that Kivu Province in eastern Congo is where losers in Rwanda traditionally end up, and it is from Kivu that they prepare to return to power in Rwanda" (Mamdani 2002:234). Many turned into loose bands and militias that joined up with other groups fighting against Mobutu, thereby creating large numbers of homeless people, mainly women and children. It was from some of these militias that many of the ADF fighters were recruited. Mamdani mentions local Congolese militias that were active in 1997, such as Ngilima operating in the Lubero and Beni areas, and Kasingien whose members came from "Congolese living on both sides of the Congo-Uganda border" (Mamdani 2002:258).[16] Likewise, an *IRIN* brief on the attack on Bundibugyo notes that the ADF "had been based around Beni in eastern DRC (Democratic Republic of Congo) where they had been used by former President Mobutu Sese Seko to fight the Zairian 'Kasindian' dissident group" (*IRIN* news item 13 August 1997).[17]

The Background of the ADF

The ADF as it appeared in Uganda was based on a Ugandan Muslim Tabliq group that was formed in the wake of President Amin's fall in 1979. It had a militant young leadership that in the first instance wished to reform the way in which Islam was practiced in Uganda. In 1984 a convert to Islam, Jamil Mukulu, joined them and, after a year as a student of Arabic in Riyadh in Saudi Arabia, he became a leading member of the group. In 1991 he led a bloody riot in Kampala in which four policemen and one Tabliq were killed and, together with 413 of his followers, he was arrested, detained, and charged with murder. After two months, however, the charges were dropped. Later on, Mukulu formed a group of militant Tabliqs, the Salafi Foundation. After a disagreement with various Muslim leaders, he went to Hoima with his followers where they established themselves. According to Gunaratna, "In 1994, Salafi Foundation of Uganda was supported by Al Qaeda/NIF (National Islamic Front [Sudan]) to develop the Ugandan Mujahidin Freedom Fighters (UMFF). ... By joining other opposition forces, UMFF evolved into the Allied Democratic Forces (ADF), which relocated to the Democratic Republic of Congo to challenge the Kampala Government. After Al Qaeda moved to Afghanistan in 1996, handpicked ADF members were trained in Afghanistan as explosives experts (Gunaratna 2002:163). The ADF camps were overrun by UPDF in February 1995 and the group was scattered. Mukulu is said to have fled to London while some of his followers fled to Sudan. Mukulu is believed to have sent his followers for training in eastern Congo while his colleagues in Sudan are said to have joined the Nile Bank Front.[18] With NALU and old Rwenzururu soldiers already established in eastern Congo, a merger between them and the Tabliqs seems to have taken place under the umbrella of the ADF. The Uganda mainstream Tabliqs, on the other hand, denounced violence and militancy after the secession of Mukulu and his followers.

Beginnings

After the first attack on Kasese in 1996, it turned out that the rebels could not go back to Congo because the Banyamulenge[19] were at that time taking over the territories where the ADF had been operating. In the first moment of enthusiasm, however, a spokesman for NALU announced that "it is NALU which is engaged in operations of liberating the country [from Museveni's rule]" (*Monitor* news item 17 November 1996).

A government official told me that many of the Ugandan young men who had joined the rebels (NALU/ADF) were younger sons in poor families who had no prospects, no education, no school fees, and no land. The lure of money and a university course in Saudi Arabia had convinced them to join. One of the captives, a MuKonzo, said he had been promised one million Uganda shillings, a good car, and a house when the war was over. Other captives revealed some of the rebels' plans: The idea had been to capture Kasese administrative centers and air strip, then proceed by boat across Lake George and eventually capture Mbarara. After this they were to go to Kabale, Rukungiri, and Kisoro districts. A standby force of 9,000 Zairian troops would come in as reinforcements after the mission had been completed (*New Vision* news item 18 November 1996).

This did not, however, happen. But from then on, Kasese district was regularly attacked by the ADF rebels. The brutal attacks on people and the wanton destruction of property caused thousands of civilians to flee from the border areas. Kasese Town authorities closed schools and community halls in order to house them, and many could not return home for several months. There was a reluctance to stay in the areas close to the border to Congo. Letters from friends in Kasese emphasized that the ADF continued their terror campaign. One friend wrote two years after the initial attack: "The ADF killings are still going on. They burn people in their houses, using petrol. In September the whole Kilembe market was burnt down."

Bundibugyo

The attack on Bundibugyo district was a major operation. According to an *IRIN* report, the rebels attacked from two angles: "Although the army had been forewarned of the attack, they were wrong-footed. While an ADF group engaged the UPDF at the border, a separate force slipped past and occupied Bundibugyo Town" (*IRIN* news item 13 August 1997). According to a newspaper story, the rebels gathered civilians at Bundibugyo Boma Ground "for a sensitization rally ... [while] the [UPDF] soldiers, unable to contain the rebel onslaught, had bolted out of town" (*Monitor* news item 27 June 1997). When the rebels spoke to the civilians they claimed to have been in Bundibugyo district for the last four months, a remark that reflects what I was told by my friend before I left.

The rebels are said to have occupied Bundibugyo Town for between four and seven hours, after which they were engaged by the UPDF and withdrew. *New Vision* reported that one thousand ADF rebels attacked Bundibugyo. Many of these were killed in the subsequent battle against the Uganda army. "Bodies of dead rebels are littered in various areas of Sempaya, Ntandi and Karugutu … Thousands of residents have fled their mountain homes and gone to camp in Bundibugyo Town," wrote the reporter (*New Vision* news item 20 June 1997). Already at the outset there were about eighty Interahamwe among the ADF attackers (*New Vision* news item 24 June 1997).[20]

A few days later, *New Vision* reported a vicious ADF attack on civilians: "Twelve people were burnt alive and at least ten others slaughtered by the ADF rebels, witnesses said today … According to a survivor: '17 civilians were rounded up and forced to enter a hut before it was set ablaze … [the witnesses] said the rebels guarded the huts to ensure that the victims perished'. All those who were rounded up were male" (*New Vision* news item 24 June 1997). The word *slaughtered* also cropped up in my first telephone call to the area: "People are not only killed, they are slaughtered with pangas and knives." And another person wrote: "Others were killed by gun shots, hoes, pangas and axes … One of the boys whom I helped with school fees burnt in that house and died."

The result of this carnage was that everyone who could get out, tried to do so. People living on the mountainsides took refuge in Bundibugyo Town, and some fled to the other side of the Rwenzori in a convoy heavily guarded by UPDF, ending up in camps in Fort Portal. The first refugee camps were also established close to the Congo border. The rebels were eventually driven by the UPDF to the mountain areas near the southern border to Congo, and continued to attack from camps in the mountains. On 1 August President Museveni came down to assess the situation and promised more troops, but this did not solve the problem. The rebels stayed on in the mountains and the Semliki forest, and now operated in small bands.

Specific actions characterized the rebels. The first I heard about the attack on Bundibugyo was the *slaughtering* of people "*with pangas and knives*," while others were *shot* and killed with pangas as well as *axes* and *hoes*. It was, in other words, an attack with ordinary weapons and tools. Already, a couple of days after the initial attack, seventeen young men were *burnt* alive in a hut, assiduously guarded by the rebels. In an early *IRIN* brief (*IRIN* news item 13 August 1997) about the attack, *beheading* was also mentioned. *Abduction*, a "terror tactic" otherwise rarely used in the area, became quite common. The ADF rebels abducted both men and women, not only to swell their numbers but also to provide assistance with everyday chores such as cooking and fetching firewood. The women were graded by the rebels: Those who were pretty were made sexually available, especially for the leaders, while the less attractive fetched firewood and cooked. Some women joined the rebel forces. Young men were frequently abducted, and few survived. Among them were men who later came back as part of a raiding band but now with Islamic names. Others were made to carry heavy loads on long marches in the mountains, and many of them succumbed to the strain and died. Another terror tactic was to *shoot people who went to their fields to dig for food.* According to the *IRIN* brief already mentioned: "According to local sources ... an average of six people are killed each week by the ADF as they work on their farms." Thus, by forcing the majority of people to flee their homes the rebels were able to live well on what was left behind. When attacking, the rebels appeared suddenly and with force, and people who were not able to get away in time were killed. This unpredictable death threat shattered people's nerves, and their fear increased with each new attack. People in Bundibugyo were, in other words, under siege and the rebels ruled their lives not only by overt terror but also by their unexpectedness and by preventing their victims to obtain food.

Relief was eventually provided by the World Food Program (WFP) and Médicines sans Frontières (MSF). Towards October the situation calmed down. People could still hear the rebels shooting in the mountains, but there were few attacks. Many went back to their homes while others stayed close to Bundibugyo Town. According to one friend: "I wish to tell you that although we were disturbed by the war, Christmas was fair." Summing up the situation at the end of the letter he said: "The main problems of the people of Bundibugyo are the war, famine and diseases."

1998

Sadly, this "fair" situation did not last. Despite heavy army presence, the rebels continued their attacks in areas near the border to Congo; houses were burned and people were killed. In February a senior secondary school at Mitandi, south of Bundibugyo Town, was overrun by the rebels and about forty students were abducted. "They [the rebels] killed some and some were later released. Others are still missing," as one letter put it. This was followed by new intense attacks in the same area. More houses were burned and more people killed. Still, in other parts of the district optimistic local projects were launched such as the "Give a goat or sheep" project intended for families whose livestock had been entirely depleted.

In March rebel activity intensified and in April MSF, which until then had worked at the hospital, left. The rebels had now firmly established themselves in the Semliki forest. On 8 June they attacked Kichwamba Technical College, not far from Fort Portal. One man described the atrocities: "I happened to travel [in an armed convoy] to Fort Portal that morning. At Karugutu we heard artillery in action. I saw with my own eyes, after the shooting had stopped, how defenseless students were burned by the rebels in their dormitories. Others, more than one hundred, were abducted. Even the surrounding villages were attacked, people were killed and abducted. There were burned bodies, people were crying. We had a massgrave burial at the school, but only skeletons were left. The rebels used petrol to set the house on fire and bullets to kill. About eighty students lost their lives, and among those who were abducted, few survived." In 1999 *IRIN* reported the story of one of the students who *had* survived the abduction. The rebels had told them that they wanted help to carry arms and supplies to the mountains, after which their captives would be freed. Once they reached the mountain camps, however, the students were tied together. For weeks they were made to march through the mountainous terrain into Congo. They were rarely fed. The bodies of many of these students were eventually found in Congo.[21]

The situation in Bundibugyo continued to deteriorate. Rebel activity became more frequent, more wide-ranging, and more brutal. In November 1998 Irema-Ngoma, the ex-King of Rwenzururu, returned to Uganda for a visit after many years in exile. It was the Norwegian Christian Network, led by Bent Rönson, who made Irema-Ngoma's visit possible as it was believed that he would have a positive influence on the situation in the area of the BaKonzo and possibly also on the rebels. Irema-Ngoma toured the whole of Konzo country and was enthusiastically welcomed by the majority of the BaKonzo. In Bundibugyo he had a somewhat cool reception. One of their grievances was that he had taken over the leadership of NALU after its leader, Amon Bazira, had been killed in Kenya at the end of 1993. Irema-Ngoma explained that this did not mean that he now condoned ADF's campaign. One man remarked that killing in 1994 [by NALU] was not different from killing in 1998 (Tom Stacy, personal communication). Irema-Ngoma promised to make it clear to all the remnants of the Rwenzururu Freedom Movement as well as to NALU that they were not fighting for *him* and should therefore lay down their arms. I was told later that many local rebels had done so, and that there were no longer BaKonzo and BaAmba in the ADF forces.

1999

Irema-Ngoma's visit heartened his followers but had little impact on the ADF's activities, and the New Year did not show any improvement on the previous one. If anything, the situation became worse. In Bundibugyo the attacks intensified. People had to leave their homes and move back to the refugee camps. WFP had withdrawn because the conflict was defined as an internal one, I was told, and the NGOs that had been there previously also left because the situation was too dangerous. The local population was, in other words, left to fend for themselves with their extremely meager resources.

The ADF rebels attacked particularly in the night, I was told, and although many of their attacks seemingly were to replenish their food supply, they "found it easier to kill a human being than a goat," as one person put it. Every night people expected to be attacked, and attacks did take place somewhere almost every night. No one dared to go out, let alone tend their fields. The food situation was precarious, and more small children died of malaria and malnutrition than ever before. Cholera also returned and a number of people died, among them someone I had known since he was a small child and played with my daughter. One of the greatest problems was the lack of firewood and paraffin, without which people could not boil their drinking water and thus avoid cholera.

A most vicious attack took place where I had once lived, and an old man I knew and had visited in 1996 "died horribly," as one friend put it. The old man had been stabbed, slashed with pangas, and shot. The frequency of attacks, and their unrelenting viciousness, became a constant pressure on everybody. Several friends expressed the same notion: "We live in fear." One man wrote: "Thursday night was a very bad night for us. In fact it was so terrible and so tense, with terrible shootings between the rebels and the UPDF ... Three civilians died, among them one of my boys who had just finished Senior Four ... It was a terrible blow to me, I am so scared. I feel anytime it may [happen] to [any] of us too."

Getting to Fort Portal on the other side of the mountains meant going in a convoy protected by UPDF armored cars. Now convoys were attacked and people killed. The son of one of my friends was in one of these convoys. Eleven people were killed. "I just thank God that I was allowed to keep my son," as his father wrote to me afterwards. Another man described his own experience of the same attack: "[I was going] together with my colleague to Fort Portal. The rebels attacked our convoy and shot at us. It was the worst experience of my life. It was life or death. The UPDF fought very hard, and I saw with my own eyes people who were dying after being shot and breathing their last. I could only cry, could not assist because it was completely impossible ... When I eventually reached Fort Portal I developed a kind of malaria and went to bed. I could not eat or drink ..."

At this time the various NGOs had contemplated to return to Bundibugyo, but with the brutal attacks on the convoys they decided not to, and the population was still without any outside help. In June and July President Museveni made a round trip to all parts of Uganda. He came to Bundibugyo at the end of his tour, in the beginning of July. "I did not know this," he lamented when children sang for him about the atrocities committed by the rebels, and promised to deploy at least two thousand more troops in the region. He had not been properly informed about the extent of rebel activities, he said, and added that he would come back. He also promised to better their situation (*New Vision* news item 8 July 1999). All this sounded wonderful, but when I later in a telephone conversation said so, the answer was: "Politics."

Afterwards the raids continued with the same force, and ADF also extended its activity in Congo. From letters and the odd telephone conversation it was clear that people were beginning to feel very strongly the pressures under which they lived. In November a friend wrote that "we have again been so scared. The situation seems to be out of control." The intense uncertainty caused by the unpredictability of the rebels and the fear that gnawed deeper and deeper into people's minds, were reflected in the tones of the letters and the pressured voices on the phone.

The New Millennium

"I tell you this month of December, no one is sure to make it to the 21st century," was the first sentence in the first letter I received in 2000. It continued to tell me about a huge battle between the rebels and the army in which the rebels had had the upper hand for quite some time, but eventually were forced to retreat. In another letter I was told that the ADF had combined with the Mayi Mayi, the Interahamwe, and the LRA forces.[22] "The WFP have not distributed food and there is acute hunger. It is almost impossible to get hold of firewood." The short telephone conversations were equally dark, with the speakers obviously on tenterhooks in case of attack. In January there was a horrendous attack on the Kirindi camp where a large number of people were killed. One friend wrote afterwards: "When we are in bed we wonder if we will rise the following day. The night drags on to the accompaniment of heavy gunfire all over the place, and we are filled with restlessness until dawn." After this the telephone was out of order for several weeks and no letters came through.

In April I at last got through on the phone again and was told the situation was much calmer. "There are days when we do not even hear a single gun shot! The rebels have been pushed into Congo by the border. There are still rebels in the mountains, also by the border, but in all the camps here now have a very strong armed guard and there are few attacks. We are no longer so frightened. But we can never know if the rebels will be coming back."

The Aftermath

Despite the obvious relief I heard on the phone that day, the situation for most people was still dire and would be so for some time to come. The population knew that the rebels were hiding in the mountains and in the Semliki forest, and continued to be afraid to move outside their camps. By now there were about fifty camps in the district. These were collections of tiny dwellings housing at least ten people each. Outside the house there would be a small area where cooking and washing took place, and a ditch leading through the whole camp. Soldiers from UPDF guarded the camps and accompanied those who had fields close by. The fear of rebels lurking in the bushes nearby prevented people from going far from their camps. Some had their houses nearby but they never slept in them. They would go, guarded by soldiers, to keep an eye on their homes, but without a chance to keep them in good repair. Their houses therefore deteriorated rapidly, as fast as the bush managed to overtake what once had been cultivated fields.

Few youngsters and adults had jobs and therefore an income. With unemployment and the lack of work opportunities, problems of alcoholism, criminality, and internal violence increased. Food was brought by WFP and other donors, but the quantities were not large enough. Bundibugyo Hospital began to function again together with small clinics dotted around in the area, but medicines were scarce, and small children continued to suffer malnutrition and illness (especially malaria), and died as before. Cholera often reappeared, particularly in the rainy season.

The people of Bundibugyo endured onslaughts of a dimension that no one who has not lived in a war zone of this kind can even begin to fathom. Not only did they fear for their lives every day and night for several years, but they also had to see their children die for lack of food combined with general malnutrition and preventable diseases. They saw their loved ones die horribly, be "slaughtered," and some had to bury some of their relatives' corpses without heads. They had their homes, their fields and their crops destroyed, and were left behind every time the situation became too dangerous, by the NGOs that brought some relief in more quiet periods.

Their normal lives, on which they were supposed to build their future, had in a sense been taken away from them, and what was left was a future of uncertainty, anxiety, and pain. They had enormous tasks ahead of them trying to reorder and reestablish their lives, and to allow themselves to mourn all those who had died. For a long time they could not know if there was any reason to begin thinking about rebuilding their lives again because the rebels could come back at any time as they had done before.

In 2002 there was a reluctant but real move out of the camps and back to the homesteads. There were enormous tasks to be done, but how to do so without tools and no money to buy them with? Most people have now managed to resettle in their homes, but the problem is still the struggle for money with which to buy tools.

ADF and the Developments in Congo

In the first half of 2000, the two high-ranking ADF leaders, Commander Benz and Rwigyema Junior, surrendered to the UPDF in Kasese (*Monitor* news item 18 April 2000). This was followed by a government offer of amnesty for rebels who gave themselves up. In Kilembe a rehabilitation center for returned rebels was established at the initiative of Bent Rönson. Many ex-rebels joined the center and were, after the process of rehabilitation, able to join their families—not always an easy process. Nevertheless, a number of former ADF rebels stayed away, some taking part in the wars in eastern Congo, some just vanishing. The many battles taking place in Congo next to the Uganda border were by the government of Uganda seen as a threat to Uganda's sovereignty, and the Uganda army entered Congolese territory, but withdrew when the UPDF was accused of exploiting Congolese natural resources on a large scale and establishing lucrative trades.

In September 2003 I got a worried phone call from Bundibugyo: "The ADF are back close to the border. We are very, very worried. The army is already in the mountains." The Ugandan newspaper *New Vision* had an article in late September confirming that UPDF had deployed near the border to Congo following reports that a Ugandan rebel group had regrouped in Congolese villages. The *IRIN* report, based on *New Vision's* article, confirmed that "a splinter group [of] Allied Democratic Front [sic] (ADF) had reformed at its former bases in Ituri District" (*IRIN* news item 29 September 2003). This new threat from across the border tempted many to return to the camps, and some did so; but after a while the panic died down, and they returned to their homes.

In October Mbusa Nyamwisi, the DRC Minister of Regional Cooperation in the transitional government, confirmed the presence of Ugandan rebel training camps in the region between Beni and Kasindi in North Kivu Province, that is, not far from the border to Uganda. According to *IRIN*, among the armed groups said to be active in the area were ADF, NALU, and PRA (People's Redemption Party) (*IRIN* news item 31 October 2003). The UN peacekeeping mission, MONUC, was asked to "keep watch of the activities of the Ugandan rebels" (*IRIN* news item 31 October 2003).

Only a few months later the UN officials hailed the repatriation of former Ugandan rebels operating in DRC. These were mainly from the former West Nile Bank front, and some may have been connected to the ADF. This was the work of the Ugandan government Amnesty Commission that had been offering amnesty for all rebels for some time. The efforts to contact rebels for peace talks earlier had fizzled out in March 2003, but now had new actuality for both the Ugandan government and all rebels. One of the problems had been that the Uganda army *violated* the cease-fire, and on a number of occasions used it to contain rebel commanders and then ambush them (*IRIN* news item 23 January 2004). In November 2004 the tensions in Congo rose due to the regrouping of the ADF and the activities of the PRA. These activities were not regarded as a threat to Uganda by the UPDF, but nevertheless, one day armed men believed to be ADF and PRA raided the Nziapande market in Bundibugyo district and rekindled the earlier fears in Bundibugyo's population (*New Vision* news item 30 November 2004).

In 2005 the Congolese army and MONUC intensified their attempts at demobilizing the various rebel bands in Ituri and Northern Kivu. In April there were reports about a considerable number of militias in Ituri that they had surrendered their weapons and were given the choice of taking part in the program of disarmament, demobilization, and reintegration (DDR) into civilian life, or to join the new national Congolese army. Some of the rebels fled, however, and hid in the forests near Uganda's border (*OCHA* report 15 April 2005).

The situation in Congo was, however, far from clarified. There were still rebel bands roaming the forests. Moreover, troops from the Congolese army defected, and some joined dissident groups while others were met by troops from MONUC and the Congolese army and persuaded to rejoin them. In September a delegation from MONUC visited the North Kivu town of Beni and announced that "the presence of dissidents from nearby Uganda"—the Allied Democratic Forces and the National Army for the Liberation of Uganda—"would not be tolerated" (*OCHA* report 17 September 2005).

In the beginning of November a great offensive was begun by the Congolese army and MONUC. The hunt was for Rwandan rebels, Mayi Mayi, and others including ADF, PRA, and NALU. Already on 9 November,

336 rebels had surrendered with their weapons. The UN estimated that 15,000 Rwandan and Ugandan rebels were still based in eastern Congo (*IRIN* news item 9 November 2005). In neighboring Congo battles between MONUC and rebel movements continued, often driving civilians to flee into neighboring countries. In January 2009 renegade rebel leader Laurent Nkunda was arrested in Rwanda, and Congo civilians began to return to their devastated homes.

Although western Uganda has on the whole been peaceful after the end of the ADF attacks in 2001, the multitude of rebel bands in the immediate neighborhood, only kept at bay by the border rivers (Lamia and Semliki), has served as a constant reminder for people in Bundibugyo not only of what they have experienced but also that they could become targets of rebel activity at any time.

Why Has Bundibugyo So Often Been Forgotten?

The geographical position of Bundibugyo vis-à-vis the rest of Uganda has made it a distant and little recognized appendix on the country. Apart from the two rebellions mentioned above, the population has, to an outsider, appeared passive, and therefore not often noticeable for the governing authorities. Poverty and increasing land shortage have not helped, and the deteriorating transport system has been directly detrimental. Educational facilities are still minimal. Because the district is "so far away," so difficult to get to, teachers do not wish to work there, and the educational standards have steadily gone down. Bundibugyo is now one of the few remaining districts in Uganda without electricity.

The government's immediate reaction to the ADF incursion was to bring in the army, but many other concerns, such as health care and food supplies, were neglected. In 1999, when President Museveni made a journey through the whole of Uganda, visiting all districts, he came to Bundibugyo *last* and found the district devastated. "I did not know," he lamented, and offered more soldiers. Aid agencies have shown very little interest in rebuilding the area after the ADF incursion. There are a few NGOs scattered around but not by far enough. A good friend wrote some time ago about how the neighboring district Ntoroko had been given a face-lift by World Vision. "Why not here?" he asked. "After all, Bwamba county was most hit by the war."[23]

In 2004 people's patience came to an end. I was told that a series of meetings were held in Bwamba in May and June where elders, district leaders, and others concerned discussed the question of how to make *their* voice heard and understood [by the Uganda authorities]. "Areas close to the large cities are OK, but we are forgotten," as one friend put it. A demonstration in front of Parliament in Kampala was planned and transport arranged for the demonstrators. This was brought to the attention of President Museveni, and he came immediately to Bundibugyo Town. Here he was met by an angry community. "Everybody, including the Chairman [of the local council] went against the President," I was told. The *Monitor* newspaper described the meeting: "The residents protested the sorry state of the Bundibugyo-Fort Portal road ... and the lack of electricity in the district. 'The Fort Portal-Bundibugyo road will be completed soon. I know you are angry with me and that is why you are booing me,' Museveni said in a mixture of English and Runyankole amidst continuous booing" (*Monitor* news item 3 July 2004). "The President then explained that there is no money for the road now, but the electrification will be completed by the end of 2005" (*Monitor* news item 3 July 2004). In a recent telephone conversation (November 2008), I asked if there had been work on the electrification, but the answer was "No."

Summary and Reflections

I have presented a close-up of a Ugandan community under siege by rebels, showing the effects of rebel activity on a local community over a period of several years. The Uganda army managed to stave off some of the attacks, but despite their presence, the rebels' inhuman violence and unpredictability devastated the population and ruined much of the land. Gradually, over a period of four years, the UPDF managed to chase the rebels back across the border to Congo. It was a bereaved and drained population who had to pick up the pieces. Any new uncertainty and threat brought back their fears, but gradually they have managed to reestablish a *modus vivendi*.

Can extreme violence be understood? In trying to understand how deliberate violence of the kind I have described can come to be, it is not for me to "sanitize" it (Last 2000). As Prunier puts it in his work on the Rwanda genocide: "this author thinks that understanding why they died is the best and most fitting memorial we can raise for the victims. Letting their deaths go unrecorded, or distorted by propaganda ... would in fact bring the last touch to the killers' work in completing the victims' dehumanisation" (Prunier 1995:xii). I fully subscribe to Prunier's sentiments, but in addition I ask the question: What caused the *extremes* of violence that took place in Bundibugyo, and can it be understood?

At the time of the ADF assault on Bundibugyo, East and Central Africa were much troubled. Decades of conflict, massacres, and political turmoil created a backdrop to Bundibugyo's tragedy. The shadows of past colonial rule were also present, coloring people's perceptions of each other. The Rwanda genocide had happened less than a couple of years before the ADF attack on Kasese, and many of those who joined the ADF were Rwandans who had participated in the genocide. The result was unimaginable horror and inhumanity.

Uganda had not treated its Rwandan refugees well, neither under Obote nor under Museveni. I would suggest that both the Hutu and the Tutsi were victims, not only of the present political turmoil but also of their long and fraught history that had structured their society in such a way that Tutsi and Hutu could not, in general, avoid deep-seated animosity against each other. Mamdani suggests that the killers' cold-blooded murders that took place during the genocide were rooted in their fate as victims of "an ongoing political drama, victims of yesterday who may be victims again. That moral certainty explains the easy transition from yesterday's victims to killers the morning after" (Mamdani 2002:233). Mamdani has chosen the political angle from which to approach the violence of genocide. He refers to Hegel's point that "humans are distinguished from animals by the fact that they, unlike animals, are also willing *to give life* for a reason higher than life. He [Hegel] should have added that humans, unlike animals, are also willing *to take life* for a reason they consider higher than life ... When the life in question is that of groups, involving large numbers, the decision is inevitably political" (Mamdani 2002:196).

The politics of violence does not answer the question of *why* violence can take such extreme forms. People in Bundibugyo were *slaughtered and beheaded* by the rebels, they were *shot* and they were *burned alive,* and many young men and women were *abducted* with horrendous consequences. The rebels created a world, not only for themselves but also for the Bundibugyo population in which there was no future, only a present where death stared them in the face.

The rebels were killers, embodying death and unleashing their frenzy on an innocent population. In the poem "Guerilla Promise" from the liberation struggle of Namibia, this embodiment of death is expressed thus:

I'll rush upon you
Like escaping new born sun ray
Then dazzle you with my lethal swiftness
'cause I'm the Fight

As unknown as an unborn battle
Labouring with steel and hand-grenade
I'm death conceived

'till my moment arrives
With pain ... blood and terror

I'm a soldier of this realm
I'm a poisoned arrow

I'm strong-bow
I'm a sharpened spear
I'm a sword

waiting in my sheath
only for your death[24]

The rebels had entered what Wyschogrod calls a *death-world* (Wyschogrod 1999). Her main concern is the man-made death that she suggests appeared in *European* history with World War I,[25] and which has since had a profound and enduring effect on human society. The beginning, the *death event*, subsequently came to include the development of nuclear, biological, and chemical warfare, and death camps (Wyschogrod 1999:xii). With the death event came the *death-world*, "a new and unique form of social existence in which vast populations are subjected to conditions of life ... conferring upon their inhabitants the status of living dead" (Wyschogrod 1999:15). The death-world is a sudden world, an unpredictable world without antecedents. It is without the reason and the ideas of a future in the *life-world*.[26]

For the people of Bundibugyo who lived in the camps, their existence consisted only of a hellish *now*. The rebels' killing methods were a source of both fear and sorrow. That relatives and friends were burned to cinders, or gruesomely slaughtered, added a feeling of utter hopelessness.

This cosmic or mythological aspect of violence has been emphasized by a number of writers. In his discussion of the origins of terrorism, Edward Said reflects on the character of violence that is beyond human comprehension. Said made a difference between the poor Palestinian who is "strapping dynamite around himself and then throwing himself into a crowd of Israelis" and those who attacked the World Trade Center and the Pentagon. The first, he says, is a human being who "feels himself being crowded out of life and all his surroundings," while the 9/11 bombers were not "poor refugee camp dwellers" but belonged to the educated middle class. "This is now transcending the political and moving into the metaphysical. It is a leap I think it is very important to keep one's eye on, because it suggests a kind of cosmic quality" (Said 2003:112–13).

This leap into the metaphysical appears also under other yet similar conditions. Liisa Malkki gives a stunning picture of the massacre of Hutus in Burundi in 1972. During her fieldwork in the Mishamo camp for Burundian refugees in Tanzania, she collected narratives that she calls *mythico-histories* told by the survivors (Malkki 1995). The mythico-histories reflect the feelings that the Hutu refugees had in relation to the Tutsi who had brought on the massacre. Malkki argues that "the Hutu mythico-history represented an interlinked set of ordering stories which converged to make (or remake) a world." She continues: "The mythico-history ... constructed categorical schemata and thematic configurations that were relevant and meaningful in confronting both the past in Burundi and the pragmatics of everyday life in the refugee camp in Tanzania" (Malkki 1995:55). In other words, through their stories the refugees created a world in which they could live, thus escaping from the death-world they had been forced into by the massacre.

Taylor, building on Kapferer, emphasizes the importance of the ontology on which the "pattern" is based that directs forms of violence. Through his knowledge and analysis of Rwandan body-symbolism, he finds that most of the methods used by the killers had their roots in the way in which the body, in its totality, is perceived. He writes: "This entails the capacity to ingest and excrete, or, in socio-moral terms, the capacity to give and receive. Consequently, two portions of the anatomy and their unobstructed connection are at issue: the mouth and the anus. By analogical extension the concern with unobstructed connection and unimpeded movement characterizes earlier Rwandan symbolic thought about the topography of the land, its rivers, roads and pathways in general" (Taylor 1999:114; cf. also the contribution in this volume). This corresponds to Hobbes' vision of the state. As Kapferer puts it: "for Hobbes the state is an extension of fundamental human nature" (Kapferer 2004:2). During the genocide, however, the terror tactics were the obverse of what would be socially accepted. The Hutu used *obstruction* of the body's pathways as well as the pathways of the landscape: "Rwanda's rivers became part of the genocide by acting as the body's political organs of elimination, in a sense 'excreting its hated internal other.' It is not much of a leap to infer that Tutsi were thought of as excrement by their persecutors" (Taylor 1999:130).

Following this argument, the victims of the Rwanda genocide were ritually killed in the obverse form of what was socially necessary and accepted. I would argue that some of the major "terror tactics" used by the ADF were in the same vein, suiting their own "death-world." Many of the ADF rebels' methods were on par with those of the Hutu during the genocide: They slaughtered, they bludgeoned, they abducted, and they shot civilians. What is striking, though, is the ADF rebels' destructive use of fire, such as when they killed the young men in Bundibugyo by burning them alive and making sure they did not escape. Likewise, they killed the students at Kichwamba Technical College by burning them in their dormitories. The burning of Kilembe market was in the same vein, although there they burned the market produce and thereby threatened people's lives by destroying their food. These are only a few of many incidents. As my friend in Kasese wrote: "They burn people in their houses, using petrol."

If we look at the ontology of these acts, we note that the population in the general area (including eastern Congo) is made up mainly of agriculturalists, and fire is necessary to clear a field in preparation for planting and sowing. Fire is also an important social element: it is used for cooking and light, for beer-brewing, and, in the not so distant past, it was a central ritual element during the spirit possession ritual, the *obubandwa*. By killing their fellow human beings by what normally is seen as life-giving, life-sustaining, and ritually important, they create their own death-world mythology where human beings are only "bare life" that can be killed (Agamben in Kapferer 2004:7)—worth less than a goat. For the rebels, killing humans is an express act of wielding power, getting rid of a population that is in the way of their own success. The victims that were burned or abducted were mainly young students, men with the promise of a future that the rebels did not have.

Fanon argues that "Racialism and hatred and resentment—a legitimate desire for revenge—cannot sustain a war of liberation. Those lightning flashes of consciousness which fling the body into stormy paths or which throw it into an almost pathological trance where the face of the other beckons me on to giddiness, where my blood calls for the blood of the other, where by sheer inertia my death calls for the death of the other—that intense emotion of the first few hours falls to pieces if it is left to feed on its own substance" (Fanon 1967:111). Although many members of the ADF were rehabilitated in 2000, a number went back to Congo and took part in the wars that continued to rage there. As already noted, the Congo government recently waged an all-out war against the remnants of the many rebel groups in eastern Congo and killed those rebels who did not give themselves up, among them members of ADF and NALU. It is possible that the small bands of rebels that fled into the forests further south and got themselves killed, would no longer have been able to live without the feeling of power and "security" that their raids and attacks had given them in their death-world.

Notes

Acknowledgements

I first and foremost wish to thank my many Ugandan friends who have contributed to this chapter with their letters and oral comments; without them it could not have been written. I wish to thank Stan Burkey of the Uganda Change Agents Association who, by sending me the first newspaper cuttings about the onslaught on Bundibugyo, jolted me into an acute awareness of what was happening. Moreover, he gave me much support during my field trip to Uganda in 1996, for which I am extreme grateful. Much gratitude also goes to Carl Emil Petersen, who has been most generous in sharing his news and his understanding of the situation in Bundibugyo with me. I am most grateful to Bruce Kapferer, who invited me to the inspirational conference "War and the State" and gave me helpful comments during the revision; to Bjørn Enge Bertelsen, who not only steered us most ably through the conference but also has given me much support since; and to the many participants of the conference who commented on my essay. Much gratitude goes to Raymond Ntalindwa and Mvula ya Nangolo for allowing me to include their poems in the text, and to Murray Last for giving me a copy of his Inaugural Lecture given at University College London. My children Beni and Patji both provided sensitive support during the time when I shared the pain of my friends in Bundibugyo and mourned people I knew who were killed. Beni and her sister Maja have also given me helpful comments and editorial advice. My anthropological fieldwork in Bundibugyo in the 1950s and 1960s was funded by the Norwegian Research Council for Science and the Humanities (NAVF). I am most grateful to the British Academy for supporting my revisit to Bundibugyo in 1996.

1. Although Congo was called *Zaire* for part of the period described here, I use the name *Congo* throughout. It was Mobutu who changed the country's name to Zaire, but when Laurent-Desire Kabila took charge in 1997, he renamed it the Democratic Republic of Congo (DRC). Presently, Kabila's son is president. The name Congo is, however, a much older name for the country, and I prefer to use it (see Nzongola-Ntalaja 2003:1).
2. I use "BaKonzo" (sing. MuKonzo) and "BaAmba" (sing. MwAmba) to denote the Konzo and Amba population in Bundibugyo, and "BaToro" (sing. MuToro) for the Toro population east of the Rwenzori. When the terms Konzo, Amba, and Toro appear alone, they are used in an adjectival meaning. The BaKonzo as an ethnicity live on both sides of the Congo-Uganda border. In Uganda they are generally called BaKonjo (Bakonjo or Konjo) while in Congo they are called Banande (or Wanande). There are strong social, economic, and kinship links between the Konzo and Nande populations in the two countries. The prefix "Lhu" indicates the language of a population group. Other population groups discussed here are called by the names used in the literature, i.e., Hutu, Tutsi, etc.
3. In 2003 there were, for instance, 11,000 refugees in Bundibugyo district. These had fled from the Ituri district in Congo. In 2005 the situation in Congo brought a new wave of refugees from Ituri to Bundibugyo.
4. Apart from the population increase, one of the main reasons for the land shortage is the creation of two national parks in the area, the Rwenzori National Park and the Semliki National Park. The establishment of these two parks, which earlier were potential areas for settlement, now make it illegal for the residents in Bundibugyo to enter the parks without a permit, let alone cultivate and hunt there. The idea for the parks came from Guy Yeoman, a veterinary surgeon who worked in East Africa. In his book *Africa's Mountains of the Moon* he wrote, "A new form of national park should be envisaged, … in which much of the forest zone of Rwenzori would be managed by the Konjo themselves … We are really talking about the Konjo domain" (Yeoman 1989:166). Sadly, although the park was established a few years later, it did not become a "Konjo domain" but is run by the Uganda government authorities that mainly employ nonlocal people as keepers.
5. One of the leaders, Nyamutswa, was a powerful healer and spirit medium. I was told that his power was so strong that he did not die until after the hangman's third attempt at killing him. After this revolt, Nyamutswa has been seen as a culture hero and regarded as a model for young BaKonzo. I was told that "even BaToro would use Nyamutswa as a symbol of rebellion. In the Toro-dominated schools a Toro teacher would ask: 'Do we have Nyamutswa here?' when Konzo children showed signs of opposition" (Alnaes 1995:132)

6. Konzo and Amba youngsters who went to Toro educational establishments suffered many indignities from their BaToro co-students. As one ex-student remembers: "I had a Mutoro friend ... with whom I used to share some 'Sumbusas.' However, [my friend] was reprimanded by some older Batoro boys for sharing a meal with me just because I was a Mukonzo" (Bwambale and Kyaminyawandi 2000:3).
7. President Amin is remembered for having established three new districts to replace the old Toro district. These were at the time called: Tooro district, Semuliki district, and Rwenzori district (Bwambale and Kyaminyawandi 2000:38). The present nomenclature is: Bundibugyo (previously Semuliki), Kasese (previously Rwenzori), and Kabarole (previously Tooro).
8. Obote II is the term used for President Milton Obote's second term of office after the fall of Amin and before the liberation of Uganda by the National Resistance Army (NRA) led by Yowevi Museveni.
9. Apart from the economic and political links that were established between Uganda and Rwanda through these population movements, cultural influences were also evident. The Nyabingi uprising in Rwanda spilled over into Uganda, especially in the southwest (Mamdani 2002:71–2; Hopkins 1970:258–336) and left behind a myth about the spirit Nyabingi—who led the uprising—that spread northward and became part of spirit possession cults (Alnaes 1995:136, 145n22). In a spirit possession ritual I recorded in Bundibugyo in 1967, the medium sang: "I have my medicine, I fetched it in Rwanda." I was told that the reference to Rwanda had to do with the distance that had to be covered in order to fetch the most potent medicine.
10. In 1982, for instance, Obote arranged a brutal attack on Rwandans in Ankole with the help of the UPC youth Wing and local chiefs. This resulted in 35,000 fleeing to the established settlements and 40,000 returning to Rwanda. Similar attacks took place elsewhere later and caused much harm among the refugees (Yeld 1996:93; Mamdani 2002: 168–9).
11. Yeld and Prunier both write that 3,000 out of 14,000 were Rwandans (Yeld 1996:94; Prunier 1995:70).
12. The Mawogola uprising took place in August 1990. It centered on the rights of pastoralists (many of whom were Rwandan settlers) to grazing land that they had used during the colonial period but, by 1990, had been divided and distributed to "businessmen and bureaucrats, politicians and military men," often as "lucrative patronage" (Mamdani 2002:176). While agriculturalists were guaranteed compensation, pastoralists were not. They were regarded as squatters who did not own property and therefore did not qualify for compensation. A long battle ensued, and the outcome was that the pastoralists lost and, especially Rwandan pastoralists, felt bitterly betrayed by the authorities.
13. Hutu Power was a part of President Habyarimana's political force. After the RPF invasion they hardened considerably and, according to Mamdani: "the genocidal tendency was born of the crisis of Hutu Power" (Mamdani 2002:185).
14. See, for instance, de Heusch 1995; Prunier 1995; Taylor 1999; Mamdani 2002.
15. The Interahamwe constituted the youth wing of President Habyarimana's party MRND(D) (Mouvement Révolutionaire National pour le Développement [et la Démocratie]). The members received intensive political training and arms before the genocide; they also kept track of all Rwandan opposition party members and all Tutsis, and many of their leaders were among the organizers of the genocide (Prunier 1995:375; Taylor 1999:33).
16. The Konzo and Amba link with their relatives in Congo was marked already in the beginning of 1962 when the secession from the Toro Kingdom was foremost in everybody's mind. The BaKonzo and BaAmba had three options for getting rid of Toro overrule: a) to demand a separate district, b) to be ruled by the Central Government, and c) to secede from Uganda and rejoin Congo (where twelve BaKonzo [BaNande] were members of the National Assembly). As the first direct elections to the Toro *Rukurato* (Parliament) were going to be held at this time, the BaKonzo and BaAmba leaders de-

cided to obtain permission to take part in the elections and to voice their grievances in *Rukurato* (Bwambale and Kyaminyawandi 2000:9; see also Alnaes 1969:247). Later, the Rwenzururu Kingdom Government established links with rebel groups in Congo, such as the Mayi Mayi militia (Bwambale and Kyaminyawandi 2000:27). Mayi Mayi is the generic term for all militias in Kivu Province linked to "indigenous" Native Authorities. They were part of the forces that mounted the first rebellion against Mobutu (Mamdani 2002:258).

17. *IRIN* is an acronym for the Integrated Regional Information Network of the United Nations.
18. This account is mainly based on Charles-Martin Jjuko: "Amin's fall, their rise" (*The Crusader* news item 7 October 1996) and the *New Vision* report 'Who are theTabliqs; what do they want?, (*New Vision* news item 17 November 1996).
19. The Banyamulenge are Rwandan Tutsis living mainly in eastern Congo.
20. During the first ADF attack, the UPDF commander was Major George Nkayarwa, a local person. When the ADF attacked he was with his men by the Congo border, but came back while the ADF were still in Bundibugyo Town and engaged the rebels at a hill called City Square. From here he managed to chase the rebels out of the immediate area. Afterwards he stayed on in the UPDF force in Bundibugyo and was most popular with everybody. As one friend wrote: "He united the Konzo and Amba together to fight a common enemy." At the beginning of 2004 he was killed in action in Northern Uganda. The intense sorrow that gripped the whole community at his death showed how important he and his actions had been when he chased the rebels out and thereby gave the population a feeling of being protected.
21. The UPDF was heavily criticized for the way in which they had handled the ADF attack on the Kitchwamba Technical College. In March 1999, six UPDF soldiers were court-martialed for failure to execute their duties, and given a two-year jail sentence. As the charge carried a maximum of the death penalty, the sentence was by many regarded as being too lenient (*New Vision* news item 31 March 1999), not least by the parents of the students who died. Less than two months later the ADF commander suspected of having led the attack on the College, Sara Nabakooza, was arrested (*New Vision* news item 18 May 1999).
22. The LRA is an acronym for Lord's Resistance Army, a group of rebels that have fought in the north of Uganda against President Museveni's rule for more than twenty years.
23. This is an area where prospecting for oil has begun.
24. The poem is from the collection *From Exile* (1976) by Mvula ya Nangolo, a member of the liberation movement SWAPO of Namibia.
25. In the text, I have emphasized *European* history because the German genocide of the OvaHerero in Namibia between 1904 and 1907 left between 60 and 80 percent of the Herero population dead (Bley 1967:36)
26. Wyschogrod quotes Husserl to describe the *life-world:* "The life-world, for us who wakingly live in it, is already there, existing in advance for us, the ground of all praxis … To live is always to live-in-certainty of the world, being constant and directly 'conscious' of the world and of oneself as living *in* the world" (Wyschogrod 1985:16).

Bibliography

Alnaes, Kirsten. 1969. "Songs of the Rwenzururu Rebellion," in P.H. Gulliver (ed.), *Tradition and Transition in East Africa*. London: Routledge and Kegan Paul, pp. 243–72.

Alnaes, Kirsten Elisabeth. 1995. "Singing With the Spirits," Ph.D. Thesis. London: London University.
Bley, Helmuth. 1967 "German South West Africa after the Conquest 1904–1914," in Ronald Segal and Ruth First (eds), *South West Africa: Travesty of Trust*. London: Andre Deutsch, pp. 35–53.
Bwambale, Bamusede and Kyaminyawandi, Augustine. 2000. *The Faces of the Rwenzururu Movement*. Kasese: Bamusede BB.
Fanon, Frantz. 1967. *The Wretched of the Earth*. Harmondsworth: Penguin Books.
Gunaratna, Rohan. 2002. *Inside Al Qaeda: Global Network of Terror*. London: Hurst and Company.
Heusch, Luc de. 1995. "Rwanda: Responsibilities for a Genocide," *Anthropology Today* 11(4): 3–7.
Hopkins, Elizabeth. 1970. "The Nyabingi Cult of Southwestern Uganda," in Robert L. Rotberg and Ali A. Mazrui (eds), *Protest and Power in Black Africa*. New York: Oxford University Press, pp. 258–336.
Kapferer, Bruce. 2004. "Old Permutations, New Formations? War, State, and Global Transgression," in B. Kapferer (ed.), *State, Sovereignty, War*. New York and Oxford: Berghahn Books, pp. 1–15.
Last, Murray. 2000. "Healing the Social Wounds of War." Inaugural Lecture given at the University College London.
Malkki, Liisa. 1995. *Purity and Exile: Violence, Memory, and National Cosmology among Hutu Refugees in Tanzania*. Chicago and London: The University of Chicago Press.
Mamdani, Mahmood. 2002. *When Victims Become Killers*. Princeton: Princeton University Press.
Nangolo, Mvula ya. 1976. *From Exile*. Printed by Zambia Printing Company.
Ntalindwa, Raymond. 2000. *Scalpels of Memory*. London: Hakuna Matata Press.
Nzongola–Ntalaja, Georges. 2003. *The Congo from Leopold to Kabila: A People's History*. London and New York: Zed Books.
Prunier, Gérard. 1995. *The Rwanda Crisis: History of a Genocide 1959–1994*. London: Hurst and Company.
Said, Edward. W. 2003. "Origins of Terrorism," in Edward W. Said, *Culture and Resistance*. London: Pluto Press, pp. 103–31.
Taylor, Christopher C. 1999. *Sacrifice as Terror: The Rwandan Genocide of 1994*. Oxford. New York: Berg.
Wyschogrod, Edith. 1985. *Spirit in Ashes: Hegel, Heidegger, and Man-made Death*. New Haven and London: Yale University Press.
Yeoman, Guy. 1989. *Africa's Mountains of the Moon: Journeys to the Snowy Sources of the Nile*. London: Elm Tree Books.
Yeld, Rachel. 1996. *Rwanda: Unprecedented Problems Call for Unprecedented Solutions*. RSP Occasional Paper. Oxford: Refugee Studies Programme.

Newspaper and magazine articles
The Crusader, Kampala.
IRIN, The UN Integrated Regional Information Network's e-mail service.
Monitor, Kampala. Also available at www.africanews.org.
New Vision, Kampala. Also available at www.africanews.org.
PlusNews, UN news email service.

Chapter Five

FEAR OF THE MIDNIGHT KNOCK
State Sovereignty and Internal Enemies in Uganda

Sverker Finnström

Independent Uganda has suffered a more or less constant postcolonial debacle, with systematic state violence especially during Idi Amin's rule in the 1970s. Milton Obote failed to reverse the violent trend during his second presidency, which began in 1980, and in 1985 he was removed from power by his own army, just as Amin had removed him from power in 1971. The 1985 coup was the result of growing mistrust in the Ugandan army regarding the violent developments during Obote's second government. Tito Okello, an army general from Acholiland, northern Uganda, was head of state for a brief period before Yoweri Museveni and his National Resistance Movement/Army (NRM/A) guerrillas seized power in early 1986.

"Politics," Karlström argues in an article on "moral rehabilitation" and "developmental eutopianism" in Buganda, central Uganda, has been a constant curse on Uganda's "moral community." It is politics, in other words, that characterizes the country's "postcolonial nightmare." The "developmental eutopianism" that is now taking root, he explains, is not the expression of a utopian impossibility but a realizable ideal, workable in everyday life (2004:595, 606, 608, passim). Indeed, most people, Ugandans as well as outside observers, argue that things have been slowly developing for the better in Uganda since Museveni's military takeover (see, for example, Whyte and Whyte's comment accompanying Karlström's article). The postcolonial nightmare is finally over, so the suggestion goes, and Uganda is held to be a success story of economic liberalization, development, progress, and increasing political stability and is, moreover, celebrated for its fight against HIV/AIDS. From this perspective, the long war in northern Uganda has often been regarded as a peripheral exception to the overall success. When commented on at all, there has been a one-sided focus on the various Holy Spirit rebel movements and thus on the religious and cosmological, even cultural aspects, of the war, by Karlström simply described as "a tragically suicidal popular uprising in northern Uganda" and "a mass movement of collective moral expiation and salvation" (2004:598).

In most respects, however, the war in northern Uganda is neither simply internal nor essentially localized. Even if it is emplaced in a local war zone, it is increasingly an international, even global, reality. By presenting four cases from everyday life in war-torn Acholiland (today's Amuru, Gulu, Pader, and Kitgum districts), where I have conducted anthropological fieldwork in periods between 1997 and 2007, I will argue that the postcolonial nightmare described by Karlström has shifted to the country's geopolitical peripheries. Museveni's no-party political system reformed politics at the grassroots, Karlström (1996; 1999) argues with ethnographic material from central Uganda. But as my material from northern Uganda will show, the same political reforms have also reproduced violent patterns that force us to question Uganda's alleged success story. In today's emerging global realities, to echo Kapferer (2004), war and violence are the very means of order and control, especially at the peripheries. More particular in the Ugandan case, war and a murky counterinsurgency industry are steadily becoming permanent. Even the involvement of the international community, I will show, is questioned by people in the war-torn north.

Thus, my aim is to reveal a violent continuity in state power as exercised in Uganda. I will situate the war in northern Uganda by outlining some thoughts on the state in Africa in general and in Uganda in particular. I will then proceed by presenting the local government council grassroots system introduced by Museveni, before finally introducing my four cases.

The Perpetration of War and Violence

After taking the oath as the new president in 1986, Museveni faced the difficult task of turning his guerrilla movement into a regular army, with the capacity to combat armed resistance that emerged in various locations in Uganda. In Acholiland, bordering Sudan, the conduct of Museveni's troops soon deteriorated. Killings, rape, and other forms of physical abuse aimed at noncombatants became the order of the day. Thousands of suspected rebels were taken into detention, and Amnesty International soon concluded that "there has been a consistent pattern of extrajudicial executions by soldiers since the NRM [Museveni's National Resistance Movement] came to power" (1992:29f.).

As time passed, elders and other influential members of Acholi society were instrumental in the increased recruitment of young people to rebel ranks. There were other people who did not explicitly support the uprising, but according to a standard version I often encountered, informants claimed that they saw no other way to survive than joining the insurgency groups in one way or the other. In many cases, joining the rebels was a direct response to the military brutality of the new government. Many of my informants claimed, not just rhetorically, that a situation had developed that was worse for them than the Amin era. Unlike Museveni's army, informants claimed, Amin's soldiers never bothered going deep into the rural areas to harass and loot, and to kill ordinary people. Lamwaka writes:

> The government's counter-insurgency campaign increasingly threatened the lives and livelihoods of people in Acholiland and allegations of atrocities resurfaced. The government's stated aim was to 'annihilate the rebels.' Part of the strategy was to deny them access to food – by destroying civilian food stocks and domestic animals – and other resources that could strengthen them politically, economically and militarily. In October 1988, the government began mass evacuation of civilians from war zones without providing adequately for their basic care. (Lamwaka 2002:32f.)

She concludes that the time that followed immediately after a partial peace agreement in 1988 actually came to reinforce war, especially in the rural areas. "Thus, in the months following the peace agreement, the war's impact on civilians became more severe and widespread" (Lamwaka 2002:33).

The war has evolved over the years, with notably Joseph Kony's Lord's Resistance Army/Movement (LRA/M) fighting Museveni's government. In what has developed into a regional war of proxies, the Ugandan government, backed by the United States, has supported the Sudan People's Liberation Movement/Army (SPLM/A) in southern Sudan. The Islamist government in Khartoum has reciprocated, offering support to the LRA/M rebels.

The 2005 peace agreement in Sudan established the semiautonomous government of Southern Sudan, and in August 2006 the LRA/M and the Ugandan government signed a historical but shaky cessation of hostilities agreement, mediated by the south Sudanese, but in late 2008 heavy fighting resumed.

Throughout the years of war, the LRA/M has systematically avoided the Ugandan army. In hit-and-run raids, the rebels have instead focused their military violence against the noncombatant population, and they have abducted thousands of minors. The rebels have orchestrated their activities from outside, from bases in remote areas of war-torn southern Sudan and eastern Congo, out of reach of Ugandan armed forces, and, at times, beyond Sudanese and Congolese state control as well. In October 2005 the International Criminal Court unsealed warrants for the arrest of the LRA/M leadership (see Allen 2006; Branch 2007).

In its counterinsurgency tactics, the Ugandan army has forced large portions of the population into squalid camps with strict curfews as a measure to deny the rebels food and other resources. This has drained the rebels' intelligence networks too. In 2005 the displaced numbered some two million Ugandans. Of the Acholi, more than 90 percent were displaced. In a slow but constant development from fully being in the world to bare life, displaced Ugandans live as marginalized noncitizens in a chronic state of emergency and exception (Finnström 2008: chap. 4; cf. Agamben 1998).

In December 2001, a few months after the September 11 attacks on the Pentagon and the World Trade Center, the global war on terror reached Uganda as the U.S. government included the LRA/M on its list of terrorist groups with which no negotiations, so it was stated, would under any circumstances be initiated. The Ugandan government immediately welcomed the rhetoric of no dialogue. In 2002, with direct U.S. support, the Ugandan army launched a campaign called "Operation Iron Fist," carried out also on Sudanese territory. In preparing for this campaign, and continuing the trend of militarization but going against the will of the parliament, the Ugandan government decided to cut by 23 percent the allocations approved by the parliament for all ministries, with the single exception of activities alleviating poverty. The funds were redirected to the military campaign against the LRA/M, to some irritation in the donor community, which continued, however, to fund around 50 percent of Uganda's government expenditure (Finnström 2008:112f.).

The Postcolonial State in Africa and Uganda

The war evokes historical antagonisms as well as deepens regional divides in Uganda. But to conclude that the war is all about ethnicity is reductionist. Reyna's description of postcolonial Chad shows something of a parallel to Uganda. "Wars that began as nonethnic clashes in a country with numerous ethnic groups," he writes, "have gradually evolved into such conflicts as whole regions have been *reimagined ethnically*" (Reyna 2003: 290, emphasis added). It is not least outside observers, as will be illustrated below, who sometimes seem keen on promoting such reimaginations.

Yet the Ugandan historian Omara-Otunnu pinpoints the development for Uganda. "What the opposition groups in the north and east of the country have in common is not ethnic identity or cultural traditions," Omara-Otunnu concludes, "but a history of being only peripherally included in the economic structures and processes of the country" (1995:230). In Acholiland, young adults with dreams of education and future employment are indeed frustrated with the way the Ugandan military elite increasingly absorbs national resources that they would have preferred to see devoted to the development of Uganda, especially its marginalized regions. The LRA/M rebels obviously tap into the local discontent with structural adjustment, privatization, and other neoliberal developments. In their manifestos the rebels acknowledge the importance of structural adjustment programs and other development measures, but they still question the way these are implemented. They hold that development is unevenly distributed and that peripheral regions of Uganda are lagging behind the central parts of the country (see Finnström 2008: chap. 3).

Young (2004) has declared the end of the postcolonial state in Africa. Since the end of the Cold War, there have been enormous pressures for economical and political liberalization in Africa, resulting in the "dramatic erosion of stateness itself," argues Young (2004:25). This has opened up the space for external organizations and a variety of more or less dubious actors. If the African state was associated earlier with a keen focus on development measures mainly in its health and educational services, built on massive aid flows, later, after years of withering, "budget reductions required by structural adjustment programmes compelled in practice cutbacks in social expenditures" (Young 2004:40). Nowadays, states have to share sovereignty with an array of transnational institutions like the World Bank, IMF, or WTO (Turner 2003:49). State accountability is less and less an internal affair only. The Tanzanian scholar Shivji forwards his bold conclusion: "The 'governors' are accountable to the 'donors' and their consultants and advisors on 'good governance' rather than to the people" (2003:9). So if the sovereign power of the state is undermined by various external corporations, to refer to Kapferer, this development also unleashes an internal and violent "wildness of state sovereignty" which in turn "contributes toward a form of structured chaos at the peripheries" (2004:10).

In other words, international actors and foreign governments implicitly or explicitly sustain the fragmentation and polarization of Ugandan society, and the perpetuation of war adds to these developments. In a simultaneous development, maintenance of African security forces tends to trump social expenditures on the continent (Young 2004:40). As an indication of the trend, between 1987 and 1997 the Ugandan army increased the number of its soldiers by 100 percent (Herbst 2004:360). And the special Presidential Protection Brigade, commanded by president Museveni's son and an organization parallel to the regular army, in recent years has grown from a few hundred elite troops to several thousand.

From Wallerstein and his followers, we may be used to conceptualizing the cores of the world system as being of the First World, while the Third World represents the drained periphery. Hardt and Negri suggest that we see beyond this merely geographical division to acknowledge a more complex geopolitical order, with the cores being globally omnipresent, all the time and by necessity out there alongside the marginalized people at the peripheries. Uganda sadly illustrates such a global organization of sociopolitical space, "characterized by the close proximity of extremely unequal populations, which creates a situation of permanent social danger" (Hardt and Negri 2000:336f., passim). But what illustrates any new world order is not only the weakening of the civil basis of states and thus also their political legitimacy. A major feature of the new order is the dramatic militarization of many states, their urban elites and rural allies, and also their oppositional groups (Reyna 2003; Sluka 2000:30ff.). At the same time, the regionalization of military violence undermines national stability. It is a paradox that the Ugandan army was to become one of many *external* fighting factions in the Democratic Republic of Congo, even as it remained incapable of defeating its most persistent *internal* enemy, the LRA/M. Thus, Uganda's military involvement in the Congo has added to the instability at both regional and national levels (see Herbst 2004:360; Prunier 2004). Still, in 2007 the Ugandan government sent troops to Somalia, and for the years 2009–2010, Uganda is accepted as a nonpermanent member of UN's Security Council.

Even though the Ugandan parliament passed a blanket amnesty bill in 1999, which the Ugandan president signed into law in early 2000, the army's hunt for rebels and rebel collaborators escalated. Ugandan authorities found murky support here from a law parallel to the amnesty law, the 2002 Anti Terrorist Act, which refers generally to opponents of the state. The army's "Iron Fist" operations and the "Anti Terrorist Act" have created internal fear and distrust of the blanket amnesty. The Ugandan army has "arrested scores of civilians, with little evidence, on suspicion of rebel collaboration; some of the detainees are supporters of the unarmed political opposition," reports Human Rights Watch (2003:5, 50ff.). The LRA/M's response was equally violent. Paradoxically, the rebels' attacks on civilian targets at the rural peripheries are undermining the Ugandan government's position, because exposed people regard the attacks as demonstrations of the army's lack of power and the government's lack of commitment to ending the war by peaceful means. My informants frequently blamed the government for its failure to protect its citizens against rebel violence.

In periods, the rebels have focused more on exposing the weaknesses and thus the lack of legitimacy of the state under the present government than on offering any alternative political legitimacy. And as will be shown below, the state does indeed expose itself in its violent counterinsurgency tactics. Uganda's international partners in development are perplexed and remain largely so, thus licensing the violent state of exception. On the structural level, the practice of war as such, which has intensified the globalization of capital and trade and the mass movement of refugees, rebels, army soldiers, and smugglers within Uganda as well as across its borders, tends to undermine the sovereignty of state power in Uganda. It is against this background that the mistrust in the government's various measures must be understood.

The Local Government System in Museveni's Uganda

In the early 1980s, during the war in central Uganda, Museveni introduced a system of resistance councils (RCs) which were renamed local government councils (LCs) in the 1995 constitution of Uganda. This constitution also formally introduced the ruling no-party Movement system and was to make restriction of the scope of action for political parties definitive for another ten years. In the 1980s and early 1990s, the local councils were subordinate to the National Resistance Council, which was led by Museveni and his guerrillas (Ngoga 1998:96). The councils, or committees, now integrated with the ruling Movement and its local government structure, are expected to function at village (LC1), parish (LC2), sub-county (LC3), county or municipality (LC4), and district (LC5) levels. According to a Movement ideologist, the LC5 "is the parliament of the district level" that is "fully equipped to run the affairs of the district" (Kabwegyere 2000:103). Similarly, and according to the Ugandan constitution, the LC5 has "the highest political authority within its area of jurisdiction," while its chairperson is the "political head of the district" who is to "co-ordinate and monitor Government functions as between the district and the Government" (Republic of Uganda 1995:120, 121).

The workings of these local councils are subject to some scholarly debate, and it is difficult to draw any general conclusion for the whole of Uganda. Karlström, who has researched them in central Uganda, concludes that they revolutionized politics there. The system "has provided Ugandans with their first significant experience of democratic governance at the local level," thus a kind of "freedom from oppression" (Karlström

1996:498f., 486). In contrast to my data from the war-torn north, his informants were genuinely skeptical toward political parties. "Political parties," as one of Karlström's informants put it, "make each man the enemy of his fellow man. They just kill each other" (1996:495). Perhaps, as a genuine alternative to parties, the local councils have worked quite well in central Uganda. It must also be emphasized that people in central Uganda lived with war in the first half of the 1980s. For them, Museveni's takeover in 1986 ended war.

Karlström (1999:119, n.19) acknowledges that attitudes towards the local government system differ from region to region. Mentioning northern Uganda only briefly, he refers to Ottemoeller, whose explanation I find stereotypically superficial. The non-armed political opposition to Museveni and the Movement in the 1996 presidential elections, Ottemoeller (1998:102) writes, was "not a significant political force outside of several ethnically defined constituencies in northern Uganda (the 'Nilotic' ethnicities of the Lango, Acholi, and Iteso), which hold Museveni and the NRM [National Resistance Movement] in deep enmity for having disposed the government of their favourite son, Milton Obote." But in what way can Milton Obote be said to be a "favourite son" of the Acholi as a group? If the constituencies in northern Uganda are "ethnically defined," which Ugandan constituencies are not? After all, it was a general of Acholi origin, Tito Okello, who in 1985 ousted Obote, of Lango origin, shortly before Museveni seized state power. My informants based their skepticism about the ruling no-party Movement on the fact that for them, perhaps in contrast to the central Ugandan case delineated by Karlström, this system has come to represent political oppression and petty harassment, increasingly so over the years. Recall the argument of Omara-Otunnu (1995:230), quoted above. His point is that opposition groups in the north and east of Uganda do not have any supra-ethnic "Nilotic" identity as primary common grounds for political mobilization. Rather, these groups share a history of being only peripherally included in the development of the country. And since 1986, they have shared the experience of having their homelands turned into a war zone.

I should hasten to add that local government councillors have had the ability to air criticism of the Ugandan army's conduct. For example, rural local councillors in the war zone have publicly raised objections to the Ugandan army's silent and often hidden recruitment of underprivileged young men, even minors, to its paramilitary groups, the so-called local defense forces. Even so, in rural areas I more often encountered people who expressed the suspicion that the local government councils were working as Ugandan army intelligence, and in several cases I found that the local government councillors indeed had contributed to an environment hostile to advocates of political pluralism and to known government critics. In the rural areas, and especially so in the congested camps, people alleged to be rebel collaborators often find themselves deserted by friends and relatives who fear harassment from Ugandan authorities and the army. Okuku's harsh conclusion has been sadly accurate for the war-torn north. "Once in power," he notes, "the RCs [now LCs] became instruments of control rather than popular participation" (Okuku 2002:26). The rebels, for their part, have found it fully legitimate to target functionaries of the local government councils.

Since, according to the constitution, the local councils are to be subordinated to the parliament, advocates of the local council system describe it as a system of genuine grassroots democracy. But as will be illustrated below, in periods the local councils have become a way for a quasi-military government, to use Oloka-Onyango's (2004:38) description of Uganda, to exercise dominance on the most local levels of society.

Experience (One): The Search for Rebel Collaborators

In early 2000, when Museveni signed the blanket amnesty passed by the Ugandan parliament, he stated at the same time that he did not believe in it. "We should apply the law of Moses; an eye for an eye, a tooth for a tooth, to bring discipline to society," he said (quoted in *The New Vision*, 21 January 2000). As a final manifestation of his unwillingness regarding the whole issue, he did not sign the new law within the thirty days stipulated by the Ugandan constitution (Republic of Uganda 1995:163). And it was to be more than one year before the first office was set up in northern Uganda, making implementation of the law extremely slow. According to the amnesty law, any rebel who "renounces and abandons involvement in the war or armed rebellion" can surrender to the amnesty. Individuals who are "collaborating with the perpetrators of the war or armed rebellion" or "assisting or aiding the conduct or prosecution of the war or armed rebellion" can also take advantage of the amnesty (Republic of Uganda 2000).

The issue of the so-called collaborators has been a source of mistrust in northern Uganda. Government representatives frequently brand individuals who support the political opposition as rebel collaborators. In a public speech in Gulu town soon after the amnesty law was declared, the region's most powerful government politician, the then chairperson of the local government council on the district level (LC5), claimed that only rebels could take advantage of the amnesty. The government, he declared, should continue to hunt for the "bad collaborators," who would face treason charges. The district chairperson even mentioned a few individuals by name, some of whom were eventually imprisoned without trial.

Most of my informants were distressed by his speech, which was given at a security meeting where he was flanked by senior Ugandan army commanders, local religious leaders and a representative of Save the Children. The religious leaders were not allowed to talk at the meeting, and the expatriate representative of Save the Children may have grasped little of the speech, which was given in the local language. The entire event fueled local discontent regarding both the government's measures to end the war and the local involvement of the international community in this. People concluded that the politician wanted to get rid of his political opponents and outspoken critics. The dilemma, as informants put it, is to criticize the government openly without being regarded as a collaborator with Kony's LRA/M. "If you say that you are pro multi-party," my friend Anthony Odiya-Labol noted, "you are straight away called Kony."

De Boeck's description of Kinshasa is pessimistic but parallel to the Ugandan case. "For most people," he writes, "the state has become the looting soldier's nocturnal knock on the door," when the soldiers are "turning the house upside down," as one of his informants described it (De Boeck 1996:96). In wartime Guatemala, notes Stepputat (2001:295), most institutions of the state hardly reached the rural areas, and state power was confined to cities and the garrisons of the military. For many years, Stepputat (2001:298) writes, governmentality was embodied in the occasional face-to-face and often violent encounters between villagers and army soldiers. In northern Uganda this encounter can take the form of the army soldiers' house searches, all part of the counterinsurgency hunt for rebel collaborators. Frequently the soldiers just break people's doors down in the middle of the night, as happened to Odiya-Labol. He had previously campaigned for an outspoken critic of the government. In early 2000, Odiya-Labol got involved in a quarrel with his neighbor over competing beer-brewing businesses. His antagonist was the chairperson on the village level in the local government council system (LC1). Odiya-Labol's antagonist tipped off the military, giving them a letter headed with the official local council logo and accompanied by all the necessary stamps. Odiya-Labol was described in the letter as a "notorious man with a gun" who had "the intention to kill Uganda army personnel on patrol."

In the middle of the following night, the military smashed Odiya-Labol's door and some twenty soldiers entered his home. The soldiers beat two of Odiya-Labol's wives and destroyed some property. They conducted a thorough search of his home before they arrested him. By walking with their army boots on the very bed in which Odiya-Labol and his wife had been sleeping a few minutes before, they violated the most private sphere of their life. Odiya-Labol was released in the morning, however, and no formal charges were made against him. No weapons were recovered during the night search. Eventually the quarrel between Odiya-Labol and the local government council chairperson was resolved through mediation by the council at the sub-county level (LC3).

This was the second time the military had come to harass Odiya-Labol, and the fourth time they had come for a violent night search in his neighborhood. In Odiya-Labol's view, the local council representative exploited his official contacts with the Ugandan army to harass political opponents and business competitors. If anything, Odiya-Labol emphasized, referring to the fact that he was a Ugandan citizen and protected by the law, the quarrel should have been taken to the police, not the army. "The LC1 chairman is using the military for his own means," Odiya-Labol concluded. The Ugandan army, as stipulated by the country's constitution, is to foster harmony in society and cooperate with the civilians, while always subordinated to the civilian authority. But if the opposite is the chief experience people have of the army on the ground, the Ugandan government—and the state—will be seen as little more than a source of unconstitutional harassment of its citizenry. As Wole Soyinka, the Nigerian Nobel laureate, generalizes from personal experience, this is "governance through a forced diet of fear, most especially on the African continent – in common parlance, the fear of 'the midnight knock'" (2004:2).

Experience (Two): The *Panda Gari* Mass Arrests

Ugandan authorities, rather than disproving people's doubts in them, make sweeping mass arrests from time to time of people alleged to be rebel collaborators. These mass arrests are referred to as *panda garis*, "get on the lorry" in Swahili. They were common during the Amin (1971–79) and Obote II (1980–85) governments (Kasozi 1999:146f.). Now yet another Ugandan government has taken up the practice. One Sunday in January 2000, for example, my friend Odiya-Labol found himself taken away in such a sweep. The military arrived early in the morning, and everyone in the neighborhood, including priests, children, and women, was arrested and taken to a large field just outside town. All morning I saw army patrols arriving with groups of people, the great majority young men, who had been arrested in the nearby villages. About five thousand people were netted, according to *The Monitor* (17 January 2000), Uganda's daily independent. The figure of the state-owned *New Vision* (17 January 2000) was considerably lower. Leaving out the issue of *panda gari*, the latter paper wrote that "about 300 people were netted in security operations in Gulu town." Former child rebels, in Uganda known as "computers," were forced to "screen" the people arrested, lined up one by one, in an effort to identify rebel collaborators. The majority of the arrested people were required to stand in the hot sun, passively waiting until late afternoon before the "computer screening" was completed. At the end of the whole exercise, besides some army deserters who were caught, fewer than five people were kept in custody. People who tried to walk away were rudely forced back by the army.

Odiya-Labol refused arrest more successfully. Always putting his words well, he questioned the legitimacy of the grounds for the whole exercise and he claimed correctly that all his papers were in order. He was eventually allowed to leave, but the army still confiscated the motorcycle we used in doing our research. Later on, Odiya-Labol and I went to the soldiers, asking rhetorically if the motorcycle was suspected of being a rebel collaborator. As one of us was a *muno*, or European, we got it back without too much arguing. Afterwards Odiya-Labol designed a rubber mudguard for the back wheel of the motorbike. *Kwo odoko tek,* it said, which means, as so many informants told us during the course of the research, "Life has become difficult."

Experience (Three): The Roadblock and Regional War Complexes

During most of 1999, there was a lull in the fighting in northern Uganda. Most LRA/M rebel units had withdrawn to base in southern Sudan. The intermission gave people new hope, although they still worried about the future as long as the conflict remained unresolved. It was now possible for Odiya-Labol and me to travel to remote places in rural areas. We even went to a cattle auction in Agoro, the northernmost part of Acholiland, bordering Sudan. The south Sudanese SPLM/A rebels came to exchange cattle for money, radios, clothes, and other things. In contrast to what they had done at previous auctions, the visiting rebels had left their guns in a nearby Ugandan army garrison. Most of them, however, wore their rebel uniforms.

The Sudanese visitors told us that they had walked for some twenty days with the cattle they had taken from the enemy. In this case, "the enemy" was people who found themselves caught in the middle. Since these people were not explicitly favoring the south Sudanese rebels, they had been accused of supporting the government in Khartoum and thus turned into legitimate targets of militarily motivated looting. This is not unique to political violence in Sudan or Uganda. One central dilemma of living with war and armed conflict, according to my informants, is to orient in life when one repeatedly finds oneself labeled "supporter of the enemy."

On the journey back from the auction in Agoro, we passed the wreck of a lorry carrying a destroyed antiaircraft gun by the side of the road. We had already learned that it once belonged to the south Sudanese rebels. About a year before our visit, there was a period of heavy fighting in Sudan and the south Sudanese rebels were pushed south by the Sudanese army. As they had done many times before, they decided to regroup their forces on Ugandan territory. They entered through Kitgum district (eastern Acholi) and eventually went back to Sudan via Amuru district (western Acholi). They hoped thereby to be in a position to counterattack the Sudanese army from the rear.

During their effort to regroup in northern Uganda, the south Sudanese rebels were ambushed by the LRA/M. This ambush was not like the arbitrary killings that international media most often write about when it comes to the war in northern Uganda. Rather, as people to whom we spoke maintained, the wreck of the lorry stood as a most concrete symbol of proxy warfare and internationally orchestrated violence on a local scene. Ugandan rebels with bases in Sudan had attacked Sudanese rebels on mission in Uganda. The wreck suggested that Uganda is deeply entangled in a larger "regional war complex," to use a term of Wallensteen and Sollenberg's (1998). In a regional war complex, "neighbouring countries experience internal or interstate conflicts" with a growing number of *"significant links between the conflicts"* (Wallensteen and Sollenberg 1998:623, emphasis added). When the Ugandan army arrived with reinforcements, the LRA/M had eventually withdrawn.

The memory of the ambush was still vivid among people in the region when we visited the scene more than one year later. The fighting had been fierce, we were told, and some forty people had died. Bodies were abandoned to rot in the sun; most of them were simply thrown a few meters into the bush. Even now, skeletons and parts of skeletons of unburied men and women lay scattered on the ground. It happens now and then that the Ugandan army purposely leaves dead bodies behind as warnings so potential rebel supporters will appreciate the danger in opposing the government. We hurried to take some photos, and went back to the motorbike. Some miles further south we passed a group of south Sudanese rebels. Their army jeep had broken down, and some of them were resting in the shade under a tree, their weaponry off-loaded on the roadside. Two of them were working on the dead engine. With the experience of the burned lorry fresh in mind, we felt uncomfortable but continued without trouble, and we slipped through the final roadblocks of the Ugandan army—again, one of us being a *muno* (Westerner)—on the road to Kitgum town. The relative calm made the Ugandan soldiers relaxed.

The Sudanese rebels were also able to pass freely, but vehicles carrying local people were stopped, as we noted, and the travelers were forced to unload their luggage for the Ugandan army's search for collaborators and rebel weapons. Again the Ugandan state was increasingly associated with petty harassment of its citizens, while various external actors, like the Sudanese rebels or the visiting anthropologist, could enjoy the freedom of movement that Ugandans are denied. As a Swede visiting Uganda, I could afford to be part of the often-celebrated cosmopolitan global flow. So could the south Sudanese rebels. Ugandans living in the war-torn region cannot even be sure they will be allowed to pass a rural roadblock. On the contrary, during some periods army roadblocks are frequent along the major rural roads. Army soldiers may stop buses and civilian vehicles every five to ten kilometers. At gunpoint, the travelers are forced to slash the roadside bush, even to cut down trees and whole forests. The army's purpose is to eliminate spots where the rebels are suspected of having mounted ambushes, but local army commanders take the opportunity to profit from this shadowy wartime logging industry.

Experience (Four): Shadow Economics and Humanitarianism

In the final case, I will highlight some of the nonformal aspects of the economy of war in northern Uganda and attempt, in Nordstrom's words, "an ethnography of the shadows." As she writes, "In the frontier realities that mark political upheaval, the people, goods, and services that move along shadow lines are often closely and visibly linked to the most fundamental politics of power and survival" (Nordstrom 2001:216). The economic and political linkages of the shadows "move outside *formally* recognized state-based channels" (Nordstrom 2004:106), but are at the same time deeply intertwined with the formal structures of the state. Many of the on-the-ground agents of the state, notably soldiers, are also powerful actors in the shadow economy. Various organizations of the international community are also entangled with the shadow economy, trust and personal ties being important aspects of the nonformal exchange. The shadows and the formal state practices intersect in a myriad of ways, *"but they do not give up their own identity in this intersection"* (Nordstrom 2001:230). In other words, a government soldier who gets involved in the shadows will in most situations remain a government soldier. Indeed this was also the conclusion drawn by my informants. Likewise, personnel of the international relief organizations who get involved in the shadows can never fully detach themselves from the organizations they represent, at least not in the experience of my informants.

The camps for internally displaced people in western Acholiland along the Karuma-Pakwach highway that connects Kampala with the West Nile region are located on the border of Murchison Falls National Park. The wild game in the park is a source of luxury food for the people in the area. Not only Acholi but also people from the West Nile region frequent the park to poach the game. In the camps, game meat is a welcome addition to the monotonous diet of home-grown vegetables and relief food. Of course, it is illegal to hunt the game. Ammunition and guns captured from rebels, or found in hidden rebel armouries in the bush, are taken to the local army quarters before they are shipped to Gulu town for registering. Sometimes Ugandan soldiers will keep some captured weapons for most dubious personal use, such as night robberies and petty harassments, often with the tacit agreement of the local army commanders (see Finnström 2008:1ff.). In the camps, army soldiers will sometimes lend captured guns to young men, who sneak into the national park to hunt wild game. In return for the weapon hire, the soldiers demand half of the collected meat, while the hunting party shares the remaining half. Obviously, on their poaching missions the young men have to avoid not only park rangers but also mobile army units, which may take them for armed rebels.

Olak, displaced to one of the camps, went to the park as a porter for a Ugandan army soldier called Opoka, who had a machine-gun. This was not the first time Olak had gone hunting in the park, and several other young men came along as porters. This time, however, they returned from four days in the park without any meat, and Opoka parted company from Olak and the other porters. After about a week, soldiers came to investigate rumors that Olak had a gun. They did not find Olak at home, as he was away working in his garden. Instead they arrested his younger brother and another young man. When Olak heard of this, he went into hiding, but the soldiers eventually located him. He was arrested and ordered to tell where the alleged gun was hidden. In the effort to make him talk, they set Olak's hut on fire, destroying his camp shelter. This is Olak's story:

> I was arrested and taken to the army barracks together with another boy called Olum. Some person claimed that we had a gun. We told the soldiers that the gun was not ours, but the owner of the gun was an army man called Opoka. So they refused our talk. They start beating us, and they tied my arms and my legs. We were beaten seriously, and they burned our bodies with a melting plastic cup. They continued beating us before taking us back to the army jail [in the camps, an empty pit latrine]. We were ordered to disclose the identity of the man who had the gun. We agreed and we were taken to his place, but the man was not around. So the soldiers thought that I was deceiving them, and then they start beating me again. They start firing their guns. They just emptied two

magazines, and two bullets hit me. From there they took me to the army barracks again, where the commander again ordered the soldiers to shoot me, as he claimed that I still did not tell the truth. However, the soldiers now objected, and I was eventually brought to [a local] hospital, where I stayed for two days. After that I was taken to Lacor [Missionary] Hospital.

The army commander did not allow Olak to leave the camp, but after two days in the camp's hospital, a sympathetic police officer provided him with an authorizing letter, thus giving him an opportunity to travel to St. Mary's Missionary Hospital in Lacor outside Gulu town, where his bullet wounds could finally be tended to.

Olak's hunting missions reflect nothing less than his everyday existential struggle with extreme poverty. Yet the stories of such illegal hunting parties do not end in the camps, or with the destinies of young men like Olak. The wild game travels farther than that. To augment their income, Ugandan soldiers usually sell their share of wild game in Gulu town, or right on the spot in the camps. The potential buyers are visitors to the camps who have the means of transport to smuggle it back to town, and who are not stopped in the army's roadblocks. In Gulu town I met a Western staff member of an international humanitarian organization, who told me that he occasionally bought game from the soldiers in the camps, which he put in the back of his white NGO pickup and took back to Gulu town. "Those who may be on the forefront of aid may as well be in the backyard of profiteering," as Nordstrom (2001:226, n. 6) notes.

The displaced people in the camps, of course, take careful notice of such exchanges. Some of the meat, my expatriate counterpart told me, he consumed himself, but some he took to Kampala, where he sold it to friends and colleagues at the Kampala headquarters. For him, however, the profit must have been insignificant and the risks equally negligible, but I was left with the impression that the whole thing boosted his ego, as he was able to offer friends and superiors some exotic wild meat. At the other end of this route of illegal trade, however, are the young men in the camps who take the full risk alone. The buyers in Kampala know little, perhaps, about the young displaced men who put themselves in jeopardy. If caught, as Olak's experience told him, they may be taken for rebels, while the providers of the guns will deny any knowledge of the whole affair.

Conclusion

"At the end of this century," Wieviorka wrote a few years back, "the dominant trend is social violence rather than political violence" (2003:129). But my argument in this chapter is that most violence—in the case of Uganda, on the part of the rebels and the Ugandan army—is part of a global and neo-imperial political structure of dominance, exploitation, and exclusion. Living through this moment in history, people existentially feel and register what is going on. They engage the world in order to be able to reflect on their experiences. And most often, despite lived uncertainties, they do so with the help of concrete and well-informed analyses, fully grasping how globalization always is emplaced to a local reality. People's lived experiences therefore reveal the violence, both in its physical and structural manifestations, as inescapably political. I have presented four cases, or experiences as I call them—of the soldiers' violent midnight knock on Odiya-Labol's door; of the *panda gari* mass arrests; of the burned lorry and the roadblock; and of Olak's hunting missions. These experiences tell the story of how globalization is always situated.

What has developed in war-torn Uganda can be described as "global peripheralization." The description is rhetorical, however, because as we know, on the surface of a globe there are no peripheral edges. Rather, as Sahlins reminds us, "People act in the world in terms of the social beings they are, and it should not be forgotten that from their quotidian point of view it is the global system that is peripheral, not them" (1999:412). But in contrast to those living in the wealthy sectors of the global village—in Uganda, in the form of soldiers, rebels, researchers and humanitarian relief workers—those at the global periphery will seldom be allowed to be part of the often-glorified cosmopolitan global flows. For people who live with war on a daily basis, the global order with its war on terror is increasingly synonymous with the state's petty harassments, in some aspects discouraged but in many aspects silently fuelled by actors of the international community. Today's global flows, of which the perpetration of war and violence is a major characteristic, are imposed upon people's lives, painfully felt on their bodies. In the process, people's rights as citizens are increasingly denied them. With the army operating in neighboring countries, and in joining the global war on terror, and more recently by sending peace keeping forces to Somalia, even with a member voice in UN's Security Council, the Ugandan government asserts *external* state sovereignty. This development must be seen against the backdrop of developments back home. As my four cases illustrate, in the shadow of the army's Iron Fist operations, the government's *internal* sovereign power is feeding on unconstitutional counterinsurgency violence in itself. Throughout the years the LRA/M rebels have done their best in the most violent ways to prove the state's internal failure, and in periods they have been acting like the terrorists the international community has labeled them as. For the Ugandan citizenry at the country's peripheries, life has become difficult indeed.

Acknowledgements

The argument in this chapter is built on material that appears in *Living with Bad Surroundings: War, History, and Everyday Moments in Northern Uganda*, published by Duke University Press (Finnström 2008). I thank Bjørn Enge Bertelsen and Bruce Kapferer for their generous input. Research in Uganda was endorsed by the Uganda National Council for Science and Technology, and financed by the Department of Research Cooperation of the Swedish International Development Cooperation Agency.

Bibliography

Agamben, Giorgio. 1998. *Homo Sacer: Sovereign Power and Bare Life*. Stanford: Stanford University Press.

Allen, Tim. 1991. "Understanding Alice: Uganda's Holy Spirit Movement in Context," *Africa* 61(3): 370–399.

Amnesty International. 1992. *Uganda: The Failure to Safeguard Human Rights*. London: Amnesty International.

Branch, Adam. 2007. "Uganda's Civil War and the Politics of ICC Intervention," *Ethics and International Affairs* 21(2): 179–198.

De Boeck, Filip. 1996. "Postcolonialism, Power and Identity: Local and Global Perspectives from Zaire," in Richard Werbner and Terence Ranger (eds), *Postcolonial Identities in Africa*. London: Zed Books Ltd, pp. 75–106.

Finnström, Sverker. 2008. *Living with Bad Surroundings: War, History, and Everyday Moments in Northern Uganda*. Durham: Duke University Press.

Hardt, Michael and Antonio Negri. 2000. *Empire*. Cambridge (Massachusetts): Harvard University Press.

Herbst, Jeffrey. 2004. "African Militaries and Rebellion: The Political Economy of Threat and Combat Effectiveness," *Journal of Peace Research* 41(3): 357–369.

Human Rights Watch. 2003. *Abducted and Abused: Renewed Conflict in Northern Uganda*. New York: Human Rights Watch.

Kabwegyere, Tarsis B. 2000. "Civil Society and the Democratic Transition in Uganda Since 1986," in Justus Mugaju and J. Oloka-Onyango (eds), *No-party Democracy in Uganda: Myths and Realities*. Kampala: Fountain Publishers, pp. 95–108.

Kapferer, Bruce. 2004. "Introduction," in Bruce Kapferer (ed.), *State, Sovereignty, War: Civil Violence in Emerging Global Realities*. Oxford: Berghahn Books, pp. 1–15.

Karlström, Mikael. 1996. "Imagining Democracy: Political Culture and Democratisation in Buganda," *Africa* 66(4): 485–505.

———. 1999. "Civil Society and Its Presuppositions: Lessons from Uganda," John L. Comaroff and Jean Comaroff (eds), *Civil Society and the Political Imagination in Africa*. Chicago: University of Chicago Press, pp. 104–123.

———. 2004. "Modernity and Its Aspirants: Moral Community and Developmental Eutopianism in Buganda," *Current Anthropology* 45(5): 595–619.

Kasozi, A. B. K. 1999. *The Social Origins of Violence in Uganda, 1964–1985*. Kampala: Fountain Publishers Ltd.

Lamwaka, Caroline. 2002. "The Peace Process in Northern Uganda 1896–1990," in Lucima Okello (ed.), *Protracted Conflict, Elusive Peace: Initiatives to End the Violence in Northern Uganda*. London: Conciliation Resources and Kacoke Madit, pp. 28–33.

Ngoga, Pascal. 1998. "Uganda: The National Resistance Army," in Christopher Clapham (ed.), *African Guerrillas*. Oxford: James Currey, pp. 91–106.

Nordstrom, Carolyn. 2001. "Out of the shadows," Thomas Callaghy, Ronald Kassimir and Robert Latham (eds), *Intervention and Transnationalism in Africa: Global-local Networks of Power.* Cambridge: Cambridge University Press, pp. 216–239.

———. 2004. *Shadows of War: Violence, Power, and International Profiteering in the Twenty-First Century.* Berkeley: University of California Press.

Okuku, Juma. 2002. *Ethnicity, State Power and the Democratisation Process in Uganda.* Uppsala: Nordic Africa Institute.

Oloka-Onyango, J. 2004. "'New Breed' Leadership, Conflict and Reconstruction in the Great Lakes Region of Africa: A Sociopolitical Biography of Uganda's Yoweri Kaguta Museveni," *Africa Today* 50(3): 29–52.

Omara-Otunnu, Amii. 1995. "The Dynamics of Conflict in Uganda," in Oliver Furley (ed.), *Conflict in Africa.* London: I.B. Tauris Publishers, pp. 223–236.

Ottemoeller, Dan. 1998. "Popular Perceptions of Democracy: Elections and Attitudes in Uganda," *Comparative Political Studies* 31(1): 98–124.

Prunier, Gérard. 2004. "Rebel Movements and Proxy Warfare: Uganda, Sudan and the Congo (1986–99)," *African Affairs* 103(412): 359–383.

Republic of Uganda, The. 1995. *Constitution of the Republic of Uganda.* Kampala: The Republic of Uganda.

———. 2000. *The Amnesty Act, 2000.* Kampala: The Republic of Uganda.

Reyna, Steve. 2003. "Imagining Monsters: A Structural History of Warfare in Chad (1968–1990)," in Jonathan Friedman (ed.), *Globalization, the State, and Violence.* Walnut Creek: AltaMira Press, pp. 279–308.

Sahlins, Marshall David. 1999. "Two or Three Things That I Know About Culture," *The Journal of the Royal Anthropological Institute incorporating Man* 5(3): 399–421.

Shivji, Issa. 2003. "Good Governance, Bad Governance and the Quest for Democracy in Africa: An Alternative Perspective." Paper presented at the *Nordic Africa Days,* Uppsala, 3–5 October 2003. Uppsala and Dar es Salaam: The Nordic Africa Institute/University of Dar es Salaam.

Sluka, Jeffrey A. 2000. "Introduction: State Terror and Anthropology," in Jeffrey A. Sluka (ed.), *Death Squad: The Anthropology of State Terror.* Philadelphia: University of Pennsylvania Press, pp. 1–45.

Soyinka, Wole. 2004. *Climate of Fear.* London: Profile Books.

Stepputat, Finn. 2001. "Urbanizing the Countryside: Armed Conflict, State Formation, and the Politics of Place in Contemporary Guatemala," in Thomas Blom Hansen and Finn Stepputat (eds), *Imagining the State: Ethnographic Explorations of the Postcolonial State.* Durham: Duke University Press, pp. 284–312.

Turner, Terence. 2003. "Class Projects, Social Consciousness, and the Contradictions of 'globalization,'" in Jonathan Friedman (ed.). *Globalization, the State, and Violence.* Walnut Creek: AltaMira Press, pp. 35–66.

Wallensteen, Peter and Margareta Sollenberg. 1998. "Armed Conflict and Regional Conflict Complexes, 1989–97," *Journal of Peace Research* 35(5): 621–634.

Wieviorka, Michel. 2003. "The New Paradigm of Violence," in Jonathan Friedman (ed.), *Globalization, the State, and Violence.* Walnut Creek: AltaMira Press, pp. 107–140.

Young, Crawford. 2004. "The End of the Post-colonial State in Africa? Reflections on Changing African Political Dynamics," *African Affairs* 103(410): 23–49.

Chapter Six

THE SHEPHERD'S STAFF AND THE AK-47
Pastoralism and Handguns in Karamoja, Uganda

Frode Storaas

Six hundred and eighty million hand weapons are out there. Eight million new ones enter the market every year.[1] While the Norwegian Initiative on Small Arms Transfers, NISAT, together with the United Nations, in 1998 hosted a conference in Oslo where they were discussing the problems associated with hand weapons with focus on Africa, I visited a 14-year-old boy by the name of Lorem at a village hospital in Uganda. His thigh had been ripped open by a bullet from an automatic weapon. He was in severe pain after being transported on a donkey for several hours to the local hospital. During the previous weeks I had been, together with him and his friends and the livestock they were caring for, on the savannah in the northeastern corner of Uganda. For some years now the shepherds have replaced their pastoral staffs with AK-47s and other automatic weapons. Strapped over their shoulders, the weapons go with the herders wherever they follow the cattle, sheep, or camels.

According to NISAT, "hundreds of thousands of people are killed every year in conflict or 'post-conflict' zones around the world. The majority of the victims are civilians. Most commonly used in wars, as well as in state repression and criminal activity, are inexpensive small arms—automatic rifles, grenades, submachine guns, high powered pistols and other weapons that a single person can easily transport and fire."[2] In parts of Africa among the pastoralists these weapons have become available for all and sundry, young and old men. Pastoralists' way of life requires access to a relative large area of land that they can utilize according to the changing

---

Notes for this chapter are located on page 158.

conditions of their natural and social environment. Evidently groups of pastoralists may clash over resources. Claims to pastureland and water sources may be lost temporarily or more or less permanently. Still, the most common threat to peace among pastoral groups is the traditional custom of raiding livestock. The affluence of weapons has encouraged young men to engage in such activities much more frequent than before. The confrontations are not between units that are commonly labeled as ethnic groups. Mobilization for raid and defense is organized on various levels, based on different principles of organizations, may split an ethnic unit, and could also include sections of a neighboring ethnic group. The flexibility inhabited in the adaptation and organization among the pastoralists and their raiding activities are seen by governments as a threat both to people and to state control. Actions for disarmament have taken place time after time. The pastoralists see these actions as harassment and a threat to their way of life. They do not trust the government to guarantee their safety as long as their enemies may still have weapons and as they have enemies crossing the national borders.

Movements

Lorem is a member of the Matheniko, a section of the Karamojong people. The Karamojong cultivate their fields when there is sufficient rain, but their ties socially and culturally are mostly connected to their livestock. Basing their subsistence mainly on the products of livestock requires access to extensive areas of land. The nature utilized by pastoralists can in most places be characterized as arid and semiarid. A vital premise for surviving is the ability to move over long distances in order to access sufficient pasture and water, and competition over resources underlies most activities. Flexibility in the way people deal with each other, as well as with nature, has always been decisive for survival and success as pastoralists. Establishing new friendships and maintaining a wide network of friendly, individual relationships provide access to pastures and livestock when needed (Storaas 1997). However, from time to time confrontations are inevitable. The way that individuals and groups deal with such challenges varies, but the presence of AK-47s has made any confrontation life-threatening.

Similar kinds of adaptation are found among neighboring people in Uganda, Sudan, Ethiopia and in northwestern Kenya. Several of these groups have the same ancestry. Over the years their relationships have been changing between enmity and friendship. Earlier studies of pastoralists such as the Maasai (Jacobs 1963, 1965), the Samburu (Spencer 1965,

1973), the Borana (Baxter 1954), the Somali (Lewis 1961), the Karamojong (Dyson-Hudson 1966), and the Turkana (Gulliver 1951, 1955), based largely upon the tenets of British "structural-functionalism" and American "cultural ecology," emphasised local pastoral systems as self-contained entities. Although the anthropologists of that time provided information about the variation of everyday life, they sought to penetrate what they felt to be trivial in order to discover organizational principles. In a reprint of *Ethnic Groups and Boundaries*—a collection of essays on social organization of cultural difference that argued against the structural-functional paradigm —Fredrik Barth writes, "similar ways of thinking are constantly being reintroduced into the social science literature, deriving either from the commonsense reifications of people's own discourse and experience or from the rhetoric of ethnic activists" (Barth 1998:5). The reification of ethnicity and ethnic groups covers up the manifold ways in which people do organize. The conflicts that we can observe on the ground seldom correspond with how the involved ethnic groups are defined. More characteristic for these societies is the fluidity of boundaries and the adaptability of populations that, in some periods, maintain extensive relationships across borders through trade, marriage, and individual friendship. In other periods, sections within the same ethnic group may clash and even develop long-lasting enmity. Men from one section may collaborate with men of a section from another ethnic group and attack any neighbors to secure additional grazing areas or conduct smaller or bigger raids to get additional herds of livestock. Furthermore, neighbors may help in bad times: the Dassanetch of Ethiopia, for instance, made available arable land along the lake shore and river courses for cultivation by destitute refugees from neighboring Hamar, Arbore, and Turkana (Sobania 1991:125). The Matheniko of Karamojong have given access to pastures to the neighboring Turkana in times when the latter need to escape drought in the Rift Valley.

However, internal tensions and conflicts often lead people to break up and move away from each other. The scarcity of resources resulting from population growth or drought could cause smaller groups to agree to seek their fortune elsewhere. Disputes over cattle and pasture are recurrent themes in legends that explain the fission of groups. Also population pressure has been focused as a decisive factor causing people to move (Sahlins 1961; Newcomer 1972). Raymond C. Kelly (1985) argues that population growth was, rather, a result of expansion, since "the Nuer assimilated very large numbers of Dinka and the Nuer population increased very substantially as a result. This strongly suggests that population growth was primarily a consequence of Nuer expansion rather than a cause, and thus casts doubt on extant explanations that invoke or depend upon 'population pressure'" (Kelly 1985:69).

Like human groups in other parts of East Africa, and elsewhere in Africa as well, local populations have been subjected to processes of expansion and division, expulsion and assimilation. Survival has revolved around the suitability of the various techniques that competing groups of people developed for exploiting natural resources. These have included techniques for selecting and breeding domestic livestock, for organizing animal husbandry, for maintaining access to grazing land, and for defending rights in animals against raiding. Over the years this has resulted in certain groups having expanded—or having split up and migrated—while others have been pushed off or have assimilated. Although people have not been continuously on the move, the history of Africa describes groups that have split, some remaining behind while others migrated. This has been a more or less continuous process for centuries, a process that still causes tensions that can lead to open and armed conflicts. Centuries ago, Tutsi pastoralists migrated south to the land of the Hutu agriculturalists in the region of Rwanda and Burundi. In recent decades many Bafuruki have migrated into the land of the Banyoro, who consider themselves to be the indigenous population of Kibaale District in western Uganda. The Bafuruki cultivated new land, and land was plenty; but not so any longer, and tensions are building up (Espeland 2006).

Oral traditions, as well as the available archaeological data, indicate that the Jiye and Toposa in southern Sudan, the Nyangatom in southern Sudan and Ethiopia, the Turkana in northwestern Kenya, and the Iteso, Jie, Dodoth, and Karamojong in north eastern Uganda (called the Karamojong Cluster of the Eastern Nilotes [Gulliver 1955] or the Ateker, or "clan" cluster [Lamphear 1994]), are all descendents of Sudanese peoples who migrated south some five hundred years ago to an area in northern Karamoja. This location they now refer to as their ancestral homeland. Some three hundred years ago, a second dispersal gave rise to today's territorial configuration of most of these groups (Lamphear 1976).

At the beginning of the nineteenth century, there was in central Karamoja a rather loose cultural confederation of disparate Ateger communities of eastern Nilotes. "Some, mainly descended from an early Ateger group based on the Koten-Magos hill country further east, were essentially pastoralists. Others, derived from a more westerly branch of Ateger, appropriately nicknamed *Ngikatapa*, 'bread people', subscribed to an economy featuring grain agriculture" (Lamphear 1994:64–65). Those who migrated east and down the rugged escarpment, which now marks the Uganda-Kenya frontier, to the Rift Valley plateau, became the Turkana. Today there are two major categories of Turkana people, which are called Ngichuro and Ngimonia. Oral tradition associates them with two separate waves of immigration, which should have taken place between six and ten generations ago. Ngichuro is said to come from the agro-pastoral Karamojong, while the Ngimonia came from the pastoral Jie. "They were Jie herders who wandered to the east and down the steep escarpment to the 'land of many caves'—*Ngaturkana*," as an old Turkana explained to me. The plains west of the lake Turkana were at that time inhabited by a loose, multicultural confederation of Cushitic-, Maa- and Southern Nilotic- speakers called Siger, to the north, and the numerous Maa-speaking Kor who lived in close pastoral association with Cushitic-speaking peoples, to the south. All of them herded a variety of livestock; the Cushitic specialized in camels and the Kor in cattle. A terrible drought decimated the Siger herds and led to a rapid disintegration of their community. Many of the survivors were absorbed by the Turkana and the Kor. As the Turkana rapidly began pushing out from the foothills, the powerful Kor alliance was forced east and south, and other people northward. "While some traditions give the impression that this dramatic expansion was essentially a military one, in fact it certainly derived from a complex combination of factors, including vital commercial relations which kept the Turkana supplied with constant flow of ironware and grain. In some cases large numbers of aliens apparently opted, for various reasons, to 'become Turkana' *en masse*, making the process of expansion as much the spread of a culturolinguistic system as a direct armed invasion" (Lamphear 1994:68).

None of the peoples now occupying the area west and north of Lake Turkana describe themselves as the original inhabitants of their territories (Turton 1991). Hunters and gathers did not compete so intensely for the same resources and retained enclaves encircled by nomads where they for the most part were left undisturbed. Hunting and gathering has always been an alternative form of adaptation for destitute pastoralists who settled for themselves or joined established groups. The presence of the Elmolo people, who subsist primarily from fishing at the south end of Lake Turkana, can be explained in this way. Similarly, groups of Irenge, with a distinct language and adaptation, have persisted until the present day in the Songot Mountains in the northern part of Turkana district, as the Tepes who occupy the Moroto hills in Karamoja. These so-called Dorobo groups are not merely hunters and gathers; many are smiths and potters and some cultivate tobacco and vegetables, products they trade for animal products with their pastoral neighbors.

Migrating agriculturalists settled in new places and could accept paying tribute to a king or a royal lineage claiming to control the area, unless the immigrants took control and forced the people to submit to them. When they entered such areas, the colonial powers could lean on the strongest of the groups, enforce their position, and use them in the service of the state. Migrating pastoralists did not settle the same way. Their form of adaptation made them difficult to control. Since animals produce more animals, this must logically have implications for the use of pastures. Ensuring sufficient forage and water for the animals is the major concern for a pastoralist. The boundaries are not fixed, and people search for ways of surviving for their livestock and themselves. The herders will at times have to move their animals close to the enemies. If they feel superior in strength, herders now and then do cross borders to find pasture and water for their livestock, and to raid the animals of their enemies. The tension between the different groups relates to land and water, and livestock raiding. Thus, pastoralists continue to stress the government.

State Policy

As the British administration took control over Uganda in the beginning of the colonial era, they pushed different groups of people around in order to pacify them. Groups of Pokot people of Kenya were relocated into a Ugandan area inhabited by a section of Karamojong, called Pian, who on their side were moved northward pushing the Karamojong-speaking Matheniko section further and north of Moroto hills. Matheniko elders still talk about, and claim, land and water at their "original" homeland. "By 1921 the British had firmly established a military administration in Karamoja, and guns were not allowed in the hands of any local people except the chiefs appointed by the British. This situation continued for the next 50 years" (Baker 2001:19). "The killing of a Bokora Chief triggered the last of the punitive campaigns carried out by the colonial administration, during which large numbers of cattle were confiscated" (Gray et al. 2003:S14). Animal confiscation continued after the collapse of colonialism. Restrictions on their movements made the pastoralists more vulnerable to periods of droughts and livestock epidemics. The Bokora, the third Karamojong section (Pian and Matheniko the others), migrated in large numbers to neighboring districts to escape starvation and insecurity. "Many women reported that they never saw members of their families again" (ibid.).

The processes of fission and migration of groups of people still lead to confrontations in several places in Africa. Current borders between countries and districts impose restrictions on the kinds of dynamic solutions to conflicts or shortages of resources. Still, as we see in central Africa, people do fight across borders when ethnicity, or attachment to any other formation of group, are utilized as a basis for mobilization.

Among the many rules and regulations that came into force in the colonial period, Sobania (1991:139) argues that the imposition of grazing boundaries had the greatest impact, as once relatively fluid societal boundaries became crystallized. The flexibility by which pastoralists had survived the changing conditions of their environment was restricted by governmental regulations. The colonial state's artificial boundaries added more stress to these societies, a stress that many have claimed was brought about because pastoralists routinely overstock and overgraze (Stebbings 1935, Brown 1971, Lamprey 1983). Ecological viability, the balance between off-take and regeneration, is a result of different factors: a) the demographic factors, i.e., birth- and death rate, and emigration and immigration; b) the grazing regime, i.e., rotation or permanent; and c) socially regulated mechanisms, such as coordination of individual investment strategies, quota regulations, and mechanisms for excluding users from a territory. The assumption that pastoralists routinely overstock and overgraze has been very strong in the development policy among nomadic people. The assumption supports the idea that governments need more control over nomads and their land use. Growth is the normal state of affairs in a pastoral production system, and, whatever the carrying capacity of the pastures may be, in case of a growing pastoral enterprise access to pastures may become a problem. Researchers have examined the carrying capacity of pastures and the numbers of livestock that could survive in given areas (e.g., Pratt and Gwynne 1977). There are well-established methods for examining this in temperate zones, but in African arid lands, in particular, these methods are inadequate and provide faulty results. The World Bank, for instance, concluded that the animal population of Mali was irresponsibly large and demanded its dramatic reduction as a precondition for support. A French consultancy firm using other models produced a very different estimate of the proportion of animals to pasture in Mali (Breman 1988).

The governments following independence have not proved to be supportive to the pastoralists in Karamoja; rather, the opposite is the case. During the 1960s, the region was heavily raided with modern firearms, especially high-powered rifles, by the Toposa from Sudan in the north and the Turkana from Kenya in the east. The armed police in the region were ineffectual in responding to these raids. When Idi Amin took over in 1971, stronger and more brutal actions were taken to stop the raiders inside and outside the region. His government sought to pacify the Karamojong by using heavy infantry and artillery, including tanks (Baker 2001). In order to civilize the nomads, traditional dressings made of skin, and women's beads, were burned in great fires. In Kenya president Moi went to visit the Turkana, assembled a lot of people in big meetings, and made big fires of their traditional dressings and ornaments (Storaas 1980). "People were compelled to abandon traditional subsistence activities to plant cash crops such as cotton" (Gray et al. 2003:S14). The Karamojongs', as the Turkanas', distrust for their governments was only intensified by these actions. In their public prayers, the Turkana cursed their government in the same way they cursed their enemies (Storaas 1980).

In the 1960s, increasingly aggressive raids had mounted between the different groups. Wars in Congo and Zimbabwe, in southern Sudan and in Uganda brought weapons to the region. Delegations of men went and brought guns of different kinds. When one group felt superior and acted according to it, it also provoked a demand for weapons among the attacked groups. Homemade guns were produced from water pipe when the development workers had left. Ammunition could be bought from local government officers, at a high price; one to three bullets for an ox. When I commented on the price to a Turkana friend, he replied: "Even with only one bullet you can raid many cattle."

The arms race between the various groups in northern Uganda accelerated with Amin's sudden flight from the country in 1979. The scouts of the Tepes people of the Moroto hills first discovered that the military barracks in the district were abandoned in a hurry. It did not take long before raiders of the Matheniko, the Karamojong section just north of the Moroto hills, joined in ransacking the abandoned armories. Some Turkana were also brave enough to steal their way to armories during nights. Tens of thousands of automatic weapons were transported by people and donkeys and distributed. Filled with newfound courage and arrogance, men carrying weapons attacked and raided for cattle and other livestock. Every attack created the desire for more weapons. At this time the civil war was starting up again in southern Sudan. The war created a nearby inlet for hand weapons to the region, weapons that were distributed to its neighboring countries.

Being somehow ahead of their neighbors in this race, the Tepes were successful in their raids. However, the cattle they raided failed to thrive in the mountains. The Tepes, being horticulturalists, hunters and gatherers, made friends with individual Karamojong pastoralists, to make them look after their cattle on the plains. As they were well armed, the Tepes were gradually welcomed to join *adakar*s of Karamojong groups. The *adakar*s are units of herders who work together to protect their livestock as well as sharing information about grazing, etc. People from different ethnic groups can belong to the same *adakar*, but generally an *adakar* consist of people who for long have lived and worked together and who are members of the same section of an ethnic group. There are many *adakar*s in one section. The *adakar* is the basic military unit for defense as well as for raiding. Most often they cooperate with other similar units.

The new National Resistance government of Yoweri Museveni from 1986 immediately launched a disarmament campaign in Karamoja. A similar campaign took place in Kenya. The campaigns were brutal and only intensified the hostility of the nomads toward the government. Rumors about military convoys being ambushed and barracks looted for weapons collected in the campaigns, were not officially verified, but the stories strengthened the local resistance.

In the 1990s, it was decided that the Karamojong should be armed so that they could defend themselves against raiders from Kenya and Sudan. A military officer in Karamoja district told me (in 1998) that the governing forces were able to disarm the Karamojong by force, but that they could not guarantee the security of people and their livestock due to lack of resources. As long as the neighbors on the other side of the state borders—in Kenya, Sudan, and Ethiopia—were heavily armed, the policy of the government was that the pastoralists in Karamoja should defend themselves. The military strategy was to get the traditional war leaders to rally on the government's side as vigilante groups. These leaders, chosen because of their personal qualifications, were heads of *adakars*, and it was accepted by their followers that they cooperated with the government. In return, the vigilantes were given ammunition and a small salary. This ammunition was to be for defense only. The military leaders claimed that a curse was attached to this ammunition, and that if it was used for attacks the results could be disastrous for the raiders. A fatal unsuccessful raid in 1997 when 116 of the Karamojong were killed, was claimed by army leaders as proof of the curse.

The government action of giving arms and ammunition to the vigilantes increased the level of conflict between Karamojong and their neighbors, especially to the west and with the Acholi and the Lango, who earlier had not been much disturbed by the Karamojongs' activities. Also, the Iteso, ethnically "cousins" of the Karamojong, were heavily raided and left with hardly any cattle.

In late 1999, BBC World reported that several hundred raiders were killed by helicopter gunships in Karamoja. And "in an attempt forcibly to suppress the raiding in 2000–2001 Kampala armed people in adjacent districts at the same time as it carried out yet another largely unsuccessful disarmament operation in Karamoja" (Gray et al. 2003:S15). Disarmament operations in Karamoja, as in the Turkana District in Kenya, have become recurrent news in the media. Rumors of young men stealing their way into military barracks, killing soldiers, and retrieving confiscated arms are hidden from media inquiries but back up the pride and the self-determination of the pastoralists.

Ever since the beginning of colonial time and the introduction of the state, governments have seen the pastoralists as too independent and unmanageable. The weapons of the colonial army were superior to the spears and bows and arrows of the nomads. The colonial government was able to more or less pacify many of the groups. Elderly people may talk about that era as a good and peaceful period of their life. The introduction of rifles, and later AK-47s and other light hand weapons, evened out the relative strength between the pastoralists and the government. Raids and other armed activities increased, while the government's ability and relative strength to handle the new challenges decreased. The pastoralists felt insecurity growing and demanded more weapons for protection of people and livestock. As more arms were distributed among people, legally and illegally, the less the government could control. Lack of governmental control made the pastoralists feel responsible for their own safety. Governmental operations toward disarming and gaining more control over the pastoralists have also provided a reason to cross national borders, as was reported in the media. "The Kenyan army has begun a massive operation to disarm cattle raiders. Six districts in the west are being targeted after the government said last year's weapons amnesty had failed. Thousands of people are reported to have fled across the border into Uganda with their animals, fearing the disarmament could end in violence" (BBC News 01.05–2006). Thus, actions taken for disarmament are experienced as moves toward eradicating people's ability to defend themselves and is therefore seen as a violent action against the pastoralists.

Raiding and Identity

The Karamojong and the Turkana being pastoralists, their major concern is the well-being of their herds. Identity, social and cultural, is geared toward the preservation of the pastoralist subsistence base. The Karamojong, more than the Turkana, do cultivate fields when there is sufficient rainfall. But the fields may be left before being harvested, if they decide that is the best for their livestock. To raid for animals has been an efficient and quick way to increase a herd. Everyone indulges in this practice, and there is a lot of prestige following a successful raid. Women, not the least, show great enthusiasm in heating up and praising their warriors. Repetitive raids may also result in controlling new fresh water resources and grazing land, and thus be part of an expansion. At a watering point a Matheniko herdsman told me that the riverbed where we were had once been taken by the Jie, who used the wells for some years. "Now we have managed to take these wells back. But the Jie can be here any time." After losing animals in a raid, mobilizing for a raid can be a quick way of rebuilding a herd. A strategy for young men not in a position to marry can be to join in raids and secretly build a herd by hiding some of the raided animals with a trusted friend. If successful, such a person may marry before an elder brother and, in the process, gain a lot of prestige. Raymond C. Kelly points out that the underlying explanation of Nuer expansion "focuses on the manner in which the Nuer bride wealth system establishes social requirements for cattle. The latter effectively determine the size, composition, and growth characteristics of Nuer herds, thereby defining the extent of Nuer grazing requirements. Recurrent shortages of dry season pasture (that are ultimately attributable to bride wealth requirements) provide the immediate impetus to successive rounds of territorial appropriation" (Kelly 1985:7). Whatever caused it, and although it was not always their explicit intention, expansion enabled groups in places such as Karamoja to secure new and perhaps larger grazing ranges for both their own stock and the animals they acquired through raiding.

In times of difficulties, the Ugandan highland in Karamoja has been a way out for the Turkana pastoralists in the Rift Valley in Kenya. When drought builds up, sections of the Turkana have been allowed to move with their livestock into the Karamoja District and even further west to the wetlands by the lakes in east central Uganda. Such questions have mainly been dealt with by the elders on each side with only limited involvement from the respective governments. The Turkana of Kenya try to maintain customary rights to the highland just inside the national border of Uganda for dry-season pastures. The long-lasting peace between the sections on each side of the border has lead to cooperation between grazing units and also to marriage arrangements. But the affluence of weapons in the area is a constant threat to any peaceful arrangements between groups.

Weapons dealing has been *longue durée* and prolific in Africa. As the western and eastern worlds have been disarming their forces, the weapon mongers are doing their bit to fuel the fires and increase demand for their services in the south. The situation in southern Sudan has been that of a virtual vacuum cleaner for weapons from all over the world. The nomads are no longer only seeking any modern weapon but rather may now choose from a wide selection. Especially popular at the moment are weapons from South Africa, as they are lighter to carry than others. At the village Pirre, close to where the borders between Sudan, Kenya, and Uganda meet, there has been a large open market for weapons and ammunition. Before the war in Sudan a man could get one or two bullets for a cow. At the market in Pirre, the traders nowadays measure the ammunition using Blue Band boxes as they do when measuring grain for sale. And it is possible for smaller merchants and dealers to exchange an automatic weapon for the price of two to four cows. Although the market in the northern parts of Uganda seems to be congested, since everyone here has arms, the trade remains lively. People are buying four to five automatic weapons, and walk by foot over the savannah and down the Rift Valley escarpment to Kenya, and then especially to the Pokot people who easily will pay double the purchase price for a weapon. The Pokot, on their side, also make a healthy profit selling the weapons further on.

In northeastern Uganda, all males from the age of twelve carry automatic weapons. The Kalashnikovs have replaced the pastoral staffs they used to carry along. And people readily fire their weapons. Our host in Karamoja, Apamago, lost a daughter a couple of months before we met. She became an accidental victim of the bullets from three drunken youths celebrating Christmas. It took three days for the gunmen to be identified, and the person who had pulled the trigger was taken by a crowd of people to the scene of the crime and executed. The body was left at the spot for the hyenas. A man staying with us at the cattle camp was in hiding after he accidently fired his gun at a party, killing a man. In January 1998, more than two hundred men were restrained on the way south to raid the Upe (i.e., Pokot of Uganda). The men were going to revenge a total failure of the raid the previous year when 116 of their people had been killed.

Peacekeeping

Conflicts of interest are latent in most relations on all levels. The presence of the weapons makes armed confrontations and killings a daily threat. Still, peace is maintained most of the time. The elders feel great responsibility for preventing open conflicts, but their authority is threatened by the young men and their modern weapons. Respect for the elders is deeply rooted in the traditions. The elders' authority is based on tradition as well as the mystical power related to cursing. Again and again, stories are told about persons and situations that show how powerful a curse can be. The stories about sufferings caused by elders' curses remind people about respect and tradition, and work to rebuild the authority of the elders. Whenever young men show off with their weapons, reactions are swift and severe. Still, when preparing for a raid, the elders may give the young men their blessings. This ambivalence refers to the cultural position of raiding as a rightful traditional way of increasing a family's herd of livestock. Every young man among pastoralists looks forward to reaching the age of being accepted to take part in a raid. The raiders organize in smaller units, attack, and collect as large a number as possible of livestock from an enemy, and the animals may be shared among the raiders immediately and spread into different herd units. The father's and the mother's herds get the biggest share from the raider, but he may hide some from his family in order to secretly build his own herd. Raiding can be a decisive way to a fast rebuild of herds lost to drought, pest infestation, or raiding. Thus, young men usually will get blessings from the elders before taking off to raid. However, the raids have become more deadly through the use of automatic weapons and the elders try to reduce these activities by refusing their blessings.

Raids are the most common reasons for clashes between pastoral groups. Frequent raids may force a group to move, and thus be a strategy to gain control over new water points and pastures. This can result in expansion of land, until the other group has restored strength and taken revenge.

There have been many peace talks between different groups over the years. Only one has lasted. After long meetings underneath the shady acacia trees on both sides of the national border, the elders of the Karamojong of Uganda and their neighbors, the Turkana of Kenya, agreed on peace in 1973. During a big ceremony a razor blade was buried. Razor blades are used to shave the heads of mourners, and were to symbolize the end of killing. A spear and a knife were buried together with the razor blade. The participants wanted to bury a bullet and a rifle as well, but claimed they did not have any, and asked the representatives of their respective governments for a weapon to bury. The government representatives on their side argued that it was not their weapons that had killed people here, and they did not want to be drawn in as a part of the ceremony. Rifles were seldom used in raids in those days, and therefore the ceremony was completed with blessings between the parties without a rifle having been buried. When this peace treaty is referred to today, this point is always emphasized. Still, an effort is made to uphold the peace. Marriages across the border tie people closer, and in-married relatives settle down together with their brothers-in-law among previous enemies. Situations threatening the peace are constantly occurring, mostly owing to young warriors feeling powerful with modern weapons. Those involved in attempted raids that threaten this peace agreement are instantly defined as criminals, spoken to, and fined—that is, forced to sacrifice an ox or two to the elders. To maintain the peace in tense situations following bad behavior by young men, the elders, at times, have established a restricted area, a fire lane, between the Karamojong and the Turkana until the situation has calmed down. People are again and again made aware of the serious curses that will follow those who break the peace. These are curses that were uttered in connection to the peace treaty.

The Raid

One of Nakorile's oxen had strayed from the herd. Two youths found the ox and herded it to town, where it was sold and slaughtered. Nakorile, a vigilante and head of an *adakar,* mobilized his men and went to town where he arranged a large meeting about how important it is to strike hard against such disrespectful behavior. The two youths, and the ones helping out with the slaughtering, should be punished and fined, he claimed.

While this meeting was going on in town, the enemy attacked the *adakar* of Nakorile. Only a few youths had stayed behind to defend the animals. When Lorem was shot, the rest of the shepherds concentrated on defending him from being killed. The *adakar* lost four hundred animals in the raid.

The footsteps indicated that the raiders were some youngsters from the Tepes. Nakorile had many friends among the Tepes, some even members of his *adakar.* Now he and his elders decided to confiscate the animals of Tepes that were kept in his *adakar.* In a meeting back in the *adakar* the following day, elders from Tepes turned up and promised to do whatever they could to retrieve the raided animals.

The relationship between Tepes and Karamojong in many places has developed in such a way that people now refer to the Tepes as a subsection of the Karamojong. This, in many ways a dramatic change, is taking place within the time span of less than one generation. Tepes children have started to use only the language of the Karamojong, and many no longer know their mother tongue, a language very different from that of the Karamojong. For the Tepes who had their livestock cared for and protected with the help of the Karamojong, any threat to the peaceful cooperation between the two groups could have been a disaster.

Conclusion

The history of Africa is a history of people migrating. Confrontations were dealt with in one way or the other. The many so-called ethnic conflicts of today are explained on the basis of recent or earlier migrations. In most cases, as the ones pointed to in this chapter, the use of the "ethnic" label raises the level of dispute above the actual settings. The confrontations in the regions of Karamoja and the neighboring people are between sections within one ethnic group or between one or more sections of one ethnic group against one or more sections of another. Ethnicity is not among the causes of the conflicts. The causes relate to disputes over resources, most often over livestock, but also over water and pastureland. For the pastoralists and their extensive land-use practice, a great deal of flexibility in dealing with land and neighbors has been necessary for survival. This in many ways fluid adaptation undermined governmental control. "The greatest risk to pastoralists' survival in the late 20th century was not drought or disease but their vulnerable position vis-à-vis governments that either punished them or exploited them according to prevailing political currents, ultimately marginalizing them and endangering their subsistence base" (Gray et al. 2003:S22). In the arid and semiarid regions occupied by pastoralists, alternative forms of adaptation, with the possible exception of hunting and gathering, have proved to be much more vulnerable than depending on livestock. Billions of dollars have been spent by governments and development agencies over the years in order to improve the life of pastoralists. No projects have come up with a solution that proves to be better than what the pastoralists already have done (Pratt and Gwynne 1977). Using livestock as the technology for subsistence has proved to be the best and only alternative way to survive in these areas. The only rationality for the pastoralists is to protect their way of living against anyone threatening them. However, this has not been recognized by the Ugandan state: "Successive post-independence governments have dealt with the 'Karamoja problem' as a problem of refusal to change and integrate, i.e. as a 'social deviance problem'" (Baker 2001:19). For the pastoralists, attacks on their culture and mode of life are attacks on their possibility to survive.

Generally, the pastoralists see the AK-47s and other hand weapons as most valuable. The weapons are necessary for protection against threat and useful when going on raids to acquire additional animals for marriage, rebuild a depleted herd, or for gaining prestige. In today's situation, the weapons are necessary for life and for living as a pastoralist. At the same time, more people than ever are killed by these weapons. The highest percentage of the dead are the young men who are most eager to obtain the deadly weapons.

Conflict prevention and management should be the responsibility of the state. In spite of sporadic disarmament operations, state presence in pastoral areas is generally nominal. Pastoral communities carry little political weight at the state level, and consequently there is no political incentive for greater involvement from the state. The repeated conflicts within and between pastoral communities are often ignored and allowed to run their course. By providing weapons, the arms dealers are pouring fuel on the many latent and simmering conflicts. While state interventions, when they take place, focus on symptoms, the worldwide economic interests involved in arms trading may be the major cause for sustaining the confrontations and killings.

* * *

Lorem spent a couple of weeks at the hospital. He swore that when he was well, he would be in the forefront to raid for revenge and to get the lost animals back home to his father. However, the Tepes' elders succeeded in their struggle to return the raided animals peacefully. After a couple of months, Nakorile got back most of the livestock that had been raided.

Two days after Lorem was shot by the Tepes, the Jie attacked our neighboring *adakar*, only a couple of miles north of Nakorile's camps. Eight men were killed and several others wounded. A few hundred animals were taken. No elders from Jie interfered.

Notes

1. This number is taken from the Small Arms Survey as listed at http://www.smallarmssurvey.org, retrieved 11 November 2008.
2. The quote is taken from http://www.nisat.org/ and retrieved 18 December 2007.

Bibliography

Barth, F. 1998. *Ethnic Groups and Boundaries: The Social Organization of Culture Difference.* Illinois: Waveland Press, Inc.
Baker, W.G. 2001. *Uganda: The Marginalization of Minorities.* London: Minority Rights Group International.
Baxter, P. 1954. "The Social Organization of the Boran of Nothern Kenya," Ph.D. Thesis. Oxford: Lincoln College, Oxford University.
Breman, H. 1988. "The Carrying Capacity of Natural Resources in Sahelian Countries: Its Abiotic and Biotic Basis; Conesequences for Development," Paper presented at SSE-seminar, *Centre for Development Studies.* Bergen: Centre for Development Studies, University of Bergen.
Brown, L.H. 1971. "The Biology of Pastoral Man as a Factor in Conservation," *Biol. Conserv.* 3(2): 93–100.
Dyson-Hudson, N. 1966. *Karimojong Politics.* Oxford: Clarendon Press
Espeland, R.H. 2006. "When Neighbours Become Killers: Land Redistribution, Ethnicity and Communal Violence in Kibaale District, Uganda." Master thesis, University of Bergen. Bergen.
Gray, S., M. Sundal, B. Wiebusch, M. Little, P. W. Leslie and I. L. Pike. 2003. "Cattle Raiding, Cultural Survival, and Adaptability of East African Pastoralists," *Current Anthropology* 44(5): S3–S30.
Gulliver, P.H. 1951. *A Preliminary Survey of the Turkana: A Report Compiled for the Government of Kenya.* Communication from School of African Studies No. 26 (N.S.). Cape Town: University of Cape Town.
———. 1955. *The Family Herds: A Study of Two Pastoral Tribes in East Africa, The Jie and Turkana.* London: Routledge and Kegan Paul.

Jacobs, A.H. 1963. *The Pastoral Maasai of Kenya: A Report of Anthropological Field Research*. London: Ministry of Overseas Development.

———. 1965. "The Traditional Political Organization of the Pastoral Maasai," Ph.D. Thesis. Oxford: Oxford University.

Kelly, R.C. 1985. *The Nuer Conquest: The Structure and Development of an Expansionist System*. Ann Arbor: University of Michigan Press.

Lamphear, J. 1976. *The Traditional History of the Jie of Uganda*. Oxford: Oxford University Press.

———. 1994. "The evolution of Ateker 'New Model Armies': Jie and Turkana," in Fukui Katuyoshi and Markakis John (eds), *Ethnicity and Conflict in the Horn of Africa*. London: James Currey, pp. 63–92.

Lamprey, H.F. 1983. "Pastoralism Yesterday and Today: The Overgrazing Problem," in F. Bourliere (ed.), *Tropical Savannas: Ecosystems of the World*. Amsterdam: Elsevier, pp. 643–666.

Lewis, I.M. 1961. *A Pastoral Democracy: A Study of Pastoralism and Politics Among the Northern Somali of the Horn of Africa*. London: Oxford University Press for Int. Afr. Inst.

Newcomer, P.J. 1972. "The Nuer are Dinka: An Essay on Origins and Environmental Determinism," *Man* (N.S.) 7: 5–11.

Pratt, D.J. and M.D. Gwynne (eds). 1977. *Rangeland Management and Ecology in East Africa*. London: Hodder and Stoughton.

Sahlins, M.D. 1961. "The Segmentary Lineage: An Organization of Predatory Expansion," *American Anthropologist* 63: 322–345.

Sobania, N. 1991. "Feasts, Famines and Friends: Nineteenth Century Exchange and Ethnicity in the Eastern Lake Turkana Region," in J.G. Galaty and P. Bonte (eds), *Herders, Warriors, and Traders: Pastoralism in Africa*. Boulder, San Francisco and Oxford: Westview Press, pp. 118–142.

Spencer, P. 1965. *The Samburu: a Study of Gerontocracy in a Nomadic Tribe*. Berkeley and Los Angeles: University of California Press.

———. 1973. *Nomads in Alliances: Symbiosis and Growth among the Rendille and Samburu of Kenya*. London: Oxford University Press.

Stebbings, E.P. 1935. "The Encroaching Sahara," *Geographical Journal* 86: 510.

Storaas, F. 1980. *How can Development be Development?* Progress Report no. 3. Turkana research Project. Bergen: University of Bergen.

———. 1997. "The Nexus of Economic and Political Viabilities among Nomadic Pastoralists in Turkana, Kenya," *Research in Economic Anthropology* 18:115–166.

Turton, D. 1991. "Movement, Warfare and Ethnicity in the Lower Omo Valley," in J.G. Galaty and P. Bonte (eds), *Herders, Warriors, and Traders: Pastoralism in Africa*. Boulder, San Francisco and Oxford: Westview Press, pp. 145–170.

Section III

SOVEREIGN LOGICS

Chapter Seven

THE SOVEREIGN AS SAVAGE
The Pathos of Ethno-Nationalist Passion

Christopher Taylor

Very frequently in the past and even today, the term *state* has been used where the term *government* would serve just as well if not better. This is the gist of an observation by Radcliffe-Brown in an early article (Radcliffe-Brown 1940). More recently, scholars of the state such as Abrams (1988) and Trouillot (2001) have seconded the objection raised by Radcliffe-Brown and have pointed out that power, construed very broadly, constitutes the central issue in understanding the state. In situating power at the center of analysis, these theorists follow the path blazed by Michel Foucault (1977). For Foucault there is no individual subject constructed in the absence of power, and there is no social institution or cultural construction that does not bear the imprint of historical struggles over power. In essence, power takes over at the micro level in the constitution of human subjectivity and at the macro level in the execution of collective action. With power so pervasively infusing human experience, there appears to be no middle ground, nothing between micro and macro where power is not the ultimate determining variable and therefore, no need of talking about anything else. Power is here; power is there. It is everywhere. History is the chronicle of the struggle for power among individuals and groups. Taken to its logical conclusion, this perspective on human social life closely resembles the Hobbesian "war of each against all."

However, it could very well be that this vision of things is a culture-bound one, steeped in the individualistic ontology of Western capitalist society. One could pose the question of whether power covers all the bases,

---

Notes for this chapter are located on page 183.

whether it by itself tells us all that we need to know in the course of social analysis. It is clear for an anthropologist like Pierre Clastres that some peoples in the world refuse the organization of society on the sole basis of power (1974). They refuse master/slave ideology and all the narratives spun from its fibers. From his work among the stateless societies of the Amazon basin, Clastres shows that many peoples reject the command/obedience dichotomy and the power of one over many. Chiefs among the Guayaki, for example, have prestige and can practice polygyny, but they must be good orators and be generous. Yet, for all their oratorical skills, their speeches are usually ignored; and, for all their generosity—or rather because of it—they are usually the most impoverished members of their communities. For these peoples, what has been perennially viewed as an absence—the lack of a state—should be seen as a presence, that is, the choice of a life where no human being rules over another. Although these societies certainly have politics, it is a politics inextricably bound up with and enracinated in the social. As Clastres terms it, these are societies against the state (1974).

Parallel to Clastres, in Marshall Sahlins' earlier work on the "domestic mode of production" (2000 [1972]), we see that, in contrast to all depictions of "primitive" economies as economies of deprivation, the people who actually live in such societies procure their subsistence with an average of less than three hours of work per day. These are economies rooted in and encompassed within the social, and it is this social factor that is their driving force rather than their by-product. These are economies against economism.

According to Sahlins' more recent work, the current Foucauldian-inspired preoccupation with power is influenced by a notion of the individual as perpetually inadequate and derives much of its impetus from Judeo-Christian cosmology (2000 [1996]). Sahlins maintains that these culture-bound assumptions underlie Western social science models that begin at the axiomatic base of the individual as a needful being. Society then, becomes either the instrument by which individual needs can be satisfied—Malinowski—or the mechanism through which conflicting individual demands can be regulated and held in check by collective constraint and pressure—Durkheim. Aspects of similar notions resurface in Foucault and others who see struggle at the basis of all human interaction. We struggle against each other in social life and even with ourselves as every individual consciousness is divided and conflictual. Although Foucault differs from Durkheim in many respects, the two thinkers share these ontological notions. In Durkheim the basis of morality lies in the collective, while for Foucault there is no so-called moral discourse outside of power/knowledge nexi that both reflect and reproduce cleavages between the empowered and the disempowered. If there are differences in the posited mechanics of repression, the two share a fundamental vision: for Durkheim, collective representations constrain and coerce; for Foucault, society is a disciplinary apparatus. In either case, the self remains the seat of desire while the collective is the locus of desire's regulation or control.

If Clastres and Sahlins are correct in their thinking, as I believe they are, there must be in addition to societies who categorically refuse the state and to those who refuse economism, state societies that cannot be adequately understood solely through the lens of a universalized *homo economicus* or a universalized *homo politicus*. Such state societies may well have been numerous in the non-Western world; it is likely that the premodern society of Rwanda was one of them. My second contention is that if we want to understand the social and cultural specifics of how war is enacted by such non-Western states, we need to understand not only the events of war, not only the political and economic calculus of maximizing individuals and their conflicting discourses, but also the ontological underpinnings of moral personhood in these societies as this is deployed in war. In this specific instance, I will attempt to show that the echoes of moral personhood as evinced in the institution of sacred kingship and in the rituals of the premodern Rwandan state were heard in the genocidal war waged by the modern Rwandan state against its Tutsi citizens. Of course, many things have changed in Rwanda over the course of the last one hundred years as a result of Rwanda's experience with colonialism, Christian evangelization, and integration into the world capitalist economy, but this does not mean that all precolonial notions of the person have been effaced, particularly where this concerns the relation of leader to polity.

One expectation, consistent with precolonial notions of the person but perhaps never stated nor ever fully manifest in postcolonial times, is that the Rwandan leader be the polity's most giving being and that the concern of prosperity for all be his foremost concern.

Violence and the State

When violence is conducted by the state, it spares no effort in legitimizing this violence according to local moral perceptions that are in harmony with subjacent cultural codes. This means that at one level the state's organized violence is supported and institutionalized by ideologies that make destructive acts appear justified for the maintenance of collective well-being. Frequently, public rituals serve as the means by which these ideologies are validated and communicated to the mass of the state's citizens. At another level, and more importantly for our purposes, these rituals convey less apprehensible messages reflecting the community's deep desires and sentiments. These latter are less accessible to conscious apperception, more archetypal in nature, and less likely to be construed by social actors as having obvious and clear-cut ideological content.

Following Aijmer's discussion of violence (2000), whose analytical scheme bears close resemblance to that used by Godelier (1996) in an apparently unrelated matter—the ambiguities left unresolved in Mauss's discussion of the gift—one could posit the existence of three dimensions to state violence and to the political rituals that enact or serve to justify state violence: the imaginary, the symbolic, and the real. At the least apprehensible level is what Godelier terms the "imaginary." The imaginary consists of iconic symbols more or less organized into diffuse cultural codes. These constitute the base of the social imagination in its envisioning of possible worlds. This material is only intuitively cognized by social actors and consists of what Roy Wagner (1986) would call "symbols that stand for themselves," or, in other words, symbols that are not readily translatable into a verbal or discursive idiom. These symbols and diffuse codes constitute the body of any community's tacit assumptions about itself and the world, while subtly and almost imperceptibly revealing its profoundest fears and desires. This level is the least accessible to the social actors themselves and to their exegesis. In those instances when an outsider indicates material from this level to the social actors who actually live it, their verbal responses are likely to be ad hoc rationalizations or secondary elaborations (Aijmer, op. cit.). Despite the relative inaccessibility of this iconic imaginary base to the persons who embody it, it precedes and conditions everything that is more conscious in nature. In this respect Godelier explicitly marks his difference from both Lacan and Lévi-Strauss, who see the symbolic as logically prior to both the imaginary and the real (1996).

At the next level, what Aijmer terms the "discursive" and Godelier terms the "symbolic," verbal elements come to the fore. It is here that agentive phenomena are manifest as social actors verbalize what their intentions are and act out these intentions in consonance with avowed pragmatic ends. This is the domain of language, discourse, and narrative. People will usually be able to identify and verbalize what the ideologies of their supporters and opponents are and explain the pragmatic ends that are served with any particular statement or action. It is here that strategization is most apparent as social actors weigh the consequences of one course of action against others and then behave accordingly. This is also the level where disagreement, conflict, and struggle are most manifest.

The most visible level of state violence is what Aijmer calls the "ethological" and which corresponds to what Godelier calls the "real." Violence has very real biological and psychological effects upon the people against whom it is applied—suffering, pain, injury, and death. Yet, even this level is dependent upon its interaction with the other two levels in order for violent acts to attain their full amplitude of social meanings. It may not be sufficient, for example, to kill one's opponent; it may be necessary to mutilate, to destroy, or to dispose of the body in such a way that the victim's spirit not return to wreak vengeance on the perpetrator of the violence. As Aijmer puts it, while physical death may be irrevocable and nonnegotiable, social death may not (2000).

Although both Godelier and Aijmer posit the primacy of the imaginary, certainly these three levels are not hermetically sealed off from one another. It is possible for people to become aware of the iconic symbols that constitute their imaginary. Certain members of a collectivity, as with individuals in psychoanalysis, may have a "prise de conscience" in which the deeper levels of their socially shared fears and desires become manifest. When this happens, the iconic enters the realm of the symbolic and becomes susceptible to verbalization. The pre-discursive rises to the discursive. In like fashion, this process can go the other way. Discursive material that had once been verbalized in the form of ideological statements and narratives can become so habitual as to become virtually unconscious. What was once stated and debated becomes tacit and implicit, joining the ranks of other phenomena constituting the *habitus* or the "things that go without saying" (Bourdieu 1977). Finally, it is also possible that at the level of the real or the ethological, the performance of violence radically reconstitutes the social and cultural order. In such a case, the older ideologies and deeper cultural layers may lose their salience, being replaced by something new. This is why we need historical as well as social analysis. In the case of Rwanda, in order to understand something about the changing relationship of the imaginary to the symbolic and to the real, we need to know something about its history as a state.

As I will demonstrate below, despite the radical changes that came in the wake of violence and revolution during the early 1960s, much of the cultural imagining of the state and the place of the sovereign in the state persisted into the 1990s.

The Premodern Rwandan State

The political entity Rwanda traces its foundation as a state to the seventeenth century C.E., when Ruganzu Ndori, coming from Karagwe-Ndorwa (present-day eastern Tanzania and southwestern Uganda), entered the central regions of what is now Rwanda and established a kingdom there (Vansina 2000). Small independent polities had existed in this area prior to Ndori's arrival. These consisted of both stateless societies and states such as that of the Renge, reputedly the most ancient, comprising much of present day Rwanda with the exception of the east (Mamdani 2001:60–63). Rwanda eventually absorbed these polities to become the territory that we now recognize with its present boundaries, although in the north and west, colonial forces were needed to fully effect this integration (Nahimana 1993). The Rwandan kingdom remained in existence until the abolition of kingship in 1962. Rwandan kings over the course of these four centuries were always members of the dominant group, the pastoralist Tutsi.

According to Jan Vansina social stratification characterized many polities in central Africa prior to the seventeenth century C.E. (Vansina 2000). At the time of Ndori's conquest then, the region's political systems were already characterized by an appreciable measure of social differentiation, as is evident from archaeological findings that show differences in ceramic use between people believed to be members of an elite and those believed to be commoners (Vansina 2000:30). With the establishment of the Nyiginya kingdom under Ruganzu Ndori and its absorption of neighboring areas, hierarchical tendencies were accentuated (Vansina 2000:30). Processes of differentiation within the Rwandan state produced three distinct ethnic groups with marked status differences among and within them. The most devalued group was the Twa, who were foragers and potters. The most privileged group was the Tutsi patron class. Low-level Tutsi herders and the mass of Hutu cultivators differed little in relative wealth, but Hutu from the early nineteenth century on were disfavored in terms of political privilege as all were subject to a form of corvée labor known as *uburetwa*, which required two days of their labor out of every four. Because of this, Hutu were more vulnerable to ecological and humanly caused catastrophes. By the time Europeans entered the area in the late nineteenth century, social differences in Rwanda had become pronounced; many Hutu were landless and impoverished (Vansina 2000). Colonialism did not instigate the ethnogenic process, but it made matters worse by adding the ideology of biological determinism to it. Early Rwanda thus conforms closely to many of the characteristics implicit and explicit in the negative portrait of the state painted by Pierre Clastres.

However, nationalistic-like processes generative of solidarity were also at work in precolonial Rwanda. An "imagined community" in the sense used by Anderson (1991) was being forged, but it was crystallizing around an ontological core of holism and hierarchy (Kapferer 1988). In this social system, every person first assessed his or her own hierarchical position in relation to every other person and then interacted accordingly. Of course, some of Anderson's conditions did not apply to early Rwanda; there was nothing like "print capitalism," for example, before the arrival of European

Catholic missionaries. Nevertheless, a vernacular language, Kinyarwanda, was widely employed in the area and in the process of supplanting other languages. Moreover, many early Rwandans whether Hutu, Tutsi, or Twa served in the army, participated in the kingdom's wars of expansion, and benefitted materially from them. However, it would be wrong to infer from all the above that the precolonial Rwandan state and quasi-nation should be understood solely through the lens of power and ideology. Examining only the competitive actions of individuals and groups involved in the struggle over power, does not bring us any closer to an understanding of the cultural specificities of the Rwandan state. Nor does it reveal the deeper ontological dimensions responsible for the construction of being and personhood in that state. Many Rwandans, for example, believed in the ritual efficacy of the kingship institution and its effects on agricultural, bovine, and human fertility as the king was charged with important ritual responsibilities. Similarly to what Sahlins and Clastres have noted for economics and politics among other non-Western societies, politics in early Rwanda was deeply embedded in the social and cannot be seen apart from religion and cosmology. It is only by understanding these aspects that we can fully understand the nature of violence directed by the Rwandan state.

Violence and the Imaginary in Precolonial Rwanda

The Rwandan king inflicted death upon the kingdom's enemies both within and without its borders, but of equal importance were his ritual actions which were thought to control the rain and to bring fertility to Rwanda's land, cattle, and citizens. According to Rwandan cosmogonic notions, the king was responsible for assuring the descent of *imaana* to the earth. According to d'Hertefelt and Coupez (1964:460), *imaana* refers to:

> a powerful quality, the dynamic principal of life and fecundity, which traditional Rwandans sought to appropriate by ritual techniques. In some cosmogonic tales, this same force is conceived of as a conscious volitional entity, that one could term Divinity. But no religion addresses itself to this anthropomorphic hypostasis precisely because the term *imaana* does not refer primarily to a personal being whom one must honor and supplicate, but a diffuse fluid that must captured. The quality of *imaana* is associated with a vast category of persons and objects through whose mediation traditional Rwandans thought they could tap its effects. *Imaana* was thought to invest certain trees and plants, royal residences and tombs, animals and objects used in divination, and protective talismans. Diviners, ritual specialists, and ancestral spirits were also believed to embody *imaana*. But, according to the concepts held by Rwandans, it is the king who is the supreme possessor of the fecundating fluid, *imaana*; the royal ritual is nothing else than the description of techniques which allow him to direct its effects to benefit the entire country.

Collective desire for the fertility of land, people, and livestock took precedence over all others and the king's role in assuring fertility was perceived as indispensable. Through the rituals prescribed by the dynastic code (*ubwiru*), the *mwami* presided over the descent of *imaana* from sky to earth. The king's power to accomplish this was contingent upon the degree to which he successfully embodied *imaana* and served as its conduit. This was manifest in his relation to liquids. As the foremost rainmaker for the kingdom, he risked his throne in the case of prolonged drought or in the case of flooding. He was expected to maintain ritual purity, eradicate impurity (*ishyano*), and to possess a body perceived to function adequately as a conduit for *imaana*. People within the kingdom thought to act as an impediment to *imaana*, "blocked beings," such as women who had reached child-bearing age without breast development (*impenebere*) or those who had never menstruated (*impa*), were the king's nemesis and it was his responsibility to eliminate them. Cattle and milk emanated from the king as *Imaana's* avatar on earth. Honey production depended upon his ritual intervention. Potency also invested the liquids of his body. His saliva was the kingdom's most important repository of divinatory *imaana* (de Heusch 1982:118). Special ritualists were charged with obtaining and guarding the royal saliva, then inserting it into the mouths of the sacrificial bulls used in divination. Power invested his semen, as can be seen from the numerous instances of ritual copulation in the royal rituals. Even when kings died, their bodies continued to possess *imaana* and to transfer this to Rwanda, for the royal tombs were located on a hill whose numerous streams coalesce to form the headwaters of the ritually important Nyabugogo River. As the kings' bodies dissolved, their *imaana* was recycled into the Nyabugogo, and it was these waters that were given to the royal cattle during the ritual of the "Watering" (Taylor 1988). Finally, potency invested the king's blood, for the *mwami* was ultimately the kingdom's sacrificial victim of last resort.

A sacrificial king, or a substitute for him, was called an *umutabazi* (liberator). This function was initiated by a Nyiginya forebear named Ruganzu Bwimba who chose to sacrifice himself in order to save Rwanda from conquest by the neighboring kingdom of Gisaka (Coupez and Kamanzi 1962:87–104). Bulls substituted for the king in ordinary court sacrifices. But there were moments of ritual danger so extreme that neither the blood of royal cattle nor the blood of ordinary mortals could keep open the conduit of beneficence between sky and earth. Such times were moments when the survival of the entire Rwandan polity was in question. In these instances diviners would determine who, among the royal coterie, should sacrifice himself for the good of Rwanda. Often the lot fell upon the king himself, for his blood was the most powerful. Spilling the royal blood upon enemy territory was thought to poison the territory for its inhabitants, rendering it easy prey to Rwandan conquest. In effect, the blood of an *umutabazi* would "buy" the land for Rwanda.

The effect of royal blood spilled in sacrifice thus resembled that of two accursed figures, *impenebere* (breastless women) and *impa* (mense-less women) whose blood when spilled upon enemy territory was thought to vitiate its fertility. In certain instances, therefore, the king could be considered the ultimate repository of *ishyano* (impurity). Some of this impurity resulted from the association between kingship and incest. For example, the earliest Rwandan kings, mythical kings of celestial origin, were said to have practiced brother-sister incest. This practice of hyper-endogamy kept the blood of royalty flowing within a closed circuit. It also precluded the possibility of outsiders sharing in the privileges of the elite. Later on, another mythical king, named Gihanga, instituted the practice of hyper-exogamy, by marrying women outside of his own celestial class. The first descendants of Gihanga continued this practice, by taking wives from the three autochthonous clans (*abasangwabutaka*): Zigaaba, Singa, and Gesera. Because of these exogamous kings, the blood of royal consanguinity began to flow in a more open manner (Taylor 1988). Ruganzu Bwimba ended this practice when his mother's brother, a Singa, refused to sacrifice himself for Rwanda despite having been chosen to do so by divination. To save Rwanda, Ruganzu Bwimba offered himself in his mother's brother's place; but shortly before his sacrificial death, he decreed that never again should potential Rwandan kings take wives from groups that were of autochthonous origin. As a result of this sudden disaffection between celestials and autochthones, the blood of royal consanguinity after Ruganzu Bwimba flowed once again within a closed circuit. Rwanda had definitively turned its back upon the possibility of equality between "celestials" and "autochthones."

The legend of Ruganzu Bwimba illustrates that the "celestial" Nyiginya had to face the problem of legitimating themselves to an already ensconced population. By intermarrying with these people, represented here by the autochthonous clans: Singa, Zigaaba, and Gesera, the Nyiginya could eventually claim enracination in the earth through kinship ties. However, in order to limit their privileged position to a restricted class, they eventually had to renounce their alliances with autochthones once their hold over the land was secure. In compensation for this reduction in the sharing of royal blood, Ruganzu Bwimba introduced the function of spilling the royal blood for the good of the entire Rwandan polity. This innovation may have been intended to place Rwandan kingship above the velleities of inter-clanic rivalry and alliances, but it also abstracted Rwandan kingship and the Rwandan polity, transforming the latter into something approaching a nation-state—an abstraction for which every citizen, following the example of the king, was supposed to be willing to sacrifice himself. The blood of Ruganzu Bwimba allegedly saved Rwanda from Gisaka,[1] but it also contributed to the creation of a collective Rwandan identity, one based upon the strict hierarchical-ethnic division of political privilege.

The Rwandan king's ritual responsibilities included those related to war and violence. Success in these endeavors was also dependent upon the degree to which the king adequately embodied *imaana*. Precolonial Rwanda was located in an area where there were other states. These states competed for the control of land and raided one another for livestock. War was thus a major preoccupation of the Rwandan state, and quite possibly one of its principal sustaining forces. Alliances between states were never respected for very long and some states seemed to be almost perpetually at war, such as Rwanda and Burundi. Yet all these states shared structurally similar institutions of sacred kingship and all of them performed rituals in which the occasional enactment of violence played an important role. Among the rituals of kingship for Rwanda, there were several that directly concerned warfare, such as the adornment of the royal drum with the genitals of slain enemies (d'Hertefelt and Coupez 1964). In other rituals of kingship not directly concerned with war, a ritual war might be fought against a neighboring polity in which a small number of the region's inhabitants would be seized and sacrificed.

The Violent Imaginary in the Modern Rwandan State: King Habyarimana—umutabazi?

The precipitating event that set off the Rwandan genocide was the killing of President Juvénal Habyarimana on 6 April 1994 when his private plane was shot down near Kigali airport by a shoulder-held surface-to-air missile. Although Habyarimana's government had been at war for almost four years with the Rwandan Patriotic Front (RPF), this event transformed the dynamics of hostilities from a tit-for-tat, attack-reprisal violence into genocide. This could be considered the war's shift from a symmetric schismogenic process (Bateson 1958) to an asymmetric one. Whereas the tacit dynamic underlying the violence had been: "We will get you back," overnight it became: "We will eliminate all of you." Preceding this shift, and to some degree catalyzing it, was the symbolism of kingship and *umutabazi* sacrifice.

No one has ever claimed responsibility for killing the president, but the two most credible hypotheses place the responsibility either on Hutu extremist members among Habyarimana's own followers or on members of the rebel group at the time, the Rwandan Patriotic Front. Felip Reyntjens, for example, once an adherent to the Hutu extremist thesis, has more recently given credence to the RPF thesis (Reyntjens 1999). Although I lean more in the direction of the Hutu extremist explanation, there is certainly merit to the RPF thesis as well. The death of President Habyarimana could have served the political interests of the extremists, just as it could have served the interests of the RPF. Many of the extremists, for example, were convinced that Habyarimana had become "soft" on Tutsi and that he needed to be replaced by someone more unequivocally "genocidaire"—the message conveyed in the cartoon. As for the RPF, they saw the president as an obstructionist who was delaying full implementation

Figure 1. Tutsi ingratitude.

"Habayarimana will die in March 1994" (*Kangura*, December 1993, no. 53, p. 3). *Kagame (top)*: On to Kigali. *Habyarimana (bottom)*: I've done everything I could to make you Tutsi happy. *Kagame:* Who asked you?

of the Arusha Accords and thus preventing their participation in a coalition government.[2]

In the two years preceding Habyarimana's death, the path was being prepared in Rwanda's print media for "king" sacrifice. At first we see hints of this in the opposition press and its portrayal of the president as a tyrannical or incompetent ruler that the country would do well to be rid of. Later, even Hutu extremists began to desert him, as is shown in the preceding cartoon from *Kangura*, a Hutu extremist magazine that predicted the president's death four months in advance! Rwandan journalists attacked the president in ways that constituted a radical departure from the timidity that had prevailed during the 1980s. This was due in part to democratization initiative, supported by France and other Western powers, that began during the late 1980s and to which Habyarimana and the MRND were forced to acquiesce in the early 1990s.[3] The press became free and open, but the sudden easing of restraints did not coincide with a corresponding rise in concern for journalistic standards. Innuendo, calumny, veiled and not so veiled, and calls for assassination characterized the printed and spoken media of the time (Chrétien 1996). More often than not, followers of the president who occupied many of the key positions in the national media, including control of the infamous "hate radio" station Radio Television Libre de Mille Collines (RTLM), used the weapons of fabrication and exaggeration against the president's perceived critics and rivals. The president's critics, however, were not above the occasional smear campaign, the use of obscenity, and the liberal use of disinformation (Chrétien 1996).

Comparing Habyarimana in the popular political literature to a traditional sacred king was not without irony, for the president was Hutu (all former kings had been Tutsi), and much of the avowed ideology of his party, the Mouvement Revolutionnaire National pour le Dévelopement et la Démocratie (MRND),[4] was anti-monarchist and, superficially at least, egalitarian. Yet, many depictions of President Habyarimana and other leading political figures in the popular literature (between 1990 and 1994) show the influence of the kingship institution. In hindsight, it is not difficult to perceive some equivalence between the Rwandan presidency and the country's former monarchy. When I began my first period of fieldwork in Rwanda in 1983, for example, I quickly became aware of the "cult of personality" surrounding President Habyarimana and the autocratic nature of his regime. At the time, Habyarimana was running for reelection and MRND party faithful were very busy campaigning. There was little chance of his losing the election, as he was running unopposed and the MRND, whose power base came largely from Habyarimana's home region of northwestern Rwanda, was the country's only authorized political party. Yet, the results of the 1983 elections strained the credulity of even uncritical observers: Habyarimana asked for and was reported to have won an incredible 99 percent of the vote. For many years afterward it seemed as if he and the MRND would hold power forever.

Rwanda was a closely controlled military dictatorship at the time, with very few people daring to raise a dissenting voice. Rarely did one hear a critical word being uttered against Habyarimana and the army's tight control of the Rwandan state. Those who did oppose the president in word or in deed usually found themselves in prison or victims of killings under mysterious circumstances. In the capital of Kigali, the presence of army and gendarmerie was pervasive. Commitment to the government was obligatory. Every Saturday morning people everywhere in Rwanda, especially employees of the state, but many others as well, would meet to participate in *umuganda*, community service. They would come with their shovels and hoes and fill in the ruts of dirt roads deeply gouged out by the rain; they would repair municipal buildings; they would plant trees. There was very little complaining. Even most Rwandan Tutsi during the 1980s supported Habyarimana, recalling the violence of 1973 when Habyarimana and the army stepped in, stopped the violence against Tutsi, and then took power from then President Kayibanda and his central and southern Hutu supporters.

At the time, adulation of Habyarimana was *de rigeur* for Rwandans; it was a key element in the enactment of their *civitas*. Virtually everyone had a portrait of the president hanging on a wall at home, and many wore the MRND party button on their shirt or blouse. On Wednesday afternoons, groups met to practice chants and skits in celebration of the Rwandan state, its overthrow of the Tutsi monarchy, its rejection of the *ubuhake* cattle contract signifying Hutu servitude to Tutsi,[5] and, most of all, to honor the country's president, Juvénal Habyarimana. Termed *animation,* it did not seem to bother anyone that these Wednesday afternoon get-togethers took people away from their jobs and did nothing to augment the country's gross domestic product. Even songs on the radio seemed to equate Rwanda, its beauty and relative prosperity, with the person of its president.

Of course, much of this adulation was self-interested. The state, with Habyarimana at its head, was the country's primary source of patronage. Showing support for it and its leader could never hurt your career. Even in contexts where there was nothing obvious to be gained, however, many people expressed their admiration of the country's president. Some people made comments about the appropriateness of Habyarimana's name, from the verb *kubyara* (to engender) and *imaana,* which together could be translated as "It is God who gives life." Nothing could have been more appropriate in a Catholic, anti-abortion, and basically pro-natalist culture;

and yet very few names could have at the same time resonated so well with the more "traditional" themes of fertility, prosperity, and good luck, manifestations of the "diffuse fecundating fluid." It seemed at the time, however, to hold true. During most of the 1980s, Rwanda was doing well economically (in comparison to neighboring states), and many Rwandans attributed this to the good stewardship of its president. The orchestrated affection for Habyarimana was part theater, certainly, but there were many who were sincere.

A close association between the country's fertility and prosperity and the person of the president is not the only way in which one can see the lingering influence of the representations of sacred kingship. Sometimes the assimilation of Habyarimana to a Rwandan sacred king was explicit; at other times it was more implicit, bordering on the unwitting. In many cases the association was intended to be flattering; in other instances, it was intended to be critical. We see the influence of the kingship institution in references to the country's rivers, the body, and violence.

Rivers

One reference to Rwanda's rivers with an explicit association to sacred kingship appeared in the popular political magazine *Zirikana*, in an article written by Bonaparte Ndekezi (1993) entitled "Habyarimana hagati ya Mukungwa na Nyabarongo." This magazine supported the viewpoint of the party known as the Coalition pour la Défense de la République, the infamous CDR, a party formed from extreme right-wing elements of the MRND and known for its anti-RPF stance and racist views against Tutsi (Chrétien 1995:386). Ndekezi, as well, was known for his extremism. The title of the article translates as "Habyarimana between the Mukungwa and the Nyabarongo" and refers to a river in northern Rwanda, the Mukungwa, and of course to central Rwanda's main river, the Nyabarongo, which in earlier times divided the Rwandan kingdom into two sacred halves. The article can be interpreted in several ways. At one level—and this is the theme that is most strongly advanced in the article—Habyarimana in 1993 finds himself in trouble and with little room to maneuver politically. The article goes on to describe Habyarimana as a good leader but, if anything, a little soft on his opponents, particularly the Tutsi-dominated RPF and the internal Hutu opposition. In other words, Habyarimana is in trouble because of his magnanimity in the face of his adversaries' treachery.

At another, less explicit level one could interpret Habyrimana's finding himself between the Mukungwa and the Nyabarongo as his being confined within the most sacred portion of his "kingdom"—the north, his natural constituency, that portion of Rwanda enclosed within the confines of the Mukungwa in the north and the Nybarongo in the center. Is the article subtly exhorting Habyarimana to be less of a peaceful, consolidating "king" and more of a warrior king? The article may carry a subtle warning to Habyarimana: "Leave the confines of your most sacred place, proceed southward, cross the Nyabarongo, and wage war! Otherwise, you will lose everything." The assertion that the author was thinking about earlier Rwanda, the days of sacred kingship, and about Habyarimana as a sacred king, is clear from one of the author's sentences: "At the level of authority, there is no difference between him [Habyarimana] and the former kings of traditional Rwanda, only the fact that he was not born clutching the *imbuto* (magic seeds of fertility) in his hand" (Chrétien 1995:4).

The allusion here to traditional Rwandan sacred kingship is interesting because it was intended to flatter Habyarimana. This is ironic, even paradoxical given its source, namely, the Hutu extremist Coalition pour la Défense de la République (CDR). After all, it was Rwandan Hutu who overthrew the monarchy in 1961. This apparent contradiction is diminished somewhat when we realize that the CDR was not really opposed to autocrats, dictators, or even monarchs as much as it was opposed to Tutsi and to the RPF. What the author appears to be saying is: "Habyarimana, a Hutu king, is every bit as worthy a king as his Tutsi predecessors; his only flaw is his reluctance to use the iron fist."

The Body and its Violation, or Adorning the Royal Drum

Rarely does one find ideological consistency among the various uses of kingship symbols before Habyarimana's assassination. About eighty popular journals, each with a different point of view, arose in the period between 1990 and 1994—quite extraordinary for a country with a population of about seven million. Some, but not all of these journals employed symbols of kingship, but it was more often the case that Hutu extremist journalists explicitly accused the Rwandan Patriotic Front of wanting to restore the monarchy, its trappings, and its rituals.[6] Routinely, Hutu extremist journalists referred to RPF members as "feudo-monarchists." Several of their cartoons recall the former custom of emasculating slain enemies and then using these body parts to adorn the royal drum. For example, in one cartoon from the extremist Hutu magazine *La Medaille-Nyiramacibiri*, RPF soldiers are depicted crucifying, impaling, and castrating Melchior Ndadaye, neighboring Burundi's first democratically elected Hutu president. Elected in October 1993, he was subsequently killed by Burundian Tutsi army officers in an abortive coup attempt.[7]

178 | Christopher Taylor

Figure 2. The assassination of Ndadaye.

Civilian RPF supporter (left): "Kill this stupid Hutu and after you cut off his genitals, hang them on our drum." *Ndadaye (center):* "Kill me, but you won't exterminate all the Ndadayes in Burundi." *Kagame (formerly RPF general, now President of Rwanda) (right):* "Kill him quickly. Don't you know that in Byumba and Ruhengeri we did a lot of work. With women, we pulled the babies out of their wombs; with men, we dashed out their eyes." *The drum:* "Karinga of Burundi."

In the annals of Rwandan Hutu extremism, very few images condense as much symbolic violence, and in so many ways, as this one. At one level, we see a clear iteration of the oft-repeated charge by Hutu extremists that the RPF were "feudo- monarchists" intent upon restoring kingship, the royal rituals, and the monarchy's principal emblem—the drum named Karinga. Another ideological claim is advanced by depicting Hutu victims of the RPF as Christlike martyrs, for Ndadaye is being crucified. Beneath these claims, however, another message touching on the imaginary is being conveyed. By impaling Ndadaye, the RPF torturers are turning his body into an obstructed conduit and, as such, are transforming his person into an inadequate, unworthy embodiment of *imaana*. In former times, Rwandans killed cattle thieves in this way (Taylor 1999: 136–140). At the ideological level, a synthesis has been forged in this cartoon between specifically Rwandan symbols possessing deep historical roots with those that are the more recent product of Christian evangelization, an appeal to two layers of Rwandan collective memory. More subtle, however, is the artist's appeal to the Rwandan imaginary, for it is as if the cartoonist were warning Hutu against insidious RPF a posteriori (il)logic: Ndadaye, as an obstructed conduit, merits his punishment.

Many references in the popular literature to the former kingship institution are ideologically motivated, and this accounts for the differences seen among the various Rwandan political factions in their depiction of Habyarimana and others. Other references cannot be explained solely as ideological, for they appeal to a deeper, more ontological level (Kapferer 1988). Indeed, the various Rwandan factions were contesting who would control the power of the state, but the contest was being waged through the mediation of a common body of symbols. Imagery of the king's body as conduit is where ideological motivation gives way to a realm of thought having to do with a specifically Rwandan way of imagining the body as a being in time and space, a being that acts as the focal point of physiological and social processes redolent with cosmological import—a being through which *imaana* should pass in its descent from sky to earth. Although the following cartoon, like the preceding one, manifests the symbolic pattern of "body as conduit," it adds to the instantiation of the pattern, its negation. Here, Hutu opponents of Habyarimana portray his body as a conduit that turns all flows back upon itself.

Much is concentrated in this illustration. At an ideological level, Habyarimana and his MRND and CDR followers are clearly being equated to cattle thieves. His wearing of banana leaves around his waist and underneath his MRND cap suggests savagery, possible association with Twa foragers (*batwa mpunyu*), and even participation in the Rwandan occult religious practice known as *kubandwa*, something that many Rwandan Christians would have considered atavistic in a modern leader. It is also quite obvious that, according to his detractors, the president is a man who eats shit. There are other ideological elements in this illustration. What serves as Habyarimana's latrine in the picture is Rwanda and its hapless population. The spoon that we see him moving from beneath his anus

180 | Christopher Taylor

Figure 3. "The politics of the cattle thieves causes problems" cartoon from *Umurangi*, no. 14, 10 December 1992.

MURI MRND BAKOMEJE KWITUMA KU MBEHE BAKIRIRAMO NO MU MAZI BAKIVOMA.

Politiki y'abashimusi b'inka idukozeho.

The headline reads, "In the MRND they continue to excrete on the plate from which they eat and into the water from which they drink." At left, an Interahamwe youth[8] holds up a severed leg and says, "Let's kill them, let's get rid of them, let's eat them." Habyarimana replies, "Yes, let's descend on them all right." To his right, one CDR man and another who is MRND exclaim sarcastically, "In the Rwanda of peace, there sure is a lot of delicious food." Beneath the cartoon are the words, "The politics of the cattle thieves causes problems."

and about to place in his mouth is labeled "taxes." The Rwandan people's taxes are swallowed by Habyarimana, excreted by Habyarimana, only to be swallowed by him again. Only if you are a follower of his are you likely to get anything to eat, as with these CDR and MRND party members who manage to grab the occasional severed limb or errant turd.

However, there are other elements in this illustration that are less directly ideological, and some that are not even logical in the ordinary sense. If taxes are like excrement and Habyarimana eats his own excrement, then wouldn't the country be spared the filth? Maybe, but notice that Habyarimana reverses the flow of beneficence. Instead of it descending downward from the sky, passing through his body and then to earth and people, it moves from below to above, from people to ruler. Once there, most of it is continually recycled in a sterile closed circuit within his body. What little passes through him gets gobbled up by his lackeys. At the imaginary level, a sentiment is being adumbrated that is more profound than the ideological message concerning Habyarimana's egoistic "politics of the belly." This sentiment concerns Habyarimana's adequacy, or more correctly his inadequacy, to serve as a proper conduit of *imaana*. Instead of a body capable of performing "open circuit flow," King Habyarimana's body performs "closed circuit flow," whatever leaves his body, reenters it. Instead of a good alliance partner, a giver and not simply a receiver of gifts, Habyarimana is an unabashed taker, the embodiment of *ishyano* (ritual impurity). He is not a worthy king. Even if all kings partake of the wild through incest and murder, this is too much: Habyarimana is a savage among the civilized. The cartoons seem to be saying—and at a level beneath, yet more powerful than the ideological—"Habyarimana must be sacrificed."

Conclusion

In this chapter I have tried to show that despite the changes brought in the wake of colonialism, Christian evangelization, and postcolonial independence, there were lines of continuity in the conceptualization of war and the state between the premodern period when Rwanda was led by a sacred king and the modern period when the state was headed by a military dictator, President Juvénal Habyarimana. These lines of continuity can be discerned through an analysis of the Rwandan imaginary as this is accessible in visual and verbal representations of the president and other political figures that appeared in the popular media during the pre-genocidal years between 1990 and 1994.

I have gone against the trend that views the state primarily as an apparatus of power productive of individual subjectivities, which must then either acquiesce to the unwelcome hegemony of the state or resist it. Analyses of the state that situate power at their center tend to reproduce Western ontological assumptions of being and personhood, positing the individual as a maximizer of utility and the collectivity as a regulator of the ensuing competition. These analyses privilege the level of the discursive and tend to neglect the level of the imaginary. Although they are necessary, they do not bring us to a full understanding of non-Western states and their performance of violence. We cannot fully understand the state, even the state as a wielder of power and destructive force, without understanding the ontological bases and cosmological determinants in which power is embedded, deployed, and interpreted. State rituals offer a means of access into this domain.

One of the central cosmological notions of premodern Rwandan society was that of *imaana*, translated variously as a "diffuse, fecundating fluid," "supreme being," or, more generally, as diverse forms of potency thought to invest certain people, objects, and substances and to insure fertility and prosperity. The diffuse and labile qualities of this notion attest to its imaginary rather than discursive properties. The most important human embodiment of *imaana* was the Rwandan sacred king or *umwami*. Understanding *imaana* requires understanding the rituals of sacred kingship and their emphasis on liquids and their movement. These include rainfall, rivers, milk, and honey and bodily fluids important in life and reproduction: blood, semen, and breast milk.

Perturbations in fluid flows were to be avoided. One of the sacred king's responsibilities was to catalyze, direct, and control them. In effect, acting as the human focal point of the polity, seen as cosmological process, the king made flows of beneficence tangible and visible. The king's body functioned as a synecdoche; he was the part of the whole that resembled the whole. His body was *imaana's* conduit in its descent from sky to earth. Yet, it was also the king who ran the risk of being perceived as the defective part in the whole responsible for complete cessation of beneficial flows in times of crisis, in which case he might be judged to be an inadequate embodiment of *imaana* and thus a candidate for elimination. Nevertheless, collective remembering of such events in dynastic histories usually followed the model of *umutabazi* sacrifice, where tragedy and defeat would be masked and the elimination of the sovereign would subsequently appear as a selfless and heroic death.

During its history the Rwandan state has had to come to grips with a number of tensions and contradictions: 1) gift sociality versus commodity sociality, 2) hierarchical holism (autocracy) versus notions of egalitarian individualism (democracy), and 3) negotiable versus hereditarian notions of ethnicity. In this process, a state based on military dictatorship replaced one based on sacred kingship. However, judging from the iconography of Rwandan popular media in the years before the genocide, the Rwandan imaginary has not been completely effaced: ontological notions and elements of a premodern cosmology coexist with the forces of modernity and globalization. We see this synthesis in the person of President Habyarimana and in the intimation that he was to become, like some sacred kings of the past, an *umutabazi*. We also perceive this in the media's move toward the veiled accusation that Habyarimana had become an inadequate "king"—a sovereign who reverses flows, retains beneficence within, and obstructs that which should pass through him. As an impediment to the descent of *imaana*, he became a candidate for elimination. Once sacrificed, however, he became a martyr to the Hutu extremist cause.

In all this we see the lingering force of the Rwandan imaginary and the encompassment of power by Rwandan cosmological and ontological notions that preexisted power's incarnation in the form of war and genocide. Power, then, even in its most obvious manifestation—that which grows from the barrel of a gun—was in this instance subsumed by other notions. A war of meaning was waged in the Rwandan popular media before the genocide in which virtually every possible ideological voice received expression. Yet, the dissension among these voices was contingent upon a common body of shared imaginary understandings. The iconic symbols that served as the vehicles of these understandings were not the simple instruments of power to be carried into battle like flags or emblems; their role was more fundamental. They provided both the base from which power was imagined and the interpretive matrix by which specific actions were judged as either powerful or impotent. As other instances of war show—like the U.S. invasion of Iraq, perhaps—the nature of power may seem obvious to those who believe they are wielding it, but its longer term effects are always lived, experienced, and interpreted through local systems of meaning; and it is ultimately these meanings that define what is powerful and what is not.

Notes

1. Although many of the legends recounting this event hail Ruganzu Bwimba's sacrifice as one that saved Rwanda from Gisaka, it was really a Rwandan defeat in which the king was killed and the Rwandan throne was taken over by Gisaka (Vansina 1962).
2. According to the Arusha accords of August 1993, a wide-based transitional government consisting of representatives from all the major opposition parties and the RPF was to be put in place. In the early months of 1994, several attempts were made to install this government but these were thwarted on every occasion by the nonparticipation of one group or another. The perception on the part of the RPF was that President Habyarimana's reluctance to have the accords implemented was the reason for this.
3. The democratization initiative pushed by Western powers during the late 1980s and 1990s also touched Rwanda. Realizing that it would have to open its political system in order to continue receiving aid from Western donors, Rwanda allowed other political parties besides the MRND to come into existence, although most power continued to reside with the president and his party. Many different political parties quickly saw the light of day, but the principal ones besides the MRND were the Mouvement Démocrate Républicain (MDR), the Parti Libéral (PL), and the Parti Social Démocrate (PSD). In an effort to confuse the situation and to use multi-partyism to its advantage, the MRND created offshoot parties that were in effect clones of itself, such as the Parti Ecologiste.

The CDR party, Coalition pour la Défense de la République, was an MRND splinter party that was more openly anti-Tutsi and anti-RPF than the MRND. Later in the 1990s, President Habyarimana and other Hutu extremists managed to split off anti-RPF factions from the MDR and the PL parties that became known as "Hutu Powa" (Hutu power) factions. Many later supporters of the genocide were recruited from the "Hutu Powa" groups.
4. The Mouvement Revolutionnaire pour le Développement or MRND changed its name in 1991 to Mouvement Revolutionnaire pour le Développement et la Démocratie after multiparty democracy was authorized in Rwanda. It retained the acronym MRND.
5. The term *ubuhake* refers to the patron-client relationship whereby the patron or *umushebuja* gives a cow to a client or *umugaragu*. All the female offspring of the cow must be returned to the *umushebuja*, but the *umugaragu* may drink the cow's milk and keep all its male offspring. Moreover, the *umugaragu* is expected to serve his *umushebuja* by occasionally providing him with labor or other service. Although it was not impossible for Hutu to become wealthy in cattle and to engage other Hutu as clients, the more frequent arrangement was a Tutsi patron with many Hutu clients. Because *ubuhake* favored patrons more than clients, it became a symbol of Tutsi oppression.
6. As part of the Arusha accords, the RPF was allowed to station one battalion of its troops in Kigali in order to protect its political representatives. Although the first violent incidents that followed the President's assassination were against prominent Hutu opponents of the genocide and some individual Tutsi, the RPF garrison was attacked early on 7 April 1994. It then asked and received permission from the United Nations Mission to Rwanda to leave the confines of its garrison in order to defend itself.
7. Melchior Ndadaye was Burundi's first democratically elected president and first Hutu president. Elected in June 1993, Ndadaye was taken prisoner in late October and then executed (not by impalement) by Burundian Tutsi army officers in a coup attempt. Almost universally condemned by other nations, the coup eventually failed, but not before it had provoked reprisal killings in which thousands of Tutsi civilians died and counter-reprisal violence in which thousands of Hutu were killed. The coup and Ndadaye's death served the cause of Hutu extremism in Rwanda quite well and extremists lost no time in exploiting it. Unfortunately the extremists' point that the Tutsi could never be trusted as partners in a democracy gained enormous credibility in Rwanda in the wake of Ndadaye's tragic death.
8. Interahamwe means "those who attack together." Most Rwandan political parties had youth wings and for the MRND party (the party in power at the time of the genocide), theirs was the Interahamwe. Recruited largely from among un- or under-employed young males who had drifted into Rwandan cities, the Interahamwe received political and arms training from MRND party officials, Rwandan Government soldiers, and possibly also from French military advisors. Practically every urban neighborhood possessed at least one Interahamwe member, and in the rural areas, every hillside. They aided the pre-genocidal apparatus in keeping regularly updated lists of all Rwandan opposition party members and all Tutsis. Before the outbreak of whole scale massacres, the Interahamwe intimidated people on their lists with actual or threatened violence and extorted "protection" money from some of them. Even before the genocide Interahamwe were occasionally given authorization to set up roadblocks and to rob, beat, and sometimes kill the people they had trapped, or to steal or damage their vehicles. On two occasions I narrowly avoided being trapped in such a roadblock, and on one of these occasions bricks hit my vehicle just beneath the windshield. On another occasion, at a small barrier consisting merely of a motor bike straddling a Kigali back street, a Tutsi friend of mine and I were caught and hassled for twenty minutes or so by a group of Interahamwe and in the presence of two Rwandan police officers. After lengthy negotiations with the police officers, who were probably nonplussed by the presence of a foreigner, the Interahamwe released my friend although not before they had cut him

slightly near the eye. During the genocide, Interahamwe weapons of choice were the machete, the nail-studded wooden club, and the grenade.

Bibliography

Abrams, Philip. 1988. "Notes on the Difficulty of Studying the State," *Journal of Historical Sociology*, 1(1): 58–89.
Aijmer, Göran. 2000. "Introduction: The Idiom of Violence in Imagery and Discourse," in Göran Aijmer and Jon Abbink (eds). *Meanings of Violence*. Oxford: Berg Press, pp. 1–21.
Anderson, Benedict. 1991. *Imagined Communities*. London: Verso.
Bateson, Gregory. 1958. *Naven*. Stanford: Standford University Press.
Bourdieu, Pierre. 1977. *Outline of a Theory of Practice*. Cambridge: Cambridge University Press.
Chretien, Jean-Pierre (ed). 1995. *Rwanda: Les Médias du Genocide*. Paris: Karthala.
Clastres, Pierre. 1974. *La Société contre l'État*. Paris: Les éditions de minuit.
Coupez, André and Théoneste Kamanzi. 1962. *Récits Historiques Rwanda*. Tervuren: Musée Royal de l'Afrique Centrale, Annales, Série in-8o, Sciences Humaines, no. 43.
Foucault, Michel. 1977. *Discipline and Punish: the Birth of the Prison*. New York: Vintage Books.
Godelier, Maurice. 1996. *L'énigme du Don*. Paris: Fayard.
d'Hertefelt, Marcel and André Coupez. 1964. *La Royauté Sacrée de l'Ancien Rwanda*. Tervuren: Musée Royal de l'Afrique Centrale, Annales, Série in-8o, Sciences Humaines, no. 52.
d'Hertefelt, Marcel. 1971. *Les Clans du Rwanda Ancien*. Tervuren: Musée Royal de l'Afrique Centrale, Annales, Série in-8o, Sciences Humaines, no. 70.
de Heusch, Luc. 1966. *Le Rwanda et la Civilisation Interlacustre*. Brussels: Université Libre de Bruxelles.
———. 1982. *Rois Nés d'un Coeur de Vache*. Paris: Gallimard.
———. 1985. *Sacrifice in Africa*. Manchester: Manchester University Press.
Jacob, Irenée. 1984. "Dictionnaire Rwandais-Français: Extrait du dictionnaire de l'Institut National de Recherche Scientifique." Kigali.
Kagame, Alexis. 1947. "Le Code Ésotérique de la Dynastie du Rwanda," *Zaire*, I(4): 364–386.
Kapferer, Bruce. 1988. *Legends of People, Myths of State*. Washington, D.C.: Smithsonian Institution Press.
Linden, Ian. 1977. *Church and Revolution in Rwanda*. New York: Manchester University Press.
Louis, Roger. 1963. *Ruanda-Urundi, 1884–1919*. Oxford (UK): Clarendon Press.
Mamdani, Mahmood. 2001. *When Victims Become Killers: Colonialism, Nativism and the Genocide in Rwanda*. Princeton: Princeton University Press.
Maquet, Jacques. 1954. *Le Système des Relations Sociales dans le Ruanda Ancien*. Tervuren: Musée Royal de l'Afrique Centrale.
Nahimana, Ferdnand. 1993. *Le Rwanda: Emergence d'un État*. Paris: Karthala.
Ndekezi, Bonaparte. 1993. "Habyarimana hagati ya Mukungwa na Nyabarongo," *Zirikana*, 30 January 1993, 4–6.
Omaar, Rakiya and Alex de Waal (eds). 1994. *Rwanda: Death, Despair and Defiance*. London: African Rights.
Ortner, Sherry. 1995. "Resistance and the Problem of Ethnographic Refusal," *Comparative Studies in Society and History* 37(1): 173–93.
Prunier, Gerard. 1995. *The Rwanda Crisis: History of a Genocide*. New York: Columbia University Press.
Radcliffe-Brown, A.R. 1970 [1940]. "Preface," in M. Fortes and E.E. Evans-Pritchard (eds), *African Political Systems*. London: Oxford University Press, pp. xi–xxiii.

Reyntjens, Felip. 1999. *La guerre des Grands Lacs: Alliances Mouvantes et Conflits Extraterritoriaux en Afrique Centrale*. Paris: Harmattan.

Sahlins, Marshall. 2000 [1996]. "The Sadness of Sweetness: or, The Native Anthropology of Western Cosmology," in Marshall Sahlins, *Culture in Practice*. New York: Zone Books, pp. 527–584.

———. 2000 [1972]. "The Original Affluent Society," in Marshall Sahlins, *Culture in Practice*. New York: Zone Books, pp. 95–138.

Smith, Pierre. 1970. "La Forge de l'Intelligence," *L'Homme* X(2): 5–21.

———. 1975. *Le Récit Populaire au Rwanda*. Paris: Armand Colin.

———. 1979. "L'efficacité des Interdits," *L'Homme* XIX(1): 5–47.

Strathern, Marilyn. 1988. *The Gender of the Gift*. Berkeley: University of California Press.

Taylor, Christopher. 1988. "Milk, Honey, and Money: Changing concepts of pathology in Rwandan popular medicine," Ph.D. Dissertation. Charlottesville: University of Virginia.

———. 1992. *Milk, Honey, and Money*. Washington, D.C.: Smithsonian Institution Press.

———. 1999. *Sacrifice as Terror*. Oxford (UK): Berg Press.

Trouillot, M-R. 2001. "The Anthropology of the State in the Age of Globalization," *Current Anthropology* 42(1): 1–24.

Vansina, Jan. 1967. "L'évolution du Royaume Rwandais des Origine B 1900," *Cahiers Internationaux de Sociologie* XLIII: 143–158.

———. 1983. "Is Elegance Proof? Structuralism and African History," *History in Africa* 10: 307–348.

———. 2000. *L'Histoire du Royaume Nyiginya*. Paris: Karthala.

Wagner, Roy. 1986. *Symbols that Stand for Themselves*. Chicago: Chicago University Press.

Chapter Eight

THE PARAMILITARY FUNCTION OF TRANSPARENCY
Guatemala and Colombia

Staffan Löfving

This chapter revolves around clandestine state violence in allegedly democratizing polities seeking their way from war to peace through implementing liberal modes of governance. More precisely, it traces the process in which paramilitarism resolves the contradiction between liberal and authoritarian practices of both law and violence in Colombia and Guatemala, and it offers a sketch toward the conceptualization of that same process.

"Transparency" occupies a particular place in this discussion. Its magic resides in a promise to make the law visible, or accessible, and thereby the disobedience of power holders to the law exposed, not allowing relations of clientelism or corruption to prevail or emerge. But the impunity of the past is more than merely lurking in the shadows in still highly militarized and quasi-democratic states of Latin America. Impunity still positions the agents of power above the law, striving to make the law invisible or inaccessible to citizens. In direct contrast, *the violence* of such regimes was notoriously ever present, excessively visible, or "spectacular." In this chapter I will combine a focus on law in the promotion of transparency with a focus on violence, also because the liberal model of openness, disclosure, and accountability—again in diametrical contrast to authoritarian states of impunity—goes hand in hand with attempts to hide the state's potential for and actual practice of violence. The nontransparent prison cell,

---

Notes for this chapter are located on page 206.

and the right to imprison, has become the paradigmatic example of state violence in neoliberal democracies.[1] They thus display authoritarianisms' inverse image of transparency in relation to *both* violence and law—where one is disclosed, the other is not; where one is concealed, the other is not. I suggest that such juxtaposition enables us to explore paramilitarism in Latin America (and potentially elsewhere) as a function of an unresolved contradiction of two political models and practices that operate with notions of visibility and clandestinity through a political and social game of transparency. Contrary to what the champions of liberal democratization are arguing for both Colombia and Guatemala, transparency is not undermining, let alone contributing to a replacement of the authoritarian model, but, instead, is providing the latter with an image of being in a process of teleological change, thereby bringing a more profound or open (to use metaphors from liberal jargon) political process to a deadlock.[2]

Paramilitarism also needs some conceptual elaboration before we move on. The *para* prefix signifies a going beyond, to one side, or aside from. The paramilitary is a private force working along with, or in place of, a regular military organization, often as a semiofficial or secret auxiliary. This secrecy, the clandestine, hidden nature of the paramilitary phenomenon is muddled by the medical or pathological connotations of the *para* prefix, namely, the functionally disabled, the abnormal, the *parafunctional*. This latter connotation would imply that more than merely working alongside the regular army, the paramilitaries are indeed beyond it, yet connected to it—a paradox signalling a serious disruption of the political-military division of labor and power in modern statecraft. My aim here is to combine the two connotations and show how paramilitarism in Colombia and Guatemala has been central to the continuous exercise of state power, and yet how recent developments are generating new non-state legalities and sovereignties in which the paramilitary agent is a key player. To be able to do this, the text will move between locations and different levels of analysis. It will first explore how the justifications of illegitimate violence in the context of "the war on terror" play out in relation to both state and imperial power. In the following section I then trace paramilitary rule in peace back to the experiences of army atrocities in and around a Guatemalan massacre. I also extend the discussion on the perpetual shifting from open to hidden state repression, a process which is compared in the subsequent section to the violent ramifications of decentralization reforms in Colombia and the corporate dimension, or logic, of the paramilitary regime. In the final section, I follow the trail of economy and suggest an anthropological approach to the kind of volatile relationships that emerged in both countries between disarmed and disempowered paramilitaries and their patron states.

The Transparent Walls of Abu Ghraib

Established on the initiative of a World Bank official in 1993, the organization Transparency International has now achieved planetary reach, present in more than ninety mostly low income countries. It deals primarily in the assessment of corruption in accordance with the OECD anti-bribery convention and of both government and private sector compliance with different policy commitments and international conventions. The strategy it promotes is aimed at making government processes like procurement, privatization, and election financing "visible" to both national and international audiences. Such an engagement with the ethics of both economic and political transaction means that it now works alongside Human Rights Watch and Amnesty International to implement a transnational norm of governance centered on the very notion of transparency. A dominant intellectual discourse embraces this development and outlines a new paradigm. The unregulated flow of information, it is argued, on topics ranging from corporate and government practice to nuclear proliferation, provides new and effective ways to hold power holders accountable. Transparency is emerging on a global scale, according to this view, thanks to the recent and dramatic breakthroughs in information technology (see, e.g., Finel and Lord 2002; Florini 2003; Holzner and Holzner 2006).[3]

The events in 2004 in the U.S.-administered Iraqi prison of Abu Ghraib come to mind when considering the role of technology in transparency and power. Writes Susan Sontag:

> The media may self-censor but, as Rumsfeld acknowledged, it's hard to censor soldiers overseas, who don't write letters home, as in the old days, that can be opened by military censors who ink out unacceptable lines. Today's soldiers instead function like tourists, as Rumsfeld put it, "running around with digital cameras and taking these unbelievable photographs and then passing them off, against the law, to the media, to our surprise." (Sontag 2004:40)

At the time, the U.S. administration's openness as to the dilemma of being obliged to follow internationally imposed rules in warfare indeed pointed at a new imperial development in which the need for paramilitary violence was diminishing owing to the superpower's self-imposed right to declare international treaties and agreements illegitimate. Secretary Rumsfeld's apparent bewilderment in the face of undisciplined American soldiers in Iraq concerned what was then only the most recent problem in a series that he and his advisors had been successfully solving since the war on terror began, and the Bush administration's gradual redefinition of torture did undercut the legal significance of the United States' obligations under the Geneva Convention (Hersh 2004; Priest and Smith 2004).

In a similar vein, Susan Sontag critiques the president's right in the context of the new U.S. doctrine of an endless war on terror to declare prisoners "unlawful combatants." This was a policy enunciated by Rumsfeld for Taliban and al Qaeda prisoners already in January 2002. Rumsfeld then stated that "'technically' they 'do not have any rights under the Geneva Convention'" (Sontag 2004:40).

Even though "global transparency" might be the catchphrase of the moment, neither the growth of a superintending legal system, restricting the doings of sovereign nation-states, nor mechanisms such as human rights monitoring organizations and "un-embedded" journalism for unveiling the covered contempt of international jurisdiction, are particularly new phenomena. The Geneva Convention itself is an attempt at making sovereign state power transparent, and it has been followed by numerous treaties and the establishment of international tribunals and courts that together build up an international system. In this chapter, I will argue that the paramilitary phenomenon emerges in both state and business *responses to* such external control, lying at the interface of prevailing structures of sovereign power and the forces at work for assessing accountability on a global level. The case of Rumsfeld's enemies—the unlawful combatants—is an inverse image of paramilitarism, since the problem of how to effectively eliminate their threat without having to face legal consequences can be solved by a removal, not only of the state's own agents as in the case of the military contracting of private companies (see Davis and Pereira 2003) but also of *the enemy* from the legal domain of legitimate soldiers (killable or detainable) and civilians (protectable or suable).

The paramilitary phenomenon, its growth and demise, is also key to an understanding of the elasticity or changeableness of the relationship between state, corporate power, and empire. Susan Sontag observed that "the meaning of these [torture] pictures [at the Abu Ghraib prison in Iraq] is not just that these acts were performed, but that their perpetrators apparently had no sense that there was anything wrong in what the pictures show" (2004:40). The perceived movement of the victim down the scale of human value makes extralegal and paramilitary violence legitimate in the eyes of many, and makes the paramilitary force a more open agent, eventually, as in the Colombian case discussed below, resembling the state itself. As in the ongoing war in Iraq, the transformation of what used to be hidden into overt techniques of punishment and humiliation could be used as a measuring rod when grappling analytically with the violent practices that themselves produce state agents and thereby predate a state in the making (see Gill 2004; Žižek 2004).

So, in order to challenge the claim that transparency constitutes a new paradigm in itself, let me explore its trajectory in regions where authoritarian states have long been struggling to contain their exercise of political power within a closed sphere free from a monitoring externality. Rather than portraying transparency as the salvation of the world from corrupted Third World regimes, my take strives for an understanding of paramilitary violence in a context of economic restructurings and political decentralization encouraged or enforced by agents of global governance (see Bates 2001; Cramer 2006).

The Guatemalan atrocities of the early 1980s aimed at annihilating the Other within—the indigenous who had turned into a threat in the shape of an armed insurrection. This combination of being disposable ("the Indian") and feared ("the rebel") embodied by the Guatemalan majority, was, as I have argued elsewhere, what unleashed the Guatemalan mayhem (see Löfving 2002). But paramilitary violence—death squad killings and counterinsurgency performed by the paramilitary civil defense patrols—even though practiced in the 1960s (Schirmer 1998:83), took on significantly new proportions during the democratization process of the 1980s, and it informed the peace process of the following fifteen years when the survival of the authoritarian state rested on its ability to *appear* democratic by delegating the act of killing to semisecret auxiliaries.

The Colombian process differs in many ways, even though a politics of fear based on excessive state and paramilitary violence is a notorious feature in both countries. Colombia's paramilitary forces have grown considerably stronger and more autonomous than their Guatemalan counterparts ever did, effectively becoming party to the negotiations with the state, and in fact taking the place of the insurgency at the negotiating table. However, it is the similarities that will concern me here. The Colombian paramilitary phenomenon, in its present shape, can be traced back to the transformations of the 1960s and 1980s when the state administration's move in democratic directions provoked a mobilization of a corporate sector that had found its power and privileges threatened (Romero 2000, 2003a, 2003b; Avilés 2006). Such a shape shifting of violence in response to political transformations also occurred in Guatemala to where this story now turns.

Disposable People and the Power of Instigating Fear

In archaic Roman law, the figure of *homo sacer* embodied "bare life"—bare since it was positioned beyond or "before" the law and could be taken by anyone without guilt of homicide, without accountability (Agamben 1998). "Homo sacer ... is the person who can be *killed but not sacrificed*" (Das and Poole 2004:11; see also Kapferer 2004:6–8). In Agamben's account, state sovereignty is exercised as much over life and death as over territory through the state privilege of declaring people "killable" by means of legislation (cf. Fitzpatrick 2001). Concentration camps represent the paradigmatic example in this discussion, but it has also come to include the ways in which the laws of sovereign states, by assessing rights and obligations of citizenry, redefine and thereby exclude categories of people such as "the refugee" and "the terrorist" (see, e.g., Žižek 2002). In response to an emergent civil rights movement in Guatemala, embodied by peasant leagues, trade unions, and radical church groups in the 1970s, the military government unleashed an open repression based on the conception of certain people as being killable *without guilt of homicide*. The Guatemalan massacres of people conceived of as disposable stand in opposition to paramilitary violence in a now increasingly transparent polity.

In present-day Guatemala, so called parallel or hidden powers (Sieder et al. 2002) operate with a maintained force and constitute viable agents of political life, exercising pressure on the government, on media, and on investors, not to mention, of course, on domestic human rights activists and grass root organizations. Their connection to sectors of the army, the business elite, and the state is well documented (see Peacock and Beltrán 2003; Beltrán 2007). In order to understand their power in "peacetime," I will now return to the Guatemalan war that officially ended in December 1996. Parts of the following event were revealed to me when I conducted fieldwork in Guatemala in the 1990s, and other parts were told to the Guatemalan Truth and Reconciliation Commission (henceforth the CEH)[4] by witnesses to the Chel massacre:

At eight o'clock in the morning, on 3 April 1982, when most of the men had left home for work in the fields, soldiers in army uniforms entered the remote mountain village of Chel. They had been marching from their base at the nearby estate—*finca* La Perla—and well inside the village they stopped those they met, ordering them not to leave. Then they went from house to house and ordered people to assemble in front of the town hall. Some were dragged; others decided to play along and walked freely. When about a hundred villagers were gathered, the commander gave a talk in which he urged people to point out the guerrillas. Out of fear or loyalty or both, or simply because those on active guerrilla duty were not around, no one said anything, which provoked the cry from the commander: "You yourselves are true guerrillas!" (CEH vol. VII p. 66). Then, the soldiers separated men from women. They locked the men up in the mayor's offices and the women in the school. In secrecy, two soldiers released six— children and adolescents—who escaped and hid on the outskirts of the village. From their hideout, the youngsters observed what happened to their relatives and neighbors. The men were deprived of their IDs and ordered to lie down on the floor. At the same time, the soldiers in the school picked out fourteen young women, whom they took to the church, where a rape continued for more than one hour. The others were taken, five at a time, to the elevated bridge at the entrance of the village. Some six to eight meters below, a wild current of water creating a stream that continues for a hundred meters surrounds the bare rocks. People were now ordered to strip, and then the killing began.

The Guatemalan Truth Commission estimates that ninety-five Chel villagers were massacred this day. The killing lasted from eleven o'clock in the morning to two o'clock in the afternoon. In the meantime, one group of soldiers completed the destruction of the village by burning houses and crops, and killing the animals.

Surviving villagers dug two graves at the cemetery; they dumped forty-nine bodies into the first and ten into the second. Six bodies were buried by the side of the river, while an estimated thirty disappeared in the current. Two women survived the fall and were found by the rebels the following day.

Upon return to the village, the guerrillas presented the survivors with two alternatives. They could either join them or leave the region and rely on the mercy of the army. Most followed the rebels, but some fifty decided not to trust either of the armed groups. They settled in the mountains close to the village of Xesaí, where the barking of their dogs and the smoke of their fires soon revealed their location to the army. Nineteen days after the massacre in Chel, on 22 April, a band of soldiers opened fire on the group. Two fled the attack and survived, and three have not been found. The survivors returned the following day to bury forty-five corpses.

In 1977 Chel, then host to approximately five hundred families, saw the arrival of the EGP—the Guerrilla Army of the Poor. The insurgent mobilization followed the customary pattern of initial encounters with individuals in the mountains surrounding the village. These contacts soon developed into meetings in smaller groups within the community at night (Löfving 2002, 2005). The Truth Commission reports on an ambivalent attitude among the villagers toward the guerrillas. Some allied with the insurgents, while some rejected their petitions for food and services. However, in 1979 EGP had formed between twenty and twenty-five revolutionary nuclei in Chel, administered by what was called the Local Clandestine Committee.

Motivated by the rumors of guerrilla presence in the region, the army established a temporary camp close by in the *finca* La Perla in 1979. The following year EGP stepped up the heat by executing a male nurse and a butcher in the village, both accused by the rebels of opposing guerrilla presence, and later the military commissioner of Chel. The military presence at La Perla became a permanent camp in 1981.

The April massacre in 1982 was not an isolated occurrence in the area. The Guatemalan Truth Commission reveals the structure of the killings: On 23 March of the same year, the army massacred ninety-six workers at the *finca* Estrella Polar. To this was added the execution of thirteen villagers in Juá and forty-five in Xesaí the same month. About one hundred people in the Ixil village of Ilom were shot to death, and thirty-four were killed in the *finca* Covadonga in April. The killing subsided in May with some ten victims in the village of Jaqchixlá. The sweep was part of what was described in military circles as "Plan Victoria 82," especially focused on the northern part of the *municipio* of Chajul. The strategy was spelled out in military documents. The purpose was to "destroy the Local Clandestine Committees (CCL) and the Permanent Military Units (UMP) of the enemy," and the means were to "localize, capture and destroy subversive groups or elements" (Plan Victoria 82, paragraphs II and IV). That these elements were unarmed civilians followed the logic of the doctrine of elimination of the rebels' popular support. The locals did not know the perpetrators within the military (as opposed to the future perpetrators within the paramilitary civil patrols). They belonged to the Mariscal Zavala Brigade based in Guatemala City but remain anonymous in the report of the Truth Commission.

Groups of forensic anthropologists exhumed the mass graves in Chel in 1997 and found the remains of a total of sixty bodies. They concluded that the overwhelming majority of the victims were female. Close to half of the massacred were children from newly born to ten years of age.

From the mid-1980s until the withdrawal of the army in 1997 and the disarmament of the guerrillas the same year, Chel marked the beginning of the army-controlled area for rebel-loyal villagers leaving for market or further travels to the capital. I conducted anthropological fieldwork in these villages, peopled by guerrillas and former rebels, displaced persons some of whom had both roots and relatives in Chel. My purpose then was the study not of paramilitarism but of the social organization of counterpower. Tensions in the area were striking, however, and conversations were filled with graphic details about the Chel paramilitaries' harassment and the countermeasures of the guerrillas on "our side" of the frontline. In such a situation, it was difficult to come to terms with the social legacy of a massacre that had occurred fourteen years earlier. I opted for a narrative approach and found that the event was used rhetorically in both the political discourse of the communities and in individuals' attempt at reordering a fragmented—indeed, violated—social world. I concluded that a massacre could be seen as the partial destruction of "selves"—that is, not the self of the killed, but the destruction of the self of the survivor. From this followed the notion of the diminished self and the analysis of narration as its slow, contested and uncertain restoration. I drew on Lewin, who writes, "The healing role of oral testimony for survivors comes with reasserting the hegemony of reality (making 'real' what had seemed 'unreal') and re-externalizing the contaminating evil of that which produced the diminished self" (1993:309).

However, demobilization in 1997 of the guerrilla, and the perpetuation of military state power in the rural areas of Guatemala, pose a challenge to go beyond the view of the massacres as historically isolated events, part of a past to be remembered or psychologically processed. Two anecdotes will guide us further.

A prominent feature in everyday narration among people "in resistance" was the expression "*Pues, así dicen*"—"well, that's what *they* say." Most often the narrative itself then referred to knowledge whose source was anonymous and about which people were ambivalent concerning both import and veracity. The very day after the demobilization of the guerrilla in 1997, assailants, dressed in the black uniforms of the army's G2 unit, robbed and threatened people on the way to market in the village of Chel. The event was soon on everybody's lips. Conversation was marked by the fear that military repression would continue despite the new peace accord. Back home in the village where I was staying, the details were various, as very few had witnessed the actual event. I was more fortunate than most. I had direct access to a credible version of what had happened since B, my host, had caught sight of the four assailants when he had been approaching Chel on horseback. He had hidden and observed the robbery for a few minutes. Then he had returned the three hours' ride, warning everyone he met on the trail. I thus had a basis on which to compare his details with those that embellished the rumors concerning the event. Everyone except B used the rhetorical devise "*Así dicen*," the generalized third person, to support information that they had not directly experienced and were uncertain about, yet were anxious to tell.

The power of this event rested both in its clandestine nature, in its very hiddenness from the immediate experience of most, in the uncertainty that surrounds the information yet which achieves a certain veracity in the kind of rhetorical device to which I have referred (a device that unifies varied accounts). But that power must also be understood against the workings of memories of violence (and of the identification of the violent agent) *in the present*, morbidly instructing on what *the future* will hold. The message of the paramilitaries in Chel was one of defying the peace agreement on military downsizing and cessation of or departure from violence.

The second anecdote is about Don J., a Chel villager in his early fifties. Don J. had always been loyal to the revolution, he claimed, and one day he told me the story about four hundred dissidents—people who abandoned the guerrilla in 1984 and who gave in to a reintegration into "legal life" and two years of residence at *finca* La Perla, the place from which the army's butchers had marched on 3 April 1982. People were forced to work "like slaves" there, Don J. said, alluding to both the lack of economic compensation and the harsh working conditions. So, in 1986 they petitioned for a return to their native village of Chel and were released by the army but ordered to keep the now established paramilitary civil patrol. Two years before, Don J. had stayed with the EGP in the mountains when a considerable number of people defected. Able to observe how his native village was repopulated, he too decided to return in the service of his poverty-ridden kin. Upon his return, however, he found his land occupied by new residents. This made him an enemy of the new authorities, the civil patrol, in which he nevertheless was obliged to serve. After all, the alliance with the army was inevitable, since the guerrilla, too, had turned into an enemy owing to Don J.'s decision to abandon the resistance for the village.

The continuously feared and militant leader of the civil patrol in Chel had once, like Don J., been a member of the guerrilla. He had remained with the rebels for only two years before changing sides. Another difference between them was that Don J. obeyed silently without taking any initiatives of his own within the Chel patrol, while the other became its unquestioned leader. A month before our first encounter and talk, and as part of the efforts to implement what the peace accord had stipulated, a call for the arrest of the civil patrol leader had been issued and a number of soldiers had entered the village. But the accused seemed to have been warned in advance. He hid successfully and was now walking the muddy streets of Chel, bragging about how difficult he was to trap, a living proof of the close ties between the army and the paramilitaries.

The Civil Defense Patrol system in Guatemala was not set up but was refined by the Rios Montt–led military junta in 1982 (Americas Watch 1986) in an effort to "restore law and order" in a country where even the military, according to the coup-maker, was running amok (Loveman and Davies 1989). In the month of the Chel massacre, the junta forcibly recruited 30,000 and was able to recruit 700,000 patrollers before it was replaced by the military government that ruled until the presidency of elected Christian Democrat Vinicio Cerezo, who took office in 1986. There were then an estimated one million Guatemalans in the patrol system nationwide, with a strong emphasis on rebel strongholds like the rural highlands (Americas Watch 1986). Army statistics reveal that "between 1983 and 1984, 1,300,000 indigenous men between the ages of fifteen and sixty … were members of Civil Patrols" (Schirmer 1998:82). The village of Chel was located at the epicenter of this violent strategy: "Integrated into various army activities, civil defense units were established in the heart of guerrilla controlled areas, especially among the repatriated at refugee camps" (Schirmer 1998:85). Officially the system prevailed until the establishment of the UN mission for the monitoring of human rights, MINUGUA, in 1994.

In presenting this case, I wanted to foreground the role of manipulating fear for strategies of politically exploiting the secrecy surrounding the role of old and supposedly disarmed or pacified agents in contemporary governance. The symbolic timing of the appearance of the men in black uniforms in the first anecdote above was the very day after the demobilization of the guerrilla, in which all of those now exposed to paramilitary threat had served, and whose ability to entrench themselves in the mountains of this region was seen as the very reason for people's survival. Many expressed the conviction that without the protection provided by the guerrillas, they would long ago have been eliminated. The peace accord and the demobilization had now rid them of the means to protect themselves, but not of the threat. And from the ashes of the war-torn village of Chel, in the second anecdote, grew not a spirit of reconciliation or any other fundament in the liberal architecture of postwar societies, but rather an ever more powerful paramilitary leader. These events, then, communicated effectively to former rebels and others that the old politics was continuing but behind the façade of the new democracy. They hid this fact from the international monitors, the pioneering "seers" in a new transparent society who, to me, seemed to be blinded by their own enthusiasm at the appearance that the conflict was coming to an end.

A State in Retreat and a State on the Rise

In attempts to break the silence caused by ontological uncertainty, produced by clandestine violence, analysts of war and states construe paramilitarism in terms of excessive responses to insurgencies too powerful to be quelled by means of conventional warfare (see, e.g., Sluka 2000; Human Rights Watch 2001). But the transmuting power of the Colombian state hints at a more complex and shifting relationship between the various practitioners of political violence; what used to be state-sanctioned rural militias have, since the early 1980s, been building their own political platform. As part of its "democratic security policy," the present Colombian government embarked on a contested process of negotiations with the nationwide paramilitary organization AUC (Autodefensas Unidas de Colombia). The goal has been stated as the restoration of an effective presence of the state and its legal institutions throughout the nation's territory. From July 2003 the AUC was openly committed to a gradual process of promoting cessation of hostilities, disarmament, demobilization, and reintegration of former combatants. From February 2004 the Misión de Apoyo al Proceso de Paz, mandated by the Organization of American States and partly funded by the Swedish and Dutch governments, was actively verifying and supporting this process. However, the developments of the last couple of years are dismal. The paramilitaries have simultaneously won a number of regional and local military battles and in the process have managed to redraw the political map in their own favor in no less than twelve districts. They have anchored their power in the national parliament, influenced the presidential elections and taken power in a vast number of towns (Romero 2007). This development confirms the views of many critics of the negotiation process, including Colombian social researchers and international human rights organizations, that the power of paramilitarism in Colombia has long been integral to the regime itself (see, e.g., Human Rights Watch 2001). Instead of focusing on the nature of the negotiations and who should be included, the time is now ripe to reverse the question and explore what the choice of parties has done to the process of peace itself, to Colombian democracy and state power. In this, an analysis of the relationship between regional elites and state administrations in different political epochs of Colombia's modern history, one provided by Colombian sociologist Mauricio Romero (2000, 2003a, 2003b), contributes to an explanation of both the role of the state for the present Colombian predicament and the paramilitary function of transparency as outlined here.

In colonial times, Colombia was split up into economic regions whereby a variety of elites came to subordinate the concept of the nation to power and influence in regional or subnational spaces (Livingstone 2004). It was roughly into these areas that, as recently as the beginning of this decade, the nation threatened to dissolve: the Northwest, dominated by counterinsurgent paramilitary groups; the Andean and central area, controlled by the constitutional armed forces; and the Southeast, occupied by guerrillas (Romero 2000:51). This very absence of state institutions in large parts of the Colombian territory is commonly emphasized as the main reason behind the development of contraband activities and the growth of a privately controlled economic network beyond the reach of the state during the first decades of the twentieth century (see, e.g., Cubides 2000; Uribe 2004:80). These networks were the seeds of the growing infrastructure for the whole industrial complex of the production and exportation of coca in the 1980s and 1990s.

Transposing a discourse on retreating states (see Strange 1996) from a European context to Latin America is thus not without problems, since the authoritarian regimes of the region have been characterized by their *lack* of ability to penetrate the entirety of their respective national territories. Two interrelated phenomena need to be addressed here. First, the ways in which a liberalizing and allegedly pro-peasant state intrudes with the purpose of containing the power of the land-owning rural elite, and how the resolve of landlords and local and regional businesses to violently counterstrike have strengthened, speak to the fact that the corporate dimension of political power risks getting lost in a sole focus on state/citizen relationships (Kapferer 2004:10). Second, the extent to which state agents are implicated in enabling the growth of private militias that safeguard corporate interest, speaks to the fact that the economy of Colombian violence does have a governmental dimension and cannot be understood through a sole focus on the relationships between workers and capitalists. Let me elaborate historically on these two points.

Liberal president Carlos Lleras (1966–70) was a supporter of the agrarian reformism that swept Latin America after the C.I.A. aborted agrarian reform in Guatemala in 1954 and after the Cuban revolution of 1959. But instead of causing any substantial and long-lasting improvement, "the modernizing policies of the Llerista Liberals opened a schism between region and centre, and proprietors have distrusted and resented state interventions ever since" (Romero 2000:56). Such "distrust" was not reserved to concealed emotions. After having put an end to the reform, regional landowners supported by the congressional opposition went through an armed mobilization, a process paralleled by drug traffickers' increasing investment in land. In a focus on the northwestern department of Córdoba, Romero shows how such a mobilization eventually led to the consolidation of a private military apparatus with connections to the Colombian state that were more fragile than hidden at the time. The ACCU (Autodefensas Campesinas de Córdoba y Urabá) rose to represent the rebels' main antagonist, coordinating its operations from headquarters in Córdoba. But even more important for the development of Colombian paramilitarism than a state open to agrarian reform, according to Romero, is the decentralizing reform of 1988 when the nationwide bipartisan agreement of 1958 between the Liberal and Conservative parties to share rule was abandoned. Before 1988, it was the president who had appointed regional governors who in turn appointed municipal mayors. Since 1988, people have elected their mayors; since 1991, mayors serve a three-year, nonrenewable term. "The new institutional opportunities for leftist groups and even the guerrillas to influence or control local government exacerbated the elites and armed forces' worries about the growing territorial reach and political leverage of the rebels" (Romero 2000:55).

As for the second point, the state represents a contested domain of power, not a monolith. This became increasingly clear in Colombia as the

Conservative president Belisario Betancur (1982–86), apart from opening a window to restructuring the bipartisan tradition of Colombian politics, initiated peace negotiations with the guerrillas. The move caused a split within the government, echoing the national divide between the armed forces, the regional elites, urban businesses, and the Catholic Church on the one hand—all opposing any talk with the insurgency—and trade unions, journalists, and intellectuals on the other. The point to be made here is that an increasingly transparent and democratic state in a context of old power induces paramilitary activity and alters its own power base in favor of undemocratic forces. Thus, the relationship between the state and the illicit Colombian economy (embodied by the narco-bourgeoisie) has shifted from cooperation to conflict and back again over the time span of the last twenty-odd years. The state's thirst for hard currency has lent it an important role in the narco-economy. In Colombia, its institutions are known for "repatriating," or laundering, narco-dollars (see, e.g., Richani 2002). The economic assets of those belonging to the narco-bourgeoisie have bought them political influence—they have financed campaigns for certain politicians, bribed judges and military officers when they have found it worthwhile to do so, and thereby created a system of economico-political interdependence. It was discovered during the presidency of Ernesto Samper, that the Cali drug cartel "had adopted the strategy of penetrating state organizations by supporting electoral campaigns and buying up the loyalty of certain politicians" (López Restrepo and Camacho Guizado 2003:263). One of them was the then incoming president Samper himself.

The role of the Colombian guerrilla in both the drug trade and the growth of the paramilitary organizations is tellingly exaggerated by both the Colombian and the U.S. administrations. It is beyond doubt that the FARC guerrilla taxes the coca paste trade in the areas it controls, but not even the U.S. Drug Enforcement Administration refers to the insurgency in terms of a major player since it lacks the contacts both within the Colombian establishment and inside the United States to be able to exploit a multibillion dollar trade (Bigwood 2003; Livingstone 2004:105). The labelling of the insurgents as "narcoguerrillas" by Lewis Tambs, U.S. ambassador to Colombia in the early 1980s, struck a chord in the political project of depoliticizing the rebellion and constructing the rebels as common criminals, but it was hardly accurate (Romero 2000:62). In contrast, paramilitaries are involved in taxing the trade and processing, storing, and transporting cocaine (Richani 2000). Moreover, large numbers of paramilitary groups were formed by the drug cartels in complex and shifting alliances with landowners, businesses, and sections of the army for the very purpose of safeguarding the drug trade. Whatever the dubious political development of the Colombian guerrilla, with both drugs and kidnappings as main sources of income the insurgency has originated and grown independently of the drug trade. Discussing paramilitaries and guerrillas under the same rubric of nonstate terrorism is therefore analytically misleading for a number of reasons other than the now well documented state-paramilitary liaisons (see e.g., Romero 2007; Gill 2009). It misconstrues the origins and developments of the different groups.

The paramilitary AUC, emanating from the ACCU in Córdoba, has in many respects acted like a state. Thus, it relied on taxes that it collected from peasants, large landowners, small businesses, and even large multinational corporations whose interests the AUC was sometimes hired to protect. It was also against neoliberal reform, which it understood as working to weaken the Colombian nation. It is not that the paramilitary network has been against foreign investment—there are in fact strong indications that British and Israeli security companies employed to secure British-, French-, and American-owned pipelines stretching through guerrilla-controlled areas in Antioquia have worked in cooperation with Colombian paramilitaries (Richani 2002)—but the issue seems to be *the control of foreign capital*. On that point, paramilitary networks have opposed a neoliberal government in political retreat from the ownership and thereby control of business.

Paramilitary organizations act like a state on a more mundane level as well. Anthropologist Michael Taussig's *Law in a Lawless Land: Diary of a "Limpieza" in Colombia*, tells the chilling story of how the paramilitaries target everyone from alleged guerrillas to delinquents and corrupt officials (Taussig 2003). Human rights organizations have reported on the persecution of homosexuals, transvestites, and prostitutes (Human Rights Watch 2001). Acting as both judge and executioner in restoring law and order and combating what is perceived as moral decay, the paramilitaries take advantage of a state of fear that they themselves have been part of creating. To Taussig's surprise, many Colombians, "many honest and honorable citizens of the republic" (Taussig 2003:xii), welcome paramilitary justice, owing to the perception that "law is worse than crime" (Taussig 2003:30). They become protagonists in a paramilitary order, in turn made possible by the retreat or absence of the institutions of the nation-state. Hence the word *limpieza*—"cleansing"—in the title of Taussig's diary. The concept, in Colombia, has the double meaning of cleansing, as in purging of the unclean, but also as in "healing a person or a home from malignity due to spirit attack or sorcery" (Taussig 2003:xiii). Transposing such a healing from the level of persons and houses to that of the nation, Romero writes: "[t]he ACCU has managed to form 'an imagined political community' and to compete for popular, middle class, and elite loyalties with both the national state and the leftist insurgents" (2000:52).[5]

The assertions of morality by agents of the contradictory "paramilitary state" are part of a process of legitimization that inevitably leads to the dissolution or transformation of either the paramilitaries or of their state. We are thus dealing with Weber's monopoly as that which constitutes a state, but we are moving from the monopoly of *any* violence (or power in terms of coercion) to the monopoly of *legitimate* violence (or power in terms of consent). In Colombia this development is traceable from the clandestine violent practices of the 1960s. Law 48 of 1968 legalized private militias throughout the country. While the law was abolished in 1989, the diverse para groups (ranging from paid assassins or *sicarios*, to private armies, to military organizations for self-defense) "have been subsumed by the organizational form that yields higher dividends, and that ends by imposing itself" (Cubides 2001:131). The loss of legal status gave rise to the AUC, an organization that constituted its own legality and was thus able to recruit combatants openly. Without taking international recognition into account, its growth makes visible the moment when paras cease to be paras; instead of acting like a state their organization, in the sense exemplified above, *becomes* a state.

The case of former AUC strongman Carlos Castaño is another illustration of paramilitary autonomy. The brothers Fidel and Carlos Castaño were among those who invested their drug-related earnings in large tracts of land in northern Colombia (Livingstone 2004; cf. Romero 2000). In the early 1990s they cooperated with the police and the Cali cartel in the assassination of the head of the Medellín cartel, Pablo Escobar. Carlos' career within the illicit Colombian economy became publicly known in 2000, and two years later he offered his services to the fifty leading drug traffickers in their negotiations with the U.S. government. He used his organization's website to communicate the offers, but he also turned to official news agencies, appearing on national television in February 2000 in a ninety-minute interview where he admitted both to having committed atrocities against civilians and to be financing "his" counterinsurgency war with 70 percent coming from drug trafficking and the rest from extortion (Livingstone 2004:109).

Perhaps struck by the contradictions of being a public paramilitary, Castaño then began making efforts to distance himself from atrocities to which he had previously pleaded guilty. In July 2003 he blamed high-profile kidnappings on "uncontrollable elements" within the AUC. Through the political act of individualizing responsibility for traditional paramilitarism (naming scapegoats in the lower ranks), he took further steps to become part of the national peace talks. The response of U.S.- and EU-backed president Alvaro Uribe proved Castaño's efforts worthwhile, since they were influential in lending the present government an excuse to unite with its former allies. The paramilitaries were dramatically pardoned on national television in 2003, following which demobilization began on 25 November.

Colombian critics remind us that neither the process of demobilization nor the actual negotiations have influenced the level of paramilitary assassinations and massacring in any radical way, and that recent developments should instead be viewed as a joint venture by the state and the paramilitaries to concentrate their efforts on counterinsurgency warfare. Wanted by the United States for terrorist activity, Castaño eventually meant trouble also to the para-friendly or para-dependent sectors of the Colombian army and administration. The rumors contesting his death (see Vieira 2004) are interesting and would have been worthy of a separate analysis. Suffice it to say that "making people disappear" was the paradigmatic exercise in the perpetuation of ontological uncertainty under the military regimes in Latin American countries like Argentina, Chile, Guatemala, and Colombia.[6] So, how to interpret the power of making *oneself* disappear, or the power over the state to make oneself disappear, with the threat of eventually coming back and continuing operations when conditions are once again favorable?

Sacrifice, Mutuality, and the Expectations of Peace

Before summing this up I will return to Guatemala and explore the legacy, not of fear *from* paramilitaries, but of relationships locally described *by* former civil patrollers as "bonds of loyalty" between themselves and their patron state.

Household economies in the Guatemalan highlands revolve about a system of a "shared workforce." Neighbors and members of the extended families work together in the fields, in efforts to restore houses, produce liquor, or carry out whatever kind of economic activity they live by. Yet no one works for free in a strict or monetary sense. The value of a day's labor, a *mozo*, is carefully recorded—which means that if I work a full week harvesting your crop with the crew that you have assembled, you owe me nothing more and nothing less than seven *mozos*, to be redeemed when it is time to deal with my own fields, house repair, liquor production, or whatever. These kinds of communal transactions produce not only goods and services but also a bond to others that in itself becomes difficult to value. Such bonds should, as Stephen Gudeman has persistently argued, be central in any conceptualization of peoples' economies, and not viewed as communal by-products of economic activity (Gudeman 2005, 2008).

Now, the act of serving in civil patrols in the 1980s and 1990s was paid neither by the government nor by the army. Many critics compared the work with slavery, and I mentioned above the economic incentives of the land-owning, army-affiliated elite when setting up this system. But among people in the villages, among the patrollers themselves, these sacrifices for the common (national) good were also assessed according to the *mozo* principle. The fact that patrolling itself was construed as work commensurate to basically any other kind of work done by the members of the reciprocally knitted communities, gave those obliged to serve a certain amount of freedom. In Guatemala back in 1990 I found it odd to see so many men from rural areas working far from home in the nation's capital and asked how they got around the army-imposed duty to patrol. It turned out that they had all cut a deal with neighbors and friends in their home villages and were now free from patrolling. Instead, they were accumulating an increasing debt to their patrolling stand-ins—a debt to be paid in *mozos*, work in exchange for work, or converted into something else valued equally, like a certain amount of money, goods, liquor, or whatever.

This economy also created a bond—albeit a strained one—with the state, or better, an anticipated or expected bond in which the patrollers, the local embodiment of law and order and "the guardians of life," were contributing their share. The many Guatemalan men who served in this system thus invested one *mozo* every twentieth day for years. But in order for the bond to be reciprocal, the other party (i.e., the state) would have to contribute too, and in Guatemala such a contribution is yet to materialize. The state is not ignorant of the importance of the principle of mutuality for social and political stability. Once installed in the early 1980s, the patrols gradually changed names (and thereby abbreviations) in order to remain a legitimate part of a regime undergoing a democratic facelift. *Defense* was added by the junta of 1982 and *voluntary* when the military handed over the government to elected president Vinicio Cerezo in 1986 (Schirmer 1998:91). Mutuality is inscribed in both of these additions—in providing people with means to allegedly defend themselves, the state can credit itself with an almost sacral generosity; and by claiming that people enrol voluntarily the state takes mutual dependencies one step further and shows how citizens are turned from receivers into givers in a restored national order.

In Colombia, rural property owners, investors, and traders found support in the cabinet in the late 1980s for their claim that regional elite exposed to threats from the insurgency had the right to defend themselves. So-called security cooperatives, CONVIVIR, were created in 1995. "These would be private surveillance organizations to bolster rural security and collect information, designed to foster cooperation between property-owning sectors and the armed forces in the work of maintaining public order" (Romero 2003:178). The measure received fierce criticism from human rights groups and was later revoked. Mauricio Romero argues that the distinction between groups for self-defense and those composed of mercenaries working for landowners and drug traffickers had lost its descriptive power by the mid-1990s, "as the different groups concurred, whether in idea or practice, with the security forces on how to solve the armed conflict" (Romero 2003:179). Here, the discursive power resides in this very conflation of paramilitary agency with self-defense, the trick of making the violator of what Jean Franco has called "sanctuary space" (Franco 1985) appear its defender (see also Feldman 1991; Löfving 2007).

Recent events in Guatemala indicate that patrollers experienced the relationship with the state as anything but reciprocal. The country has seen the resurfacing of paramilitaries as an open political force claiming their right to economic compensation from the state for services in the patrol system during the war. Such frustrated claims indicate that the grand expectations that energize peace processes might eventually turn into a very violent disappointment. An apparent democratic progress with its fetishism of both peace and democracy seems instead to be a step backward, allowing the continuity or more open emergence of antidemocratic forces (Löfving 2004).

Conclusion

Paramilitary or extralegal violence occurs beyond the reach of both national and international law. It ranges from "murder with deniability" (Campbell and Brenner 2000) to acts of punishment and retaliation construed as righteous in a context where the law is perceived as unrighteous or ineffective. In this chapter, I have sought to combine a focus on hidden and open paramilitarisms and suggested, first, that in war-torn regions of Latin America the delegation of acts of killing to semisecret military auxiliaries is a response of authoritarian power to the liberal notions and practices of transparency, emerging with the development of an international legal system and superintending presence and not, as implied by recent scholarship, with the advent of cell phones and digital cameras. The development of paramilitarism in both Colombia and Guatemala supports such a claim. From the 1960s, but especially during the democratization processes of the two countries in the 1980s, extra-judicial assassinations on a grand scale hid the responsibility of the state for the exercise of executions, disappearances, and terror from the gaze of the "international community" and the national judiciaries developed and funded by it. Second, by temporarily feeding on the promise of change and by simultaneously exercising power through paramilitary networks, transforming and allegedly more open regimes do create the conditions under which paramilitary violence, spectacular yet clandestine, can be legitimized and perceived as "a necessary evil."

Notes

Acknowledgements

The arguments of this essay were discussed and developed in the 2006 Conference of the Latin American Studies Association (LASA) in San Juan, Puerto Rico, and also in the universities of Bergen, Edinburgh, Sussex and Stockholm. I am indebted to the many engaged participants of these conferences and seminars, and especially to Bjørn Enge Bertelsen, Bruce Kapferer, Lesley Gill and Stef Jansen for insightful commentary.

1. Loïc Wacquant sees the penalisation of that which itself is generated by the diffusion of social insecurity as a marker of a regime that he characterizes as liberal-paternalist: "it is liberal at the top, towards business and the privileged classes, at the level of the causes of rising social inequality and marginality; and it is paternalistic and punitive at the bottom, towards those destabilised by the conjoint restructuring of employment and withering away of welfare state protection or their reconversion into instruments of surveillance of the poor (2001:402). I am interested in the coexistence and simultaneous *separation* of these "levels" in contemporary liberalism and suggest that the notion of transparency operates in relation to law when regulating "the top," but that non-transparency or concealment is more accurate a description of the politics of violence regulating "the bottom" (see also Jansen and Löfving 2008).
2. I would also stress the difference between my take here and the argument that neoliberalism should be seen as a linear extension of oligarchic rule. David Harvey's influential elaboration of Marx's notion of primitive accumulation as "accumulation by dispossession" (Harvey 2003) indeed does contribute to an understanding of how both paramilitarism and free market policies feed on war and disaster (see Klein 2007; Gill 2009). But if, instead, free market reform is viewed as part of a broader political and indeed socially regulating project, involving a promotion of individual accountability in liberal democratisation and human rights (see, e.g., Brown 2004, Englund 2006), the task becomes one of analysing how, when and why that which is often portrayed as an opposition to authoritarian rule (i.e., neoliberalism) operates in producing perpetual but always contradictory power effects. The role of transparency in that process is the focus of this chapter.
3. A growing recognition of "the perils of transparency" is also noted in the literature. For example, Fung, Graham, and Weil (2007) seek explanations of the prevalence of conflict and corruption in the fact that transparency reforms and economic restructurings have been *insufficient* and that the open society is yet to be fulfilled or implemented. Others (see, e.g., Lord 2006) maintain that technologies of transparency can also be used by authoritarian governments themselves to spread "lies and hatred" which, in turn, stirs conflicts and hampers processes of democratization. A useful survey of the transparency literature and a successful attempt at measuring a politicized discourse against ethnographic case studies in the fields of business and organization, but also more broadly in politics and society, is provided by Garsten and Lindh de Montoya (2008).

4. Comisión para el Esclarecimiento Historico – Commission for the Historical Clarification. The following is based on cases 15634, 15635, 15636, 3082, 3466, 3221, 161, 3515 and 3389 of the CEH.
5. See also Colombian historian Álvaro Camacho's account of how the drug traffickers in the department of Valle de Cauca became accepted members of society in spite of their involvement in illicit trade and allegedly illegitimate violence (Camacho 1993), and Swedish anthropologist Oscar Jansson's tracing, in southern Putumayo, of this power through an astute analysis of "the capacity of [paramilitary] terror to present [or accommodate] the abject" (Jansson 2008:163). James Ron, for the case of Serbian paramilitaries operating in Bosnia, even testifies to the locally perceived heroism of paramilitary war lords, credited with the power and resolve that the government (in this case in Belgrade) is lacking (Ron 2000).
6. See Taussig (1992) for the power of making people disappear and the forms of resistance it evokes.

Bibliography

Agamben, Giorgio. 1998. *Homo Sacer: Sovereign Power and Bare Life*. Stanford: Stanford University Press.
Americas Watch. 1986. *Civil Patrols in Guatemala*. New York: The Americas Watch Committee.
Avilés, William. 2006. "Paramilitarism and Colombia's Low-Intensity Democracy," *Journal of Latin American Studies* 38: 379–408.
Bates, Robert H. 2001. *Prosperity and Violence: The Political Economy of Development*. New York: W. W. Norton.
Beltrán, Adriana. 2007. *The Captive State: Organized Crime and Human Rights in Latin America*. Washington, D.C.: Washington Office on Latin America.
Bigwood, Jeremy. 2003. "Doing the US's Dirty Work: The Colombian Paramilitaries and Israel," *The Narco News Bulletin* issue 29, 8 April 2003.
Brown, Wendy. 2004. *Regulating Aversion: Tolerance in the Age of Identity and Empire*. Princeton: Princeton University Press.
Camacho, Álvaro. 1993. "Villa Pujante: Une 'narcocratie' regionale," in A. Labrousse and A. Wallon (eds), *La Planete des drogues*. Paris: Seuil, pp.:48–52.
Campbell, Bruce B. and Arthur D. Brenner (eds.). 2002. *Death Squads in Global Perspective: Murder with Deniability*. New York: Palgrave.
CEH (Comisión para el Esclarecimiento Histórico). 1999. *Guatemala: Memoria del Silencio*. Guatemala City: United Nations Office for Project Services (UNOPS).
Cramer, Christopher. 2006. *Civil War is Not a Stupid Thing: Accounting for Violence in Developing Countries*. London: C. Hurst and Co Publishers Ltd.
Cubides, Fernando C. 2001. "From Private to Public Violence: The Paramilitaries," in Charles Bergqvist, Ricardo Penaranda and Gonzalo Sanches (eds.). *Violence in Colombia 1990–2000: Waging War and Negotiating Peace*. Wilmington: SR Books.
Das, Veena and Deborah Poole (eds). 2004. *Anthropology in the Margins of the State*. Santa Fe: School of American Research and James Currey.
Davis, Diane D. and Anthony W. Pereira (eds). 2003. *Irregular Armed Forces and their Role in Politics and State Formation*. Cambridge: Cambridge University Press.
Englund, Harri. 2006. *Prisoners of Freedom: Human Rights and the African Poor*. Berkeley: University of California Press.
Feldman, Allen, 1991. *Formations of Violence: The Narrative of the Body and Political Terror in Northern Ireland*. Chicago: University of Chicago Press.

Finel, Bernard I. and Kristin M. Lord (eds). 2002. *Power and Conflict in the Age of Transparency.* Basingstoke: Palgrave Macmillan.

Fitzpatrick, Peter. 2001. "Bare Sovereignty: Homo Sacer and the Insistence of Law," *Theory and Event* 5(2): 67–81.

Florini, Ann. 2003. *The Coming Democracy: New Rules for Running a New World.* Washington D.C.: Island Press.

Fung, Archon, Mary Graham and David Weil 2007. *Full Disclosure: The Perils and Promise of Transparency.* Cambridge: Cambridge University Press.

Franco, Jean. 1985. "Killing Priests, Nuns, Women, Children," In M. Blonsky, ed. *On Signs.* Baltimore: Johns Hopkins University Press, pp. 413–420.

Garsten, Christina and Monica Lindh de Montoya (eds). 2008. *Transparency in a New Global Order: Unveiling Organizational Visions.* Cheltenham: Edward Elgar.

Gill, Lesley. 2004. *The School of the Americas: Military Training and Political Violence in the Americas.* Durham: Duke University Press.

———. 2009. "The Parastate in Colombia: Political Violence and the Restructuring of Barrancabermeja," *Anthropologica* 51(2).

Gudeman, Stephen. 2005. "Realism, Relativism and Reason: What's Economic Anthropology All About?" in Staffan. Löfving (ed.), *Peopled Economies: Conversations with Stephen Gudeman.* Uppsala: Uppsala University, pp. 115–155.

———. 2008. *Economy's Tension: The Dialectics of Community and Market.* Oxford and New York: Berghahn Books.

Harvey, David. 2003. *The New Imperialism.* New York: Oxford University Press.

Hersh, Seymour M. 2004. *Chain of Command: The Road from 9/11 to Abu Ghraib.* New York: Harper Collins Publishers.

Holzner, Burkhart and Leslie Holzner 2006. *Transparency in Global Change: The Vanguard of the Open Society.* Pittsburgh: University of Pittsburgh Press.

Human Rights Watch. 2001. *The "Sixth Division": Military-Paramilitary Ties and U.S. Policy in Colombia.* New York: Human Rights Watch.

Jansen, Stef and Staffan Löfving 2008. "Introduction: Towards an Anthropology of Violence, Hope and the Movement of People." In Stef Jansen and Staffan Löfving (eds.), *Struggles for Home: Violence, Hope and the Movement of People.* Oxford and New York: Berghahn Books, pp. 1–23.

Jansson, Oscar. 2008. "The Cursed Leaf: An Anthropology of the Political Economy of Cocaine Production in Southern Colombia," Ph.D. Dissertation. Uppsala: Uppsala University.

Kapferer, Bruce. 2004. "Introduction: Old Permutations, new Formations? War, State, and Global Transgressions," in Bruce Kapferer (ed.), *State, Sovereignty, War: Civil Violence in Emerging Global Realities.* Oxford: Berghahn Books, pp. 1–15.

Klein, Naomi. 2007. *The Shock Doctrine: The Rise of Disaster Capitalism.* New York: Metropolitan Books.

Lewin, Carroll. 1993. "Negotiated Selves in the Holocaust," *Ethos* 21(3): 295–318.

Livingstone, Grace. 2004. *Inside Colombia: Drugs, Democracy and War.* New Brunswick, New Jersey: Rutgers University Press.

López Restrepo, Andrés and Álvaro Camacho Guizado. 2003. "From Smugglers to Warlords: Twentieth Century Colombian Drug Traffickers," *Canadian Journal of Latin American and Caribbean Studies* 28(55–56): 249–75.

Lord, Kristin M. 2006. *The Perils and Promise of Global Transparency: Why the Information Revolution May Not Lead to Security, Democracy, or Peace.* New York: State University of New York Press.

Loveman, Brian and Thomas M. Davies, Jr. (eds) 1978. *The Politics of Antipolitics: The Military in Latin America.* Lincoln: University of Nebraska Press.

Löfving, Staffan. 2002. "An Unpredictable Past: Guerrillas, Mayas, and the Location of Oblivion in War-torn Guatemala," Ph.D. Dissertation. Uppsala: Uppsala University.

---. 2004. "Paramilitaries of the Empire: Guatemala, Colombia and Israel," in Bruce Kapferer (ed.), *State, Sovereignty, War: Civil Violence in Emerging Global Realities*. Oxford: Berghahn Books, pp. 150–166.

---. 2005. "Silence, and the Politics of Representing Rebellion: On the Emergence of the Neutral Maya in Guatemala," in Paul Richards (ed.), *No Peace No War: An Anthropology of Contemporary Armed Conflicts*. Oxford and Ohio: James Currey and Ohio University Press, pp. 77–97.

---. 2007. "Liberal Emplacement: Violence, Home, and the Transforming Space of Popular Protest in Central America," *Focaal – European Journal of Anthropology* 49: 45–61.

Peacock, Susan C. and Adriana Beltrán 2003. *Hidden Powers in Post-conflict Guatemala: Illegal Armed Groups and the Forces behind Them*. Washington D.C.: Washington Office on Latin America.

Priest, Dana and R. Jeffrey Smith. 2004. "Memo Offered Justification for Use of Torture: Justice Department Gave Advice in 2002," *The Washington Post*, 8 June 2004.

Richani, Nazih. 2000. "The Paramilitary Connection," *NACLA Report on the Americas* XXXIV (Sept/October): 38–41.

---. 2002. *Systems of Violence: The Political Economy of War and Peace in Colombia*. Albany: State University of New York Press.

Romero, Mauricio. 2000. "Changing Identities and Contested Settings: Regional Elites and the Paramilitaries in Colombia," *International Journal of Politics, Culture and Society*, 14(1): 51–69.

---. 2003a. "Reform and Reaction: Paramilitary Groups in Contemporary Colombia," in Diane D. Davis and Anthony W. Pereira (eds.), *Irregular Armed Forces and their Role in Politics and State Formation*. Cambridge: Cambridge University Press, pp. 178–208.

---. 2003b. *Paramilitares y autodefensas 1982–2003*. Bogotá: Editorial Planeta Colombiana.

---. (ed.). 2007. *Parapolitica: la ruta de expansión paramilitar y los acuerdos políticos*. Bogotá: Intermedio Editores.

Ron, James. 2003. *Frontiers and Ghettos: State Violence in Serbia and Israel*. Berkeley: University of California Press.

Schirmer, Jennifer. 1998. *The Guatemalan Military Project: A Violence called Democracy*. Philadelphia: University of Pennsylvania Press.

Sieder, Rachel, Megan Thomas, George Vickers and Jack Spence 2002. *Who Governs? Guatemala Five Years After the Peace Accords*. Cambridge, MA.: Hemisphere Initiatives.

Sluka, Jeffrey. 2000. "State Terror and Anthropology," in Jeffrey Sluka (ed.), *Death Squad: The Anthropology of State Terror*. Philadelphia: University of Pennsylvania Press, pp. 1–45.

Sontag, Susan. 2004. "Regarding the Torture of Others: Notes on What Has Been Done – and Why – to Prisoners by Americans," *The New York Times Sunday Magazine*, 23 May 2004,

Strange, Susan. 1996. *The Retreat of the State: The Diffusion of Power in the World Economy*. Cambridge: Cambridge University Press.

Taussig, Michael. 1992. *The Nervous System*. New York: Routledge.

---. 2003. *Law in a Lawless Land: Diary of a* Limpieza *in Colombia*. New York: The New Press.

Uribe, Maria Victoria. 2004. "Dismembering and Expelling: Semantics of Political Terror in Colombia," *Public Culture* 16(1): 79–95.

Vieira, Constanza. 2004. "La conveniente desaparición del paramilitar Carlos Castaño," *Inter Press Service News Agency*, retrieved 17 August 2004 from www.ipsnoticias.net.

Wacquant, Loïs. 2001. "The Penalisation of Poverty and the Rise of Neo-Liberalism." *European Journal on Criminal Policy and Research* 9: 401–12.

Žižek, Slavoj. 2002. *Welcome to the Desert of the Real*. London: Verso.

---. 2004. *Iraq: The Borrowed Kettle*. London: Verso.

Chapter Nine

SORCERY AND DEATH SQUADS

Transformations of State, Sovereignty, and Violence in Postcolonial Mozambique

Bjørn Enge Bertelsen

In late November 2005 I was sitting in a bar in one of the poorer bairros, *the slum quarters of town, in Chimoio, central Mozambique, drinking beer with a friend and some acquaintances of his. We were talking about the problems of crime and of how things had gotten worse since the death of Samora Machel, the legendary president of Mozambique from independence in 1975 until he was killed in 1986. Many people attribute a certain nostalgia to him. "During his rule, there were no thieves, no criminals," one of them said. "Yes, and after him it has always gotten worse—with [former president Joaquim] Chissano it deteriorated rapidly," my friend said. "It is true," said an older man, smiling, "but now it might start again." "What might start again?" I asked. "They are killing off people," my friend said. "Who are being killed? And who are killing them?" I said, somewhat bewildered. "The police, of course!" was the answer I got. The others around the table were nodding, sipping their beer, some smiling shyly. "But … killing whom?" I said, still uncertain what they were talking about. "The police are killing off the criminals here in the* bairros. *It happens during daytime as well, not just at night; they just come on their motorbikes and BAM! They are dead!" the older man said, striking his hand on the table. The others laughed, all nodding. "But why are the police killing them?" I asked. "Ah, they receive orders from above—[the new president of Mozambique Armando] Guebuza orders them to get rid of the criminals. It is good!" one of the men around the table replied, smiling contently. The others nodded, seemingly in accordance with this, also smiling.*

Notes for this chapter are located on page 233.

Reports from the last couple of years in Mozambique support that what some texts call "summary executions by police" and others "police killings" are well known practices in all major cities in Mozambique. For example, the Mozambican League for Human Rights documents a number of cases from 2003 (LDH 2005), and various newscasts from July 2007 similarly report police officers confessing to the execution of three young men on a Maputo soccer field (Mozambique. Murders point to police brutality 2007). In the Chimoio case from 2005, the particular story above of people being killed by the police was cross-checked with a great number of informants both during 2005 and later fieldworks in Chimoio.[1] Everyone, from the impoverished young man peddling pirate DVDs (the "micro-entrepreneurs of the informal market" in IMF/World Bank parlance) to the judges and members of the jury at local community courts in the *bairros*, agreed in seeing recent deaths of criminals in Chimoio in the same way: The police in Chimoio and, as some alleged, in other places in Mozambique as well, were executing criminals after president Guebuza's inauguration in January 2005. Most claimed this was due to president Guebuza having voiced that crime should be targeted and not accepted. The informants varied, however, as to how directly he had ordered the police to kill criminals.[2]

When listening to stories about the brutality of the impoverished *bairros* of Chimoio in general or allegations of veritable police death squads, it is perhaps easy to be in agreement with Jeffrey Sluka's insistence on the need for an "anthropology of state terror" (2000). However, if the anthropology of "state terror" is, indeed, a subject we should seek to contribute to, then we need to undertake an analysis of both "the state" and "the terror"—probing the relations between state and violence in different forms. In the Mozambican context, this is irreducibly related to questions concerning continuities or discontinuities between war and peace as the country came out of a protracted period of warfare only in 1992. Beyond the Mozambican context and as Agamben has pointed out, "the police are perhaps the place where the proximity and the almost constitutive exchange between violence and right that characterizes the figure of the sovereign is shown more nakedly and clearly than anywhere else" (2000:104). The probing of these Mozambican forms and practices of sovereignty and state on the one hand, as well as violence and war on the other is the purpose of this chapter.

The Postcolonial State, Sovereignty, and Violence

This probing of relations between state and violence in the Mozambican context rests on the paradox of simultaneous pervasiveness and transformation of the state form. However, the state form, as Aretxaga points out, need not have a unitary form despite its continued power and presence (2003:395). This recognition of the state's non-unitary centers, its multiple shapes and guises, its capacities and potential to transform itself, and its non-stability, is crucial for understanding also the Mozambican state. As Hansen and Stepputat put it (2005:4), "although sovereign power always seeks to project itself as given, stable and natural, it never completely manages to achieve the status of a 'master signifier' that can stabilize a social order and a set of identities." This implies that the state, in any context, never will be the *only* sovereign power, and, consequently, will *always already* be challenged by other logics, sets of knowledges, practices, or forms of power. However, the force of the social in this continued challenge to the state form, as argued by Pierre Clastres (1998 [1974]), is an element not duly recognized by Hansen and Stepputat (2005). For, the Mozambican postcolonial state has been constantly challenged not only by other powers, dominant aid organizations, the superpowers of the Cold War, etc., but also by other internal logics of sovereignty. The dynamics of sovereignty and violence during Mozambique's civil war (1976/77–1992), the transformations and potencies of tradition, and the important dimensions of sorcery and violence of the postwar condition underline aspects of the state's non-sovereignty and non-stability. Theoretically, this condition may be analyzed by the concepts of *war machine* and *the state* as introduced by Deleuze and Guattari (2002). By understanding these concepts as *modalities* and *practices* of power rather than as institutional units in a formalistic sense, the state's tense relation to war and violence as well as the predicaments of the postcolonial state in relation to its citizens/subjects (Mamdani 1996) become clear. At one level, the tensions between the modalities of power, the war machine and the state, befits the two dominant bellicose practices of the civil war in Mozambique, usually thought of in organizational terms as the government forces of Frelimo and Renamo guerrillas. This chapter will argue that one may—after the general peace agreement in 1992 ending the war formally, and in line with Deleuze and Guattari's important point about the interrelatedness of war machine and state—see in the Mozambican state how the war machine and the state represent two "state logics" and, as such, also expose divergent violent, or wild, sides of a non-unitary sovereign power.

Implicitly, the police death squads as exemplified above represent some dimensions of this multi-faced state, but in a particular sense, and perhaps contrary to what one might think, an action that asserts and reconfirms state authority: If we are to see state authority as based on violence—on the state *being* violence, as Agamben persuasively argues—then sovereignty needs to be performed to be *real*. The notion of Agamben's *bare/naked life*

(1998) will be introduced in the latter part of the chapter to probe the ways in which lives seem to be imbued with a certain "dispensability" in the face of power in postcolonial Mozambique.

Further, as Hansen and Stepputat argue, sovereignty "is made real and reproduced through ritualized, everyday confirmations of this royal violence: the giving and enforcement of laws, the killing of criminals as well as enemies of the state, or of those who did not pay due respect to the king, and so on" (2005:7). Following Hansen and Stepputat's stressing of the performative aspect of sovereignty, the power over life and death seems to be central to the postcolonial state in both war and peace.

However—and this aspect is not acknowledged fully in generalized accounts and in some ways state-centric approaches as in Hansen and Stepputat—the violence of the war and postwar period in Mozambique, and the ways in which the modalities of power, the war machine and the state, evolved from war to peace in Mozambique, also relates heavily to the sphere of what one might call *tradition*. "Tradition," or *tradição* in Portuguese, is a term in the Mozambican context popularly employed to explain a wide range of practices and institutions, from the Portuguese colonial system's reliance on chiefs to the current situation in which sorcery is experienced as rife. Throughout recent Mozambican history, the cosmology and practices of "tradition" have been violently altered—for example, bent to bellicose purposes by Renamo in the civil war, and violently rejected post-independence by modernist Frelimo state politics as "obscurantist." These shifts between tentative appropriation by the colonial state apparatus and the Renamo war machine and the tentative erasure by the post-independence Frelimo state have imbued the whole sphere of tradition with tension and ambivalence, but it has not meant the demise of its importance, its potentialities or capacities. An important empirical focus in this chapter, therefore, is exploring the ways in which tradition is violently altered but remains potent in the face of violence in different settings.

This chapter will aim to map dynamics central to past and present violence in Mozambique, doing so through focusing especially on the developments of the Mozambican post-independence state. Central to this exploration will be an argument of the transformation of the practices and logics of violence and sovereignty from war to peace. It will be argued that especially *the postcolonial state*, far from being marginalized or weakened, in many contexts, as in Mozambique, is powerful, and yet must be understood as having multiple shapes and not necessarily a unified center.[3] Conversely, instead of arguing for the shrinking of the state and its capacity in connection with the increased "free" circulation of goods—both views central to dominant so-called neoliberal discourses—one may argue for the shift indicating a strengthening of the state in many areas. This is even so, or perhaps logically most evident, in so-called Third World countries where the Structural Adjustment Programs (SAPs) from the Bretton Woods institutions heavily impact the formal state system. As in other countries, the Mozambican state and its domains of control underwent processes of privatization of former state companies and enterprises in the 1980s and 1990s, as well as other forms of structural adjustment "in what was the largest privatisation programme in sub-Saharan Africa in the 1990s" (Cramer 2007:266; see also Cramer 2001; Hanlon 2000; Pitcher 2002). Gruffydd-Jones (2002:126) is one of those seeing in this situation a harsh irony in that the Mozambican economy is again enmeshed in and dominated by a global politico-economic system:

> Today national policies of market liberalization, export-oriented production, creating an "enabling environment" attractive for investment of international capital are implemented not under the colonial direction of the Portuguese metropole, but under the technocratic direction of transnational capital and the western industrialized states, above all the US, by means of international economic institutions of the World Bank, IMF and so on.

This view of Mozambique as a particular form of the corporate state—as argued in the introduction to this volume—in some ways parallels the visions of empire and the global dominance of neoliberalism as voiced by Arrighi (2005a; 2005b), Hardt and Negri (2000; 2005), and others. However, although this meant that the Mozambican state formally withdrew from parts of the economic sector, it did not mean that the state as such weakened. Rather, it transformed and is now a postcolonial state secured and supported by the aid from international donors and adhering to SAPs and other programs of economic adjustment (see also Macamo 2005).

However, it will also be argued that the non-unitary state and its continuous transformations allow for contestations and alternative logics such as through the language of tradition and sorcery. Empirically, the chapter will take as points of departure cosmologies and experiences of violence based on fieldwork in and around Chimoio, Mozambique, especially focusing on the transformation of "tradition" in this context. Arguably, the post-liberation and postwar state of Mozambique emerged in the period after the civil war ended in 1992 as stronger than ever and dominated by one party, Frelimo—the liberation movement of old. What was the background for this dominance of the one party and the reemergence of a strong state?

Colonialism, State, War

The space on the East African coast that gradually became Mozambique was under Portuguese colonial rule for almost five hundred years until the country's liberation in 1975. This freedom was achieved, perhaps, more as a result of a coup d'état on 25 April 1974 in Portugal that toppled the Fascist government and led the new regime to take heed of the soaring costs of the country's various colonial wars in Angola, Guinea Bissau, and elsewhere. However, from 1964 onward the guerrilla movement Frelimo, Front for the liberation of Mozambique, fought independence, operating both from so-called liberated areas in Mozambique where Frelimo governed protected villages inside the country and from army bases outside.[4] The protracted struggle between the Portuguese colonial army and Frelimo drew large parts of the country into the armed conflicts through the Portuguese use of dirty tactics and massacres together with the "protective" encapsulation of people into protected villages. On the other hand, Frelimo fought guerrilla-like, living among and off the so-called civilian population. The dynamics of waging war in Mozambique meant that the civilian population to a significant extent became enmeshed in the *modus operandi* of two different formations of military and political power, the guerrilla movement and the colonial state. With the transition to independence in 1975, the guerrilla movement was "sedentarized" and became the sovereign power in its area of dominance: It became a territorial state.

The nascent independent Mozambican state was in crucial ways shaped by the militancy embedded in the Frelimo movement since its inception in fighting for liberation.[5] This militancy was evident in the figure of the Mozambican President Samora Machel—the leader of Frelimo and the president of Mozambique from independence in 1975 until he was killed in a plane crash in 1986.[6] During his period, the one-party state with a strong, centralist leaning was established and the organization of the people into different militant sections serving the nation and the party (one organization for women, one for youths, local "dynamizing groups" to support and organize people around party initiatives, etc.) were established.[7] However, despite increased use of a Marxist-Leninist rhetoric from the end of the 1970s onward, measures taken to decolonize the state (and nation) by nationalization programs, the introduction of universal schooling, the creation of state-run agricultural collectives and rural farm shops, etc., the order of the colonial state was in profound ways continued in the postcolonial period—in terms, for example, of spatial and administrative organization (Sidaway 1991, 1992).

However, equally important for shaping the current postcolonial state was the so-called period of civil war between the Frelimo state and the guerrilla movement Renamo that was initiated in 1976–77 and lasted until the General Peace Agreement (GPA) in 1992.[8] What is generally acknowledged is that Renamo was to a certain extent created by Rhodesia around 1976 as a direct result of Mozambican independence in 1975. Rhodesia's explicit dual aims were, firstly, to target mainly ZANLA guerrillas,[9] which were fighting for a liberated Zimbabwe and which operated from bases in Mozambican hinterlands, and, secondly, to wreak havoc on the new majority-ruled state of Mozambique.

Around Zimbabwe's independence in 1980, it is pointed out by most researchers, control of Renamo changed from Salisbury to Pretoria's BOSS (South African Bureau of State Security) and SADF (South African Defence Forces). Renamo thereby became an integrated part of South Africa's regional "destabilization strategy." But from here on, diverse views and conflicting analyses emerge. Many scholars lay the heaviest responsibility for the dynamics and development of Renamo on *exogenous factors* such as Rhodesia and South Africa, also arguing that SADF forces were directly involved in battles, army bases, logistics, and in the killing of Frelimo activists abroad.[10] This claim is contested by some, who stress *endogenous factors* evidenced by Renamo's popular base from which it drew support among the disgruntled Mozambican civilian population owing to two much-criticized Frelimo strategies: the socialist inspired strategy of forced villagization for increasing agricultural production, and the refusal to recognize traditional authority, especially the *régulo* (chief) based on the rhetoric that traditional practices (however conceived) were "obscurantist" and therefore nonproductive. Both policies, they claim, contribute strongly to explaining widespread rural support for Renamo.[11]

What is evident from these sketches of colonialism and post-independence civil war is a country in which relations between state and violence, however one might conceive of these entities, have been crucial, visible, and tangible from the liberation struggle onward. Regarded superficially, an argument may be made for these social, political, and cosmological issues to have ceased to be important with the ending of the war in Mozambique with the General Peace Agreement (GPA) in 1992.[12] Such a view is dangerous for several reasons, but perhaps its largest flaw is that it under-communicates (or worse, miscommunicates) the prolongation of war in different guises in peacetime on several levels. Firstly, an argument for the end of war in 1992 is peculiar if one zooms out of particular localities and focuses on the national level of politics in Mozambique, where bellicose rhetoric still looms large within and outside election campaigns and periods (see Bertelsen 2002; 2003). This was evident in the first, second, and third presidential and parliamentary elections in 1994, 1999, and 2004 respectively.[13] Secondly, and perhaps more importantly, the war and its violence is seen as continuing in popular experiences of war, illnesses derived from spirits born of war and wartime identities still in operation, negation, and contestation. It is to these experiences of the civil war and its logics of violence that we now turn.

"Leaving Culture for the Bush": State and Guerrilla War Practices

A central feature of the "civil war" or the "post-liberation war" is that on the ground the fronts were everything but "clear-cut," in a Clausewitzian sense. The chess-pieces representing military units were not moved by generals and warlords on maps as the fronts were militarily renegotiated, as in the logic of military theaters of war. Rather, various armed groups with shifting agendas and aims targeted the civilian population, accosting people and sacking villages, making up a complex situation in which it was hard to distinguish between the two parties fighting. However, at a *structural* and *systemic* level, different logics of war may be related to state forces' and Renamo's practices. Renamo as an opposition group, relied heavily on coerced support from the civilian population, and their methods of enforcing cooperation included widespread terror and massacres comprising forcing young men to kill family members in order to become one of their group with little or no possibility to return.[14] One man, a local musician based near Chimoio, told me of how he was captured when local Renamo forces came one day in 1981:

> They came when I was working on the *machamba* [field]. Many fled, but I just heard noise from a compound nearby. I went to see, and they were robbing goats and other things. I knew them from before. They were from [X]. When I asked what they were doing, they said "war is war." They forced me to come along with them. I was six years with them in a base near Muzingaze. I was forced to play music for them on my guitar from early morning. They danced and drank. If I stopped they said they would kill me, so I played. There was very little food in the base, and I was often hungry. When I ran away in 1986 to Zimbabwe, there was very little food there as well. It was hard.

Stories also abound of forced recruitment to the Mozambican state's army, FAM, and one in particular emphasizes the brutal ways in which this was perceived.[15] During the war, towns were for the most part controlled by FAM, and young men and some women were sought and recruited to it. However, the poor state of FAM and the dangers of war attracted few volunteers, so drafting recruits by force was used: from time to time when the cinema in Chimoio was operating, the army would cordon the building off, combing the audience for men between seventeen and forty who were herded into army trucks to be taken off to war. The violence of the state was embedded in recruitment practices as well as in more tangible aspects of waging war.

The fear of violence and nocturnal attacks, the sights of violated bodies and charred homesteads and granaries, are all present in memories of the destruction of the war. As such, violence as destroying sociality, attacking the very cores of meaning, is central to what is recounted. This is also evident in the following parts of a story from a young man, Younas, who recounts atrocities committed during the mid-1980s:

> During the war, a lot of bad things happened here, a lot of bad things indeed. If you walked down the road you would see all sorts of things. Often, you saw people who had had their heads cut off. Or people impaled with the sticks coming out of their mouths or their sides. Often they had bananas stuck in their mouths, just like animals. But no one, not even their families, dared to bury them. The corpses were left to rot. There are still a lot of problems from this. Eh pah! A lot of problems, my friend.

This type of story is not unusual among those circulating in "Honde," the name I have given to my fieldwork site outside Chimoio. Others elaborated on and addressed the themes of the destruction of artifacts and buildings. This seems in no way to be a uniquely local situation, as descriptions from other parts of the country reflect similar razing of physical structures. An important aspect of this particular violence was attributed to Renamo, namely the obliteration of structures of Frelimo and *the state*, perceived as one: Concentrating on wiping out visibly important physical structures that the post-liberation state had constructed, schools, health clinics, and agrarian seed and equipment shops for peasants were razed, and a number of teachers, nurses, and shopkeepers were killed, abducted, or beaten.[16] In one sense, the violence and destruction of Renamo was directed toward the *deterritorialization* of the Mozambican state through erasing its points of visibility (buildings, communication, people). Also, almost all of Honde's inhabitants had had their houses consumed by fire, destroyed by mortars, or burned. Reflecting on this, many that were able to flee when armed soldiers came emphasize how the violence that took place transformed the very core of their being. In the voice of a middle-aged woman:

> It was hard to know where they were, so when you heard rumors that someone was coming, you fled. You brought your sleeping mat and a few things and ran into the night. Sleeping in the bush at night, sometimes up trees. And then eating wild fruits because of hunger as we were like monkeys. Ah! It was bad, really bad. Living like that, like animals is no good. When you return home, your house would maybe be burned, the chickens gone, the maize gone, the goat gone. All had gone. Eh pah! It is hard seeing that. Everything had changed.

Violence as encapsulating and total, stemming from people roaming around—"someone" not necessarily identified as Renamo or Frelimo (or Rhodesian soldiers or Zimbabwean fighters, for that matter)—the story emphasizes not merely the acts of inflicting physical hurt, but how mortal fear instilled flight. The flight and how it is perceived is very significant in this respect, where the locus of the home and the social is left for "the bush" where one is turned into living like an animal.[17] Violence is experienced as destructive and erasing of meaning, that which effaces and debases households and kinship, and it is not possible to reduce this to aggression or pain-provoking physicality. Most explicitly, this perspective of the *erasing* and *effacing* dimension to perceptions of the violence of the war came across to me when sitting with a peasant informant:

> You know it [the war] started here in Manica? Ah, it was bad in the times of the war. They put children into mortars [for crushing maize meal] and the mother or father had to crush it, killing their own child.[18] They burned the houses, and often the maize meal too. They put heads on sticks just to say "here we kill people." Can you imagine that? They destroyed everything. I did not want that. I did not want to leave culture for going into the bush.

The image of "they" (contextually being Renamo) as a destructive force cannot possibly be expressed in stronger terms: The image of leaving "culture" (*cultura*) for the bush provides a potent local metaphor for the destruction and violence, and in this context Renamo is portrayed as belonging to the very same bush.[19] The debasing effects of violence, the animal-like and bush-like behavior, is contrasted with the threatened "culture," a cherished world of houses, children, and *machamba*, the small plots of agricultural land each family cultivates. The view of "meaningless" violence (as with no intent but destruction) is dominant in this story: there are no clear perpetrators or victims other than "they." Conversely, there are others, telling explanatory stories that seem to "understand" if not endorse violence, not merely as acts of utter destruction but rather as, within the political context of violence, seeming to imply a *re-inscription* of meaning through violence: Violence was necessary to readjust certain societal contexts. Such a story of how past violence *redressed* certain structures may be represented by what another young man from Honde told me:

> Before there was *aldeia comunal* [communal village] and Frelimo had all the power. Renamo did not want that. They wanted people to return to the bush. So they destroyed the *aldeia comunal*. But why did they kill people? They had to rob and loot to survive.

In this narrative, the violence is both clearly attributed to Renamo, and their intentionality is narrated and explained as wanting to disrupt workings of the *aldeia comunal* and the alleged omnipotence of the Frelimo state.[20] The use of violence represents a means to an end, and the killing of people explained as due to the necessity of looting to survive. However, not merely, "Renamo" or "they," but also "Frelimo" is invoked as *erasing* and *re-inscribing* society and the landscape with new meaning through violence. In Chimoio there is a mountain whose peak stands some 200 meters above the rest of the terrain. The profile of the mountain, when viewed from the east and west, forms the face of an old man, hence the Portuguese name "Cabeça do Velho," meaning "The Old Man's head." Artur (1999a) probes some of the meanings of this prominent part of local cosmology and topology, attributing it with the local term Chindaza (my informants call it Bengo). Important ancestral spirits inhabit the mountain and an important local *régulo* (chief) resides close by so as to be within close proximity of the autochthons.

In light of this, the fate of the so-called sacred goats at Cabeça do Velho carries considerable import. Prior to the post-liberation war, the goats grazed the grassy slopes of the mountain. The animals would not be eaten and were in general reverently left alone save for ritual occasions, as they are viewed as having important relations to ancestors.[21] But in many of the stories in popular circulation, the goats were killed by Frelimo soldiers during the war, who also, savagely, devoured them, consuming their flesh, intestines, and genitalia. The wide circulation of the story of this sacrilege in killing the goats epitomizes Frelimo's and the state's antagonistic role toward "tradition" for local people. In distinct ways, the relations to the ancestors were perceived as having been shattered and/or transformed by the killing of goats, which were physical manifestations of these important relations and presences. In the context of this story, violence amounts to erasing tradition and re-inscribing new meaning in the landscape. By being inscribed with the death of sacred goats, Cabeça do Velho has become, ambivalently, both "bush" in the local sense of outside culture as well as an area *reterritorialized* by the Frelimo state. For many in Honde, this particular story evidences the Frelimo state's aggressive purging of things traditional and sacred from the landscape and people's lives. However, there is also a somber underside to the goat-consumption: by transgressing the boundaries of the traditional and by devouring the goats, the Frelimo soldiers may be seen to have engaged in dark acts of sorcery by challenging and appropriating the spiritual ancestral forces and territory. This interpretation, also proposed by many informants, is in keeping with the view of the Frelimo-related elites engaging in sorcery, as will be developed below. The particular example of the soldiers transgressively devouring goats may be seen to represent metaphorically also the violent and nebulous form of accumulation of power and material goods experienced to be undergirded by sorcery.

Despite the civil war's enormous complexity, it should be evident from the above that violence was not randomly performed. An important aspect of it was related to the confrontation of or violent appropriation of the sphere of tradition, the "bushification" of villages and physical structures related to state and society, to processes of *territorialization* and *de-/reterritorialization*.[22] These specific trajectories of violence are integral to dynamics of power and sovereignty.

War Machine and the State

> The war destroyed a lot. When Frelimo came, they came as enemies. When Renamo came, they came as enemies. (*Tchirenge*, local rainmaker.)

Anthropologically, *war* has been thought of in terms as "an armed contest between two independent political units, by means of organised military force, in the pursuit of a tribal or national policy" (Malinowski, quoted in Ferguson 1984:3); "the sanctioned use of lethal weapons by members of one society against members of another" (Wallace, quoted in Ferguson 1984); or simply "intergroup aggression" (Livingstone, quoted in McCauley 1990:1). Quite a few of these older anthropological approaches conjure up images of structured and formalized armed conflicts in the Clausewitzian mold. As argued initially, and as also Simons has pointed out, "the orderly Clausewitzian connections between governments, armies, and people have largely been dissolved" (Simons 1999:94). Against a Mozambican context, these types of distinctions come across the same problems as outlined above in delimiting the war in Mozambique to a "civil war" between two struggling parties represented by FAM and Renamo. As war is a contested field, no one story of war may, of course, represent it. Just as violence can be imagined polysemically and as containing both processes of erasure and inscription of meaning, a great array of different versions of war were captured by the stories told in Honde. There, the war was rarely viewed as "a long-term condition of violent interaction between clearly established groups" (Schröder and Schmidt 2001:15). Rather, the confusion, the suffering of a civilian population, the shifting alliances and (international) complexity was constantly emphasized.

Nevertheless, very often the conflict in Mozambique is represented as bifurcated into distinct groups at the same time producing orderly, clean dichotomies: soldiers and civilians, guerrilla and state, Renamo and Frelimo. This view is what, for example, Dolan and Schafer (1997) perpetuates in their analysis of Manica province.[23] Much of this and other literature on Mozambique tends to propose a nationwide universality of Renamo and Frelimo, instrumentally dividing regions into "being Renamo" and the others, by default, "being Frelimo." By construing as universal the main dichotomy of parties in the country, this approach effectively excludes the many local interpretations, experiences, and contestations of the dualism that is glossed over for the sake of completing the clear-cut "big picture."[24]

However, as, for example, F. Legrand (1993a) has pointed out, for Manica province during the post-liberation war, people constantly moved between zones, to and from other provinces and Zimbabwe as movement and periodical halts were one of the most prominent features of the period. "The border between Renamo zones and Government areas has not been as 'waterproof' as we had thought and many circulated from one zone to another. People living in the Renamo zone close to a Government locality often got access to some facilities like health services and markets" (F. Legrand 1993:21).

Following Legrand, I found that the zones were not total in absolute terms with people being identified as having the one or the other political identity, but there was (and is) rather a multiplicity of shifting identities. This flux may go some way in accounting for the strict policies of control tentatively and violently enforced in and between the zones. The control of bodies through herding, coercing, or kidnapping people in a zone is such that the conceptual and experienced differences between being imprisoned and punished, enslaved and protected, become hazy. Many stories encircle this theme of abduction, punishment, coercion, and, in the end, transformation to becoming "one of them"—the story of the guitar player above being merely one. The importance of controlling (and enrolling) "civilians" through the war further blurs the distinction in locations in Manica province and elsewhere between the categories.

Manica province's so-called Beira corridor has the main oil, gas, and petrol pipeline to Zimbabwe cutting across the landscape surrounding Chimoio, and the pipeline was the object of much fighting. Armed groups, often alleged to be Renamo, blew up parts of the pipeline numerous times purportedly to damage the Frelimo-state and Zimbabwe. But postwar analysis suggest that Lonrho in 1982 "signed a secret protection agreement with Renamo leaders covering the Beira oil pipeline" (Vines 1998:2). On the other hand, South Africa as a main Renamo backer in the 1980s, prioritized the destruction of the pipeline, and a compromise was made that "Renamo would carry out symbolic attacks on the pipeline" (Vines 1998:2). Be that as it may, the involvement of Rhodesian troops, ZANLA fighters, Renamo troops, FAM soldiers, and so on, make up complex trajectories of war in Honde, reflected in the stories above.

The climate of fear and uncertainty may account for some of the punitive measures taken against "traitors" or "informers," as it was important to inscribe the bodies with violence, and thus, to erase other options. The bodies displayed along the roadside in Honde may have served to demarcate bodily the zones and their borders, thus stressing what happens to traitors and squealers.[25] This point indicates why borders, zones, and bodies constituted such important categories for enforcing control and legitimacy. The presence of the post-liberation war and its violence in Honde has hopefully been made clear, and, as Nordstrom (1997, 1998), Werbner (1991), and others have shown, delimiting the phenomenon of war temporally or by means of body count hampers a thorough, in-depth analysis of causes and consequences, dynamics and structures.

Given that the war was largely fought in rural areas and over the control of population, its violence may also be seen to be a dynamic practice of power and control. Two of Deleuze and Guattari's (2002) concepts, "state" and "war machine" (hereafter unbracketed), may elucidate two of these modalities of power in operation in the Mozambican post-liberation war. As Kapferer notes, employing the terms in the context of the dynamics of power and Sinhalese sorcery, "the war machine ... and the state describe power *in its dynamic* as this materializes in a diversity of structurating processes on the ground" (Kapferer 1997:284, italics retained). However, the fruitfulness of the terms in the context of Honde is that they may aid in describing processes on the ground without reducing these to *institutional approaches*. For Deleuze and Guattari, the notions of the war machine and the state, as Kapferer's description illustrates, are best seen as concepts that are meant to analytically capture practices of power. These are interwoven but separate, antagonist but dependant; hence, one cannot be perceived without the other. What, then, are the traits of these concepts? The *war machine* is "rhizomatic," implying that "it connects any point to any other point, and its traits are not necessarily linked to traits of the same nature" (Deleuze and Guattari 2002:21) and "has no beginning or end" (Deleuze and Guattari 2002:25). This indistinct, complex shape is complemented by a fluidity and mobility, and its form is exterior to the state apparatus. *The state,* on the other hand, is characterized by territory and control, sedentation and lack of mobility, where hierarchy is an important feature; and Deleuze and Guattari assert that "the State has no war machine of its own" (Deleuze and Guattari 2002:355). The two concepts illustrate well some of the practices and features of Renamo and Frelimo, but more important, some of the logic inherent to the dynamic of the war in Honde.[26]

Frelimo, in control of the government for most of the post-liberation period, partially fits the concept of the state in that, throughout, it sought to control territory. As Deleuze and Guattari write, "one of the fundamental tasks of the State is to striate the space over which it reigns" (2002:385). As was noted above, a central feature of the state in general and in the case of Mozambique and Chimoio in particular, is the inscribing of meaning to urban and rural space, which was also an important priority for Frelimo. The reordering of agricultural practices and the transformations of the communal village to the protected village in Honde, as elsewhere in Mozambique, illustrate these practices. Through this, structures that were deemed "colonial" by Frelimo, such as the *régulo* (chief), in part were substituted and transformed into becoming party secretaries and other party organs.

Renamo's practices conforms to the features of the *war machine*, as it confronts and "dehierarchizes" the structures of the state: razing physical structures such as roads and buildings, and killing representatives of the state. In erasing signs of the state, the war machine, in Deleuze-Guattarian terms, "deterritorializes" the state as it loses its grip on the rural areas: "the war machine is directed against the State, either against potential States whose formation it wards off in advance, or against actual States whose destruction it purposes" (Deleuze and Guattari 2002:359). Renamo also fits the notion of the war machine in terms of how the 'non-battle' is central to guerrilla warfare (Deleuze and Guattari 2002:416). Fluid entities such as tradition, magic, and sorcery are, again in Deleuze-Guattarian terms, "metamorphosized" so as to serve the war machine that recruits through violence, coercion, and abduction. Movement and action of the war machine also follow, and feed on, existing structures as kinship systems, neither necessarily adhering to military strategies of warfare nor limiting waging war to a national context. In a brilliant ethnographic work on the Kaerezi on the Zimbabwe-Mozambique border, Moore (2005) portrays how the memories of Renamo attacks are vivid among people. Moore claims that Kaerezi dwellers allege that attacks by Renamo in Kaerezi "followed kinship or political networks across the border; reprisals and the settling of old scores produced collateral damage" (Moore 2005:44).[27] Thus, the shape of the war machine does not aim at control of territory or the battle, as the state does, but rather exploits and is fueled by for example logics of kinship and the politics of traditional authority. By way of fighting the war machine, the state creates spaces of control— as in the Frelimo state's creation of communal villages, safe roads—but it also *transforms* itself into a war machine as it engages in war. In this dynamic the state form of sovereignty may be seen to expose its powerful and violent potential and practice. Likewise, Renamo is drawn toward sedentarization, creating zones where captured are held (as in the entertaining guitarist above), camps are built, etc., and gravitates towards state order. Both processes are evident in Honde, where the state, Frelimo, rarely emerges as merely controlling and executing power but is also seen as "dirty" or as "doing a lot of bad." Further, as has also been demonstrated, wartime and postwar distinctions were and are difficult, and the stories and contestations reflect the ambivalence and opacity of the wartime practices of the present political parties. In Honde, the operations and practices of Renamo, Frelimo, ZANLA, Rhodesian troops, Zimbabwean troops and soldiers, and armed bands in general entailed violence with an unending and ambivalent presence. Both the metamorphosis of the war machine (as in appropriation of tradition) and the transformation of the state (as in the institution of *régulos*) entailed contested processes of erasure and re-inscription of meaning through violence impinging on postwar political processes.

As the concepts of war machine and the state are ways in which one may see modalities of power only, they do not correspond fully to what may be classified as either Renamo or Frelimo practices. Rather, the dynamics of war machine and the state serve to illustrate different dynamics of power and violence which are especially evident during wartime. However, if the dynamics of war machine and the state are particularly evident during war, what then of the period after the negotiated end of the war in 1992? Do the concepts still have explanatory power for the postwar, postcolonial state of Mozambique?

Postwar? Sorcery, the State, and "Naked Life"

The period after the peace was negotiated in 1992 and to the first general parliamentary and presidential election of 1994 was one marked by tension and fear of war returning to Mozambique. Important in relation to an argument regarding state and violence, however, is that the Mozambican state during this period restructured its troops and integrated elements of Renamo into its new Mozambican national army. The new national defense force, Forças armadas de Moçambique, FADM, was created. However, seemingly Mozambican society embarked on a peaceful transition to a prosperous post-conflict situation, and the country has had by regional standards quite a substantial economic growth—8.4 percent GDP growth annually from 1993 until 2001 (Stern 2002:63). From 1992 on, the peace process was supervised by a very costly UN operation, ONUMOZ, which oversaw and facilitated all aspects of the transition from war to peace.[28] Also, through the successful holding of elections in 1994, 1999, and 2004—all won by Frelimo—Mozambique has become a "poster child" (Moran and Pitcher 2004) of the international aid and NGO business, signifying that the country is a democratic, peaceful one. The term "success story" is used rather indiscriminately (see, e.g., Gruffydd-Jones 2002:108n2).

On the other hand Mozambique is riddled by conditions of abject poverty, and the dominance of Frelimo at the state level—which verges on being a one-party state—is propped up by great amounts of international aid contributed each year. Hence, the unity of the state is intertwined with the interests of international aid units—sovereignties in their own right—which contributes to the continued social, political, and economic power of the business and political elite related to the Frelimo party.

However, this apparent unity of state, party, and elite has been threatened for some time for various reasons. Firstly, the regionalist (and, to some extent, ethno-political) rhetoric of Renamo in which the national cosmology of unity in history, nation, and territory has been challenged (Bertelsen 2003; 2004). Secondly, and perhaps of even greater significance, one may argue that postwar there has been a process of "de-sovereignizing" the Mozambican state through its aid dependence, donor dominance, and being open to (almost solely) foreign capital investments. This has made the state and its agents to a large degree catering to foreign donors and passively administering aid and projects rather than developing its own politics of administration and political initiatives (Bowen 2000; Hall and Young 1997). Thirdly, the appropriation of the violence of the war—the war machine—by the state (in line with Deleuze and Guattari's vision of the relation between the two) has created a multifaceted, more unpredictable state. This co-optation (or cannibalization, if you will) of the war machine by the state at its most basic and wide-ranging level may be seen as the continuation of the violence of the civil war by the Mozambican state. This shift to a more unpredictable dominating force is evidenced by, for example, the state's co-optation of the field of the traditional—a field exploited and cannibalized by the war machine during the civil war as shown above: Through its creation of so-called "community leaders," meant to be a recognition of de facto local leaders, the state intervenes in the tense cosmology and logics of tradition and traditional authority. As demonstrated above, this is a field that was violently transformed, appropriated, and/or contested by both war machine and the state during the civil war. Now employing the rhetoric of "local democracy," the Mozambican state creates new authority figures with a highly problematic and ambiguous loyalty toward both the state and the local community (see Buur and Kyed 2005).

Thus, at the same time as the Mozambican state is stronger than ever with no internal or external military threat and severely weakened political opposition by Renamo and all others, Mozambican society is experiencing a time in which friction within its elite and between different organs of the state manifests itself as a wilder, self-contradictory, and, at the same time, more dominant state. Through the merging of the war machine and the state at end of the war and embroiled in an international system of conditioned aid, the Mozambican postcolonial state must be seen as a non-coherent unit expanding into the sphere of the traditional. However, despite the economic growth and the status as an international "poster child," the non-coherence of the state postwar and the unrelenting (and, some argue, increasing) popular poverty work together to create a situation in which uncertainty, anxiety, banditry, corruption, and para- and extrastatal judicial bodies and practices (e.g., the necklacing of alleged thieves at markets) prevails in many urban and peri-urban locations in Mozambique.

In this context, several features of the postcolonial situation become apparent. As already mentioned, despite its non-coherence, the sovereignty of the state needs to be performed through, for example, the killing of thieves by police death squads in Chimoio in 2005. Thus, one may argue that the ferocious battles and violence between Renamo and Frelimo, between war machine and state, have transformed the violence of the dirty war of the past into new constellations and spheres in peace time.

A real transformation of violence has taken place in which the violence and arenas of confrontation are not only of visible kinds, although the goods and riches are as visible as ever. This continued dominance of the state, the growing riches of its elite, and the state's expansion into the sphere of the traditional is popularly addressed, understood, and contested in the language of *sorcery*. In the logic of sorcery, sorcerers transgress social and human boundaries in order to harm or accumulate wealth, and these logics coincide with the perceived practices of the state with the killing of thieves. For example, in the town of Chimoio, there are examples of the abduction and killing of children and babies allegedly for the extraction of body parts for purposes of dark and powerful sorcery. Although these practices more often than not seem to be visions of the power of sorcery rather than actual deaths, some murders are documented, complete with information about the removal of kidneys, hearts, brains, and/or genitals. In the cosmology of the sorcery of accumulation, the transgression of boundaries for civilized human behavior is enacted through the killing and devouring of body parts of young, pure children and youths (that is, bodies not yet contaminated by sorcery or drugs). This is a dark path chosen by greedy men and women. Practically, in a context where accumulation and riches occur in very opaque ways, as in the Mozambican case, these modes of understanding power and wealth become increasingly prevalent. On a theoretical level, however, one may see this transgressive violence of sorcerous accumulation and power as the denuding and anti-social violence of the civil war continued in the creation of an increasingly detached, wild, and seemingly irrational state in the hands of the rich.[29]

The continued accumulation of wealth and money, the conspicuous consumption of goods and the visions of well-clad, corpulent party cadres parading their new cars or the splendor of *nouveau riche* with party connections, underline the existence of a dark, sorcery-fueled economy of which the poor are the targets for and vehicles of accumulation. Informed by knowledge of the annual cycles of agricultural production in which "hunger months" are an all-too-well-known fact, the idiom of "eating," *comer*, is very often used to describe these transgressive acts of consuming the flesh, working power, fertility, or resources of the other by both sorcerers and the rich.[30] Thus, the field of the "traditional" is misleadingly often portrayed as static and should, as has been argued in this chapter, be seen as a dynamic and contested field. This creates a situation in which, at the hands of a greedy, ruthless, and dominant sovereign employing sorcery, the "disposable" or "naked life," in Giorgio Agamben's parlance (1998), is in dire need of protection. Employing Agamben's critical vision of the state, sorcery and police death squads in Mozambique may represent some of the aspects of this multi-faced state. Again: Contrary to what one might think, sorcery and violence are actions that assert and reconfirm its authority. If we are to see state authority as based on violence, on the state *being* violence, then sovereignty needs to be performed to be *real*.

The empirical examples of sorcery and death squads are also arguments about the centrality of power over life and death, which is key also to Achille Mbembe's vision of *necropolitics* in the postcolonial age (Mbembe 2003). Lives, in the context of *necropolitics,* or lives as "naked" or "bare," to echo Agamben, are then imbued with a certain "dispensability" in the face of power in postcolonial Mozambique. Such visions of the violent state necessitates a counter-sorcery for protection of life and property resisting the nebulous arts of accumulation through transgressive acts. In this context, violence, fear, and power are interlinked with accumulation, riches, and transgression, constituting a cosmology of the occult where sovereignty is integral to abominable acts of dark sorcery—for example, the abduction and killing of children and the consumption of their body parts. These sorcerers are widely experienced to be living and working in the impoverished *bairros* surrounding Chimoio, and from time to time witchcraft and sorcery accusations are vocalized in the public sphere.

However, more often accusations and experiences of these dark forces and their agents are semiprivate in nature and the forces and spirits related to sorcery need to be sought repelled in sessions with *n'anga* or *profete*. The *n'anga* is an important traditional healer-diviner in Mozambique, while the *profete* is a particular healer that has emanated from the context of Pentecostal churches. In Chimoio, some of these measures are *kufunga muiri*, "the closing of the body," and *kufunga taiyao*, "the closing of the property." Both are seen as necessary to ward off potential and often nocturnal attacks from sorcerers and other ill-doers. However, during nighttime in the *bairro*, not only sorcerers are dangerous but also the agents of the state. Recent reforms to decentralize different bodies of state authority include the creation of so-called *polícia comunitária*, "community police," members of which are recruited locally in the *bairros*. The workings of these agents and how much they are seen to be accountable—to borrow a "rights and democratization" term—to local populations varies greatly, it must be assumed. However, what is important for the present discussion is how these figures represent emerging forms of sovereignty at the margins of the formal state apparatus, sometimes violently pursuing "justice" through corporal punishment during their nocturnal rounds. In many cases, being armed with sticks and sometimes knives, the groups of young local men patrol the *bairros* at night to frighten off thieves or to intercept troublemakers if encountered.

However, in late 2005 this community police, at least in one *bairro* in Chimoio, had developed into a structure that had the reputation for operating on both sides of the law, and its members were said to be involved in everything from extortion and protection schemes to outright break-ins and violent crime. As community police seem, to a large extent, to be recruited locally, to receive very little if any remuneration from the state, to sometimes not be given uniforms or other forms of identification cards, they develop according to logics of violence already existing from the time of the war and the state. Interestingly, they sometimes also turn *against* the state and its party, Frelimo, as the following example from the second largest city of Beira demonstrates. There, the head of the community police in the *bairro* Ndjalane, Afonso Henriques, is accused by residents of having established corporal punishment as the main means of, in Henriques' own words, "establishing order." Beira being a staunch Renamo area, it is interesting that especially members and local party secretaries of Frelimo seem to have been targeted by the spanking by Henriques' community police. But more interesting, Henriques denies all charges of acting politically and says that he is a "slave of the people":

> My party is the people. I was a soldier before and now I sought to use my talent for protection in our bairro. I am an honest citizen who manages to support my family through fishing on the beach of Ndjalane.[31]

What is interesting in this respect is not whether or not the local head of the community police was informed by party sympathies (themselves relating to the period of the war in which identities and loyalties were shaped, albeit ambiguously), but the fact that the logics of military protection and violence is seen as informing local police duties.

Both examples of community police work, that is, the nocturnal vigilante groups of Chimoio and the head of community police in Beira, demonstrate the different shapes and constellations of sovereignty that have developed in the *bairros*, emerging from and feeding on prior logics of the war machine and the state. Together with the ongoing transformation of the sphere of tradition as exemplified in the increasingly important role of sorcery of protection and destruction in the *bairros*, this means that different sovereignties contribute to a social and existential climate permeated with a fear of "being disposed of," being attacked and violently consumed by the flesh-eating appetites of sorcerers, of receiving a bullet in the forehead by more or less corrupt community police, ordinary police, or thieves. Or being killed by death squads.

Let us retrace the trajectory of the Mozambican state and Frelimo's development in a way that may be described as the transformation of a guerrilla movement (war machine) to a state. Although tactics varied, an important element in Frelimo's liberation war against the Portuguese colonial regime aimed for the *non-battle,* conforming to the practice of the war machine as described by Deleuze and Guattari.

As Coelho (1993:174) argues in his description of early Frelimo military strategies directed against the colonial power, Frelimo's methods were heavily inspired by contemporaneous Chinese ideas on revolutionary insurgencies: "The guerrilla forces operated through hit-and-run raids, according to Mao's strategy of the 'thousand small cuts,' without confronting the enemy in direct face-to-face battles" (Coelho 1993:174). This strategy was enacted in the case of Frelimo's attack on an important part of the Portuguese forced villagification program during the Liberation war: settling large segments of the rural population in villages under Portuguese "protection" during the war "was seen as the best way of insulating the population from Frelimo propaganda" (Newitt 1995:473); and toward the end of the war the Portuguese had settled around one million people in so-called *aldeamentos* (Coelho 1993:203n110). The villagification strategy, a phenomenon well-known from other war-contexts such as Vietnam, Malaysia, and Rhodesia, was attacked viciously by Frelimo during the liberation war. However, at independence Frelimo, it could be argued, transformed from a guerrilla organization to a party and even a party-*state,* and it now endorsed the *aldeamentos* it previously attacked.

Perhaps one should rather say that Frelimo as a guerrilla movement oscillated between several modes of domination and practices of power. On the one hand, its movements, its nonpermanent presences and organizational features, its plasticity in adapting to local contexts and structures of authority, highlight the nomadic and, in Deleuze and Guattari's terms, war machine–like features of guerrilla practice. On the other hand, with its few "liberated areas" it operated more or less as a "parastate"—perforating the Portuguese colony with liberated spots that could be said to have provided the prototype for the post-liberation state order. Coelho writes: "People escaping from colonial control into the areas controlled by Frelimo had been organised in villages of a new type, where the traditional and colonial rules no longer held, but where replaced by Frelimo's political organisation" (Coelho 1993:330).[32]

After liberation, Frelimo was in some senses "sedentarized." In the late 1970s and early 1980s, it executed policies that only partly restructured colonial systems of administration despite being aimed at creating a new post-independence politics inspired by Marxist-Leninist ideals. This translated into the abolishment of the system of *régulos*, the system of chiefs that the Portuguese colonial state had in part co-opted and in part interacted with. The chiefs were replaced by party secretaries and other party officials, and the party also sought to abolish "obscurantist" beliefs in sorcery, traditional medicine involving spirits, and so on, in its aim to create *o homem novo*, the rational and socialist "new man." Together with its continuation of a villagification program where the *aldeamentos* of the Portuguese in part were replaced by *aldeias comunais*, Frelimo's antitraditional stance was widely unpopular among large segments of the rural population.[33] The unpopularity of these measures was exploited actively by Renamo, which, tapping into the potentialities of traditional polities and practices, claimed to fight "a war of the spirits" during the civil war.

These measures, continued villagification (but now within a socialist or Afro-Marxist context), and the replacement of traditional leaders by party secretaries led to the whole area of tradition being imbued with profound ambivalence and potency in the postwar period.[34] Given the ways in which the whole context of tradition had been violently forged and shaped, firstly through colonization, secondly through having been an important object for control and coercion during the liberation war, and thirdly through the ways in which Renamo cannibalized it through its violent practices, its presence in postwar Mozambican society is important and forceful.

Endnote: The Violent Sovereign

A quintessential point regarding the predicament of the "nakedness of life," to paraphrase Agamben, in postwar Mozambique is that the multifaceted bodies of the state are compatible with a non-centric and non-totalistic form. This postcolonial shape is, again, subjected to and transmogrified by the emerging new empire, a system in which the economic and political gains by the domination of the centers is related to, in fact necessitated by, the unruly lack of unified states with full economic and political control at the peripheries (Joxe 2002)—a situation in which the corporate state form is also increasingly present. In this postcolonial situation of a multifaceted state in which several sovereign logics of violence and territorialization seem to compete or, at least, coexist, the "naked life" of its subjects will necessarily be subjugated to, and be vulnerable and open to, lethal violence as evidenced by the conversation about the executions of criminals at the outset of this chapter. Within this structural logic, criminals are seen to be void of human value and thus are dispensable. Consequently, to cleanse the social body of criminals is inherently logical to the *modus operandi* of death squads. The fact that these death squads may or may not be directed according to internal logics of corrupt agendas in which one may be threatened to be killed if not paying bribes or protection money to the police, does not thwart the argument. Rather, it demonstrates the way in which the perceived logic of the apex of the system, President Guebuza, is transformed and appropriated locally. This case indicates the analytical virtue of studying violence and its state in specific contexts if we are to understand the violent conditions of postcolonial contexts at the global peripheries. Moreover, a localized focus, and one informed by the specific historical trajectories and configurations of violence and sovereignty, will also avoid, on the one hand, the vague generalizations of some postcolonial studies and, on the other, contribute to avoiding the reproduction of empirically faulty images of different national unified and sovereign states.

Further, in a context where the dynamics of traditional structures have been violently altered, the experience of being vulnerable in profound but also direct physical ways is constitutive of people's very existence in urban, peri-urban, and rural contexts. Sorcery—more than an explanatory mode for riches and evil or a social commentary to the alleged onslaught of "modernity"—is crucially also the logic of protection, of preventing harm being done unto physical bodies, of preventing theft, rape, or summary executions at the hands of death squads. In this way, the violence of the civil war and, before that, colonialism is continuously transformed and confronted through the logic and practice of sorcery. Through employing protective measures such as encircling one's plot and house or protecting one's body from magical attacks, the nakedness of life is effectively clad in the dress of sorcery for protection against wild and antisocial consumption by the wealthy and by the death squads of the violent state.

Notes

1. The fieldwork referred to in this article was carried out mostly in and around Chimoio in 1999–2000, 2004, 2005, 2007 and 2008. An early version of this text was published as Bertelsen 2007.

2. A 2005 article in the Mozambican newspaper *Savana* (Catueira 2005) documents that there was at the time, indeed, a case against fourteen police officers in Chimoio charged with "acts of summary executions of individuals suspected of various criminal practices" [my translation]. In the article, the charged are also quoted as alleging that the orders came from above. In 2006, a more definite piece of evidence for the existence of death squads surfaced as eight police officers were sentenced to prison for having executed eight people in the period 2001–2005. These had been abducted from Chimoio's prison and executed on Chimoio's outskirts (see Police murderers sentenced to long prison terms 2008). For the unflattering record of police in Mozambique in general, see also Baker (2003), Ellis (1999:65), Cahen (2000b), Kyed (2007), and Seleti (2000).

3. Albeit the influence of what we might call globalization, with its increased directed flows of capital, people, information, and goods (Nonini 2003), may be seen to decenter, weaken, and make more opaque the vision of the state, it is dangerous to, as some have argued (see, e.g., Appadurai [1996] or Strange [2004]), envision a universal tendency of the withdrawal of the state from society and people's lives. As for example Balakrishnan (2005) makes clear in recent discussions on the state, the market, and globalization—although disagreeing on many central questions pertaining to the transformations/continuation/demise of U.S. and/or capitalist hegemony—flows and structures so central to parts of the globalization rhetoric are *not* haphazardly organized and structured. There *are* centers where power and wealth condense and have clear material effects, benefiting from and also being central to the construction and management, continuation, and policing of these flows. The specificities of these globalized flows of the postcolonial state of Mozambique and others needs to be related to the seemingly growing number of dirty, covert, international wars and states of aggression. Within the last decade or so, there has been a strengthening of an increasingly unipolar international system of aggressive policing and military intervention of conspicuously selective areas spearheaded by the United States of America. Military conflicts and interventions as well as "civil wars" or "dirty wars" need to be contextualized in relation to this emerging global system in which the violent forging of economical relations, political allegiances, and dependencies as well as aggressive belligerent practices need to be viewed as intertwined with geopolitical interest and humanitarian motives. These increasingly important formations of violence, economic power, and war have been analyzed critically by many, most famously in the analysis of this as "empire" (Hardt and Negri 2000). But this may also be seen as the constitution of a new form of political order as coined by Alain Joxe's term "empire of disorder" (Joxe 2002). Joxe argues that "the geographical prevalence of armed violence in the *Souths* should not lead us to think that these are new examples of 'cultural savagery': they are the result of a strategy by the dominant countries to spatialize violence and push the most virulent causes of violence into the South" (2002:8, italics in original). Thus, the changes in the global politics of security seem to reaffirm the visions and, indeed, tangible presences of particular kinds of states in the global centers and peripheries. I here follow Joxe and others in avoiding seeing the state as a static, total unit to be empirically identified and analyzed; there is a need, rather, to explore how one may perceive the transformation of the many forms of the state and its potential and actual use of violence—as is also argued in the introduction to this volume. This is an important key to understanding the various ways in which the state, neither weakened nor fading, is not giving way to create a utopia of unrestrained movement of global citizens, as the most ardent supporters of a particular kind of globalization would have it. Rather, the state seems to reassert itself, changing, participating in, and relating to nonstate sovereign forms of power and control like international bodies. As Aretxaga remarks: "Even as operations of state (or state-like) power exceed the boundaries of the nation-state to be deployed by actors such as transnational nongovernmental organizations, private corporations, guerrilla groups, or narcotraffick-

ers, the state form shows remarkable tenacity and adaptability (2003:393)." The global periphery with its many postcolonial states provides a position from which to analyze these transformations, and the Mozambican transition from states of war to peace is here taken to be an example of such a shift in state power, entailing not a weakening of the state but a turn to a more complex and, perhaps, stronger state.

4. See e.g. Coelho (1993), Nwafor (1983), and Saul (1979).
5. On the origin, nature, and early political shaping of the liberation movement Frelimo (Frente de Libertação de Moçambique), see Opello (1975), Alpers (1979), and Mateus (1999).
6. On the importance of Samora Machel for Mozambican early independence, for the Frelimo party and as a political strategist and president at war, see Christie (1988) and Sopa (2001). For a revisionist view of Samora Machel, see Cabrita 2005.
7. For details on the dynamizing groups, see Egerö (1990) and Hanlon (1990 [1984]), and for critical perspectives on the Frelimo-dominated state and its importance, see Cahen (1993; 1997; 2000a).
8. As will also be explored below, this transition of Frelimo from a mobile, multiple movement to a sedentarized, unitary, territorially oriented organization is also what Deleuze and Guattari describes as one of the directions the rhizomatic guerrilla movements may gravitate toward by becoming "arborified" (2002:506): "It is not so much that some multiplicities are arborescent and others not, but that there is an arborification of multiplicities. That is what happens when the black holes scattered along a rhizome begin to resonate together, or when the stems form segments that striate space in all directions, rendering it comparable, divisible, homogenous."
9. Zimbabwean African National Liberation Army (ZANLA) and Zimbabwean African People's Union (ZAPU) fought for the liberation of Zimbabwe (see Bhebe and Ranger 1995; 1996).
10. See i.e. Alden (1996:43ff), Beinart (1992:484), Roesch (1992), and Vines (1991).
11. See Geffray (1990), J.C. Legrand (1993), and Cahen (1993) for this view. An early anthropological attempt at analyzing the Mozambican conflict not only as external aggression was done by Meillassoux and Verschuur (1985).
12. The signing of the peace agreement between Renamo and the Mozambican state (effectively Frelimo as it was a one-party state) followed months of negotiated talks initiated 8 July 1990 in Rome and spanning twenty-seven months (Alden 2001:19ff; see also Morozzo della Rocca 1997).
13. Both the 1994 and the 1999 elections were generally regarded as formally "free and fair" by the international community. See e.g. Carter Center (2000) and Mazula (1995). This is, alas, not the case with the 2004 election (see e.g. Ostheimer 2005).
14. This method of forced conscription is widely documented, see Gersony (1988) and Wilson (1992) especially.
15. Forças Armadas de Moçambique (FAM), the armed forces of Mozambique, was the country's post-independence army until the uniting of FAM forces and those from the Renamo guerrillas as part of the peace process after the GPA in 1992 when FADM was formed (Young 1996).
16. This has often been interpreted as "directly instrumental": "Officials of FRELIMO, and of the administration, are priority targets. In rural areas their physical elimination serves to isolate communities and remove them from *the rival authority of central power*" (Hall 1990:52, emphasis added). For analyses of Renamo violence in general, see e.g. Geffray (1990) and Wilson (1992).
17. The tropes of the bush, the wild, and becoming like an animal are recurring perspectives in many conflicts. See e.g. Alexander, et al. (2000) and Malkki (1995).
18. "Their own" here means the child of their household, neighboring households, relatives, visitors, or from their *dzindza*. *Dzindza* connotes kin group or family group, nor-

mally patrilineal relations. "Their own" has, then, wider connotations to the dissociation *from* and *of* community such an act entails.
19. The image of the bush is also relevant in relation to views on contemporary politics as when one informant told me that due to electoral fraud in the general presidential and parliamentary election in 1999, Renamo had really won. Therefore there was a lot of discontent among people. "But", he said, "no one wants to return to the bush. No one wants more war."
20. *Aldeia comunal* (communal village) was an important post-liberation institution which was initially implemented to augment peasant agricultural production, also in Honde.
21. The importance of male goats, preferably black, called *gotokoto* in chiTewe (and Shona) is related to the handling of evil spirits. Some types of evil spirits, especially the wandering kind and not the type sent directly from a sorcerer to harm, must be treated ritually. In a ceremony with a *n'anga*, a ritual healer-diviner, the type and preferably the name and other information of the spirit is brought out. If the spirit is of a wandering and evil kind, then a male goat must be arranged; and in a ceremony typically some coins will be tied with a red cloth around its neck and the animal will be set free to roam. In the context of Bengo, many of the *gotokoto* type goats and related spiritual goats were inhabiting this.
22. Elsewhere (Bertelsen 2002; 2007) I have discussed at length the understanding of the civil war in Mozambique in terms of erasure and inscription of meaning—also critiquing Nordstrom's important contribution to understanding the war in *A different kind of war story* (1997).
23. See, for example, their use of the categories "soldiers" as opposed to "civilians" in their analysis of reintegration, simplifying extraordinarily the complexity of the war (1997:106ff). This construction of monolithic and mutually exclusive categories is a general problem in much of the "developmentalia" that makes up a substantial portion of the literature on Mozambique.
24. This simplification and post-hoc ordering, which entails a construction of two (or more) monolithic parties is not, of course, a phenomenon unique to the peace process in Mozambique, but may rather be seen as a general feature of post-conflict consolidation.
25. The mutilated body inscribed with violence corresponds perhaps to what Feldman has noted, where the individual body "becomes the material and visual bearer of discriminating histories" (Feldman 1998:229).
26. It should be noted that the "war" of the war machine and the state for Deleuze and Guattari is probably meant as potentiality and not actuality, although I here apply their terms to look at larger structures of war practice.
27. See also J.-C. Legrand (1995) for a review of the multiple reasons for and the historical context of Renamo raids and forced capture of the civilian population in Manica province, also supporting the fact that these practices may not be reduced to merely strategic and military dispositions.
28. For details of this operation, see Alden (2002); Dept. of public information (1995), or Venâncio (1998).
29. Mozambique is in no way unique in this respect, and there are numerous examples of the increased attention to sorcery and the state's appropriation or increased relations with the sphere of the traditional in other postcolonial African countries. See Ashcroft, et al. (2005); Ashforth (2000, 2005); Crais (2002); Geschiere (1997); Geschiere and Nyamnjoh (2000); Perrot and Fauvelle-Aymar (2003), and/or West and Sanders (2003).
30. This idiom of "eating" in relation to power and sorcery is well documented for many parts of Africa, but for a Mozambican example see West (2005:45-47 especially).
31. All quotes taken from the 16 November 2005 article 'Na Beira: Polícia comunitária acusada de agredir membros de Frelimo' in *Notícias de Moçambique* and all translations mine.
32. This oscillation between shapes is in accordance with Deleuze and Guattari's vision of the state needing—in fact, transforming—into a war machine. An additional example

of this is the Portuguese creation of small, indigenous units of African soldiers, the *Grupo Especiais* (Special Groups) from 1972 on to be units "supposed to go back to their home areas to act as a specially prepared militia combating the guerrillas in the 'same element' as theirs" (Coelho 1993:192). The Portuguese acknowledged in the same way as Renamo later did, the force of the sphere of tradition and created during mid- to late 1960s small units that "placed contact with village population before fighting the guerrilla forces, and integrated local population carrying traditional weaponry and led by their head of village" (Coelho 1993:177n46).

33. Coelho alleges that in 1982 there had been created 1,360 *aldeias comunais* in which 1,8 million people lived (1993:345).
34. See also Artur (1999b), Buur and Kyed (2005), Fernando (1996), Florêncio (2005), Lourenço (2002), Lundin (1996), and West (1998).

Bibliography

Agamben, Giorgio. 1998. *Homo Sacer: Sovereign Power and Bare Life*. Stanford: Stanford University Press.
———. 2000. *Means Without Ends: Notes on Politics*. Minneapolis: University of Minnesota Press.
Alden, Chris. 1996. "Political Violence in Mozambique: Past, Present and Future," *Terrorism and Political Violence* 8(4): 40–57.
———. 2001. *Mozambique and the Construction of the New African State: From Negotiations to Nation Building*. Houndmills and New York: Palgrave.
———. 2002. "Making Old Soldiers Fade Away: Lessons from the Reintegration of Demobilized Soldiers in Mozambique," *Security Dialogue* 33(3): 341–356.
Alexander, Jocelyn, JoAnn McGregor and Terence Ranger. 2000. *Violence and Memory: One Hundred Years in the Dark Forests of Matabeleland*. Oxford: James Currey.
Alpers, Edward. 1979. "The Struggle for Socialism in Mozambique," in C.G. Rosenberg and T.M. Callaghy (eds), *Socialism in Sub-Saharan Africa: A New Assessment*. Berkeley: University of California Press, pp. 267–295.
Appadurai, Arjun. 1996. *Modernity at Large: Cultural Dimensions of Globalization*. Minneapolis and London: University of Minnesota Press.
Aretxaga, Begoña. 2003. "Maddening States," *Annual Review of Anthropology* 32: 393–410.
Arrighi, Giovanni. 2005a. "Hegemony unravelling I," *New Left Review* (32): 23–80.
———. 2005b. "Hegemony unravelling II," *New Left Review* (33): 83–116.
Artur, Domingos do Rosario. 1999a. *Cidade de Chimoio*. Chimoio: Arquivo do Património Cultural.
Artur, Domingos do Rosario (ed.). 1999b. *Tradicão e Modernidade: Que Lugar para a Tradicão Africana na Governacão Decentralizada de Mocambique?* Maputo: Projecto de Descentralizacão e Democratizacão (PDD), Ministério de Administracão Estatal/Direccão de Administracão Local e Agência Alemã de Cooperacão Técnica (GTZ).
Ashcroft, Bill et al. 2005 *Post-colonial Studies: The Key Concepts*. London: Routledge.
Ashforth, Adam. 2000. *Madumo: A Man Bewitched*. Chicago: University of Chicago Press.
———. 2005. *Witchcraft, Violence, and Democracy in South Africa*. Chicago: University of Chicago Press.
Baker, Bruce. 2003. "Policing and the rule of law in Mozambique," *Policing and Society* 13(2): 139–158.
Balakrishnan, Gopal. 2005. "States of War," *New Left Review* (36): 5–32.

Beinart, William. 1992. "Political and Collective Violence in Southern African Historiography," *Journal of Southern African Studies* 19(3): 455–486.
Bertelsen, Bjørn Enge. 2002. "'Till the Soil – But Do Not Touch the Bones': Histories and Memories of War and Violence in Mozambican Re-constructive Practices," Cand. Polit. thesis. Bergen: Dept. of Social Anthropology, University of Bergen.
———. 2003 "'The Traditional lion is dead': The Ambivalent Presence of Tradition and the Relation between Politics and Violence in Mozambique," C. Goirand (ed.), *Lusotopie 2003. Violence et Contrôle de la Violence au Brésil, en Afrique et à Goa*. Paris: Éditions Karthala, pp. 263–281.
———. 2004. "'It Will Rain Until We Are in Power!': Floods, Elections and Memory in Mozambique," H. Englund and F. Nyamnjoh (eds), *Rights and the Politics of Recognition in Africa*. London: Zed Books, pp. 169–91.
———. 2007. "Violence, Sovereignty and Tradition: Understanding Death Squads and Sorcery in Chimoio, Mozambique," A.M. Guedes and M.J. Lopes (eds), *State and Traditional Law in Angola and Mozambique*. Coimbra: Ediçoes Almedina, pp. 201–61.
Bhebe, Ngwabi and Terence Ranger (eds). 1995. *Soldiers in Zimbabwe's Liberation War*. Harare: University of Zimbabwe Publications.
———. 1996. *Society in Zimbabwe's Liberation War*. Harare: University of Zimbabwe Publications.
Bowen, Merle. 2000. *The State Against the Peasantry: Rural Struggles in Postcolonial Mozambique*. Charlotteville: University Press of Virginia.
Buur, Lars and Helene Kyed. 2005. *State Recognition of Traditional Authority in Mozambique: The Nexus of Community Representation and State Assistance*. Uppsala: Nordic Africa Institute.
Cabrita, João M. 2005. *A Morte de Samora Machel*. Maputo: Edições Novafrica.
Cahen, Michel. 1993. "Check on Socialism in Mozambique: What Check? What Socialism?" *Review of African Political Economy* (57): 46–59.
———. 1997. "'Entrons Dans la Nation': Notes Pour une Étude du Discours Politique de la Marginalité. Le cas de la RENAMO du Mozambique," *Politique Africaine* 67: 70–88.
———. 2000a. «Mozambique du Marxisme Protestant au Néolibéralisme Transcendental?» *Africultures* 26. Retrieved 12 November 2008 from http://www.africultures.com/index.asp?menu=revue_affiche_article&no=1257&rech=1.
———. 2000b. "Mozambique: L'instabilité Comme Gouvernance?" *Politique Africaine* 80: 111–135.
Carter Center. 2000. *Observing the 1999 Elections in Mozambique: Final report*. Atlanta, GA: Carter Center.
Catueira, André. 2005. "Em Plena Acareação: Procurador de Manica Escapa a Baleamento," *Savana* (Maputo), 25 November, 5.
Christie, Iain. 1988. *Machel of Mozambique*. Harare: Zimbabwe Publishing House.
Clastres, Pierre. 1998 [1974]. *Society Against the State: Essays in Political Anthropology*. New York: Zone Books.
Coelho, João Borges. 1993. "Protected Villages and Communal Villages in the Mozambican Province of Tete (1968–1982): A History of State Resettlement Policies, Development and War," Ph.D. thesis. Bradford: Dept. of Social and Economic Studies, University of Bradford.
Crais, Clifton. 2002. *The Politics of Evil: Magic, State Power and the Political Imagination in South Africa*. Cambridge: Cambridge University Press.
Cramer, Christopher. 2001. "Privatisation and Adjustment in Mozambique: A 'hospital pass'?" *Journal of Southern African Studies* 27(1): 79–103.
———. 2007. *Violence in Developing Countries: War, Memory, Progress*. Bloomington and Indianapolis: Indiana University Press.
Deleuze, Gilles and Félix Guattari. 2002. *A Thousand Plateaus: Capitalism and Schizophrenia*. London: Continuum.

Dept. of public information, United Nations. 1995. *The United Nations and Mozambique: 1992–1995*. New York: United Nations.
Dolan, Chris and Jessica Schafer. 1997. *The Reintegration of Ex-Combatants in Mozambique: Manica and Zambezia Provinces*. Oxford: University of Oxford
Egerö, Bertil. 1990. *Mozambique, A Dream Undone: The Political Economy of Democracy, 1975–84*. Uppsala: Scandinavian Institute of African Studies.
Ellis, Stephen. 1999. "The New Frontiers of Crime in South Africa," in J.-F. Bayart, S. Ellis and B. Hibou (eds), *The Criminalization of the State in Africa*. Oxford: James Currey, pp. 49–58.
Feldman, Allen. 1998. "Retaliate and Punish: Political Violence as Form and Memory in Northern Ireland," *Eire Ireland* 33(1–2): 195–235.
Ferguson, R. Brian. 1984. "Introduction: Studying War," in R.B. Ferguson (ed.), *Warfare, Culture and Environment*. Orlando: Academic Press, pp. 1–81.
Fernando, Domingos. 1996. *Autoridade Tradicional em Moçambique: A Organização Social na Sociedade Tradicional*. Volume 2. Maputo: Ministério da Administração Estatal, Núcleo de Desenvolvimento Administrativo, Projecto "Descentralização e Autoridade Tradicional."
Florêncio, Fernando. 2005. *Ao Encontro dos Mambos: Autoridades Tradicionais vaNdau e Estado em Moçambique*. Lisboa: Imprensa de Ciências Sociais.
Geffray, Christian. 1990. *La Cause des Armes au Mozambique: Anthropologie d´une Guerre Civile*. Paris: Karthala.
Gersony, Robert. 1988. *Summary of Mozambican Refugee Accounts of Principally Conflict-Related Experiences in Mozambique*. Washington: Bureau for Refugee Programs
Geschiere, Peter. 1997. *The Modernity of Witchcraft*. Charlottesville: University of Virginia Press.
Geschiere, Peter and Francis Nyamnjoh. 2000. "Capitalism and Autochthony: The Seesaw of Mobility and Belonging," *Public Culture* 12(2): 423–452.
Gruffydd-Jones, Branwen. 2002. "Globalisation and the Freedom to be Poor: From Colonial Political Coercion to the Economic Compulsion of Need," *Portuguese Studies Review* 10(1): 108–128.
Hall, Margaret. 1990. "The Mozambican National Resistance Movement (Renamo): A study in the Destruction of an African Country," *Africa* 60(1): 39–68.
Hall, Margaret and Tom Young. 1997. *Confronting Leviathan: Mozambique since Independence*. London: Hurst and Company.
Hanlon, Joseph. 1990 [1984]. *Mozambique: The Revolution under Fire*. London: Zed Books.
———. 2000. "Power Without Responsibility: The World Bank and Mozambican Cashew Nuts," *Review of African Political Economy* 27(83): 29–45.
Hansen, Thomas Blom and Finn Stepputat. 2005. "Introduction," in T.B. Hansen and F. Stepputat (eds), *Sovereign Bodies: Citizens, Migrants and States in the Postcolonial World*. Princeton: Princeton University Press, pp. 1–36.
Hardt, Michael and Antonio Negri. 2000. *Empire*. Cambridge: Harvard University Press.
———. 2005. *Multitude: War and Democracy in the Age of Empire*. London: Hamish Hamilton.
Joxe, Alain. 2002. *Empire of Disorder*. Los Angeles and New York: Semiotext(e) / MIT Press.
Kapferer, Bruce. 1997. *The Feast of the Sorcerer: Practices of Consciousness and Power*. Chicago: University of Chicago Press.
Kyed, Helene. 2007. "The Politics of Policing: Recapturing 'Zones of Confusion' in Rural Post-war Mozambique," in L. Buur, S. Jensen and F. Stepputat (eds), *The Security-Development Nexus: Expressions of Sovereignty and Securitization in Southern Africa*. Uppsala and Cape Town: Nordic Africa Institute and HSRC Press, pp. 132–51.
Legrand, Françoise. 1993. "Evaluation of Health Services for Possible Integration of Refugees and Displaced People in Manica Province." Chimoio: Mozambique Health Committee, Seattle.
Legrand, Jean-Claude. 1993. "Logique de Guerre et Dynamique de la Violence en Zambézia, 1976–1991," *Politique Africaine* (50): 88–104.

———. 1995. "Passé et Present Dans la Guerre du Mozambique: Les Enlèvement Pratiques par la RENAMO," in M. Cahen (ed.), *Lusotopie 1995: Transitions libérales en Afrique lusophone*. Paris: Éditions Karthala, pp. 137–49.
Liga Moçambicana dos Direitos Humanos (LDH). 2005. "Relatório de direitos humanos em Moçambique 2003." LDH: Maputo.
Lourenço, Vitor. 2002. "Estado e Eutoridades Tradicionais no Moçambique: O Caso de Mandlakazi," Dissertation for obtaining the "Grau de Mestre em Estudos Africanos." Lisboa: Instituto Superior de Ciências do Trabalho e da Empresa (ISCTE).
Lundin, Irãe. 1996. "The Role of Traditional Chiefs: Relics from the Past or Vehicles of Social Change?" in C. Marias, P.H. Katjavivi and A. Wehmhormer (eds), *Southern Africa After Elections: Towards a Culture of Democracy*. Gamsberg: Friedrich-Ebert Stiftung with University of Nambia, UNESCO and Macmillan Publishers, pp. 103–12.
Macamo, Elísio S. 2005. *O abecedário da nossa dependência*. Maputo: Ndjira.
Malkki, Liisa. 1995. *Purity and Exile: Violence, Memory, and National Cosmology among Hutu Refugees in Tanzania*. Chicago: University of Chicago Press.
Mamdani, Mahmood. 1996. *Citizen and Subject: Contemporary Africa and the Legacy of Late Colonialism*. Princeton: Princeton University Press.
Mateus, Dalila. 1999. *A Luta pela Independência: A Formação das Elites Fundadores da FRELIMO, MPLA e PAIGC*. Mem Martins: Editorial Inquérito.
Mazula, Brazão (ed.). 1995. *Moçambique: Eleições, Democracia e Desenvolvimento*. Maputo: Patrocínio.
Mbembe, Achille. 2001. *On the Postcolony*. Berkeley: University of California Press.
———. 2003. "Necropolitics," *Public Culture* 15(1): 11–40.
McCauley, Clark. 1990. "Conference Overview," in J. Haas (ed.), *The Anthropology of War*. Cambridge: Cambridge University Press, pp. 1–25.
Meillassoux, Claude and Christine Verschuur. 1985. "Entre l'État et les «bandits» Armés par l'Afrique du Sud. Les Paysans Ignorés du Mozambique," *Le Monde Diplomatique*, 14 October, 14–15.
Moore, David. 2005. *Suffering for Territory: Race, Place and Power in Zimbabwe*. Harare: Weaver Press.
Moran, Mary and M. Anne Pitcher. 2004. "The 'Basket Case' and the 'Poster child': Explaining the End of Civil Conflicts in Liberia and Mozambique," *Third World Quarterly* 25(3): 501–519.
Morozzo della Rocca, Roberto. 1997. *Mozambique de la Guerre à la Paix: Histoire d'une Méditation Insolite*. Paris: L'Harmattan.
"Mozambique: Murders point to police brutality, raising human rights concerns." 2007. *IRIN News Item*. Retrieved 12 November 2008 from http://www.irinnews.org/Report.aspx?ReportId=73143.
Newitt, Malyn. 1995. *A History of Mozambique*. London: Hurst and Company.
Nonini, Donald. 2003. "American Neoliberalism, 'Globalization', and Violence: Reflections from the United States and Southeast Asia," in J. Friedman (ed.), *Globalization, the State, Violence*. Walnut Creek: Altamira Press, pp. 163–201.
Nordstrom, Carolyn. 1997. *A Different Kind of War Story*. Philadelphia: University of Pennsylvania Press.
———. 1998. "Terror Warfare and the Medicine of Peace," *Medical Anthropology Quarterly* 12(1): 103–121.
Nwafor, Azinna. 1983. "Frelimo and Socialism in Mozambique," *Contemporary Marxism* 7: 28–68.
Opello, Walter. 1975. "Pluralism and Elite Conflict in an Independence Movement: FRELIMO in the 1960s," *Journal of Southern African Studies* 2(1): 66–82.
Ostheimer, Andrea. 2005. "Mozambique's Tainted Parliamentary and Presidential Elections (December 2004)," *Afrika Spectrum* 40(1): 125–137.

Perrot, Claude-Hélène and François-Xavier Fauvelle-Aymar (eds). 2003. *Le Retour des Rois: Les Autorités Traditionelles et l'État en Afrique Contemporaine*. Paris: Éditions Karthala.

Pitcher, M. Anne. 2002. *Transforming Mozambique: The Politics of Privatization*. Cambridge: Cambridge University Press.

"Police murderers sentenced to long prison terms." 2008. *Agencia de Informação de Moçambique* News article posted to web 31 July 2008, retrieved 03 September 2008 from http://allafrica.com/stories/200807311197.html.

Roesch, Otto. 1992. "Renamo and the Peasantry in Southern Mozambique: A View from Gaza Province," *Canadian Journal of African Studies* 26(3): 462–484.

Saul, John. 1979. *The State and the Revolution in Eastern Africa*. New York: Monthly Review Press.

Schröder, Ingo and Bettina Schmidt. 2001. "Introduction: Violent Imaginaries and Violent Practices," in B. Schmidt and I. Schröder (eds.), *Anthropology of Violence and Conflict*. London: Routledge, pp. 1–24.

Seleti, Yonah. 2000. "The Public in the Exorcism of the Police in Mozambique: Challenges of Institutional Democratization," *Journal of Southern African Studies* 26(2): 349–364.

Sidaway, James. 1991. "Territorial Organization and Spatial Policy in Post-Independence Mozambique in Historical and Comparative Perspective." Ph.D. thesis. London: Dept. of Geography, University of London.

———. 1992. "Mozambique: Destabilization, State, Society and Space," *Political Geography* 11(3): 239–258.

Simons, Anna. 1999. "War: Back to the Future," *Annual Review of Anthropology* 28: 73–108.

Sluka, Jeffrey. 2000. "Introduction: State Terror and Anthropology," in J.A. Sluka (ed.), *Death Squad: The Anthropology of State Terror*. Philadelphia: University of Philadelphia Press, pp. 1–45.

Sopa, António (ed.). 2001. *Samora: Homem do Povo*. Maputo: Maguezo Editores.

Stern, Nicholas. 2002. "The Role and Effectiveness of Development Assistance Lessons from World Bank Experience." United Nations International Conference Financing for Development, Monterrey, Mexico, 2002. World Bank.

Strange, Susan. 2004. *The Retreat of the State: The Diffusion of Power in the World Economy*. Cambridge: Cambridge University Press.

Venâncio, Moisés. 1998. "Can Peace-Keeping Be Said to Have Worked in Mozambique? (Bye Bye ONUMOZ)," in M. Venâncio and S. Chan (eds), *War and Peace in Mozambique*. Basingstoke: Macmillan, pp. 98–116.

Vines, Alex. 1991. *Renamo: Terrorism in Mozambique*. London: James Currey.

———. 1998. "The Business of Peace: 'Tiny' Rowland, Financial Incentives and the Mozambican Settlement," *The Mozambican Peace Process in Perspective*. Retrieved 12 November 2008 from http://www.c-r.org/our-work/accord/mozambique/business-peace.php.

Werbner, Richard. 1991. *Tears of the Dead: The Social Biography of an African Family*. Edinburgh: Edinburgh University Press.

West, Harry. 1998. "Betwixt and Between: 'Traditional Authority' and Democratic Decentralization in Post-War Mozambique," *African Affairs* 98(393): 455–484.

West, Harry and Todd Sanders (eds). 2003. *Transparency and Conspiracy: Ethnographies of Suspicion in the New World Order*. Durham: Duke University Press.

Wilson, Ken. 1992. "Cults of Violence and Counter-Violence in Mozambique," *Journal of Southern African studies* 18(3): 527–582.

Young, E. 1996. "The Development of the FADM in Mozambique: Internal and External Dynamics," *African Security Review* 5(1): 19–28.

Chapter Ten

COLLECTIVE VIOLENCE AND COUNTER-STATE BUILDING
Algeria 1954–62

Rasmus Alenius Boserup

This chapter is about collective violence and counter-state building during the war of national independence in Algeria.[1] The war, which took place from 1954 to 1962, was one of the bloodiest struggles for national independence in Africa and the Middle East. Scholars estimate that about 30,000 French citizens and 350,000 to 500,000 Algerian Muslims were killed,[2] that one million were wounded, and that about two million others were internally displaced.[3] The French army's harsh methods of counterinsurgency in Algeria, which comprised of extrajudicial killings, systematic torture of suspects, and other war crimes,[4] provoked indignant responses from scholars and intellectuals whose criticisms in the decades after the war materialized in what has been called an "anticolonial perspective" of French Middle East Studies.[5] With few exceptions, scholars inscribed in this tradition have mainly focused on the French repression,[6] and in general analyzed the events in Algeria in this period as an external war between the Algerian guerrilla and the French forces of order.

In the present chapter I analyze both the violent conflicts between the guerrilla and the French forces of order, and the violent conflicts between the guerrilla and the local population in Algeria that the guerrilla claimed to represent. Combining unpublished classified documents in French and Arabic produced either by French officers serving in Algeria or by members of the guerrilla with published documents and scholarly literature,[7]

Notes for this chapter are located on page 258.

I present seven small cases of collective violence that the guerrilla group perpetrated in Algeria during the war. Each episode, I argue, represents a sociological type of collective violence that I name according to a core intention that I claim the guerrilla had with the violence. I designate these types: "intimidating violence," "disciplinary violence," "polarizing violence," "terrorizing violence," "monopolizing violence," "cohesive violence," and "power-staging violence" (a complete typology and a few methodological remarks are found in Annex 1). Two arguments emerge from this typological analysis. First, that the guerrilla fought two distinct wars in Algeria: an external war against the French army and the European settlers, and an internal war against elements in the Muslim population. Second, that the guerrilla combined the different types of collective violence in the external and in the internal war in order to build a particular type of social organization that was capable of competing with, and eventually replacing, both the existing colonial state and competing social organizations. Developing a term introduced by Mohammed Harbi, I call this enterprise "counter-state building."[8]

The Colonial State

When FLN (National Liberation Front) started the armed insurrection in 1954, Algeria had been under French domination for more than a century. In 1830, the French state invaded the Turkish Regency in Algiers, which since the sixteenth century had been the western frontier of the Ottoman Empire. After three weeks of fighting the French army had taken control over the capital and dismissed the Ottoman administration. Initially, the French army only conquered the major coastal cities, but when the French state in 1834 adopted Algeria as a "colony" a total conquest of the entire former Ottoman territory was begun. In 1848 the political status of Algeria was again altered when the territory was fully integrated in the French state as consisting of three *"departements."*[9] Another twenty years passed before the French army in 1871 declared that the territories were pacified by the military.

At this time a rapid modernization of the infrastructure and communication lines had already laid the foundation for the development of a modern capitalist state structure in Algeria.[10] Parallel with the modernization of transport, commerce, and communication, the productive system in Algeria was transformed as technological innovations in agriculture, irrigation and draining paved the way for capitalist production of export-oriented crops like wine and tobacco.[11]

It was, however, mainly a white European settler community originating from southern Europe and France that benefited from the modernization.[12] After the military conquest and with renewed intensity after the military pacification in 1871, the French state encouraged white Christians from France and southern Europe to settle in Algeria. The first large group of 100.000 French settlers arrived in Algeria after the loss of Alsace and Lorraine to Prussia in 1871. From this moment until the French withdrawal from Algeria in 1962, the number of settlers stabilized to make up around 10 percent of the total population (Ageron 1994). The settlers had a privileged position in the colonial state owing to their strong connections to the colonial center. They had their own political advisory bodies, a special system for obtaining control over the best agricultural land, exclusive trade unions where locals were denied access, and they had a strong colonial lobby working for them in Paris.[13]

The powerful position of the settlers was reflected in the administrative categorizations of the inhabitants in colonial Algeria. These categories were conceived in terms of a nineteenth-century racist and cultural essentialist ideology, which held that Christian cultural and racial superiority had accredited France with a superior position among the world's civilizations. This position obliged France to spread humanity and fight barbarianism outside Europe through a "civilizing mission."[14] When France officially adopted Algeria as an integral part of the state in 1848, all inhabitants in the adopted territory were accordingly given "French nationality" (*nationalité française*) without regard to religious or ethnic affiliations. However, it was only Christians, and from 1871 also Jews, who were given "French citizenship" (*citoienté français*). Muslims, for their part, were judged in separate courts relying on local custom. They were underrepresented in the political system, and their civil rights were severely restricted by the so-called "law of the indigenous population," which among other things prohibited Muslims from circulating and assembling freely (Ageron 1994: 60–69). It was only through conversion to Christianity or Judaism that the Muslim majority in Algeria could acquire the civil rights that the French Republic had declared universal after the Revolution in 1789. Less than 2 percent of the Muslim population in Algeria opted for this solution (Ageron 1994:60–69)).

When Algerian Muslims in the early twentieth century formed the first Algerian nationalist movements and parties in order to participate in the political system of the colonial state, their idea about the "Algerian nation" logically reflected the racism and cultural essentialism of the confessional categories that upheld the powerful position of the white European Christian settler population.[15]

Algerian Nationalism

The first attempts to create a nationalist party operating within the political system in colonial Algeria was made by Emir Khaled, whose grandfather, Abd al-Kader, had been an important figure in the early resistance against the French occupation. Inspired by his encounters with early Arab nationalists during his upbringing in political exile in Damascus in the late nineteenth and early twentieth centuries, Khaled entered Algeria secretly in 1907 and formed a political party called *hizb Khaled* or Khaled's Party (Koulakssis and Meynier 1987). Ideologically, Khaled's Party appealed to the educated Muslim elite by agitating for political reforms within the framework of the colonial state. In 1917, during the First World War, the colonial authorities exiled Khaled and banned his party. However, during the former ten years of political activism, Khaled's Party had helped introduce a series of core nationalist concepts that survived in the Algerian political culture. Gradually during the 1910s Khaled's Party replaced the colonial category "Muslim" with the Arabic expression *al-muwāṭin al-jazā'irī*, meaning "Algerian patriot" (Koulakssis and Meynier 1987). This new conceptualization of the preexisting colonial category of indigenous Muslims combined the Arabic word "*al-waṭan*," meaning "homeland," "fatherland," or "nation-state," with the Arabic word for Algeria. In the late 1920s and throughout the 1930s and 1940s, a new group of young urban-based nationalists from lower proletarian and middle-class origin rallied behind the charismatic Messali Hadj, who saw the Algerian nation (*waṭan*) as a historical and cultural reality that should be realized in an independent Algerian state through a French withdrawal from Algeria.[16] Messali's different political parties and movements were continuously repressed by the colonial authorities, and after a popular uprising instigated by nationalist agitators in May 1945, the colonial forces of order killed thousands of suspected Muslims in reprisal and imprisoned the political leadership of Messali's group.[17] The repression in 1945 is often seen as one of the radicalizing factors behind the Algerian nationalism. In 1947, a special unit called the "OS" (Organization Speciale or Organization Secrète) was created within Messali's nationalist group. OS was supposed to provide the nationalist leadership with a strategy for an armed struggle against the colonial state as well as a group of trained and armed activists.[18] In 1950, the OS was dismantled by the French intelligence services. Four years later a group of young radicals from Messali's movement and members from the former OS formed a small guerrilla group and started the armed struggle against the colonial state.

FLN's Two Wars in One

In the early morning hours of 1 November 1954, more than a hundred coordinated acts of sabotage, and a few ambushes and armed attacks against the colonial forces of order, were perpetrated simultaneously in Algeria. In a one-page proclamation edited in Arabic and French and loosely distributed an unknown group, whose members kept their identity secret, claimed responsibility for the events.[19] The group called itself FLN, which was an acronym of Front de Libération Nationale, which again was a translation of the Arabic name *jabha at-taḥrīr al-waṭanī*. In the proclamation, FLN declared "war" (*ḥarb*) on "colonialism" (*al-istiʿmār*) but simultaneously offered the colonial authorities what it called an "honorable platform of negotiation." Condemning the internal power struggles in the Algerian nationalist movement, FLN presented itself as a common front open for "all patriots" (*jāmiaʿ al-muwāṭinīn*). While the FLN did not present a detailed political program, the group listed two parallel war projects: A "War of Independence" (*ḥarb al-isitqlāl*) against what the group called its "enemy" (*ʿadū*), and a "War of Liberation" (*ḥarb at-taḥrīr*) against "traitors of the nation" (*khawana lil-waṭan*).

According to the available statistics produced by the French army, FLN's external war resulted in the violent death of about 15,000 French citizens in Algeria between 1954 and 1962. In the same period FLN killed between 200,000 and 300,000 Muslim Algerians.[20] Proportionally, the guerrilla killed fifteen Muslim Algerian "traitors" each time they killed one French "enemy." The two wars were manifested in seven distinct types of collective violence, which I will illustrate in the seven case studies below.

Intimidating Violence

When the FLN started the insurrection in November 1954, the group encompassed only a few hundred poorly armed activists. During the first two years of combat, however, the FLN managed to incorporate the majority of other nationalist and anticolonial groups in Algeria, ranging form the reformist religious group *al-ʿulamā* to the Algerian Communist Party (Harbi 1975). Simultaneously, thousands of young men and women joined the guerrilla's armed branch, ALN, which was an acronym for *Armeé de Libération Nationale* (as the front and the army were de facto overlapping, I collectively label them FLN.) The exact number of guerrilla warriors engaged in the FLN remains unknown. However, scholars agree, that from early 1956 and throughout the war, FLN had few problems mobilizing the

Algerian population. An intelligence report from the French army dating from July 1956, estimates that the ALN numbered around 18,000 weapons-bearing guerrilla soldiers called *mujāhidūn* or *junūd,* and could mobilize at least as many civilian supporters, the so-called *musābilūn*.[21] Historians roughly agree that FLN at its peak in early 1957 numbered about 23,000 *mujāhidūn* and 50,000 *musābilūn* (Ageron 1998).

The guerrilla group faced a colonial state that in November 1954 had about 50,000 men in uniform in Algeria, but which quickly mobilized its coercive capacities as the insurrection spread. In January 1956, the French forces of order in Algeria numbered 200,000 men, and by the end of 1957 the total number surpassed 450,000. The colonial state also mobilized about 120,000 Muslim Algerian auxiliary troops, the so-called *harkis*.[22] Besides the human capacities, the colonial forces of order relied on the republican air force to survey the borders and the navy to block the maritime access to Algeria.[23]

Already the OS had realized the impossibility of an Algerian uprising inflicting military defeat on the French army in traditional open combat (Harbi 1981:15–49). Instead, the FLN adopted a classic guerrilla strategy, which combined rural ambushes and surprise attacks (Harbi 1994:20–25). An episode of this type of collective violence took place an afternoon in January 1955. A French military convoy consisting of three cars had left a base in the Aurès Mountains in the eastern part of central Algeria and was heading for the Tunisian boarder. After driving a few kilometers, a motor problem forced the car in the middle to stop. In order to provide protection while the motor was repaired, the last car also made a hold. Apparently, the soldiers in the first car did not take notice of the incident. They continued driving and soon turned a corner on the mountainous road. After a quick repair the two cars set off again, but after turning a few corners they found the first car burning in the roadside. A paratrooper who had driven the car and the commanding lieutenant of the convoy lay slain on the road killed by several bullets, and the incinerated bodies of two other soldiers were found inside the burning car. Reinforcements were called in, and the area was surveyed until nightfall. The survey revealed that between five and ten guerrilla fighters had participated in the ambush, but in a report written a few days later, the leader of the investigation concluded: "nobody can say exactly what has happened."[24] The only thing that was clear was that the guerrilla fighters had attacked the car, killed the soldiers, and taken a few weapons and some ammunition before disappearing.

The FLN was of course not always successful in its guerrilla tactics. As the French army professionalized its counter-guerrilla warfare, the FLN experienced increasing military difficulties. However, in spite of observable variations in intensity over time and place, the FLN continually perpetrated such acts of collective violence against the external enemy throughout the war. Close to 12,000 French soldiers were killed in such episodes.[25] While there exists examples of war crimes being committed by the FLN against the French soldiers, the empirical documentation in the French archives reveals that the FLN's leadership throughout the war insisted that the guerrilla fighters should treat the French soldiers in accordance with the international conventions of warfare.[26] Hence, while the FLN often boasted of the guerrilla's invincibility and willingness to inflict military defeat of the French army in their propaganda, my analysis suggests that the main function of the collective violence perpetrated by the guerrilla against the colonial forces was to force the French political system to engaging in political negotiation with the guerrilla through the proposed "honorable platform." I call this type of collective violence "intimidating violence," since it was intended not to exterminate but to intimidate a respected enemy whom the guerrilla recognized as an equal partner of negotiation.

Disciplinary Violence

Another type of collective violence, which appears in the records of the FLN throughout the eight years of the war, is what I call "disciplinary violence." While the intimidating violence targeted members of the French forces of order, the disciplinary violence targeted civil Muslim Algerians that the guerrilla group suspected of collaborating with the colonial state. One such episode dates from September 1960.

Late at night, six men dressed in military uniforms arrived on horseback in a small village in Western Algeria named Ouled Bouchena. Here the group stopped outside the house of Kamil, a retired soldier and small-scale peasant farmer. In an interrogation made by the French police the day after, Kamil's wife related that three men had entered their house and told her husband to follow them.[27] The group made six other stops in the village, beginning at the house of Kamil's neighbor, Asad. Asad's wife later told the French police that she had waited up all night, but in the morning, when Asad had not returned, she went to alert her brother-in-law who lived in the village. "It was at this moment that I saw a horribly mutilated creature with a bleeding face coming towards me. I soon discovered that it was my husband. His ears had been cut off. And so had his nose, his upper lip, and his tongue." Alarmed by the events, the villagers gathered and followed Asad's blood-stained path back to a nearby riverbed where his nose, tongue, ears, and upper lip lay besides the dead body of Kamil. A bit further away close to the main road leading to the nearest town they found the bodies of three other men from the village. The guerrilla group had killed all four men by slitting open their throats with a knife. When the police closed their investigation of the case ten days later, two more men from the village were missing. On that same day it was reported that Asad had died at a clinic specializing in facial amputations.

Apparently the violence in Ouled Bouchena was motivated by the fact that the villagers, against the orders of the FLN, had continued working for a group of French settlers in the area. I call this type of collective violence "disciplinary violence," since its main purpose was to establish and maintain undisputed discipline among the members of the "Algerian national community" that the FLN claimed to represent. The French military archives contain hundreds of reports that document such episodes.[28] In the majority of these cases, the FLN systematically killed the civil "traitors" by slitting their throats and often they would mutilate the victims' bodies. While the majority of the cases concern episodes of small-scale collective violence, there occasionally appear examples of smaller massacres of twenty to thirty persons in which typical war crimes such as rape, torture, and plundering are observable. In contrast to the intimidating violence that the guerrilla perpetrated against the French soldiers, which was perpetrated in order to comply with the internationally recognized rules of warfare, the disciplinary violence against the Algerian "traitors" was designed to signal the FLN's disregard of the "traitors" by systematically using degrading forms of violence, such as mutilations, rape, and throat slitting.[29]

Polarizing Violence

In accordance with FLN's willingness to comply with the international rules of warfare in the external war against the French enemy, the guerrilla group deliberately avoided targeting civilian Europeans in Algeria during the first months of the insurrection. In August 1955 this momentarily changed. In the morning of 20 August, a few hundred FLN members and thousands of Muslim civilians had assembled in small groups outside some twenty villages in northeast Algeria.[30] Armed with pick-axes, knives, hunting rifles, and a few automatic weapons, the groups entered the villages around noon. Here they attacked the European forces of order and European civilians.[31] Depending on the resistance of the forces of order, the insurrection lasted for a few hours or throughout the day. According to the official statistics, 123 people were killed in the events—70 were Europeans (Ageron 1997:40). In the following weeks the region was sealed off, and the French forces of order assisted by militias composed of armed

European civilians undertook a rough repression of suspects in the Muslim population. The official number of killed Muslims in the repression was put to 1,200, but the FLN and other nationalist groups immediately claimed that the number was much higher and eventually put forward the number of 12,000.[32]

The FLN's political leadership condemned not only the rough repression but also the use of the civil population as perpetrators and as targets in the uprising. Apparently, it had been planned and carried out by a local guerrilla leader without prior coordination with the political leadership. Scholars agree that the intention with the events in August 1955 was to polarize the two communities of civilians living in Algeria.[33] By attacking European civilian settlers and by incorporating Muslim civilians in the group of perpetrators, the FLN forced the colonial forces of order to react with harsh repression of the Muslim population in the area. I call this "polarizing violence."

Monopolizing Violence

In March 1956, the dead bodies of sixteen Muslim Algerians dressed in combat clothes were found in a roadside in Kabylia. Their throats had been slit open and their faces were mutilated. A handwritten letter in Arabic entitled "Proclamation and Warning" issued by the local FLN leader was stuffed into the nostril of one of the corpses. "Let it be known for everybody that these soldiers (*junūd*) were from the army of Messali (*jaysh massālī*), which deviates from the Algerian national unity (*ittiḥād al-waṭan al-jazāirī*)," the short text begins (Etat Major 1957:54). The author finishes the text by affirming that "the Army of National Liberation, which has the honor to belong to the Front of National Liberation, has condemned them to death (*al-ḥukm bil-'i'dām*). This will be the destiny (*masīr*) for everybody that breaks away from the national unity."

In late 1956, such killings were becoming increasingly common, notably in Kabylia. As mentioned above, the FLN grew out of the nationalist mass movement created by Messali Hadj in the 1930s.[34] In 1953, Messali's movement was split into three fractions with different tactical preferences for how independence should be acquired (Harbi 1980): the *Centralists*, who opted for legal political action; the *Messalists*, who stayed loyal to Messali Hadj's pragmatic nonviolent revolutionary tactics; and, finally, the *Activists*, who believed that only armed struggle could force the colonial state to engage in political negotiations. In 1954, members from this last fraction created the FLN in collaboration with members of the former OS. In early 1955, the *Centralists* joined the ranks of the FLN. In contrast, the

Messalists created a competing armed guerrilla group in December 1954, which they called MNA (Mouvement National Algérien). After a relatively peaceful coexistence, the FLN and the MNA became increasingly antagonized during the latter half of 1955. The central issue in the conflict was not ideological but concerned leadership. Neither Messali nor the leaders of the FLN were willing to grant a leading position to the other, and a compromise was never reached (see e.g. Meynier 2002:448). In September 1955, important voices in the FLN accused the MNA of being "auxiliaries of colonialism," and a few months later, in February 1956, FLN's political leadership proclaimed that all "Messalists" from the MNA should be "killed without prior judgment" (Abbane cited in Meynier 2002:451). In spring 1956, the two groups had several bloody confrontations, notably in Kabylia where a former Messalist had created a disciplined guerrilla group loosely attached to the MNA (Planche 2000:2). The violent confrontations between the two groups inevitably involved the civil population, which was often accused of providing assistance to one of the two guerrilla groups. An example of this was the so-called "Red Night of Soummam" where a lieutenant in the FLN killed 500 to 1,200 Muslims civilians within a few days in reprisal for being betrayed to the French army (Benyahia 1988:46–48; Meynier 2002:446). In August the same year, FLN's political leadership unanimously decided that all Messalists were "traitors," and that Messali himself was guilty of "conscious treason" (*khiyāna 'an khabra wa-dirāya*).[35] During 1957, the FLN gradually gained the upper hand in Algeria. Sometimes MNA members simply rallied to the FLN, but it also happened through armed confrontations and harsh repression of suspects in the civil population, as, for instance, the infamous Melouza massacre in Kabylia where four hundred villagers who had collaborated with the MNA were killed by the FLN. I call this type of collective violence "monopolizing violence" since the FLN's core intention was to eliminate competitors and ensure the group's total monopoly to represent the Algerian national community.

Terrorizing Violence

While the FLN in 1956 was quickly moving toward a position as the sole representative of the Muslim population in Algeria, the political results in the external war were sparse. After two years of armed combat, the French continued to regard the FLN as an illegitimate terrorist organization.[36] In August 1956, the political leadership of the FLN decided to bring the war from the rural areas into the urban heart of the colonial state.[37]

A month later, 30 September 1956, three bombs exploded simultaneously in two bars in central Algiers, the Milk Bar and La Cafeteria. The bars were frequented exclusively by settler youth. Two people died and sixty were wounded in the explosions.[38] Throughout 1957, this type of urban terrorism supplemented and in certain regions and periods replaced the guerrilla activities of the FLN.[39] In January 1957, a new wave of explosions ravaged three more bars frequented by European settler youth, Otomatic, Coq Hardi, and, again, La Cafeteria. Four people died and forty were wounded. In February the same year, ten bombs exploded in a stadium in Algiers during a football match. Twenty died and a hundred were wounded. In June, bombs placed in street lamps killed seven and wounded ninety-two. A bomb explosion in Casino de la Corniche on the beach killed eight and injured eighty-one.[40] Close to two thousand European civilian settlers were killed in these and similar episodes, which soon became known as "the Battle of Algiers." The majority of these were killed during 1957 (Pervillé 2002:240).

While some scholars have argued that the urban terrorism aimed at attracting international mass-media coverage, FLN members themselves have explained it as revenge for the executions of imprisoned FLN members that the French state had begun in early 1956.[41] In my analysis, the FLN's decision to widen the target group to encompass civilians from the enemy's community and thereby intentionally break the international rules of warfare, served to intensify its pressure on the French government by creating a feeling of terror in the settler community. I call this type of collective violence "terrorizing violence."

The "Battle of Algiers" not only put the French political system under internal pressure from the settler community but also brought international awareness to the "Algerian question" and notably the French forces' harsh methods. However, the terrorizing violence also intensified French repression of the guerrilla. By the end of 1957, FLN's urban terrorist networks in the major cities in Algeria were more or less annihilated by the French paratroopers. Several of the group's important leaders had been killed and the political leadership had fled the country and installed itself in the newly decolonized Tunisia. Although guerrilla warfare continued in certain regions, the FLN had been seriously weakened. 1958 was in this respect the year that the French army gained the military initiative in the external war and marked several victories over the guerrilla. In late 1958, the French army therefore concluded that the FLN had been militarily defeated.[42] Yet, 1958 also became the year when the French authorities, under the strong leadership of General De Gaulle, initiated secret negotiations with the FLN. From then on the collective violence against its external enemy and its community remained at a low intensity until a cease-fire was agreed in 1962.

Cohesive Violence

By the end of June 1958 an extraordinary military court headed by the FLN leader in Kabylia, Colonel Amirouche, was set up in the Akfadou forest in Kabylia.[43] The court was supposed to investigate a conspiracy that, according to the leadership of the guerrilla, had been orchestrated by the French intelligence services in collaboration with infiltrated spies in the FLN.[44] The military court was conveyed for the first time during a three-day meeting in the Akfadou forest in late July. It was directed by one of Amirouche's closest officers, Larbi Touati. In his memoirs, a former lower officer from the FLN, who assisted the meeting, recalled the interrogation by the military court of a guerrilla fighter named Arezki.

> Arezki is attached to a tree. Four guerrilla fighters and lieutenant Larbi Touati hit him with sticks one after the other. Another guerrilla fighter lights a fire, and with a flaming bamboo stick burns him on his sexual organs and in his armpits. To suppress his screams they force a rag into his mouth. Large drops of sweat run down his face. When it becomes intolerable, Arezki lifts his head to signify that he is ready to talk. The rag is removed and in a gurgle of desperation he says: "there is no God but Allah, and Mohammed is his prophet. I assure that I am a true *mujāhid,* and that I have never betrayed anyone." Each time Touati shouts: "Oh really! Are you making fun of us?" Then he orders the other guerrilla fighters to put the rag back into Arezki's mouth and resume the torture. The scenario is repeated several times. When the night falls, Arezki dies, without having confessed to any of the accusations. (Benyahia 1988:61)

Benyahia's accounts of brutal torture in Akfadou is confirmed by several documents in the French military archives.[45] A report written by a French intelligence officer a few months later estimates that more than 400 guerrilla fighters were interrogated, tortured, condemned, and executed during the three-day meeting in Akfadou.[46] While other documents from the French intelligence service estimate that at least 1,000 guerrilla fighters were killed in Kabylia during the summer,[47] scholars assume that close to 2,000 members of the FLN were executed in the Kabyle region alone in 1958.[48] By the end of 1958, these so-called "purges" in the FLN had spread to several other regions of Algeria. While some former French officers have suggested that 10,000 guerrilla fighters were killed in the purges, scholars have pointed out that written documentation can be found for "only" a little less than 5,000 victims.[49]

The motives for the purges remain disputed. The documents produced by the French intelligence services in Algeria leave little doubt that the FLN was not infiltrated in a way that could explain thousands of killings. While some French intelligence officers considered it possible that the guerrilla leader Amirouche had been the object of a "murder attempt" and therefore reacted by purging his troops,[50] others have claimed that Amirouche simply "went mad."[51] I propose another interpretation. After four years of combat, the FLN was in 1958 facing serious military and political difficulties. The successful French repression of the FLN's urban networks in 1957 was followed by a rural counterinsurgency in 1958. Lack of provisions and the increasing military pressure created serious problems for the guerrilla in upholding the morale of the guerrilla fighters. In the summer of 1958, the guerrilla leaders in the Kabyle region reacted by initiating internal executions of potential deserters (in part for symbolic purposes). I call this type of collective violence "cohesive violence" since its aim was to reestablish internal cohesion in the guerrilla group in a time of crisis.

Power-Staging Violence

In late summer 1962, the situation in Algeria was chaotic. On 2 July the population had voted for a French withdrawal and a complete takeover of the state institutions by the FLN. However, eight years of counter-guerrilla warfare and internal power struggles in the guerrilla had considerably weakened the FLN. In the words of Mohamed Harbi, the FLN "imploded" into competing factions unable to make any decisions the moment the French state withdrew from Algeria (Harbi 2000). When the so-called "external army," which had been built up in Morocco and Tunisia since 1958, moved into Algeria and fought the guerrilla fractions, violence increased dramatically. On 5 July 1962, 75 Muslims and 20 Europeans were killed in the city Oran (Meynier 2002:641). The next day more than 300 Europeans were kidnapped in apparent retaliation, and in the following weeks another 2,000 to 3,000 Europeans were kidnapped (Meynier 2002:642). A few months later more than 800,000 Europeans had left Algeria together with the French army (Pervillé 2002:252). In the same period, the FLN organized a systematic repression of Algerian Muslims who had been engaged in the French army as auxiliary soldiers, or "*harkis*," during the war.[52] In a report from August 1962, a French intelligence officer notes that a "campaign of generalized repression" had begun in some of the areas where the guerrilla fighters still held power. From there it spread to the rest of Algeria between July and September 1962 and only gradually decreased in early

1963.[53] As with any other death toll from the war, it is difficult to ascertain how many *harkis* were killed. While some authors have claimed that the total is close to 100,000 (Hamoumou 1993), others have estimated that the number should be fixed somewhere around 10,000 (Meynier 2002).

An early episode of collective violence against the disarmed *harkis* took place the day after independence. A group of guerrilla fighters kidnapped two former *harkis* at a train station in northeast Algeria. The *harkis* were brought to the local FLN headquarter outside the village. Here they were interviewed together with a former cook, who had prepared food for a local unit of *harkis*.[54] During the interview, the guerrilla leader explained that the war was over and that the men had nothing to fear. They had been picked up at the station because the FLN was in an urgent need of men who knew how to use a gun. The cook therefore replied that he was of little help since he had never taken part in any fighting. In contrast, the first *harki* reported that he personally had killed six FLN fighters during the war. The other *harki* said that he had killed close to eighty FLN members. After the interview the men were imprisoned. A few days later the cook was released after a severe beating. The FLN also confiscated his identity papers and told him not to join his family. The same day the two former *harkis* were presented for a crowd of local civil Muslims who had assembled at the FLN headquarters. In front of the crowd the first *harki* was severely beaten and finally killed by having his throat slit. The other *harki* was also beat up. Then a guerrilla fighter took an axe and cut him into what was announced to be "as many pieces as he had killed rebels."

The punishment of the *harkis* was framed in symbols that served to publicly promote an image of the local guerrilla fighters as capable leaders who could correct the historical injustice imposed on the Algerian national community by the colonial state and thereby ensure a just order in independent Algeria. This political message was communicated through a penal logic that resemble the premodern European "punishment as public spectacle," where painful physical punishment was carefully measured to counter the pain inflicted by the criminal on the community (Foucault 1979:7–8): One blow with the axe for each killed *mujāhid*. I call this type of collective violence "power-staging violence," since its main purpose was to present, or "stage," the FLN as a legitimate power holder in the postcolonial state.

Counter-State Building

In this chapter I have argued that FLN's war against colonialism in Algeria comprised two parallel but qualitatively distinct war projects. Discursively, the group referred to these as the "war of independence" (*ḥarb al-istiqlāl*) directed against a French "enemy" (*'adū*), and the "war of liberation" (*ḥarb at-taḥrīr*) directed against a Muslim "traitor" (*khā'in*). From 1954 to 1962 the guerrilla group fought these two wars through the different sociological types of collective violence that I have described in the above cases.

Fought as a classic guerrilla war, the external war of independence against the French colonial state was fought by the FLN not to inflict military defeat. Through forms of collective violence designed to intimidate the external enemy's soldiers and polarize, and later terrorize, the external enemy's community of civilian (white) settlers, the FLN sought to force the French state to engage in political negotiations. Thereby the FLN implicitly demanded that the French state should recognize it and treat the organization as an "equal"—that is, as representative of a state and not as a terrorist group. By prohibiting the guerrilla fighters from committing war crimes against the external enemy and by condemning them when they occurred, the FLN sought to follow the rules of warfare laid down by international conventions and hence acted as if it represented a recognized state in war with another recognized state. When two years of fighting had passed and the French state continued to refuse to recognize both the FLN and the Algerian state that it claimed to represent, the guerrilla group officially changed its strategy and began targeting civilians of the external enemy's community.

Between 1954 and 1962, the FLN killed 15,000 French citizens in Algeria in order to intimidate, polarize, and terrorize the French enemy and gain recognition as a legitimate negotiating party. In the same period and within the same territory, the same guerrilla group killed 200,000 to 300,000 internal enemies, or "traitors of the nation," from the Muslim population in Algeria. While the FLN conceived the external war as a war between equal states, it conceptualized its internal war as a legitimate repression of members of the national community of the state that it represented. The internal war was manifested in four types of collective violence. Through *disciplinary violence* the FLN enforced its authority over the national community of Muslim civilians. Through *monopolizing violence* the FLN eliminated other nationalist guerrilla groups, which claimed authority over the Muslim population and the right to represent the Algerian state in international relations. Through *cohesive violence* the FLN ensured its own survival in times of moral crisis involving the guerrilla fighters. And, finally, the guerrilla fighters in the FLN used *power-staging violence* to present itself as legitimate regime in the independent Algerian state.

The central argument here is that these two distinctively conceptualized and enacted wars—one external and the other internal—shared the intention of creating a position for the FLN as representative of an independent Algerian state. I call this "counter-state building." However, by "countering" the French colonial state in Algeria, the FLN appropriated and reinterpreted the categories, taxonomies, and even state ideologies of the colonial state. Like former generations of Algerian nationalists, the FLN created a national community of "Algerians" that reflected the colonial state's confessional and racial categories, which distinguished between the "European," who was white, Christian, and settler, and the "Muslim," who was a colored and indigene.

It would be hazardous to compare directly the micro-historical analysis that I have made of the FLN's use of collective violence in the state building during the war of independence in Algeria with the macro-historical analyses of state formation and collective violence in Europe made by Charles Tilly and his collaborators (Tilly 1975). However, the phenomenon of intimation and reproduction of colonial categories in the Algerian case deserves further discussion. In the European case, the creation of a system of consolidated nation-states happened according to Tilly and his collaborators as an unintended result of centuries of warfare and mobilization for war. In Algeria, and in the Middle East in general, the creation of the existing nation-states was also the result of violence, coercion, and war between local and international actors, such as the FLN, the Messalists, and the French state. But in contrast to state formation in early modern Europe, state building in Algeria and in the Middle East was a *conscious* and *intended* process of imitation and reproduction. In certain cases, the European colonial powers in the Middle East themselves created colonial states that imitated the colonial metropolises. In other cases, the European colonial powers created independent states in the Middle East that were modeled upon the European colonial metropolis.[55] My argument in this chapter is also that local actors—namely, the FLN—imitated the hegemonic political concepts of the modern European nation-state in an attempt to create an independent political entity. Hence, whether exported by colonial powers or imported by local actors, the creation of nation-states in the Middle East was, in contrast to the European state formation through war, a conscious process of imitation of an already existing principle and form of social organization manifested in the European national state.[56]

Annnex 1: Methodology and Typology of the FLN's Collective Violence

The typology below consists of seven sociological ideal type of collective violence. I define collective violence, in line with the work of Charles Tilly, as episodes of social interaction that involve at least two coordinating per-

Table 2. Typology of forms of violence

	External War of Independence (*istiqlāl*)			Internal War of Liberation (*taḥrīr*)			
Types \ Variables	Intimidating Violence	Terrorizing Violence	Polarizing Violence	Disciplinary Violence	Monopolizing Violence	Cohesive Violence	Power-staging Violence
Target's affiliation	Enemy's group (army)	Enemy's community	Enemy's community	Own community	Competing group	Own group	Own community
Designation of target	"Enemy"	"Enemy"	"Enemy"	"Traitor" *"collaborator"*	"Traitor" *"messalist"*	"Traitor" *"agent"*	"Traitor" *"harki"*
Form of violence	Ambush and surprise-attack by fire arms	Mass-casualty bombs	Lynching and popular riots	Mutilations and throat slitting, collective reprisals	Combat by fire arms and executions by throat slitting	Execution by throat slitting	Lynching, public mutilations, and public executions
Location	Rural	Urban	Rural and Urban	Rural and urban	Rural and urban	Rural	Rural and urban

| Chronology | 1954–62 | 1957–58 | 1955 | 1954–62 | 1956–58 | 1958–59 | 1962–63 |

petrators and that immediately inflict physical damage on persons or objects (Tilly 2003:3). Each type of collective violence listed in the typology has a distinct combination of four subordinate variables. The first subordinate variable is the target's affiliation to a group or community. There are five differing categories in this variable: (a) members of the enemy's group of soldiers serving in the French army; (b) members of the enemy's community of civil European settlers living in Algeria; (c) members of the guerrilla group's own community of civil Muslims living in Algeria; (d) members of competing Algerian nationalist guerrilla groups operating in Algeria; and (e) members of the guerrilla group itself. The second subordinate variable is FLN's discursive nomination of the target. Here two main categories are found: First, an *external* enemy that the FLN called "the enemy" (*al-'adū* in Arabic, and *l'ennemie* in French). Second, an *internal* enemy that the group called "the traitor" (*al-khāin* in Arabic, and *le traître* in French). In certain cases, the guerrilla group would further specify the internal enemy into subcategories such as "collaborator," "Messalist," and *"harki."* The third subordinate variable is the form of the violence, or more precisely, the way the FLN took the target's life. This variable comprises several differing forms of collective violence: Ambush, massacre, mass-casualty bombing, throat slitting, mutilations, combat, execution, and lynching. The fourth and last subordinate variable is the location of the violence, which could be either urban or rural—or both.

On the basis of varying combinations of these four subordinate variables, I attempt to identify some of the major "core intentions" for the episodes of collective violence that the guerrilla perpetrated during the war.

Notes

1. The chapter draws on three years of research in the French military archives, which in 2001 was presented to École des hautes études en sciences Sociales in Paris as a *mémoire de diplôme* entitled "Violence et trahison – Les violences politiques du FLN et de l'ALN contre les Algériens musulmans pendant la Guerre d'Indépendance 1954–62." In 2002 the work was honored with the yearly *Prix du meilleur diplôme de l'EHESS*.
2. Death toll quoted in Stora 1998:182, and discussed in Pervillé 2002:240–45.
3. Most of these were Muslim peasants whom the French forces moved from the so-called "prohibited zones" where the guerrilla operated and resettled in surveyed camps. For a sociological analysis of the forced displacements, see Bourdieu and Sayad 1964.
4. Already during the war French intellectuals denounced the use of torture by police and military in Algeria. Most well known is the essay entitled *La Question* in which the French communist Henry Alleg testified to the torture that he had endured in the hands of the French paratroopers in Algeria (Alleg 1957). After the war notably Pierre Vidal-

Naquet has investigated the war crimes committed by the French forces of order in Algeria (Vidal-Naquet 1973). Based on documents from the military archives, Raphaëlle Branche (2001) and Slyvie Thénault (2001) have lately expanded the understanding of both judicial and administrative aspects of the French repression.
5. While the writings of influential intellectuals like Frantz Fanon fit well into this perspective (Fanon 1959 and 1961), also certain of the early works of a scholar like Pierre Bourdieu present a critical attitude to French colonialism in Algeria (e.g. Bourdieu and Sayad 1964). Furthermore, the early studies of the war focused predominantly on the activities of the French army. Only in the late 1970s a generation of Algerian scholars educated in France began publishing studies of the guerrilla groups (Harbi 1975; Teguia 1980; Cheikh 1998 [1980]). With the opening of the French military archives in 1992, a large body of scholarly literature about both the guerrilla's activities and the colonial army's repression has appeared. A survey of the development of the historiography of the war was published yearly by Guy Perville between 1976 and 1992 in *Annuaire de l'Afrique du Nord*. A critical discussion of the anticolonial perspective in French Middle Eastern studies is found in Liauzu 1998.
6. An interesting study of the FLN's strategic use of different forms of terrorism was published in 1978 by Martha Crenshaw Hutchinson (Hutchinson 1978).
7. The French military archives from the war in Algeria are kept by the *Service historique de l'armée de terre* (SHAT) in Chateau de Vincennes outside Paris. The collection notably contains documents produced by the French military bureaucracy, but also encompasses a variety of documents written in French and Arabic by members of the guerrilla, and collected by the French forces of order. The majority of the documents that I refer to in this essay are still listed as "classified." Consulting these dossiers requires a written permission from the French Ministery of Defense.
8. Focusing on the political development of the FLN, Mohammed Harbi has argued that the FLN during the war aimed at building a "counter-state" (*contre-État*) in opposition to the existing French colonial state (Harbi 1980).
9. As a "*departement*" in the French state, Algeria was more closely tied to the colonial metropolis than were the other North African and Middle Eastern territories that in the late nineteenth and early twentieth centuries came under French colonial domination in the form of "protectorates" (Tunisia, 1881–1956; Morocco, 1912–56) and "mandates" in Syria and Lebanon (1920–44).
10. It was the colonial state that developed regularly scheduled transportation that linked Algeria to the colonial metropolis through a system of railways and steamships, and later build the infrastructure inside the Algerian territory that again laid the foundation not only for the military pacification but also for the development of commerce and capitalist production and export (Carlier 1997).
11. A critical analysis of the development of a capitalist state structure in Algeria is found in Bourdieu and Sayad 1964.
12. In contrast to the Algerian colonial model in which the white settler community "directly" administered the colony, many European colonies in Africa, Asia, and the Middle East were organized as a system of "indirect rule" in which the white European settler minority ruled through a group of local notables and/or ethnic and religious minorities. For an overview of the different manifestations of colonial rule, see Osterhammel 1997, chapter 5.
13. For a definition of the specific pattern of control and domination called the "colonial state" in a Middle Eastern context, see Owen 2000 and Zubaida 1993.
14. For an analysis of the French colonial *mission civilisatrice,* see Porterfield 1999 and Lorcin 1999.
15. Sami Zubaida has argued that the European colonial state in the Middle East introduced what he calls a "new political field." On the basis of the coercive, economic and institutional power of the colonial motherland, the colonial state, according the Zubaida,

forced both preexisting and emerging social actors to adapt their political strategies to the realities of this new field (Zubaida 1993).
16. In the 1950s, the Messali's movement had about 20,000 activists and 18,000 supporters in Algeria as well as 5,000 activists and 3,000 supporters in France (Harbi 1975:88).
17. A detailed account of the repression is found in Mekhaled 1995.
18. In 1948, the OS presented a detailed program for how a guerrilla war against the French colonial state should be fought (the text is published in Harbi 1981:15–49).
19. A French version of the text can be found in Harbi 1981:101–103, and an Arabic one in FLN 1987:3–6.
20. Altogether, more than 30,000 French citizens died in unnatural ways in Algeria between 1954 and 1962. Of these, about 15,000 died in accidents. The rest were killed by the FLN (Stora 1998:182).
21. Fiche Sur la Situation en Algérie. SHAT 2R 166–2 (classified).
22. In 1954 these Muslim troops numbered about 7,000, but by 1961 the number had risen to 120,000 (Chauvin 1995:23 and Ageron 1995:11).
23. For a complete list of the colonial forces of order, see Jauffret and Vaïsse 2001.
24. Rapport du Chef d'Escadron relatif à l'embuscade tendue par les rebelles le 4 janvier 1955 dans la région de Chélia. SHAT 2R 166–1 (classified).
25. According to Guy Pervillé, around 2,000 French citizens were killed in acts of urban terrorism (Pervillé 2002:240).
26. Many examples from the military archives indicate that the guerrilla had a strict policy of treating the French prisoners of war with respect. One such example was when a local FLN leader in late 1958 decided to execute a captured lieutenant from the French army in reprisal for an extrajudicial killing of an FLN officer by the French forces of order. Before acting he sent a notice to the FLN's political leadership in Tunisia explaining that the case was a necessary exception and that he continually respected his orders to treat the French prisoners of war correctly (Tract ALN d`Amirouche: 'La loi de talion'. SHAT 1H 2584–4 [classified]).
27. Procès verbal de l'enquête préliminaire du 1er octobre 1960. La Brigade de Trezel (Tiaret). SHAT 1H 1985 bis –1 (classified).
28. See for instance the dossiers in SHAT: 1H 1691–4, 1H 1790–1, 1H 1793–1 and 2, 1H 1983–3, 1H 1984–1 and 2, 1H 1985–1 and 2, 1H 1985–1bis and 2bis, 1H 1986–1, 1H 2584–2, 6 and 7.
29. The FLN designed its forms of violence against "traitors of the nation" in order to transform local customs into socially degrading violence. For instance, throat slitting, which in Arabic is called *dhabh*, is the way Muslim tradition prescribe that animals destined for eating or sacrifice must be slaughtered. By systematically employing methods intended for animals rather than human beings, the FLN signalled its disrespect for the "traitor." For a semiotic analysis of the forms of violence perpetrated by the FLN against the Muslim traitor and the French enemy, see Boserup 2004.
30. The number of participants in the uprising remains uncertain. Charles-Robert Ageron, for instance, quotes documents whose numbers range between 600 and 900 ALN members and between 3,000 and 20,000 civilians (Ageron 1997:38).
31. A detailed chronology of the events can be found in Courrière 2001 [1968]: vol. 1.
32. The numbers for the Muslim casualties during the war are objects of constant discussion among historians. Slimane Cheikh argues that the FLN did establish a verified list of about 12,000 persons killed in the repression (Cheikh 1998 [1980]), Charles-Robert Ageron pragmatically proposed that the number is to be found somewhere between 1,200 and 12,000 (Ageron 1997:34).
33. E.g. Ageron 1997 or Hutchington 1978. According to Charles-Robert Ageron, August 1955 was a decisive turning point in the external war: "It was no longer a question of armed resistance or acts of rebels [*felleghas*] whom it was said came form Tunisia. This

was a war of a an entire people animated and lead by the FLN and the Army of National Liberation" (Ageron 1997:27).
34. For a detailed analysis of the development of the Algerian nationalist movement, see Harbi 1975.
35. The declaration was published as an integral part of the FLN's forty-page political program called the "Soummam Platform" (*minhaj al-sūmām*), which was developed at a secret meeting in Kabylia in August 1956 (FLN 1987)
36. On 12 November 1954 the French president Pierre Mendes France publicly stated: "One does not negotiate when it is about defending the internal peace of the nation and the integrity of the republic" (cited in Pervillé 2002:129). The French political authorities upheld this attitude toward the FLN until 1958.
37. The influential FLN leader in Algiers, Abane Ramdane, expressed the motives behind the urban terrorism in the following terms: "It is better to kill one French citizen in an Algerian city that will be mentioned on American television the following day, than to kill 10 in the countryside where nobody will hear about it" (Fairbairn 1974:284).
38. *Echo d'Alger*, 1 October 1956.
39. According to Guy Pervillé, the period from November 1954 to January 1957 was characterized by the appearance and aggravation of the urban terrorism in Algeria. Yet, from 1957 to 1960 the French forces of order successfully repressed FLN's urban terrorist networks. From December 1960 to June 1962 the French militant settlers reintroduced urban terrorism under the leadership of the OAS (Pervillé in Jauffret and Vaïsse 2001:450).
40. For an account of the events see Horne 1977: chapter 9 and 10, or Hutchinson 1978:89–90.
41. According to the leader of the terrorist unit of the FLN in Algiers, Yacef Saadi, the executions of imprisoned FLN members in the central prison in Algiers enraged not only the radical militants but also large parts of the Muslim civil population. Saadi explains that in the spring of 1956 he had told one of his officers: "the machine gun, the pistol, and the knife no longer can hold back the rage of the ultras. There is only one way to calm them: bombs" (Saadi 1984:277).
42. Several scholars analyzing the military aspects of the external war have reached the same conclusion. See, e.g., Schrader 1999.
43. Fiche de Renseignements. 22 September 1958. SHAT 1H 1699–1 (classified).
44. Dossier Amirouche. Exemplaire n° 14/15. SHAT 1H 1700–1 (classified).
45. One such example is the substantial thirteen-page eyewitness account told by a former member of the FLN to the French intelligence services in august 1958. Témoignage de X. Rallié aux F.O. le 6.4.1959. SHAT 1H 1699–1 (classified).
46. About 400 corpses carrying the marks of torture were found by the French army in late September 1958 in the Akfadou Forest. Fiche de Renseignements. Le 22 septembre 1958. SHAT 1H 1699–1 (classified).
47. Note de renseignements. Tizi-Ouzou le 14 avril 1959. SHAT 1H 1699–1 (classified).
48. Quoted by Charles-Robert Ageron (Ageron 1998:19). Mohammed Harbi and Droz and Lever, for their part, quote a former FLN fighter who has proposed that the death toll in Kabylia was 2,000 (Harbi 1980:235 and Droz and Lever 1991:209). Mohammed Téguia, on the other hand, estimates that the death toll was "a little above one thousand" (Téguia 1980:374). Yves Courrière suggest that "more than 3,000 young people" died in the purges (Courrière 2001[1968] vol. 2:374).
49. Charles-Robert Ageron considers this "strongly exaggerated" and recalls that the guerrilla's total membership never surpassed 23,000, or 50,000 with the *musābilūn*. In contrast, he recalls that written documentation has indicated that the number of killed is a bit less than 5,000 persons (Ageron 1998:26).
50. Note Concernant l'épuration menée au sein du FLN en Wilaya III. SHAT 1H 1699–1 (classified).

51. E.g. *"Annexe V"* [without date]. SHAT 1H 1699–1 (classified).
52. As the official peace settlement gave complete amnesty for all war crimes, many former *harkis* stayed in Algeria after the independence.
53. Situation des ex-harkis en Algérie depuis le cessez-le-feu. 13 August 1962. SHAT 1H 1793–1 (classified).
54. It was the cook who reported the events to the French military. Rapport de général de Brigade Frat – Annexe 1. 18 August 1962. SHAT 1H 1793–2 (classified).
55. This was notably the case in the "mandates" of the former Ottoman territories that after World War I were administered by Great Britain and France.
56. Charles Tilly himself has noted this possible difference between state development in Europe and the Third World (Tilly 1985).
57. All the listed documents are classified and can, according to French law, only be consulted with special permission from the Ministry of Defense.

Bibliography

Ageron, Ch.-Robert. 1994. *Histoire de l'Algérie Contemporaine, 1830–1994*. 10 ed. Paris: Presses Universitaires de France.

———. 1995. "Les supplétifs algériens dans l'armée française pendant la guerre d'Algérie," *Vingtième siècle* 48 (Octobre-novembre): 3–20.

———. 1997. *La guerre d'Algérie et les algériens 1954–1962*. Paris: Armand Colin.

———. 1998. "Complots et purges dans l'armée de libération algérienne," *Vingtième siècle* 59 (juillet-septembre): 15–27.

Alleg, Henri. 1957. *La question*. Paris: Minuit.

Benyahia, Mohammed. 1988 *La conjuration au pouvoir*. Paris: L'Arcantère.

Boserup, Rasmus Alenius. 2004. "Semiotics of Violence: Examples from the War in Algeria [in Danish]," *Tidsskriftet Antropologi* 46: 77–88.

Bourdieu, Pierre and Abdelmalik Sayad. 1964. *Le déracinement: La crise de l'agriculture traditionnelle en Algérie*. Paris: Minuit.

Branche, Raphaëlle. 2001. *La torture et l'armée pendant la guerre d'Algérie (1954–1962)*. Paris: Gallimard.

Carlier, Omar. 1997. *La révolution du rapport à l'espace et au temps et la recomposition du lien social: le cas de l'Algérie coloniale (1830–1930)*. Collective publication from Université d'Oran, CRASC.

Chauvin, Stéphanie. 1995. "Les appelés français de souche nord-africaine," *Vingtième siècle* 48 (Octobre-novembre): 21–30.

Cheikh, Slimane. 1998 [1980]. *L'Algérie en armes, ou le temps des certitudes*. Paris: Economica.

Courrière, Yves. 2001 [1968]. *La guerre d'Algérie*. (2 vol). Paris: Fayard.

Droz, Bernhard and Evelyne Lever. 1991. *La guerre d'Algérie, 1954–1962*. 2d ed. Paris: Seuil.

Etat Major. 1957. *True Aspects of the Algerian Rebellion*. Alger.

Fairbairn, Geoffrey. 1974. *Revolutionary Guerilla Warfare: The Countryside Version*. Harmondsworth: Penguin.

Fanon, Frantz. 1959. *Sociologie d'une Revolution: L'an V de la revolution algérienne*. Paris: Maspero.

———. 1961. *Les damnés de la terre*. Paris: Maspero.

FLN. 1987. *An-nusūs al-asāsiyya li-jabha at-taḥrīr al-waṭanī 1962–1954*. Alger: nashar wa-tawzī' qiṭā' al-i'lām wal-thaqāfa wal-takwīn.

Foucault, Michel. 1979. *Discipline and Punish*. New York: Vintage Books.

Hamoumou, Mohand. 1993. *Et ils sont devenus harkis…* Paris: Fayard.

Harbi, Mohammed. 1975. *Aux origines du FLN*. Paris: Bourgois.

———. 1980. *Le FLN: Mirage et réalité, des origines à la prise du pouvoir*. Paris: Jeune Afrique.
———. 1981. *Les archives de la révolution algérienne*. Paris: Jeunes Afrique.
———. 1994. *1954 - La guerre commence en Algérie*. Bruxelles: Complexe.
———. 2000. "L'implosion du FLN (été 1962)," in Gilbert Meynier (ed.), *L'Algérie contemporaine: Bilan et solutions pour sortir de crise*. Paris: L'Harmattan.
Horne, Alistar. 1977. *A Savage War of Peace: Algeria 1954–1962*. London: Macmillan.
Hutchinson, Martha Crenshaw. 1978. *Revolutionary Terrorism: The FLN in Algeria 1954–1962*. Stanford: Hoover Institution Press.
Jauffret, J-Ch. and M. Vaïsse (eds). 2001. *Guerre et guérilla en Algérie (1954–1962)*. Bruxelles: Complexe.
Koulakssis, Ahmed and Gilbert Meynier. 1987. *L'Emir Khaled, Premier Za'îm? Identité algérienne et colonialisme français*. Paris: L'Harmattan.
Liauzu, Claude. 1998. "Décolonisations, guerres de mémoires et histoire," *Annuaire de l'Afrique du Nord*, tome xxxvii. Paris: CNRS.
Lorcin, Patricia. 1999. *Imperial Identities: Stereotyping, Prejudice and Race in Colonial Algeria*. London: I.B. Tauris.
Mekhaled, Boucif. 1995. *Chroniques d'un Massacre: 8 mai 1945, Sétif, Guelma, Kherrata*. Paris: Au nom de la mémoire.
Meynier, Gilbert. 2002. *Histoire intérieure du FLN 1954–1962*. Paris: Fayard.
Osterhammel, Jürgen. 1997. *Colonialism: A Theoretical Overview*. Princeton: Marcus Wiener Publishers.
Owen, Roger. 2000. *State, Power and Politics in the Making of the Modern Middle East*. 2nd edition. London: Routledge.
Pervillé, Guy. 1976–1992. "Historiographie de la Guerre d'Algérie," *Annuaire de l'Afrique du Nord*. Paris: CNRS.
———. 2001. "Le terrorisme urbain dans la guerre d'Algérie (1954–1962)," in J.Ch. Jauffret et al. (eds), *Guerre et guérilla en Algérie (1954–1962)*. Bruxelles: Complexe.
———. 2002. *Pour une histoire de la guerre d'Algérie*. Paris: Picard.
Planche, Jean-Louis. 2000. "De la solidarité militante à l'affrontement armé: M.N.A. et F.L.N. à Alger, 1954–1955," in D. Rivet and A.-L. Pathé (eds), *La guerre d'Algérie au miroir des décolonisations françaises*. Paris: SFHOM.
Porterfield, Todd. 1999. *The Allure of Empire*. Princeton: Princeton University Press.
Saadi, Yacef. 1984. *La bataille d'Alger*. Alger: ENAL.
Schrader, Charles R. 1999. *The First Helicopter War: Logistics and Mobility in Algeria 1954–1962*. London: Praeger.
Stora, Benjamin. 1998. *La gangrène et l'oubli: La mémoire de la guerre d'Algérie*. Paris: La Découverte.
Teguia, Mohammed. 1980. *L'Algérie en guerre*. Alger: OPU.
Thénault, Sylvie. 2001. *Une drôle de justice: Les magistrats dans la guerre d'Algérie*. Paris: La Découverte.
Tilly, Charles (ed.). 1975. *The Formation of National States in Western Europe*. New Jersey: Princeton University Press.
———. 1985. "War-making and State-making as Organized Crime," in P. B. Evans et al. (eds), *Bringing the State Back in*. Cambridge: Cambridge University Press.
———. 2003. *The Politics of Collective Violence*. Cambridge: Cambridge University Press.
Vidal-Naquet, Pierre. 1973. *La torture dans la république*. Paris: Maspero.
Zubaida, Sami. 1993. *Islam, the People and the State*. London: I.B. Tauris.

Unpublished documents kept by SHAT[57]

1H 1699-1: Fiche de Renseignements, 22 Septembre 1958; Témoignage de X. Rallié aux F.O. le 6.4.1959; Note de renseignements, Tizi-Ouzou le 14 avril 1959; Note Concernant l'épuration menée au sein du FLN en Wilaya III, Annexe V.

1H 1700–1: Dossier Amirouche, Exemplaire n° 14/15.
1H 1793–1: Situation des ex-harkis en Algérie depuis le cessez-le-feu, 13 August 1962.
1H 1793–2: Rapport de général de Brigade Frat – Annexe 1, 18 August 1962.
1H 1985 bis –1: Procès-verbal de l'enquête préliminaire du 1er octobre 1960, La Brigade de Trezel (Tiaret).
1H 2584–4: Tract ALN d`Amirouche: "La loi de talion."
2R 166–1: Rapport du Chef d'Escadron relatif à l'embuscade tendue par les rebelles le 4 janvier 1955 dans la région de Chélia.
2R 166–2: Fiche sur la Situation en Algérie.

Chapter Eleven

MALIGNANT ORGANISMS
Continuities of State-Run Violence in Rural Liberia

Mats Utas

> [P]ower everywhere and continuously refers and appeals to emergency as well as laboring secretly to produce it. (Agamben, Binetti, and Casarino 2000:6)

According to Hardt and Negri (2001), the abstract network organism that the authors have called the *Empire* feeds on its fringe zones. These zones clearly constitute geographically marginal areas including entire states, such as Liberia and several other West African countries, which provide textbook cases. The focus of this chapter is the contested sovereignty of the Liberian state during the 1990s civil war in the country. I provide an examination of historic accounts of organized violence, both on local and national levels, and argue that what we today often perceive to be failed or weak states must be seen as historically continuous rather than as representing a new phenomenon. My specific examination of state-run violence aims at clarifying this point.[1] In taking the multifaceted (and certainly not unproblematic) work of Hardt and Negri as a theoretical base for the discussion, I further try to link historical processes in its Liberian peculiarity with an international dimension. *Empire* pinpoints for anthropologists the importance of taking global patterns into account and urges us to move well beyond ideas of globalized cultural flows in our efforts of reading "the local." Compressed, Hardt and Negri's notion of *Empire* could be described as:

> The empire is organized by "imperial sovereignty"—constituted by the fast-growing networks of international legal regulation of trade, economic transac-

---

Notes for this chapter are located on page 285.

tions, along with globalized concepts of human rights and development, global cultural flows, the configuration of the international community as a moral and political network of powerful states, as well as complex networks of military alliances backed up by the overwhelming size and sophistication of American military power. (Hansen and Stepputat n.d.)

The Empire according to Hardt and Negri is no longer based on national control over geographical areas or human bodies—"our postmodern empire has no Rome" (Hardt and Negri 2001:317)—but rather it is an abstraction without core, based on global economic transactions with large multinational corporations as main engines. The Empire feeds on fringe zones—zones that are not necessarily geographical but any areas where the Empire's networks grow thin—of the world economy as areas of expansion and/or production. According to an inherent capitalist logic, these areas are not formally incorporated in any sense, and at times are even prevented from being incorporated into the Empire. As such, it is a hierarchic world order.[2] The Empire is not deliberately causing disorder at its fringe areas, and this is in clear opposition to how the traditional empire is conceived as going about its business. For instance, in Alain Joxe's *Empire of Disorder* (2002) we find a vision of a classic "Roman" empire constructed of state and nation and currently personified by the United States, a modern—not postmodern as in Hardt and Negri's version—empire that maintains political and socioeconomic control by creating chaos in geographic fringe zones.[3]

Even if we in the Empire find certain key cities of control (Hardt and Negri 2001:297) as the nexus for a wide spectrum of bodies functioning as global constitutional elements (Hardt and Negri 2001:309), it is evident that even the postmodern Empire needs fringe zones; but in contrast to the national empires, it breeds on local differences rather than on state-orchestrated homogeneity processes. The Empire does not wish to rule out regional or local conflicts but rather aims at manipulating differences to keep populations at bay (Hardt and Negri 2001:339–43). In fact the logic of the Empire prospers by permitting difference—collapsing the inherent drive for homogeneity of the modern nation-states that at times has led us toward extreme genocides, as argued by Zygmunt Bauman (1989), Michel Foucault (1977), and Achille Mbembe (2003). By promoting frontierless cultural difference, the Empire also gives voice to, and choice of, localism, or autochthony, yet decisively aims at preventing collective sentiments of outright regional separatism. From the Empire's point of view, the *ethnie* is not a threatening entity but rather a stepping-stone in superseding troublesome borders.

Observers such as journalists experience and advocate for the local as consisting of naturalized sociocultural varieties. By describing inherited cultural differences, they comply to the bio-power of the Empire. This is clearly observable in many accounts of the news media in, for instance, descriptions of ethnic warfare in Africa (for an anthropological critique see, e.g., Allen and Seaton 1999; Richards 1996; Shaw 2003; Utas 2000). Such "ethnic" images are depictions of internal warfare, in Africa in particular, as struggles based on tradition, and by rebel movements that are directly antimodern (read anti-West), all to the contentment of the postmodern Empire. But it could, quite contrarily, be argued that conflicts like the Liberian Civil War are modern rather than postmodern or antimodern (Utas 2003; 2004c).

Social scientists would also be at risk of carrying such ideas, as our intellectual base is after all part of the bio-politics of the Empire. Through an overemphasis on ethnicity and by localizing mechanisms of violence, we might go about the business of the Empire. Jonathan Friedman is to the point when in *Globalization, the State and Violence* (2003) he underlines the necessity of starting any analysis of violence from the state downward and not by overemphasizing the body—as contemporary anthropology could be accused of. But he subsequently overstates the possibility of an *in praxis* separation of space and body. In his emphasis, violence in an ethnic landscape can be clearly formulated toward a coherent Other, and collective violence has thus only to do with space, as bodies are abstract or even absent, easy to slaughter, easy to rape, appearing as faceless objects. As is evident from my own Liberian research (Utas 2003; 2005a; Utas 2005c; 2008) and in, for instance, Christopher Taylor's book *Sacrifice as terror* (1999), on the Rwandan genocide, bodies and territories are often conflated. Targets of violence are frequently neighbors, people that have ambivalent backgrounds. Any ethnic project is driven forward precisely by the cleansing of familiar bodies of ambivalence—they form part of, and thus embody, contested social territories. By disconnecting control over space from control over bodies, we overlook one of the most important building stones of Hardt and Negri's Empire, namely, the complex of bio-politics and biopower that they have adopted from Michel Foucault's work on governmentality (see, e.g., Foucault 1979). On the other hand, disregarding the embodiment of power sources is exactly what the Empire thrives upon.

In the following text I will take space and bodies of rural Liberia into special consideration. After discussing the Liberian Civil War in brief, I will discuss the sociopolitical setup of events that preceded the war. I aim at presenting *local* forms of violence as means of control.[4] I continue with a discussion on the use of state-run violence as the disciplining of subjects by the nation-state from the time of the arrival of freed slaves from the Americas in the 1820s to their subsequent "colonization" of Liberian territory. In the next part of the chapter, I will compare structural use of violence by local leadership as well as state actors in prewar Liberia with that of rebel-run violence of the war years. As I have already indicated in the chapter title, I find more structural resonance between state-run violence and rebel movements than between local non-European armies of the history books and recent rebel movements. Yet, one has to comply with the fact that certain administrative issues and forms of symbolic violence of "local" sociopolitical organization have filled essential functions during the civil war. In the final discussion I will reconnect to topics presented above with a discussion on discipline, bio-power, state, local authorities, and the implications of the Empire.

The Liberian Civil War

The Liberian Civil War commenced on Christmas Eve 1989, when a group of roughly 150 ill-equipped rebel soldiers, supported by Libya and Burkina Faso, crossed into Nimba county, Liberia, from the adjacent Ivory Coast (Ellis 1999). This group, which became known as the National Patriotic Front of Liberia (NPFL), initially enjoyed massive popular support, with many young men and women joining it, armed only with single-barreled guns and at times sticks. The government forces, the Armed Forces of Liberia (AFL), were soon driven out of Nimba county. Later, following an internal struggle, the NPFL split into two factions: the NPFL, as led by Charles Taylor, and the Independent National Patriotic Front of Liberia (INPFL) under Prince Y. Johnson. Taking different routes, and at times fighting each other, both defeated the AFL and reached the Atlantic coast and Monrovia in July 1990. In August of that year a West African peacekeeping force, ECOMOG, was created under the leadership of Nigeria and sent to take control of the situation in Monrovia. Prince Y. Johnson seemingly struck a deal with the peacekeepers and lured President Samuel Doe into a trap, capturing him, torturing him in front of a video camera, and eventually killing him.[5] The struggle that at the outset had been viewed as a popular rebellion by the Gio and Mano ethnic groups in Nimba county, in due course turned the whole of Liberia into a war zone, where young rebel fighters not only fought each other but terrorized, looted, and committed gruesome atrocities against the entire civilian population.

After the killing of Doe, the INPFL continued playing an active role in Monrovian politics until Johnson was brought into exile in Nigeria in late 1992. Meanwhile several other rebel factions appeared. The United Liberation Movement of Liberia (ULIMO) was one, formed in Freetown, Sierra Leone, with assistance from the Sierra Leonean government. Soon

ULIMO itself split into two: ULIMO-J and ULIMO-K. The Liberian army, AFL, continued fighting and was later aided by another faction, the Liberian Peace Council (LPC) originating in the southeast of the country. Other factions, often enjoying localized regional support, came and went; such as the Lofa Defence Force (LDF) and the Congo Defence Force (CDF). A main incentive to continue the war was financial (Reno 1996)—but, as we shall see below, there were other motivations as well. Soldiers fought to obtain instant booty, while warlords aimed at gaining control over productive geographic areas, especially those having gold and diamonds, as well as timber and rubber, coffee and cocoa plantations. Rebel movements kept some amount of popular support alive by feigning the protection of the interests of particular regions and ethnic groupings, which were further politicized by the war itself (Atkinson 1999). In reality, the brutality of combatants toward the very people they claimed to serve kept civilians submissive. Shady international businessmen, conglomerates of West African states, and at times foreign departments of powerful Western states all supported the warlords (Keen 1998; Reno 1996).[6]

After seven years, the war came to a halt, culminating in democratic elections in 1997. Ironically, Charles Taylor and his National Patriotic Party (NPP)—formed out of the NPFL—won a landslide victory and thus succeeded in achieving what they had not been able to accomplish through warfare (see Harris 1999). The war had by then caused between 60,000 and 200,000 deaths.[7] Without relying on uncertain statistics, it is fair to say that during the course of the war most Liberians were displaced at some time. Areas across the borders in Sierra Leone, Guinea, and the Ivory Coast were at times flooded with refugees (see, e.g., Utas 2004a [1997]). Internally displaced persons (IDPs) moved up and down between temporary safe havens in search of the protection of some form of authority. The coastal cities of Monrovia and Buchanan, zones guarded by the peacekeepers, received most of the IDPs; and to this day, Monrovia, for instance, has more than doubled its population since the onset of the war.

During 1998 and 1999, the security situation in Liberia remained uncertain. Parts of the country experienced moments of unrest verging on the brink of war, with heavy shooting and civilians fleeing helter-skelter. Even so, most observers regarded the war as over. Yet, in late 1999, upper Lofa county experienced the first of a series of armed incursions. By mid-2000, groups of subversive soldiers were entering from neighboring Guinea on a regular basis. Liberians saw the birth and growth of a new rebel movement, ironically named Liberians United for Reconciliation and Democracy (LURD). LURD rebels operated in Lofa county, on occasions advancing toward Monrovia. During the first half of 2002, LURD made a series of successful raids in Bong, Bomi, and Montserrado Counties, temporarily taking control of the major towns. The tide changed, however, and during the autumn of 2002 LURD was forcibly driven back.

A new advance followed in the spring of 2003 that during the summer months brought the rebel faction all the way to Monrovia. With a core of soldiers recruited from Liberian exiles in Guinea, LURD was also to enlist young people from within Liberia, yet still relied heavily on mercenaries from Sierra Leone and Guinea. Various governmental security forces and pro-governmental paramilitaries also succeeded in drawing fresh support and recruitment among young Liberians, mainly from Monrovia and surrounding counties. LURD split up along old ULIMO-J/ULIMO-K lines in April 2003 into two LURD, with continued presence in the north, and MODEL (Movement for Democracy in Liberia) operating in the south. Rapid advances by both movements toward Monrovia, and unified international political and economic pressures on the government, forced Taylor to leave office and go into exile in Nigeria. An interim government was formed and the UN engaged a large military force to establish peace. Since then Liberia has gone through a democratic transformation and is, under the leadership of President Ellen Johnson-Sirleaf, rebuilding state capacity and consolidating peace.

Even though forced conscription took place during the Liberian Civil War, most combatants, whatever their age, joined out of "free" will.[8] At the outset of the war, as noted above, the people in Nimba county viewed the war as a rebellion designed to free them from a repressive government seen as anti-Nimbadian. Parents sent their children off to fight in what was seen as a righteous war. However, young people also saw it as a youth revolution, a possibility to get rid of an elitist urban leadership made up of autocrats (as described in Clapham 1976; Liebenow 1987), but also a rural gerontocratic leadership (Bellman 1984; Murphy 1980). It is evident that in the minds of young Liberians, leadership—urban or rural notwithstanding—showed no concern for them and many regarded the war as "pay-back time." Thus, war was fought to a large extent by marginalized peoples, predominantly youth, who saw the hostilities as possibly the only opportunity for them to experience mobility from the margins into the center of politics and the economy.

The war gradually shifted shape, and as rebel groups increased their terror against civilians and as looting excursions increasingly became the raison d'être for war, the grounds for joining as combatants also changed. Many young ex-combatants that I interviewed during fieldwork in Liberia during 1998 (see Utas 2003) admit that it was the possibility of personal advantage that caused them to join the war. These advantages worked both ways: certainly in direct gains, but also in escaping the disadvantages of being a civilian. Advantages included loot from raids, payoffs waged during security assignments, and fees levied from protecting locals. A direct advantage would also be the acquisition of power in local communities. The leap from being a powerless young boy, under the strict authority of parents, guardians, and community elders, to being a commander with a gun is both tremendous and momentous. Being a soldier would also imply having girlfriends, often many at a time, a sensation for young men of a social strata that prior to taking up arms, were nearly disqualified from the spheres of mating. On the other hand, when young people talked about escaping the disadvantages of being a civilian they would primarily allude to preventing other rebel soldiers from harassing oneself and one's family. During the war, it was crucial for every family to have someone—a son, a daughter, an uncle, or another close relative—in the rebel army in control of the area; otherwise, family members would constantly be harassed and farms and property looted.

Warfare and State-Run Violence: Local/Non-European Formations

There is a general agreement among most historical commentators that warfare was endemic in the precolonial history of the peoples of present-day Liberia. One voice proposed that "whatever the vocation of the primitive African, his avocation was formerly war" (Schwab 1947:228). This inference is drawn from superficial first-hand material, but suggests that small-scale warfare was probably a common occurrence. It is also established that the historical colonial presence of the Liberian state pacified the Liberian hinterland, mainly through coercion and in part through imposing a system of indirect rule—thereby actively suppressing "tribal" warfare (Akpan 1973; 1988; Ford 1989; Harley 1941a; Liebenow 1969; Massing 1988). This period of pacification resulted in a situation where the structures of warfare became eclipsed. Thus, anthropological accounts of the country show very little written content on matters of protection and expansion through violent measures. Writing on the Krahn people of eastern Liberia, Schröder and Seibel note that, concerning military organization, "when no military action was in progress, these offices, along with their quite considerable authority, were virtually deactivated" (1974:60). In the absence of hostilities, warfare until recently has been a topic only scantily described in anthropological studies of Liberia (see, e.g., Bellman 1975; 1980; Bledsoe 1980; Leopold 1991; Moran 1990; Tonkin 1992).

Most references to warfare in Liberia are instead found in the literature of early missionaries or civil servants, or by the pen of those who could loosely be referred to as colonial ethnographers (see, e.g., Schwab, Harley). Most of these were written during early colonial days and as sources are generally accounts of cultural exotification, largely having been produced in an evolutionary paradigm. It is not until the onset of the current civil war that observers and researchers appear to have recommitted themselves to the study of cultural factors in Liberian warfare. Relying mainly on data from these "colonial" sources often entails the risk of over-essentializing the "traditional" or the "tribal" aspects of contemporary wars, as is evident in the works of Stephen Ellis (1995; 1999; 2001).[9]

In recapitulating a Liberian history of local, subnational warfare we should be wary of geographic generalizations picked up from area-specific data. Mary Moran (2002a; 2002b) has recently pointed out that by a scholarly overemphasis on Mande-speaking peoples in Liberia, disproportionate attention has been given to the strictly hierarchical elements found in Liberian political society, and as a result the more egalitarian traits of the Kruan-speaking peoples of the southeast have been neglected. Her point is relevant also to ideas of "traditional" warfare. If we look at general ethnographic accounts of war structures, we actually find more traits of egalitarianism among the Kruan peoples and a more pronounced hierarchy among the Mande peoples. However, even within Kruan ethnic groups, such as the Krahn, relations of hierarchy and egalitarianism differ substantially from region to region (Schröder and Seibel 1974). As my intention is to present additional general points concerning forms of early colonial, or "traditional," warfare, it would be important to bear these flaws of generalization in mind.

In the small-scale polities that were dominant in precolonial and early colonial Liberia, most fighting forces comprised a small core of professional warriors,[10] often including individuals originating from outside of the group (Westermann 1921)—what today we would regard as mercenaries. Undoubtedly, the loyalty of these warriors lay with the war chief and not the local community per se. In addition to professional warriors, during times of war and unrest, ordinary citizens were also mobilized in considerable numbers. According to Fulton (1968) there was no standing army, nor a police force, deployed among the Kpelle peoples he studied. Instead, what he labels a "nephew group" was the leading organizer of warriors, headed by the war chief. Positions in these war structures were open to all able-bodied men, and as such, it was an important path to local power for politically ambitious young men born outside of the dominant lineages. Fulton (1968; 1972) points out that among the Kpelle, the position of war chief itself was open to all young men who could prove their bravery and ability in the battlefield (see also Korvah 1971 on Loma and Mandingo).

During times of conflict, the war chief was the society's most powerful person. He also maintained control over captured "village mini-states and turned them into private domains" (Fulton 1968:15), using his "war powers to set himself up as a virtual warlord" (Fulton 1972:1222). Spoils of war, such as looted goods, cattle, and slaves, formed an important incentive to the war endeavor. All spoils were invariably brought to the war chief(s) and redistributed to the wider society according to customary rules (Fulton 1968; Schröder and Seibel 1974). Warriors who had fought bravely obtained proportionately larger shares, and it should be emphasized that great warriors often obtained substantial wealth from their war activities (Fulton 1968; Westermann 1921; Schröder and Seibel 1974). "Big men," or senior warriors, at times kept their own group of combatants (Schröder and Seibel 1974), resembling private armies. It is suggested by Massing (1988) that among the Gio peoples, warriors with modern firearms even extended status and power beyond their immediate vicinity, allowing for speculation that contacts formed with trade and the colonial government that might have, albeit temporarily, increased the individual powers of these big-men warriors.

If the standing professional army comprised only a limited number of men, the group of irregulars, by contrast, included "alle kampffähigen Männer und Junglinge," that is, "all men and youth fit for warfare" (Westermann 1921:108). Among the Krahn, these irregulars "were organized into paramilitary age-groups, which in wartime served as the organizational structure of fighting, but in peacetime provided the basic structure for workgroups of various sorts" (Schröder and Seibel 1974:68).[11] Even if warriors were often labelled as "young," as found in Schwab's account of the Mano peoples warrior class (1947:237), there is still little evidence as to the actual ages of warriors. Among the Mano peoples, the *Ge yumbo* cult functioned mainly for the military training of young men (Harley 1950). Likewise Tonkin (1992) states that Jlao (Kru) people's public initiation into the army was the time when males became adult citizens.

Magic and war medicines were widely used both collectively and individually; boy mascots were but one example. Harley (1941a) accounts for ten different types of war magic in use by the Mano peoples at that time. Power and invulnerability, as well as the lack of the same, were all ascribed to magical causes. During the war against the LFF (Liberian Frontier Force) in Nimba in 1911, the death of the legendary warrior Wonkpa was attributed to the destruction of his magic invulnerability, summoned by the wife of a local trader (Massing 1988). Powerful warriors had to possess strong medicines that both protected them and caused harm to their enemies. Once a fighter had become "famous for his medicines, his mere appearance often sufficed to disperse an enemy, and his threat to apply medicine often was enough to prevent actual conflict" (Schröder and Seibel 1974:68). Practicing medicine men (called *Zo, Nzo,* or *Zoe* in many of the Mande languages) filled important roles in the war endeavor, producing war medicines, blessing the warriors upon departure, and performing sacrifices (Fulton 1968). Certain rituals carried out by these medicine men were often violent in appearance (i.e., human sacrifice and cannibalistic acts) and were effective to instil fear into the enemy.[12] In addition, masks usually worn during rituals and partly carried on to the battlefield along with various bells and drums, both imitated fearless and victorious deceased warriors and dangerous animals, and were used to strengthen the confidence of one's own warriors as well as to weaken the morale of the enemy (Harley 1950).

Secret societies have long been a favored topic among anthropologists studying the region, resulting in a plethora of ethnographic studies on secret societies in Liberia and the Sierra Leonean/Guinean borderlands (see, e.g., Bellman 1984; d'Azevedo 1980; Fulton 1972; Gibbs 1962; Hoejbjerg 1990; Little 1965; 1966; Siegmann 1980; Zetterström 1980). In such studies, a significant focus has been given to the central secret organizations: Poro (male) and Sande/Bundu (female). Many other secret societies more or less subordinated or connected to the Poro and Sande do exist, but by no means receive the same attention. If one returns to the earlier idea that warfare was endemic in the region prior to Liberian colonial presence, surprisingly little is written about these secret societies in relation to their functions during times of war. However, we ought not to forget that war systems were actively suppressed during times of peace, and Liberian pacification was precisely indicative of such a state of affairs. Thus, the current generation of anthropologists can only observe fragments of these dormant war organizations—which rose again to view by the second half of 1980s. Stephen Ellis, among others, has pointed toward the importance of secret societies in the current civil war (e.g. Ellis 1995; 1999; 2000; 2001), yet it would be insufficient to point toward the concept of Poro as being all-encompassing, as other semisecret societies played roles more central than the Poro.

Among the Liberian societies involved in Poro—e.g., the Kpelle, Mano, Loma, Guissi, Gio, Gola, Bella, Mende, and Bassa peoples (Bellman 1975)— it is worth noting that all warriors belonged to the Poro, simply because their initiation was a requirement to become an adult man.[13] This was so even if the level of actual involvement in Poro issues differed widely, depending on status and power in any given local society:

> No boy or young man is considered a member of the tribe until he has been initiated by suitable rites into the company of his elders. The adolescent must

undergo certain ordeals to prove that he is ready and worthy to take on the responsibilities of citizenship—until then he does not count. (Harley 1941b:3)

As a powerful organizer of most activities on all levels of society in Liberia, the importance of Poro should not be underestimated. However, we need to take into account that in issues of warfare, Poro seem to have enjoyed quite limited direct influence. There would often appear to be a built-in conflict within a given society between the Poro leadership and the senior warrior nomenclature—Fulton calls this "an interesting balance of the polity's power" (1972:1222). Even if the war chiefs and secret societies that are preoccupied in war issues in part fall under the authority of Poro, the warriors still form a pool of hard-to-rule individuals, often in opposition to Poro leadership. Fulton's account of self-serving war chiefs points toward that. Bellman also suggests that, among the Kpelle peoples he studied, secret associations other than Poro are involved in war activities—for example, the *Mina* (horn) and *Moling* (spirit) societies. These organizations require membership in Poro and provide services to both Poro and Sande, although they are formally outside the Poro itself (Bellman 1984, and personal communication 14/3–01). To Harley (1941a; 1941b; 1950), in contrast to Bellman's account, Poro society appears to encompass all other secret societies. Harley also points out that the peace initiatives of the Poro, as masked men of the Poro (*ge's*) could be sent out to the battlefront to also stop ongoing warfare. In Harley's words:

> The fixed functions of the *ge's* extended with some local variation, across the borders of the clan or tribe, and even across language barriers. They even exerted control over warfare. This was carried to such an extent that arbitration through the *ge's* was more final than the result of war. (Harley 1950:42)

Fulton proposes further that "Poro may have been an alternate means of arbitrating disputes" among the Kpelle (Fulton 1968:14), and indeed d'Azevedo (1969–1970) points out that the Gola Poro, during the expansion of Gola peoples, turned into both a "pan-tribal" and "inter-tribal" institution of *diplomacy and solidarity*. Certainly Poro officials did enter the battlefields, but in the history of Gola warfare:

> Pan-tribal training in obedience to Poro codes was more frequently utilized to resolve hostilities before or even after they had occurred. … Secret agreements among Poro officials of warring chiefdoms could result in the sudden cessation of hostilities in the midst of battle. (d'Azevedo 1969–1970:11)

Thus, Poro ought to be seen primarily as a mechanism for the resolution of conflict (Sawyer 2005:30) rather than an instigator and organizer of further hostility. Poro leadership actually seeks to control subjects in society attempting to use violent measures on neighboring communities. The power of Poro, as a gerontocratic organization of established families and lineages, is continuously being contested by those who would seek power. War chiefs, warriors, and some of the secret societies with their relative youthfulness (or marginality) could all be put into this category. Power obtained through bravery on the battlefield would normally appear to be the only passable route to fulfilment of such an individual endeavor. A way to summarize would be to create an imagined scheme of binary opposition: placing Poro, gerontocracy, peace, and social stability on one side, opposed by war societies, youth/marginality, and conflict-proneness on the other. In doing so, a delicate balance is maintained between Poro and the war chief/war societies.[14] Governmental as well as missionary efforts to subdue the Poro over the years have clearly restrained gerontocratic control of local government. Such a tilting of the balance of power may well have paved the way for the armed youth rebellion of the 1990s.

A Colonial Army of Brutes: State Organisms

In order to grasp the Liberian Civil War we must consider the project of nation building in Liberia. Colonial Liberia's culture of military force forms a central source of information to understand current Liberian warfare. It was repatriated U.S. slaves, arriving from 1822 onward, who actually founded Liberia.[15] Settling in clusters mainly along the Atlantic coastline, the so-called Americo-Liberians established themselves as local elites, forming small colonies resembling city-states.[16] In 1838 they established the Commonwealth of Liberia, and in 1847 the settlers declared Liberia an independent republic.[17] As Akpan has noted, "settlers on whom the government of Liberia thus devolved ... were essentially American rather than African in outlook and orientation" (1973:219); thus Liberia as a state project ought to be viewed as being colonial in its own right (Akpan 1988; see also d'Azevedo 1971; 1989). "Like its colonial equivalents, the Liberian state imposed itself on the hinterland by force, and to some extent maintains itself the same way" (Clapham 1978:122).

Stephen Hlophe (1973) has pointed out that Americo-Liberian immigrants did not constitute a unified group of settlers, and that their interests were often in conflict; thus, constructing "natives" as a common enemy was one way of consolidating group identity. In a study on Liberian nation building and state use of symbols in historical documents, Blamo (1971–72) finds that officials among the Liberian elite, i.e. the Americo-Liberians, repeatedly used words such as "aggression," "aggressors," "insubordination," "interdictions," "punitive missions," "internecine warfare," "military intervention," "native raids," "pacification," "rebels," "rebellion," and "war" to mobilize public support for governmental operations, with the objective of gaining control over the Liberian hinterland.

The formation of the Liberian nation in 1847 had little direct effect on the hinterland. The control and political influence of the Liberian state was in reality quite insignificant. However, the uncomfortable prospect of losing part of its predominantly imagined "domains" when European states commenced the Scramble for Africa (1880–90) through the formal regulation of territorial interest at the Berlin Conference (1884–85), caused the Liberian government to establish firm military outposts at strategic positions throughout the interior (Ford 1989; Akpan 1973).[18] With the aim of controlling and pacifying the Liberian hinterland, the Liberian Frontier Force (hereafter LFF) was instituted in 1908. From the outset, it comprised mainly Mende and Loma soldiers, originating from both Sierra Leone and its immediate Liberian borderlands. It also came to include other subdued Liberian peoples (Ford 1989; Wilson 1980).[19] In this "pacification" exercise of the early nineteenth century, the LFF was often engaged in several battles with indigenous groups, simultaneously over vast territories. Victory over a particular group of people, however, rarely led to total conquest; and although conflicts were often low-intensity, they could nevertheless flare up and spread countrywide as rebellions (Ford 1989).[20] With a bifurcated state (Mamdani 1996), the overall setting of rural Liberia was that of a colonial "space of death" (as elaborated by Taussig 1992) where state, state-supported companies (in Liberia's more recent history, as in Taussig's Columbian material, foremost those in the rubber business), and state-backed "civilized" strongmen used any means of violence they wanted to control its subjects.[21] The logic of locating socioeconomic space within the state to individuals with civil servant or semi–civil servant status has prevailed up to current day. Postcolonial states paying insignificant salaries make space for ingenuities of the individual civil servants according to a pay-yourself logic—the multitude of checkpoints in West African states being an obvious case (Ferme 2004; Roitman 2004).

Available historical sources give an unequivocal picture of the LFF as an army of badly trained, poorly disciplined, and inadequately equipped soldiers. The government of the day seldom paid salaries, forcing soldiers to "live of the land" (Ford 1989:47), implying: "soldiers indulged in wanton pillage, rape, and harassment of the Africans in their districts, and commandeered food, labourers, and carriers without payment" (Akpan 1973:230). In the annual report by the British Consul General in 1912, the LFF is described with the epithet "that rabble of bloodthirsty cut-throats called the LFF" (cited in Massing 1988:70). Even the Liberian president, Arthur Barclay (1904–12), revealed his concerns by stating that the militia was "tending to become a greater danger to the citizen, and his property, which it ought to protect, than to the public enemy" (cited in Liebenow 1969:53–54). In the wake of LFF "pacification," a system of indirect rule followed, along with the birth of a rural tax system (the hut tax) (Liebenow 1969; Akpan 1973). Using violent means, civil servants—commissioners, superintendents, custom officials—of the Liberian state, worked in close cooperation with the LFF, but frequently with conflicting incentives (Massing 1988). They blatantly extorted their counties, levying illegal fees and fines, and at times sharing this with government functionaries in Monrovia (Akpan 1988).[22]

For more than a century, the tiny minority of Americo-Liberians controlled state affairs and commerce through an intimate network of privilege and dominance.[23] Even if the government in Monrovia gradually increased its presence in the interior, much remained the same. The indirectness of rule, although not as official policy, remained a system of divesting the countryside of goods and labor up until the present day. The LFF was reshaped into the Liberian army and later became the Armed Forces of Liberia (hereafter AFL); but to a considerable extent it continued to harass local communities in brutal fashion: manhandling and rape were routine.[24] The AFL was, to use the words of political journalist Bill Berkeley, "a malignant organism in the body politic, inherently opportunistic, unlikely to be a source of progressive change." And he continues:

> In retrospect it's clear that the institution of the army was a microcosm for what ailed Liberia. A gang culture flourished. Violence was rampant. Ties of blood and ethnicity were paramount. The construction of ethnic patronage systems by rival soldiers would become one of the most important causes of Liberia's subsequent collapse. (Berkeley 2001:31)

The structurally sanctioned violence of the Liberian army became evident in the events that followed the 1980 coup, when Master Sergeant Samuel Doe rose to presidential power. The coup that put an end to the long-standing dominance of the Americo-Liberian elite released a hatred for the Americo-Liberians that had long existed among other Liberians (Bøås 1997). However, the public execution of the members of the Tubman government, which became known as "the Liberian Beach Party," was not only "people's justice" but also had its roots in military culture.[25] The Liberian army, under Doe's rule, resumed its violent patrols, and after a failed coup attempt following rigged elections in 1985, AFL soldiers paraded the corpse of the plot leader, Thomas Quiwonkpa (one of the senior members of the 1980 coup who had fallen out with Doe), in downtown Monrovia. Apparently soldiers in the parade publicly hacked off body parts, to be kept as souvenirs or even to be consumed to obtain some of the great powers possessed by "the warrior" Quiwonkpa (Ellis 1999).[26]

In the aftermath of the 1985 coup attempt, AFL troops set out to pacify the ethnic Gio strong men of Monrovia, and primarily in Nimba county from where Quiwonkpa and many of the other coup plotters originated. The wanton violence wrought on innocent civilians in Nimba county (1985–89) remains to this day a vivid historical predicament to most people from the area.[27] It also paved the way for the National Patriotic Front of Liberia (NPFL) insurrection of Christmas Eve 1989. The Krahn/Gio ethnic axis of the coup in 1980 had within a few years turned into an ethnic cleavage that spilled over from Doe/Quiwonkpa personal competition over power in the military barracks, into the country itself (Ellis 1999). "Soldier time," as the period of Doe rule between 1980 and 1990 is called, was at the time referred to as "a time of fear and economic hardship"; and at the onset of the civil war the soldier "had become completely discredited, a figure of derision, corrupt, cowardly, and ineffectual in the face of a real adversary" (Moran 1995:78).

Discipline and Bio-Power: State, Local Authorities, and the Encroaching Empire

Modes of social organization, structures of power, and violent technologies in Liberian warfare have been subjected to continuous change over the past few hundred years. Ethnic, national, as well as generational identities breed on reimaginations of diverse pasts, putting sociocultural practices to new and at times disastrous effects. Practices of secret societies, early warlord politics, warrior myths, and the economy of magic and the occult make up the constant cultural processes of continuity and change that we can observe in the Liberian organization of warfare. Within the LFF and AFL, we can see how meaning and content of earlier warfare is maintained as well as broken. We can see how symbols and social structures are reinvented and used for different purposes. This is continuing well into the Liberian Civil War of the 1990s, and the war itself is a bricolage of such flows of knowledge. In this final part of the chapter I shall try to tie up these issues and fit them into the logic of the global Empire.

I want to suggest that we have two sets of cleavage lines that we will have to account for in our analysis of rebel factions in the civil war. Firstly, there is the line between local communities and the nation-state, as opposed to that between competing ethnic groups. The troublesome relationship between state and local community exceeded that of any ethnic logic. Politicized ethnicity should rather be recognized as a further consequence. Secondly, I would argue that a cleavage line between youth and gerontocratic leadership became increasingly evident in the conflict. The tension between youth and elders was heightened even prior to the war but became paramount in the war in 1992. Even if, in what follows, I make a rather clear-cut distinction between the driving forces of local/national during the 1990–92 part of the war and youth/gerontacratic leadership in the post-1992 wars, needless to say there is no exact chronological breaking point. Further, things also differs in the Liberian geography from setting to setting. Local support remained strong in certain areas and differed from community to community and in the choices of individuals.

In 1990 and 1991, the war drew popular support in many predominantly rural areas. Most local communities in Nimba county accommodated NPFL and INPFL troops, offered supplies, and actively aided them in order to clean out the Liberian army and other persons viewed as pro-government. In this task local leadership and family actively influenced sons, husbands, and, at times, daughters to take up arms. Secret-society leadership and medicine men also encouraged the rebels by providing spiritual and medicinal protection. Hastily gathered groups of young men structurally complied with ideals of warriorhood, as discussed above. Medicine men provided protecting medicine, or charms, for their warriors. Warriors had in their turn to act in accordance with strict taboos—not having intercourse while under the protection of the medicine, not stepping over the chili mortar, etc. Local conduct of soldiers dressed in women's clothes in 1991/1992 caught the media world's attention as it hardly complied with our perception of military and army and was, needless to say, left unexplained. However, Mary Moran has explained this practice well by stating that in the tradition:

> [w]arriors are free to play with gender identity, to draw power from the deliberate conflation of categories, to demonstrate that qualities of courage, strength, and supernatural prowess are not limited to biological endowment. (Moran 1995:80)

During roughly two years, rebel soldiers in the rural areas drew to a large extent support from local dignitaries in the villages. My informants tell me of how this relationship gradually deteriorated. The visual proof of this was that traditional paraphernalia of the fighters, for instance women's clothes, was supplanted by clothes and gear of Western origin. Moran describes this makeover on the individual plane as a transformation from *warrior* to the *commando*, a character drawing on American film imaginary (Moran 1995:81–82). In the symbolical sense, the use of Western items was still based upon concepts within local cosmology, namely, the abstract appropriation of power from commodities. Structurally, however, it indicates how the rebel movements changed in setup. By loosing local popular support they were forced into a position similar to that of the Liberian army. Instead of being the protectors of territory and peoples, the rebel movements started preying on them; levying fees, looting property, torturing men, raping women. By structurally mimicking the cycles of conquest of the Liberian hinterland by the AFL, the rebel movements turned into the same malignant organisms that they a few years back had risen in opposition to.

"The Kalashnikov lifestyle is our business advantage," noted a NPFL fighter in an interview with William Reno (1998:15). Other rebel soldiers make a parallel between their weapon and a credit card. It opens up a discussion of a socioeconomic dimension of the war, detached from the culturally passionate similes of ethnic warriors. William Reno has taken the economic perspective of the Liberian Civil War furthest. In his view warlords, supported by foreign governments and private companies, in essence fought over resources of the weak state. Governments form but are yet another actor in what he has dubbed warlord politics (Reno 1998). In this vein, weak states are forced into the tactical behavior of market-based non-bureaucratization/informalization (see Reno 1995). This may well be a direct outcome of post–Cold War decline of state-to-state patronage, but from my outlook on Liberia I would *first* like to point out that this warlordism is in many ways business as usual. It is the continuation of state-run violence on the Liberian hinterland. As I have shown above, the various state actors of prewar Liberia sustained themselves on resources that were taken from the rural areas by force, through forced labor, by a system of sustained terror carried out by tax commissioners, immigration forces, and the army. It is intimately linked with African colonial administration as pointed out by Mamdani (1996), where colonial rulers "relied heavily on indirect rule, on a somewhat random brutality, and on local notables to whom many details of governance and tax collection were entrusted" (Hansen and Stepputat 2001:11). The Liberian state has never been in a sovereign position, its sovereignty has always been contested, and we are thus better off studying the interplay of various "sovereign bodies," as proposed by Hansen and Stepputat (2005).[28] In this chapter I have thus tried to grasp this complexity of competing bureaucratic logics sanctioned by violence. *Secondly*, although the current state of affairs in Liberia clearly demonstrates a logic of continuation regarding the Liberian state rather than a clear break, considerable changes have occurred over the last fifty years. I agree with Reno's analysis that with the growth of a Shadow State (Reno 1995), and an increase of shady business activities by international conglomerates, weak states are exactly too weak to shield themselves. This has cleared the floor for the logic of Warlord Politics (Reno 1998), and if we read Hardt and Negri this is exactly the Empire doing business in its fringe zones. Liberian warlords have thus been dancing to the tunes of the Empire.

Thirdly, from a foot-soldier perspective, individuals hook up with warlords in individual pursuit for socioeconomic power. We here observe a similar logic as that of migration. Migration, according to Hardt and Negri, forms another cornerstone of the Empire—in opposition to the modernist state-based world order that saw as its task to limit population movements. We might thus see endless political discussions concerning migration to the West as a battle between modernist identity-based states and the ideals of fluidity of the Empire. Powers within the networks of the Empire are striving for a borderless world. Migration as a process aims at breaking down the states formed after a modern logic; thus exodus is, in the eyes of Hardt and Negri, a critique of national state order (2001:210–13). Deserting the nation is in their work an extended form of class struggle, a mode of resistance equal to sabotage (in the era of disciplinary statehood). I would argue that in Liberia sabotage, exodus, and *participating in armed struggle* in opposition to leadership draw the same kind of support. Migration, in the form of urbanization, or labor migration to plantation or mining areas, is a long-standing technique of opposition to rural leadership. It is a path for young men outside the local power spheres to obtain individual power—a return to the home community with newfound power is imagined as leaving as a slave returning as a master (Utas 2004c). Armed combat in this vein is equally a mode of resistance in relation to both local and national leadership. The direct targeting during the civil war of both national and local forms of leadership as well as the sabotage of state structures is evidence of that.

It is clear, however, that armed combat is not solely an act of resistance; rather, it is also a *walk* in the De Certeauian sense (1984). Henrik Vigh calls it *social navigation* in his work on militias in Guinea Bissau (Vigh 2003, 2006).

> [N]avigation, when used to account for social action covers exactly the duality of action as related to both present and future orientation, as it is to draw a course as well to keep a course along an imagined trajectory; it is simultaneously to navigate the immediate obstacles in front of you, plotting getting ready to navigate the next as well as keeping an eye on ones imagined trajectory. (Vigh 2003:136)

We ought not forget that enrolment in a militia or a rebel movement might at certain times, for certain people, be a completely rational move. On the social chessboard individuals make their moves. That is from the perspective of the chessmen themselves, but from the perspective of the players, rebel soldiers remain mere pawns.

Bill Berkeley (as quoted above) suggested that the Liberian army was "a microcosm of what ailed Liberia." Ties of blood and ethnicity were, according to him, paramount in the Liberian army. Others have also noted that ethnic tension within the army became acute during the 1980s (Moran 1995:78). Ethnicity and more immediately kinship and village ties play central roles in social networks. However, it has been individuals of the same social microcosm (the army or other state agencies) and not entire peoples, ethnic groups, or clans that have been awkwardly involved with one another. If blood ties people together as well as keeps people apart within microcosms such as the Liberian army, these animosities might extend to ethnic targeting in the country as a whole. It does not, however, follow naturally that local people of the same origin will take whatever measures necessary to support any aspirant ethnic leadership. Within local communities, it often takes direct acts of violence and terror directed toward ambivalent categories of people to transform those who wish not to comply with violent ethnic politics into a mass of collaborators. As functions of the Liberian state, such as the army, have been able to acquire only the most rudimentary forms of bio-power and at the same time have lost most of their disciplinary powers, we can observe acute problems of state legitimacy. If ethnification in the Liberian army was rampant, it might be suggested that the army's lack of public legitimacy and lack of force prevented the effective spread of ethnic sentiments to the larger Liberian population.

In the Hobbesian sense, the social contract of the modern state has never been signed in Liberia, as there has never been any established reciprocity between state and citizens. How well can we then use Michel Foucault's distinction between disciplinary society and control society when discussing the Liberian state? I have in the text above made use of the notions bio-politics and bio-power. If control society is characterized by immanence, where structures of dominance and power are naturalized and embodied in citizens, the Liberian state has not successfully gone down that path. It is further a matter of fact that the Liberian state never has obtained control over the disciplinary apparatuses (prisons, factories, hospitals, psychiatric facilities, universities, schools, etc.) that characterize the disciplinary society; instead, it has rested heavily on direct force. I would thus, as Mariane Ferme has done in the case of Sierra Leone, argue for a hybridization of the territorial state and the bio-political regime where "political subjects are more at home in the 'control' models of the state ... than in the purely biopolitical ones" (Ferme 2004:89).

During and after the war, Liberia has been/is experiencing a massive surrender of state and civil society functions to the international community via UN and international NGOs. When they take over schools, hospitals, and even prisons—i.e., much of the disciplinary apparatuse in Liberia—they and, in the extension (in Hardt and Negri's vision), the Empire establish an increased presence in, and control over, the production of bio-power in Liberia—that is the external side of Foucault's bio-politics (Dean 2001:47). The promoting of local community and local difference gives them a head start over the Liberian state. Meanwhile, the Liberian state is in chaos. Indeed, the state is left with some rebuilding capital offered by the UN "nation-state ideal," and opportunities offered by international business powers generate hesitancy over how and with whom to make up legal business documents in the absence of a state actor.

With sovereignty being constantly contested and reasserted by a number of players on the Liberian arena, we have seen that certain levels of control over disciplinary society as well as bio-power have remained with (and have been regained by) local leadership. As a strategy of protection, local communities sanctioned the war at its onset in order to (re)gain power from the state. However, as rebel armies started to maim local communities, big men and elders withdrew their support, leaving rebels in a position that was structurally similar to that of the national army prior to the war. Deliberate disconnection from state matters and war became strategy, as villagers moved from their roadside "towns" into the bush to reside on their farms. During 1998, international staff in the EU aid projects in Nimba county expressed bewilderment when "traditional" masked dancers prevented EU employees from repairing bridges and roads in the rural areas. From an emergency-aid perspective, it is difficult to understand why people do not want reconstruction of infrastructure. However people's "deliberate efforts to make their site remote" (Ferme 2001:37) is quite certainly not a new strategy invented during this war; rather, it was used also prior to the war in order to avoid the predatory state. In fact, as historians (see, e.g., Arthur Abraham and La Ray Denzer in Shaw 2000:35) and anthropologists (Ferme 2001; Richards 2000) point out, this was a major technique for the neighboring Sierra Leonean population to avoid slave raiders. Rosalind Shaw has in fact argued that such a hiding away of places and sociocultural issues during the times of slavery fundamentally changed people's culture and even cosmology, something central to Sierra Leonean society today (Shaw 2000; Shaw 2002). One could assume that life in Liberia was affected in a similar way. Thus, to this day Liberian citizens, in times of war and peace, are finding hideouts to get away from a predatory state that uses violence in order to "pay themselves" in lieu of the malignant Liberian state.

At a very low point in the Liberian state's checkered career, in 1996, I was struck by a feeling that Liberian exiles in the Ivory Coast saw George Weah, the Liberian footballer who was voted world footballer of the year in 1995, as the only remaining social capital of Liberia. He was then "the Lone Star" of Liberia, a name that was originally given to the Liberian flag with pride. On a somewhat ironic note, in the democratic election of 2005, the social capital that *was* George Weah, became the social capital *of* George Weah, allowing him to become a powerful political player in his own right as one of the main contenders for the Liberian presidency.

Notes

1. State-run violence is violence orchestrated by a state-like administration directed toward a specific population that it at least symbolically protects, but such violence is not monopolized or systematized according to the logic of the Weberian state.
2. Yet, Hardt and Negri seem at times to contradict themselves by, for instance, discussing networks of the Empire as non-hierarchic, or flat, rhizomes. This contradiction will not be dealt with here.
3. In my view, Hardt and Negri's work is more stimulating and challenging in all its diversity and theoretical complexity than Joxe's, mainly in that it is trying to foresee processes and products of an emerging world order. Joxe's argument, on the other hand, largely remains in the old school. It is, however, unfortunate that in the last part of Negri and Hardt's book, when the reader yearns for patent prospects of what is to come, we are left with a wishful, highly hypothetic political manifesto. In this sense, I very much agree with Kapferer's critique of the book: "while the abstract philosophical discussions are important and frequently illuminating the book suffers from an excessive straitjacketing of social and political phenomena to the terms of abstract philosophical concepts"; and, further: "the forces upon which they pin their hopes could just as easily spell disaster for humankind" (Kapferer 2002:179).
4. For lack of a better term I shall in this chapter use *local* to denote regionalized socioeconomic fields less influenced by European state forms of governing, their economic impacts, etc. Such fields are alternatives to state order, at times contesters of state sovereignty, but as we know under mutual influence, rather than in mutual opposition to a global and/or state order of things. Local, as we have seen above in the discussion on Empire, is at times the output and outlook of the Empire itself, thus local imagined, and should be used free from connotations of "original" or "primordial" that the word *traditional* often entails.
5. For an analysis of the video of the Doe torture, see (Utas 2006).
6. One of the best known of the businessmen is the Dutchman Gus Kouwenhoven, a large-scale drug trafficker who has made Liberia a base for his illegal operations in drugs, arms, diamonds, and timber (see Global Witness 2001). Kouwenhoven was in 2005 indicted by ICC in the Hague.
7. Popular estimations point towards 200,000 war-related deaths, but in a recount, Ellis (1999) argues convincingly for a much lower figure (60,000).
8. Structural constraints are naturally more severe in times of war and armed conflicts. This article is indeed highlighting some of the structures working toward a "voluntary" conscription into rebel armies. I use voluntary or "free" will when direct force does not appear in the moment of conscription. My research findings on the high number of voluntary conscripts in the Liberian Civil War are contradictory to most popular and aid-directed research in the field of child and youth soldiers in Africa, but I argue

elsewhere that such findings are generally the outcome of faulty, or partial, research methods (Utas 2004b).
9. To give but one example, he discusses the secret-society Poro as if it has remained static since the time of the doctor/missionary Harley (in Liberia 1926–60), whereas the socializing capacity and control of Poro is far from the same today. (For example, the Poro initiation is today typically completed within a few weeks time as compared with earlier year-long initiations). In parts of Liberia Poro remains powerful, yet only to a limited extent from a spiritual viewpoint rather than as a political organizing force.
10. I use the term *warrior* for the historical or "traditional" soldier. For contemporary soldiers, I use the term *fighter* or *combatant*. Influenced by western film, the term *commando* is often used emically as a crossover category of "warrior" and rebel soldier. See Moran (1995; 1997) for an extended discussion concerning these categories.
11. This point is also valid for the current situation in post-conflict Liberia, as I have pointed out elsewhere (Utas 2005b).
12. In the minds of early researchers such as Harley (1941a; 1941b; 1950) and Schwab (1947), acts of human sacrifice and cannibalism were very real. In the light of the exotification of peoples during those days and with the knowledge of how important violence is in rituals of war, one ought to handle these sources with care. To a great extent, such rituals seem to conform to images of "eating" on a symbolic level.
13. Hoejbjerg points out that several authors have warned against regional generalizations, especially in regard to the Poro associations (Hoejbjerg 1999:535).
14. Hoejbjerg (1999:539) points out that among the Loma in the Guinean forest zone, the political chief and the "senior war father" is the same person. In this case, the idea of balance between gerontocratic leadership and war leadership appears invalid.
15. By 1900, about 15,000 settlers with African background had arrived from the United States, as well as about 300 from the Caribbean (Akpan 1973).
16. In popular discourse, Americo-Liberians are often, in somewhat derogatory parlour, called "Congos." This label originates from another settler group comprising recaptured Africans seized from slavers in the Atlantic Ocean by the U.S. Navy between 1845 and 1862. Many came from the region of the Congo River, hence the label "Congo." Over time, this group became assimilated with the Americo-Liberians.
17. On Liberian state building and its maintenance see, Akpan 1973; Blamo 1971–72; Clapham 1976; 1978; 1988; and the Liebenow trilogy (1969; 1980; 1987).
18. Liberia claimed territory far up into what is today the heartland of Guinea, following Benjamin Anderson's Journey to Musardu in the late 1860s (Anderson 1870) and in current Mali, Medina, and Djenne (see Akpan 1973).
19. In 1912 the U.S. ambassador to Liberia also sent Afro-American army officers (Buffalo Soldiers) to assist the LFF. With a primary aim of training the army, it was also believed that they would "serve as an 'inspiration' to the people" (Rainey 1996:212).
20. On indigenous rebellions see, e.g., Akpan (1988) on Vai, Gola, and Gbandi; d'Azevedo (1969–1970) on Gola and Mandingo; Wilson (1980) on Kru, Bassa, Dey, Grebo, Mende, and Kissi; Massing (1988) on Gio; Ford (1989) on Gio and Mano.
21. See De Boeck (1998; 2000) for a similar argument on DR Congo and Mbembe (2001) for Africa in general.
22. Yet it is important to point out that many people of the Liberian interior voluntarily complied with ideals and ways of the Liberian state, e.g. those discussed by Tonkin as "civilised natives" (Tonkin 1981).
23. Liebenow's trilogy (1969; 1980; 1987) gives a fabulously detailed account of Americo-Liberian rule.
24. Anthropologists Elizabeth Tonkin and David Brown have in personal communication (both on e-mail 21 July 2004) pointed out that in their various fieldwork locations in the years before the 1980 Samuel Doe coup, the army "behaved well towards the citizenry" and had a subdued role. The 1980 coup reversed that scenario.

25. For a detailed account of the coup and what followed, see Schröder and Korte (1986); see also Bienen (1985) for a discussion on the Doe coup in relation to similar coups in West Africa, and Liebenow (1984) for study of politics under the Doe administration. After Taylor's victory in the 1997 elections, it took hardly a month before people in Monrovia started complaining about the Kongos (Americo-Liberians) having returned to levels of influence equal to the pre-Doe era.
26. Quiwonkpa is a *nome de guerre* taken from the legendary Gio warrior Wonkpa, briefly mentioned above.
27. It is estimated that as many as 3,000 civilians were killed in Nimba county by government forces (Cain 1999:270).
28. Sovereign bodies range "from nations, communities, self-appointed big-men and leaders, to mobile individuals and political outfits" (Hansen and Stepputat 2005.:4).

Bibliography

Agamben, Giorgio, Vincenzo Binetti, and Cesare Casarino. 2000. *Means Without End: Notes on politics*. Minneapolis: University of Minnesota Press.

Akpan, Monday B. 1973. "Black Imperialism: Americo-Liberian Rule over the African Peoples of Liberia, 1841–1964," *La revue canadienne des Études africaines/ The Canadian Journal of African Studies* vii(2): 217–236.

———. 1988. *African Resistance in Liberia: The Vai and the Gola-Bandi*. Bremen: Liberian Working Group.

Allen, Tim, and Jean Seaton. 1999. *The Media of Conflict: War Reporting and Representations of Ethnic Violence*. London: Zed.

Anderson, Benjamin J. K. 1870. *Narrative of a Journey to Musardu, the Capital of the Western Mandingoes*. New York: S. W. Green, Printer.

Atkinson, Philippa. 1999. "Deconstructing Media Mythologies of Ethnic War in Liberia," in T. Allen and J. Seaton (eds), *The Media of Conflict: War Reporting and Representations of Ethnic Violence*. London: Zed Books, pp. 192–218.

Bauman, Zygmunt. 1989. *Modernity and the Holocaust*. Ithaca: Cornell University Press.

Bellman, Beryl. 1975. *Village of Curers and Assassins: On the Production of Fala Kpelle Cosmological Categories*. The Hague: Mouton.

———. 1980. "Masks, Societies, and Secrecy Among the Fala Kpelle," *Ethnologische Zeitschrift* (Zuerich) 1: 61–78.

———. 1984. *The Language of Secrecy: Symbols and metaphors in Poro ritual*. New Brunswick, N.J.: Rutgers University Press.

Berkeley, Bill. 2001. *The Graves Are Not Yet Full: Race, Tribe and Power in the Heart of Africa*. New York: Basic Books.

Bienen, Henry. 1985. "Populist Miltiary Regimes in West Africa," *Armed Forces and Society* 11(3): 357–77.

Blamo, J. Bernard. 1971–72. "Nation-building in Liberia: The Use of Symbols on National Integration," *Liberian Studies Journal* iv(1): 21–30.

Bledsoe, Caroline. 1980. *Women and Marriage in Kpelle Society*. Stanford: Stanford University Press.

Bøås, Morten. 1997. "Liberia – the Hellbound Heart? Regime Breakdown and the Deconstruction of Society," *Alternatives* 22: 353–379.

Certeau, Michel de. 1984. *The Practice of Everyday Life*. Berkeley: University of California Press.

Clapham, Christopher. 1976. *Liberia and Sierra Leone: An Essay in Comparative Politics*. Cambridge and New York: Cambridge University Press.

———. 1978. "Liberia," in. J. Dunn (ed.), *West African States: Failure and Promise*. Cambridge: Cambridge University Press, pp. 117–131.

d'Azevedo, Warren. 1969–1970. "A Tribal Reaction to Nationalism," *Liberian Studies Journal* i, ii, iii (2,1,2,1): 1–21, 43–63, 99–115, 1–31.

———. 1971. "Tribe and Chiefdom on the Winward Coast," *Rural Africana* 15: 10–29.

———. 1980 "Gola Poro and Sande: Primal Tasks in Social Custodianship," *Ethnologische Zeitschrift* (Zuerich) 1: 13–23.

———. 1989. "Tribe and Chiefdom on the Winward Coast," *Liberian Studies Journal* xiv(2): 90–116.

De Boeck, Filip. 1998. "Beyond the Grave: History, Memory and Death in Postcolonial Congo/Zaire," in R. Werbner (ed.), *Memory and the Postcolony: African Anthropology and the Critique of Power*. London: Zed Books, pp. 21–58.

———. 2000. "Borderland Breccia: The Mutant Hero in the Historical Imagination of a Central-African Diamond Frontier," *Journal of colonialism and colonial history* 1(2): 1–43.

Dean, Mitchell. 2001. "'Demonic Societies': Liberalism, Biopolitics, and Sovereignty," in T. B. Hansen and F. Stepputat (eds.), *States of Imagination: Ethnographic Explorations of the Postcolonial State*. Durham and London: Duke University Press, pp. 41–64.

Ellis, Stephen. 1995. "Liberia 1989–1994: A Study of Ethnic and Spiritual Violence," *African Affairs* 94: 165–197.

———. 1999. *The Mask of Anarchy: The Destruction of Liberia and the Religious Dimension of an African Civil War*. New York: New York University Press.

———. 2000. "Armes Mystiques: Quelques Éléments de Réflexion à Partir de la Guerre du Liberia," *Politique Africaine* 79(Octobre): 66–82.

———. 2001. "Mystical Weapons: Some Evidence From the Liberian War," *Journal of Religion in Africa* xxxi(2): 222–236.

Ferme, Mariane. 2001. *The Underneath of Things: Violence, History, and the Everyday in Sierra Leone*. Berkeley: University of California Press.

———. 2004. "Deterritorialized Citizenship and the Resonances of the Sierra Leonean State," in V. Das and D. Poole (eds), *Anthropology in the Margins of State*. Santa Fe: School of American Research Press, pp. 81–116.

Ford, Martin. 1989. "'Pacification' Under Pressure: The Political Economy of Liberian Intervention in Nimba 1912–1918," *Liberian Studies Journal* xiv(2): 44–63.

Foucault, Michel. 1977. *Discipline and Punish: The Birth of the Prison*. New York: Pantheon Books.

———. 1979. "Governmentality," *m/f a feminist journal*, 3(July): 5–21.

Friedman, Jonathan. 2003. "Globalization, Dis-integration, Re-organization: The Transformations of Violence," in J. Friedman (ed.), *Globalization, the State, and Violence*. Walnut Creek: Altamira Press, pp. 1–34.

Fulton, Richard. 1968. "The Kpelle Traditional Political System," *Liberian Studies Journal* i(1): 1–17.

———. 1972. "The Politics, Structures and Functions of Poro in Kpelle Society," *American Anthropologist* 74: 1218–1233.

Gibbs, James. 1962. "Poro Values and Courtroom Procedures in Kpelle Chiefdom," *Southwest Journal of Anthropology* 18: 341–350.

Global Witness. 2001. *Taylor-made: The Pivotal Role of Liberia's Forest and Flag of Convenience in Regional Conflict*. London: Global Witness/International Transport Workers Federation.

Hansen, Thomas Blom, and Finn Stepputat. 2001. "Introduction," in T. B. Hansen and F. Stepputat (eds), *States of Imagination: Ethnographic Explorations of the Postcolonial State*. Durham and London: Duke University Press, pp. 1–40.

———. 2005. "Introduction," in T. B. Hansen and F. Stepputat (eds), *Sovereign Bodies: Citizens, Migrants and States in the Postcolonial World*. Princeton: Princeton University Press, pp. 1–36.

———. n.d. "On empire and sovereignty." Unpublished manuscript.

Hardt, Michael, and Antonio Negri. 2001. *Empire*. Cambridge, Mass.: Harvard University Press.

Harley, George Way. 1941a. *Native African Medicine: With Special Reference to Its Practice in the Mano Tribe of Liberia*. Cambridge: Harvard University Press.

———. 1941b. *Notes on the Poro in Liberia*. Cambridge: Peabody Museum of American Archaeology and Ethnology, Harvard University.

———. 1950. *Masks as Agents of Social Control in Northeast Liberia*. Cambridge, Massachusetts: Peabody Museum of American Archaeology and Ethnology, Harvard University.

Harris, David. 1999. "From 'Warlord' to 'Democratic' President: How Charles Taylor Won the 1997 Liberian Elections," *The Journal of Modern African Studies* 37(3): 431–455.

Hlophe, Stephen. 1973. "The Significance of Barth and Geertz' Model of Ethnicity in the Analysis of Nationalism in Liberia," *Revue canadienne des etudes africaines/Canadian Journal of African Studies* 7(2): 237–256.

Hoejbjerg, Christian Kordt. 1990. "Beyond the Sacred and the Profane: The Poro Initiation Ritual," *Folk: Journal of the Danish Ethnographic Society* (Copenhagen) 32: 161–176.

———. 1999. "Loma Political Culture: A Phenomenology of Structural Form," *Africa* 69(4): 535–554.

Kapferer, Bruce. 2002. "Foundation and Empire (with Apologies to Isaac Asimov): Consideration of Hardt and Negri's *Empire*," *Social analysis* 46(1): 167–179.

Keen, David. 1998. *The Economic Functions of Violence in Civil Wars*. Oxford and New York: Oxford University Press for the International Institute for Strategic Studies.

Korvah, Paul M. 1971. "Notes on the Traditional History of the Tribes in the Voinjama District of Lofa County," *Rural Africana* 15: 30–36.

Leopold, Robert Selig. 1991. "Prescriptive Alliance and Ritual Collaboration in Loma Society," Ph.D. Thesis. Bloomington: Indiana University.

Liebenow, J. Gus. 1969. *Liberia: The Evolution of Privilege*. Ithaca: Cornell University Press.

———. 1980. *Liberia: The Dissolution of Privilege*. Hanover, NH: American Universities Field Staff.

———. 1987. *Liberia: The Quest for Democracy*. Bloomington: Indiana University Press.

Little, Kenneth. 1965. "The Political Function of Poro, Part 1," *Africa* 35(4): 349–365.

———. 1966. "The Political Function of Poro, Part 2," *Africa* 36(1): 62–71.

Mamdani, Mahmood. 1996. *Citizen and Subject: Contemporary Africa and the Legacy of Late Colonialism*. New Jersey: Princeton University Press.

Massing, Andreas. 1988. "Towards an Ethno-history of Liberia: The Early Colonization of the Dan," *Liberia-Forum* 4(6): 65–73.

Mbembe, Achille. 2001. *On the Postcolony*. Berkeley, CA: University of California Press.

———. 2003. "Necropolitics," *Public Culture* 15(1): 11–40.

Moran, Mary. 1990. *Civilized Women: Gender and Prestige in Southeastern Liberia*. Ithaca, NY: Cornell University Press.

———. 1995. "Warriors or Soldiers? Masculinity and Ritual Transvestism in the Liberian Civil War," in C. R. Sutton (ed.), *Feminism, Nationalism and Militarism*. Washington DC: Association for Feminist Anthropology/ American Anthropological Association, pp. 73–87.

———. 1997. "Warriors or Soldiers? Masculinity and Ritual Transvestism in the Liberian Civil War," in L. Lamphere, H. Ragoné, and P. Zavella (eds), *Situated Lives: Gender and Culture in Everyday Life*. New York: Routledge, pp. 440–50.

———. 2002a. "Imagining Democracy on the Guinea Coast," *American Anthropological Association Conference*, New Orleans: American Anthropological Association.

———. 2002b. "Towards an Indigenous Democracy for Liberia: Concepts, Voice and Autonomy in Local Political Practice," *Liberian Studies Association Meeting, April*. New York: Liberian Studies Association.

Murphy, William. 1980. "Secret Knowledge as Property and Power in Kpelle Society: Elders Versus Youth," *Africa* 50: 193–207.

Rainey, Timothy A. 1996. "Buffalo Soldiers in Africa: The US Army and the Liberian Frontier Force, 1912–1927, An Overview," *Liberian Studies Journal* xxi(2): 203–238.
Reno, William. 1995. *Corruption and State Politics in Sierra Leone.* Cambridge: Cambridge University Press.
———. 1996. "The Business of War in Liberia," *Current History* May: 211–215.
———. 1998. *Warlord Politics and African States.* Boulder, CO: Lynner Rienner Publishers.
Richards, Paul. 1996. *Fighting for the Rain Forest: War, Youth and Resources in Sierra Leone.* Oxford: James Currey.
———. 2000. "Chimpanzees as Political Animals in Sierra Leone," in J. Knight (ed.), *Natural Enemies: People-wildlife Conflicts in Anthropological Perspective.* London: Routledge, pp. 78–103.
Roitman, Janet. 2004. "Productivity In the Margins: The Reconstitution of State Power in the Chad Basin," in V. Das and D. Poole (eds), *Anthropology in the Margins of State.* Santa Fe: School of American Research Press, pp. 191–224.
Sawyer, Amos. 2005. *Beyond Plunder: Toward Democratic Governance in Liberia.* Boulder: Lynne Rienner.
Schröder, Günter, and Werner Korte. 1986. "Samuel K. Doe, the People's Redemption Council and Power: Preliminary Remarks on the Anatomy and Social Psychology of a Coup d'État," *Liberia Forum* 2(3): 3–25.
Schröder, Günter, and Dieter Seibel. 1974. *Ethnographic Survey of Southeastern Liberia: The Liberian Kran and the Sapo.* Newark, Del.: Published for the Tubman Center of African Culture by Liberian Studies Association in America.
Schwab, George. 1947. *Tribes of the Liberian Hinterland.* Cambridge, Mass.: The Museum.
Shaw, Rosalind. 2000. "'Tok Af, Lef Af': A Political Economy of Temne Techniques of Secrecy and Self," in I. Karp and D. A. Masolo (eds), *African Philosophy as Cultural Inquiry.* Bloomington and Indianapolis: Indiana University Press, pp. 25–49.
———. 2002. *Memories of the Slave Trade: Ritual and the Historical Imagination in Sierra Leone.* Chicago: University of Chicago Press.
———. 2003. "Robert Kaplan and 'Juju Journalism' in Sierra Leone's Rebel War," in B. Meyer and P. Pels (eds), *Magic and Modernity: Interfaces of Revelation and Concealment.* Stanford: Stanford University Press, pp. 81–102.
Siegmann, William. 1980. "Spirit Manifestation and the Poro Society," *Ethnologische Zeitschrift* (Zuerich) 1: 89–95.
Taussig, Michael. 1992. "Culture of Terror – Space of Death: Roger Casementís Putumayo Report and the Explanation of Torture," in C. Besteman (ed.), *Violence: A Reader.* Houndmills: Palgrave Macmillan, pp. 211–43.
Taylor, Christopher C. 1999. *Sacrifice as Terror: The Rwandan Genocide of 1994.* Oxford and New York: Berg.
Tonkin, Elizabeth. 1981. "Model and Ideology: Dimensions of Being Civilised in Liberia," in L. H. a. M. Stuchlik (ed.), *The Structure of Folk Models.* London: Academic Press, pp. 305–30.
———. 1992. *Narrating Our Pasts: The Social Construction of Oral History.* Cambridge: Cambridge University Press.
Utas, Mats. 2000. "Liberian Doomsday Carnival: Western Media on War in Africa," *Antropologiska Studier* 66–67: 74–84.
———. 2003. "Sweet Battlefields: Youth and the Liberian Civil War," Ph.D. Thesis. Uppsala: Department of Cultural Anthropology and Ethnology, Uppsala University.
———. 2004a. "Assiduous Exile: Strategies of Work and Integration Among Liberian Refugees in Danane, Ivory Coast," *Liberian Studies Journal* 29(2): 33–58.
———. 2004b. "Fluid Research Fields: Studying Excombatant Youth in the Aftermath of the Liberian Civil War," in J. Boyden and J. d. Berry (eds), *Children and Youth on the Front Line: Ethnography, Armed Conflict and Displacement.* Oxford: Berghahn Books, pp. 209–36.

———. 2004c. "The Violent Logic of Marginality: Youth and the Liberian Civil War," *News from the Nordic Africa Institute* 2: 23–26.

———. 2005a. "Agency of Victims: Young Women's Survival Strategies in the Liberian Civil War," in F. d. Boeck and A. Honwana (eds.), *Makers and Breakers: Children and Youth as Emerging Categories in Postcolonial Africa*. Oxford: James Currey, pp. 53–80.

———. 2005b. "Building A Future? The Reintegration and Re-marginalisation of Youth in Liberia," in P. Richards (ed.), *No Peace, No War: An Anthropology of Contemporary Armed Conflicts*. Oxford and Athens: James Currey and Ohio University Press, pp. 137–54.

———. 2005c. "Victimcy, Girlfriending, Soldiering: Tactic Agency in a Young Woman's Social Navigation of the Liberian War Zone," *Anthropological Quarterly* 78(2): 403–430.

———. 2006. "War, Violence and Videotapes: Media and Localized Ideoscapes of the Liberian Civil War," P. Kaarsholm, (ed.), *Violence, Political Culture and Development in Africa*. Oxford: James Currey, pp. 161–181.

———. 2008. "Abject Heroes: Marginalised Youth, Modernity and Violent Pathways of the Liberian Civil War," in J. Hart (ed.), *Years of Conflict: Adolescence, Political Violence and Displacement*. Oxford: Berghahn Books, pp. 111–138.

Vigh, Henrik. 2003. "Navigating Terrains of War: Youth and Soldiering in Guinea Bissau," Ph.D. Thesis. Copenhagen: Institute of Anthropology, University of Copenhagen.

———. 2006. *Navigating Terrains of War: Youth and Soldiering in Guinea Bissau*. Oxford: Berghahn Books.

Westermann, Diedrich. 1921. *Die Kpelle: Ein negerstamm in Liberia*. Gottingen and Leipzig: Vandenhoeck and Ruprecht; J. C. Hinrichs.

Wilson, Henry. 1980. "Nation-building, Ethnicity and the New Imperialism: Dilemmas of Development in Liberia," in B. K. Swarz and R. E. Dumett (eds), *West African Culture Dynamics: Archaeological and Historical Perspectives*. Haag: Mouton Publ., pp. 563–86.

Zetterström, Kjell. 1980. "Poro of the Yamein Mano, Liberia," *Ethnologische Zeitschrift* (Zuerich) 1: 41–54.

Chapter Twelve

ISRAEL'S WALL AND THE LOGIC OF ENCYSTATION
Sovereign Exception or Wild Sovereignty?

Glenn Bowman

I wrote the bulk of the following chapter in the Autumn of 2003 after witnessing first hand the depredations being imposed by the Israeli state on a community I had worked with closely for nearly fifteen years. The chapter is supplemented by—or is itself a supplement to—an annotated photographic slide show which attempts to offer audiences a palpable relation to the people who are being disinherited, dislocated, and worse by the Wall and by the militaristic manoeuvres which have accompanied its erection and maintenance.[1] I have decided, in reworking the essay for inclusion in the present volume, not to attempt substantially to update the description of what is being done to Bethlehem, Beit Sahour, and the West Bank (although I have, where appropriate, provided new information). As anyone attending to the news will know, the process described here has continued apace (and has in fact accelerated in the wake of the *soi disant* "withdrawal" from the Gaza Strip); the wall has engulfed more land, the settlements have grown larger, and the Palestinians have experienced higher levels of unemployment, of emigration, and of malnutrition.[2] My decision to retain much of the original text is based on the fact that the process I described in Bowman (2004), a process I call "encystation," is the same as what Palestinians (and those of us attentive to the news) continue to observe today. This slow process of ethnic cleansing (all the more effective for its unhurried inexorability) has been openly operating in Gaza and the West Bank since the Oslo Accords (1993), and will continue

---

Notes for this chapter are located on page 302.

Figure 4. Palestinian graffiti.

Palestinian Graffiti on the inside of the Wall encircling Qalqilya. Local residents refer to themselves as "bottled," and this image resonates intriguingly with the dual sense of "encystation" explored in this chapter. Photograph by Glenn Bowman, 22 October 2007.

to work with brutal efficiency either until the last Palestinian leaves (or blows him- or herself up in an emotive but fruitless suicide bombing) or until a sustained international outcry calls a halt to it.

The Architecture of Entombment

In the summer of 2003 I spent several weeks in Beit Sahour, the West Bank town in which I have carried out fieldwork since the late 1980s, observing—among other things—the rapacious hunger with which Israel's "Anti-Terrorist Fence" (more commonly known as "the Wall") consumed Palestinian lands and infrastructure, biting off roads, wells, housing projects, community centers, and other supports of Palestinian life. On the northern border of Beit Sahour, the Wall was for the most part a bulldozed strip of between twenty and forty meters in width containing two three-meter barbed wire–topped fences, a ditch, another fence with electronic movement sensors, two raked sand "trace strips," and a paved patrol road. It meandered through the countryside in what appeared to me to be an aimless and extravagant manner (extravagant insofar as it costs on average 2.27 million U.S. dollars per kilometer, Cook 2003) until I recognized that it ran right along the edge of the inhabited sectors of Beit Sahour and neighboring Bethlehem and Beit Jala, gathering behind it nearly all of the vineyards, the olive groves, the orchards, and other agricultural lands of the local people.[3]

The Wall, however, was not the only bit of caging being erected. Since September 2000, when the Second Intifada erupted after Ariel Sharon's armed "visit" to Jerusalem's Haram esh-Sharif took place, Bethlehem District has been ghettoized through the programmatic erection of fifty-nine barriers across its roads, fifty kilometers of "Anti-Terrorist Fence," and a tight bracket of "bypass roads" which, to the 170,000 Palestinians trapped inside, were functionally indistinguishable from the rest of the Wall. To the east of Beit Sahour, the Wall linked up with the "Za'tara Bypass Road" (a militarily guarded "settler road" between Jerusalem and Tequ'a that neither passes through nor allows access to or from Palestinian towns or villages). To the West it sliced through residential and commercial areas of Bethlehem and Beit Jala (devastating them through its imposition of an emptied security zone stretching variously from the Wall between fifty and one hundred meters into Palestinian territory) before butting up against Route 60, a settlement "motorway" running from Jerusalem south to Efrat and its satellite settlements, which, again, cannot be accessed by vehicle from the Bethlehem townships. All roads out of Bethlehem district to the south had been cut, often by simply bulldozing up the roadbed and turning it into a three-meter high wall of rubble. Armored fencing separating the extensive settlement complexes of Tequ'a, Efrat, and Migdal Oz from nearby Palestinian villages was expanding into Palestinian lands at a rate exponentially related to the growth of the settlements themselves. There was only one road in and out of Bethlehem district and that, fiercely guarded at checkpoints by the Israeli Defense Force, could only be traversed by yellow-plated (i.e., Israeli-licensed) vehicles bearing soldiers, settlers, journalists, and the occasional tourist. Palestinians who wanted, or needed, to get in or out of Bethlehem District went by foot, either—if they had "permissions"—trudging through the long, slow queues at the checkpoints or—if not—clambering illegally over the remains of their broken roadways so as to gain access to the busy traffic of everyday Israeli life.[4]

What I saw that summer in Beit Sahour was far less dramatic than what I knew was happening in other regions of the West Bank and the Gaza Strip. Qalqilyah and Tulkarm, in the north of the West Bank, were being encircled by single-gated, eight-meter-high stretches of concrete wall crowned with smoked-glass-windowed watchtowers and protected by ditches, patrol roads, and supplementary fences. The ghettoization of these cities was not only preventing their inhabitants from working in either Israel or the

West Bank but also depriving those living in satellite villages of access to markets for buying necessities, selling their produce and labor, and accessing basic services such as medical care and education.[5] There, where the "sealing" was much more efficient, entry to and egress from the cities was only available to those willing, or able, to wait in long and faltering queues for bored Israeli soldiers to interrogate them—often publicly strip-searching and humiliating them—before deciding whether or not to let them, one by one, in or out.

Encystation

It seems obvious that the horrific grandiosity of the Wall's "sealing off" of Qalqilyah and Tulkarm serves to reassure a nervous Israeli electorate in the coastal cities so near to these West Bank conurbations that "Arabs" won't be able to get to them. The "quieter" rhetoric with which the section of "fence" surrounding Bethlehem District "speaks," seems more appropriate to addressing the foreign diplomats, journalists, and tourists likely to be traveling in the vicinity of Jerusalem. Such differences in appearance and address are, however, deceptive. Beneath these diverse visual rhetorics operates a unitary logic of what I call "encystation."[6] Encystation is the process of enclosing within a cyst, and the encirclement of Palestinian communities within the territories over which Israel claims sovereignty—in violation of the Fourth Geneva Convention and numerous United Nations Security Council resolutions—is indisputably a matter of quarantining "matter" believed to put the surrounding social body at risk.[7]

It is unclear whether or not there is a "goal" at the end of this process. Arguments can convincingly be made that the walling is meant to bring about either the voluntary emigration or the involuntary expulsion of Palestinians—or both. Rates of emigration in Bethlehem and elsewhere in the Occupied Territories are currently at an all-time high, and the increasing popularity of the phrase—"Jordan is Palestine"—that Sharon promoted since the 1950s (see Shlaim 2000:477 and *passim*) does little to quiet fears that what the Israeli historian Benny Morris called the "mistake" of the "non-completion of the transfer [in 1948]" (Shavit 2004:8) might be forcibly rectified in the not-too-distant future. Regardless of whether the ultimate motive for walling is making people leave or simply making them invisible to the Israeli population, it is indisputable that life within Palestinian "gated communities" is being etiolated by an intentional crippling of the economy, the strangling of access to food, water, medicine, and education, and the imposition of a sense of isolation and political impotence.[8] Palestinians, or at least those within these enclaves surrounded by Israeli settlements and highways, are certainly not treated as part of what is popularly known as "the only democratic state in the Middle East."

Nor, for the most part, do Palestinians in the West Bank and Gaza want to be; they want their own state in the 17 percent of Mandate Palestine left under "Arab" control (albeit by fiat that of Egypt and Jordan rather than of the local Palestinians) in the wake of the Arab-Israeli War of 1948. Although the liberal European press and the European Parliament has tended, since the summer of 2003, to condemn Israel's building of the Wall, it has done so on the assumption that the Wall is intended to constitute the border between a nascent Palestinian state and a state of Israel in retreat from its current maximalist position. They assume that the Wall should run along the "Green Line"—the internationally recognized armistice line established at the close of the 1967 war, which is 190 miles in length—and are outraged that government plans announced in April of 2006 project a total length for the Wall of 437 miles. None of the circuitous wanderings of the existing wall take place on the Israeli side of the Green Line, while at a number of points it bulges dramatically into the West Bank to incorporate Israeli settlements. The Wall's "land grab" threatens to expropriate more than 10 percent of the West Bank, and commentators feel that this puts the viability of a Palestinian state at risk—especially in light of the fact that the most fertile lands, and the largest aquifiers, are within the territory being consumed by the security fence.

But is the Wall meant to be a border? It is important to note, in my descriptions of Bethlehem, Qalqilyah, and Tulkarm above, that the encircled towns are cut off as much from the West Bank as from Israel; Palestinians must cross through checkpoints to access other sectors of Palestine. Numerous other towns and villages are being "enclaved" by supplementary fences built around them, while the effects of road cuttings and roadblocks (as detailed above in Bethlehem district) on countless other Palestinian conurbations do not even show up on the detailed map of the Wall the Palestine Land Development Information Systems drew up in 2003 on the basis of the Israeli Defense Force plans (see Stop the Wall 2003 for details). Also not shown on that map is that the city of Jenin, a considerable distance from the projected path of the fence, is currently being walled.[9]

Meanwhile, despite the outrage expressed by "outside" critics of the Israeli state for its pushing of the Wall up to three and a half miles into the West Bank so as to incorporate Israeli settlements such as Alfe Menashe, the projected path of the "western" Wall (that taking its bearings from the Green Line) leaves 98 percent of West Bank settlers on the east side of the Wall. This population (which holds Israeli citizenship despite being "extra-territorial") can move without hindrance along its own roads and through roadblocks designed only to stop Palestinians. Long-term plans (announced by Ariel Sharon in March of 2003) envisage another wall running down the entire length of the Jordan Valley's western rim, effectively caging the entirety of the West Bank. Even now, while this more draconian project remains on the drawing boards, towns and villages left on the outside of existing walls are stranded in the midst of hostile territory, severed from other Palestinian communities. Palestinian communities "inside" are similarly quarantined insofar as walling divides the territories into three discontinuous "cantons" containing forty five to fifty percent of the West Bank's current territory, three "depth barriers" (fully encircled domains with single entry and exit points), and six fenced enclaves (see Cook 2003).

It is hard to imagine the borders of a Palestinian state that is comprised of a series of noncontiguous *bantustans* around, between and through which swarm armed settlers and the tanks, bulldozers, and personnel carriers of an antagonistic foreign military. Furthermore, as Eyal Weizman has saliently pointed out, while under the Oslo Accords "the Palestinian Authority was given control over isolated territorial 'islands,' ... Israel retained control over the airspace above them and the sub-terrain beneath" (Weizman 2002:n.p.). As a consequence, the aquifiers beneath the Palestinian communities are drained by underground pipes into Israel from whence, during frequent water shortages in the Territories, commercial tank trucks venture out to sell water at exorbitant prices to the Palestinians. The air above those communities is filled, day and night, with the sonic booms of Israeli jets and the thrumming of Apache helicopters, any of which might suddenly rain bombs or missiles down on Palestinians deemed "terrorists," or on those standing or living nearby. This is not a national territory, but a bubble—or series of scattered bubbles—pressured and threatened with extinction by an antagonistic outside.

The Concept of a "Border"

The concept of "border" has been both central to and multivalent in Israeli practice and discourse since the early days of the state, as Adriana Kemp has shown in her study of the role of the border and of military border violations in the shaping of Israeli identity (Kemp 1998). She contends that:

> [T]he territorialist idiom of settlement, which presented the boundary as the ultimate symbol of state sovereignty, did not take root in the Israeli mind. The army gradually initiated practices which transferred activity to the other side of the border[10] ... [so that] the breaching of the border became a symbolic practice, a genuine territorial ritual, which had the effect of both trivialising the border and instilling a sense of lordship over the territories across the lines. (Kemp 1998:89f, 92)

Kemp is talking of cross-border violations in the period when the West Bank was in Jordanian hands (although a favorite Israeli destination for the incursions of that period was Petra, well to the east of the Jordan River). The "frontierist" conception of borders she claims characterizes Israeli attitudes toward state and sovereignty is still in play in Israeli state policies, not only toward Lebanon and Syria but also with regard to what international law declares is the illegally occupied territories of the West Bank, the Golan Heights, and (until recently) the Gaza Strip. Here, the state establishes settlements, builds roadways and other infrastructural "facts on the ground" and also maintains the citizenship of "extraterritorial" settlers. In the period that Kemp discusses (1949–57), border crossings by the Israeli military were designed to punish Palestinian communities for allowing attempts to access Israel by refugees (who, for the most part, were attempting to return to houses and properties from which they had been forced in the course of the 1948 war and subsequent "mopping up" operations):

> Crossing of the lines by the Palestinians was portrayed as a "gross violation of the armistice agreements" and was called "infiltration." However, when border-crossing became a habit of the Israeli army, even if unacknowledged, it was known as "routine security measures" and depicted as part of the attempt to achieve "border discipline." (Kemp 1998:87)

Today, as evident both in Israeli incursions into Gaza and the West Bank to assassinate activists or arrest government ministers and in the recent invasion of Lebanon, a similar logic operates; "Arabs" must remain passive and in place while the Israeli military can go anywhere it wants to ensure that quiescent immobility.

The fact that borders continue to be delineated as devices for encysting Palestinians is manifest in the contemporary operations of the "Border Police," a "police" unit under the command of the military that is supposed to patrol borders as well as ports and airports. In practice, the Border Police go into operation wherever Palestinians confront Israelis in what the authorities perceive as a political manner. Thus, when Ariel Sharon's 28 September 2000 "visit" to the Haram esh-Sharif (which provoked the Second Intifada) sparked demonstrations in "Arab" towns and cities within Israel's 1949 borders, it was the Border Police who were sent into the Galilee to suppress the activities, at the cost of thirteen "Israeli Arabs" shot dead. Borders, whether those drawn by the Wall or those of "Closed Military Areas" that any officer can declare at whim, pertain to Palestinians and are erected wherever and whenever a Palestinian is seen to impinge upon or question Israeli sovereignty over "the land."

Giorgio Agamben's concept of the "sovereign exception" may illuminate the logic that has led Israel simultaneously to enclose the Palestinians of the West Bank and Gaza and render them "extra-territorial"—a term used here not to describe persons or communities belonging to a national collectivity located outside national territory (such as Israeli settlers or Jews outside of Israel), but rather to signify persons excluded from the conceptual and legal domain of the nation-state within which they nonetheless live. Agamben, in his *Homo Sacer: Sovereign Power and Bare Life*, writes:

> The exception that defines the structure of sovereignty is ... complex. Here what is outside is included not simply by means of an interdiction or an internment, but rather by means of the suspension of the juridical order's validity—by letting the juridical order, that is, withdraw from the exception and abandon it. The exception does not subtract itself from the rule; rather, the rule, suspending itself, gives rise to the exception and, maintaining itself in relation to the exception, first constitutes itself as a rule. The particular "force" of law consists in this capacity of law to maintain itself in relation to an exteriority. We shall give the name relation of exception to the extreme form of relation by which something is included solely through its exclusion. (1998 [1995]:18)

As was the case for those imprisoned in the concentration camps (a case that lies at the core of Agamben's argument), the withdrawal of the juridical order from the Palestinians "behind the wall" is not a matter of disregard but one of dehumanization—the production of what Agamben terms "bare life". The "enclosed" populations are carefully regarded—profiled, branded with identity cards, confined to specified areas, tracked—while simultaneously being denied the rights or legal status accruing to citizens of the incorporating state. The encysted are brought far more under the control of the state than its citizens but, rather than enjoying protection by the state correlative to that control, stand in constant risk of extermination by it.[11] For Agamben this construction of an "inside" (the sovereign juridical order of the state) by the inclusion of an excluded population (the threatening "other") is a central rhetorical (and practical) move by modern sovereign powers. This interiorization of a national exteriority not only provides its citizenry with evidence of the protective power of the state but simultaneously grounds—on the threat that incorporated other presents—that state's demands to increase its power over, and reduce the rights of, that citizenry (see King-Irani 2006; Agamben [2003] 2005).

Certainly the perspective provided by Agamben's concept of the sovereign exception provides an alternative understanding of the Oslo Agreements, which served to entice the diasporic "Palestinian Government in Exile" into a territory claimed and controlled by the Israeli state where it eventually found itself confined to and impotent within the walled camps of Gaza and the West Bank. From here too the recent (24 October 2006) incorporation into the Israeli government of Avigdor Lieberman's extreme right-wing Israel Beitenu ("Israel Our Home") party seems less bewildering; Israel Beitenu proposes the handing over of Arab majority regions within Israel to the Palestinian Authority in exchange for territory occupied by Israeli settlements. Both strategies further encyst the Palestinian populations—in the former case, bringing the activist cadres "outside" within the Israeli controlled areas; in the latter, realigning the wall so as to ensure that all Palestinian populations within areas controlled by the Israeli state areas are concentrated behind the wall—while presenting, to Israelis as to the world, the image of a strong state committed to a peaceful and just resolution of the Arab-Israeli conflict.

Citizens of the World

If borders for Israelis exist in large part for what Kemp calls the "symbolic practice" of breaching them, how does one discern the limits of "the land of Israel"? This question concerns not only the legal rights of settlers to benefits accruing from Israeli citizenship, which are refused their "Arab neighbors" in the Occupied Territories. It also has "extraterritorial" applications. Israel's Law of Return (5710–1950) promises that "every Jew has the right to come to this country as an *oleh* [an immigrant]" (Ministry of Foreign Affairs 1950), which in practice grants automatic citizenship and benefits to any Jew who makes *aliyah*. Jewish immigrants receive better benefits than non-Jewish immigrants, including guaranteed housing, ulpan (Hebrew language study), full tuition for graduate degrees, and other benefits including discounts on major purchases, such as cars and appliances (Weiner 2008). Beyond, however, easing *aliyah* (immigration), the Law of Return implies that, by virtue of being Jewish, Jews outside of Israel are in effect always already Israeli citizens (a parallel instance from Former Yugoslavia is analyzed in Dimitrijevic 1993:50–56). In line with the effective extension of Israeli state sovereignty that this guarantee of automatic citizenship entails, Israel has, in the past few years, intervened, either directly or by providing asylum, in cases in which Jews were on trial for crimes committed outside of Israel, as though these were cases in which its own citizens were being tried by a foreign state. It has also, in Iran, Iraq and Ethiopia, organized massive "rescue missions" taking Jewish citizens of other countries out of those countries and "resettling" them in Israel.[12] If Israeli sovereignty is extensible to anywhere Jews exist, then there are in effect no borders at all.

Certainly, in terms of its violation of international borders in defense of its self-ascertained interests, Israel acts as though they do not exist. In several instances, dating from the earliest days of the state until the present, Israel has ignored extradition processes and kidnapped persons it deemed criminals from foreign states. Strikes against and invasions of Lebanese territory are virtually routine, and it is worth noting that Israel has in the last twenty-five years alone laid claim to the following violations of other states' sovereignty as expressions of its right of self defense: the 7 June 1981 bombing of the Osiraq nuclear power plant in Iraq; the June 1982 invasion of Lebanon; the April 1988 assassination of Abu Jihad in Tunis by a military squad; the bombing on 5 October 2003 of Ein Saheb refugee camp northwest of Damascus; and the July 2006 invasion of Lebanon. If within Israel and the Occupied Territories every Palestinian has a border inscribed around him or her, in the global context Israeli sovereignty is extensible to everywhere Israeli-defined "Jewish" interests can be discerned.

Imperial Sovereignty

I return, in closing, to the concept of "encystation." Like the term *border* in Israeli discourse, and that of *extra-territorial* in this chapter, *cyst* has a double meaning: it is both a closed sac in which morbid matter is quarantined so as to protect the surrounding body and a "cell containing an embryo," which provides a defensive membrane within which that fetal entity can develop until it has grown sufficiently strong to emerge into the world outside. It is in the latter sense that Israel, as a homeland for the Jewish people, was conceptualized by Theodor Herzl and the late-nineteenth-century Zionist pioneers who saw the land as a place distant from Europe and its anti-Semitism where Jews, weakened by centuries of discrimination, could shelter while developing into what Herzl termed "real men" (*Complete Diaries* I, 19 cited in Kornberg 1993:166; see also Bowman 2002:456–463). Unsurprisingly, as a protected space within which a people could shelter and grow strong without encountering debilitating competition and challenges, Israel's founders envisaged not only the need for strong defenses against an "outside" but also means for ensuring that any internal challenge to the development of sovereignty would be contained, expelled, or destroyed.[13]

Modern day Israel, which—with its massive army, its nuclear capabilities, and its high technology economy—certainly has entered forcefully into the global community of mature states, nonetheless still wants to pose itself as a protective womb for a fetal people. As a result it encysts non-Jewish populations within the territory over which it imposes de facto sovereignty, refusing them even the semblance of self-determination (see Kimmerling 2003), while simultaneously extending its protective wall outward so as to encompass and protect all the members of a globally distributed ethno-religious population it sees as its "concern." Like the United States, which, with the demise of the Soviet Union, is able to celebrate its power to defend its citizens and its interests everywhere, Israel has, with its victories over the antagonisms against which it established itself, become unrestrained in its will to sovereign power both within and beyond its borders.

Notes

1. The slide show was presented to accompany the essay's presentation at "Vital Matters: War and the State," a workshop hosted by Bergen University between 21 and 22 February 2004. See http://www.global.uib.no/home/files/uplink/Visit_to_Beit_Sahour_Israeli_Occupied.ppt or look under Glenn Bowman, Powerpoint presentation, at http://www.svf.uib.no/sfu/vitalmatters/war.htm.
2. Readers looking for a succinct description of what has happened since the "Gaza Withdrawal," the collapse of Sharon, and the Palestinian elections can do no better than to look at Tanya Reinhart's *The Road Map to Nowhere: Israel/Palestine since 2003* (2006). Joel Beinin and Rebecca Stein's edited *The Struggle for Sovereignty: Palestine and Israel 1993–2005* (2006) and Jeff Halper's *Obstacles to Peace* (1995) offer incisive contemporary assessments of the situation.
3. According to a 2004 report by the Applied Research Institute, Jerusalem (ARIJ) walling in the Bethlehem district resulted in the alienation of 70 square kilometers of the total 608 square kilometers that make up the district (ARIJ 2004). The "wall" around Bethlehem and Beit Jala has, since 2004, been literalized as an eight-meter-high, guard-towered concrete edifice, and while a few checkpoints have been removed the majority have simply been rendered extraneous by the wall's cutting of the roads.
4. A striking exemplification of the disjunction between these two worlds is displayed when the two potential suicide bombers of Hany Abu-Assad's film *Paradise Now* (2005) move, cutting through the "Security Fence," from desolated Nablus into the affluence of Tel Aviv.
5. See Bornstein 2002 for an analysis of the fostered economic dependency of Tulkarm residents on Israel in the days before the Wall's erection.
6. A cyst is a "sac containing morbid matter, parasitic larvae etc.; cell containing embryo, etc" (Concise Oxford English Dictionary). *Encystation* differs from the term *encapsulation* as used by Boal (1994) and *enclavement* in Douglas' work (2001) in emphasizing a bodily metaphorics of disease and generation that resonates with a bio-politics deeply embedded in Israeli conceptions of nation and statehood. The particular nature of Israeli border conceptions must be understood within the extensive body of anthropological work on borders, usefully assessed and critiqued in Donnan and Wilson 1999 and 2005, and Wilson and Donnan 1998.
7. Or, in the neutralized speech of government websites, "it cannot be clearly stated that the Palestinians' right to freedom of movement must take precedence over the right of Israelis to live" (Ministry of Foreign Affairs 2004).
8. Ilan Pappe, commenting on the situation in the "hermetically sealed" territory of Gaza in September 2006, wrote "the conventional Israeli policies of ethnic cleansing employed successfully … in the West Bank are not useful here. You can slowly transfer

Palestinians out of the West Bank [via Jordan] ... but you cannot do it in the Gaza Strip once you sealed it as a maximum security prison camp" (Pappe 2006).
9. *Behind the Walls: Separation Walls between Arabs and Jews in Mixed Cities and Neighborhoods in Israel* (Ibrahim 2005) documents the growing popularity in Israel proper (behind the Green Line) of municipalities and developers constructing (without the consent of the Palestinian communities) four-meter-high concrete walls between Jewish and Arab communities. Case studies are presented from Qisariya, Lid, and Ramle.
10. Michel Warschawski, in his excellent *On the Border* (2006 [2002]), writes that "in May 1966, while out hiking with some friends, I wound up in Jordan without knowing it, and it was an Israeli patrol that brought us back to the railway zone, an extraterritorial zone, and made us get on the next train. None of us even questioned then what an Israeli patrol was doing inside Jordanian territory" (Warschawski 2006 [2002]:12).
11. In an interview with Ulrich Raulff, Agamben asserted that the situation "of the prisoners in Guantánamo ... is legally-speaking actually comparable with those in the Nazi camps. The detainees of Guantánamo do not have the status of Prisoners of War, they have absolutely no legal status. They are subject now only to raw power; they have no legal existence. In the Nazi camps the Jews had first to be fully 'denationalised' and stripped of all the citizenship rights remaining after Nuremberg, after which they were also erased as legal subjects" (Raulff 2004: 610).
12. On Iran and Iraq see Giladi 1990 [1988] and Swirski 1989; on Ethiopia see Ashkenazi and Weingrod 1987 and Wagaw 1993.
13. This position is elaborated by Ze'ev Jabotinsky, Zionist leader and founder of the clandestine anti-British militant organization *Irgun*, in his 1923 manifesto for a Jewish state, *The Iron Wall (We and the Arabs)*; see Shlaim 2000:11–16.

Bibliography

Agamben, Giorgio. 1998 [1995]. *Homo Sacer: Sovereign Power and Bare Life*. Meridian: Crossing Aesthetics. trans. Daniel Heller-Roazen. Stanford: Stanford University Press.
———. 2005 [2003]. *State of Exception*. trans. Kevin Attell. Chicago: University of Chicago Press.
Applied Research Institute of Jerusalem (ARIJ). 2004. "Bethlehem 59," *ARIJ*, 25 February 2004. Retrieved 11 November 2008 from http://www.poica.org/editor/case_studies/view.php?recordID=347.
Ashkenazi, Michael and Alex Weingrod (eds). 1987. *Ethiopian Jews and Israel*. New Brunswick: Transaction Books.
Beinin, Joel and Rebecca L. Stein (eds). 2006. *The Struggle for Sovereignty: Palestine and Israel 1993–2005*. Stanford Studies in Middle Eastern and Islamic Societies and Cultures. Stanford: Stanford University Press.
Boal, Frederick. 1994. "Encapsulation: Urban Dimensions of Ethnic Conflict," in S. Dunn (ed.), *Managing Divided Cities*. Keele: Keele University Press, pp. 30–40.
Bornstein, Avram. 2002. *Crossing the Green Line between the West Bank and Israel: The Ethnography of Political Violence*. Philadelphia: University of Pennsylvania Press.
Bowman, Glenn. 2002. "'Migrant Labour': Constructing Homeland in the Exilic Imagination," *Anthropological Theory* II(4): 447–68.
———. 2004. "About a Wall," in Bruce Kapferer (ed.), *State, Sovereignty, War: Civil Violence in Emerging Global Realities*. New York and Oxford: Berghahn Books, pp. 147–158.
Cook, Catherine. 2003. "Final Status in the Shape of a Wall," *Middle East Report Online*, 3 September 2003. Retrieved 11 November 2008 from http://www.merip.org/mero/mero090303.html.

Dimitrijevic, Vojin. 1993. "Ethnonationalism and the Constitutions: the Apotheosis of the Nation State," *Journal of Area Studies* 3: 50–56.
Donnan, Hastings and Thomas M. Wilson. 1999. *Borders: Frontiers of Identity, Nation and State.* Oxford: Berg.
Donnan, Hastings and Thomas Wilson (eds). 2005. *Culture and Power at the Edges of the State: National Support and Subversion in European Border Regions.* Munster: Lit Verlag.
Douglas, Mary. 2001. *In the Wilderness: The Doctrine of Defilement in the Book of Numbers.* Oxford: Oxford University Press.
Giladi, Gideon. 1990 [1988]. *Discord in Zion: Conflict Between Ashkenazi and Sephardi Jews in Israel.* Trans. R. Harris. London: Scorpion.
Halper, Joel. 2005. *Obstacles to Peace: A Re-Framing of the Palestinian Israeli Conflict.* Third Edition. Jerusalem: The Israeli Committee Against House Demolitions.
Ibrahim, Tarek. 2005. *Behind the Walls: Separation Walls Between Arabs and Jews in Mixed Cities and Neighborhoods in Israel.* Nazareth: Arab Association for Human Rights.
Kemp, Adriana. 1998. "From Politics of Location to Politics of Signification: The Construction of Political Territory in Israel's Early Years," *Journal of Area Studies* 12: 74–101.
Kimmerling, Baruch. 2003. *Politicide: Ariel Sharon's War Against the Palestinians.* London: Verso.
King-Irani, Laurie. 2006. "Exiled to a Liminal Zone: Are We All Palestinians Now?" *Third World Quarterly* XXVII(5): 923–36.
Kornberg, Jacques. 1993. *Theodor Herzl: From Assimilation to Zionism.* Jewish Literature and Culture. Bloomington: Indiana University Press.
Ministry of Foreign Affairs of Israel 2004. "The Anti-Terrorist Fence – An Overview." Retrieved 11 November 2008 from http://securityfence.mfa.gov.il/mfm/Data/48152.doc.
———. 1950. "Law of Return 5710–1950." Retrieved 11 November 2008 from http://www.mfa.gov.il/MFA/MFAArchive/1950_1959/Law%20of%20Return%205710-1950.
Pappe, Ilan 2006. "Genocide in Gaza," *Electronic Intifada*, 2 September 2006. Retrieved 15 November 2007 from http://electronicintifada.net/v2/article5656.shtml.
Raulff, Ulrich. 2004. "Interview with Giorgio Agamben. Life, A Work of Art Without an Author: The State of Exception, the Administration of Disorder and Private Life," *German Law Journal* V(5). (Translation Morag Goodwin, original *Suddeutsche Zeitung* 6 April 2004.) Retrieved 11 November 2008 from http://www.germanlawjournal.com/print.php?id=437.
Reinhart, T. 2006. *The Road Map to Nowhere: Israel Palestine Since 2003.* London: Verso.
Shavit, Ari. 2004. "Survival of the Fittest? An Interview with Benny Morris." Originally published in *Haaretz* (Friday Magazine), 9 January 2004. Retrieved 11 November 2008 from http://www.logosjournal.com/morris.htm.
Shlaim, Avi. 2000. *The Iron Wall: Israel and the Arab World.* London: Allen Lane.
Stop the Wall Campaign. 2003. "The Wall in the West Bank." Electronic document downloaded from http://stopthewall.org/downloads/maps/wallpostermap2.69mb.pdf, retrieved 11 November 2008. Jerusalem: PENGON/Stop the Wall Campaign.
Swirski, Shlomo. 1989. *Israel: the Oriental Majority.* Trans. Barbara Swirski. London: Zed Books.
Wagaw, Teshome. 1993. *For Our Soul: Ethiopian Jews in Israel.* Raphael Patai Series in Jewish Folklore and Anthropology. Detroit: Wayne State University.
Warschawski, Michel. 2006 [2002]. *On the Border.* Trans. Levi Laub. Cambridge, Massachusetts: South End Press.
Weiner, Jessica. 2008. "Who is a Jew." Retrieved 11 November 2008 from http://www.jewishvirtuallibrary.org/jsource/Judaism/whojew1.html. Chevy Chase, MD: The Jewish Virtual Library.
Weizman, Eyal. 2002. "The Politics of Verticality," Published at *OpenDemocracy* 24 April 2002. Retrieved 11 November 2008 from http://www.opendemocracy.net/conflict-politicsverticality/article_801.jsp.
Wilson, Thomas and Hastings Donnan, eds. 1998. *Border Identities: Nation and State at International Frontiers.* Cambridge: Cambridge University Press.

Contributors

Kirsten Alnaes is a social anthropologist, who was born in Norway and completed first-degree studies at Oslo University. She lived in Africa for twelve years and in London for thirty-three; in 2002 she moved to Norway. Alneas has conducted fieldwork among the BaKonzo in Western Uganda (1957–60, 1964, 1967, 1995, visit 2006), studying song as a code of communication, general cosmology, and political developments. She has also done extensive fieldwork among the OvaHerero in Ngamiland, Botswana (1976, 1977–78, 1980, visit 1994) on the topics of Herero history, local politics, ritual, and cosmology. She has held full-time and part-time teaching posts at London University, and has also published a prize-winning children's novel, *PIO*, (1978) based on experiences in Uganda.

Bjørn Enge Bertelsen is a Ph.D. student of social anthropology at the University of Bergen. He has done extensive fieldwork in and around Chimoio, Mozambique, from 1999. The context of the civil war, violence and postwar reconstructive practices were the subjects of his Cand. Polit. thesis (2002), and currently his research interests include the relations between tradition and state. Publications include "'It will rain until we are in power': Floods, elections and memory in Mozambique" (in H. Englund and F. Nyamnjoh, eds. *Rights and the Politics of Recognition in Africa*, Zed Books, 2004) and "The traditional lion is dead: The ambivalent presence of tradition and the relation between politics and violence in Mozambique" (*Lusotopie*, 2004).

Rasmus Alenius Boserup is Director of the Danish-Egyptian Dialogue Institute in Cairo. He holds a doctorate degree in political sociology from École des Hautes Études en Sciences Sociales in Paris, and a doctorate in Arabic and Middle East Studies from the University of Copenhagen. He has taught modern Middle Eastern history for several years at the Department of Near Eastern Studies at the University of Copenhagen. His academic research focuses on contemporary Islamic and national political movements in North Africa, paying special attention to their changing action repertoires varying between violence and nonviolence.

Glenn Bowman was trained in social anthropology at Oxford. His doctoral fieldwork (1983–85) focused on Jerusalem pilgrimage and led to his subsequent interest in Palestinian communities under occupation. He has consequently been involved in a longitudinal study of the West Bank town of Beit Sahour, begun during the first *intifada* and continuing until the present day. He has carried out field research in Yugoslavia on nationalist mobilization and the production and dissemination of contemporary art in Belgrade. He is currently engaged in writing a book on "shared shrines" in both Palestine and Macedonia. Bowman teaches in the Anthropology Department of the University of Kent (Canterbury, UK), where he coordinates the MA program in the Anthropology of Ethnicity, Nationalism and Identity.

Sverker Finnström teaches anthropology at Stockholm University (Sweden). He is the author of *Living with Bad Surroundings: War, History, and Everyday Moments in Northern Uganda* (Duke University Press, 2008). His current research investigates Pan-Africanist reorientations among Africa's young intellectuals, exemplifying how today's young Africans seek inspiration and societal hope as the contemporary world develops toward increased global inequalities and different democratic and political standards for the West and the Rest.

Caroline Ifeka is an Honorary Research Fellow in the Department of Anthropology, University College London. Ifeka is currently a member of the Editorial Working Group of *Review of African Political Economy*. Since the early 1990s, she has been based in the UK and Nigeria, where she is Chairperson of the Board of Trustees of Rural Empowerment Initiative (REIWA), a leading Nigerian NGO working with schools, adults, and literacy groups to integrate ICTs and e-connectivity in learning. On account of their extreme marginalization, REIWA targets in particular pastoralists. She is also Senior Adviser to the Board of Directors of the African Research Association, a leading Nigerian NGO working with farmers for more sustainable agriculture and forest conservation. Ifeka is completing a volume on corruption, the state, and political violence.

Bruce Kapferer is Professor of social anthropology at the University of Bergen. Kapferer has held chairs at several other institutions, including the University of Adelaide and University College London. He has conducted extensive fieldwork in Southern Africa, Sri Lanka, India, and Australia, and has published several monographs on themes including forms of ritual healing, sorcery, nationalism, and urbanization, among them *Aesthetics in Performance: Formations of Symbolic Construction and Experience* (2007, ed. with Angela Hobart), *Beyond Rationalism: Sorcery, Magic and Ritual in Contemporary Realities* (2003, ed.), *Legends of People, Myths of State* (1998 [1988]), *The Feast of the Sorcerer* (1997), and *A Celebration of Demons* (1991 [1983]).

Staffan Löfving is a researcher at the Department of Social Anthropology at Stockholm University. His doctoral project at Uppsala University explored the war–peace transition in Guatemala as experienced in displaced and rebel-affiliated communities in the Highlands. Since then, he has been Research Fellow in the Centre for Multiethnic Research, Uppsala University (2003) and Assistant Professor in the Institute of Latin American Studies, Stockholm University (2004–08), with research projects on neoliberalism, violence, and poverty in Colombia and Central America. His books include *Struggles for Home: Violence, Hope and the Movement of People* (co-edited with Stef Jansen, Berghahn Books, 2008) and *Peopled Economies: Conversations with Stephen Gudeman* (Uppsala University, 2005).

June Nash is Distinguished Professor Emerita at the City University of New York, Graduate Center and City College. Nash has taught at Yale University and New York University. She has published extensively on her work in Chiapas, Mexico, with Mayas in the late 1950s and 1960s and return field stays in 1990 to the present. Her work in tin-mining communities of Bolivia from 1969 to 1984 is published in Spanish and English as well as a documentary film of the same title. Her engagement in feminist and working-class movements resulted in the co-editing of several anthologies in the 1980s, when she was engaged in field research on the military-industrial complex during the Reagan years as it was played out in the General Electric plant. She returned to Chiapas to record the transition from a semisubsistence economy of cultivators and artisans to producers in a world market in the 1990s. Soon after, the uprising of Maya migrants to the Lacandon rainforest burst into global headlines and is played out in the ongoing conflict as Mayan claims for pluricultural autonomy are countered by state counterinsurgency. Her return study of General Electric workers in Pittsfield was the basis for interviews for the present article. Her interest in the comparative study of social movements in the process of globalization is expressed in recently published books such as *Social Movements and Practicing Ethnography in a Global World* (Altamira Press, 2007). She continues to revisit field sites in Chiapas, Guatemala, and the United States.

Jakob Rigi is Associate Professor at Central European University Budapest, holding a Ph.D. from London University (1999). He taught at Cornell University (2002–08) and London University (2001–02). He has been a fellow at New York University, Edinburgh University, and Manchester University. His major publication is *Post-soviet Chaos: Violence and dispossession in Kazakhstan* (Pluto Press, 2002). His research interest includes state, law, and capital in Russia. He is completing a book on sovereignty in Russia tentatively entitled *The Spectacle of Law: Coercion and Sovereignty under Putin.*

Since 1993 **Frode Storaas**'s base has been Bergen Museum at the University of Bergen. Before then he had different positions at the Department of Anthropology at UiB in between work for aid organizations in Sudan and East Africa, as NORAD, NCA, FAO, a two-year scholarship from Norwegian Research Council, and a year as a visiting scholar at Program for Visual Anthropology at the University of Southern California, Los Angeles. Storaas' anthropological research has mainly dealt with pastoralists and agro-pastoralists in Sudan, Kenya, and Uganda and issues concerning adaptation, economy, ethnicity, and local politics. As an ethnographic filmmaker he has been involved in projects in Eastern and Southern Africa, the Middle East, Mexico, the United States, China, and Norway.

Since 1991 **Christopher Taylor** has been a Professor of anthropology at the University of Alabama at Birmingham (UAB). He has done anthropological fieldwork in Rwanda on several occasions and has also done applied work there on questions related to STDs and HIV/AIDS. He was present in Rwanda at the start of the genocide in 1994. His principal theoretical interests are: symbolism, cosmology, and medical anthropology. His published works include *Milk, Honey and Money* (Smithsonian Institution Press, 1992) and *Sacrifice as Terror* (Berg Press, 1999).

Mats Utas is Senior Researcher at the Nordic Africa Institute and the Royal Swedish Academy of Letters, History and Antiquities. He received a Ph.D. in cultural anthropology from the University of Uppsala in 2003 and has since published numerous journal articles and book chapters on themes such as youth, civil wars, gender, and media. Utas is the co-editor of *Navigating youth, generating adulthood: Social becoming in an African context* (Nordic Africa Institute, 2006). He has conducted fieldwork in the Ivory Coast (1996), Liberia (1998), and most recently Sierra Leone (2004–06). His current research centers on socioeconomic networks of street-corner youth in postwar Sierra Leone.

INDEX

9/11. *See* September 11, 2001

abduction
    of foreign nationals (Israel), 301
    of foreign nationals and journalists (Russia), 54, 68, 70, 79n16, 79n17
    of minors as part of LRA/M tactic (Uganda), 127
    of people in Bundibugyo (Uganda), 107f, 116, 118f
    and Renamo tactic (Mozambique), 218
    and FLN tactic (Algeria), 253f
    as paramilitary and guerrilla tactic (Colombia), 200–202
    and control of people (Mozambique), 222, 224
    and murder of children and youth (Mozambique), 227f
    and killing of prisoners and thieves (Mozambique), 233n2
Abrams, Philip, 163
Abu Ghraib, 31, 45, 48, 189–191. *See also* torture
Acholiland, 124–128, 131, 135f, 138, 151
accumulation. *See also* capitalism, corporate state, corporate control
    and coercion, 60
    and state, 65
    by dispossession, 206n2
    conspicuous a., 220, 227f
    global capitalist a., 31

Adivasi movement, 9
Adorno, Theodor, 5
Afanas'ev, M.N., 57
Africa, 90, 134, 143, 146
    East and central A., 115f, 146, 148, 168, 214
    Southern A., 1f, 17
    Sub-Saharan A., 214
African
    racial stereotypes of Africans, 80n22
    states, 84, 92n7, 125, 128. *See also* state
Agamben, Giorgio, 7f, 60f, 119, 127, 191, 211f, 228, 231, 265, 298f, 303n11
Ageron, Charles Robert, 243, 246, 248, 260n22, 260n30, 260nn32–33, 261nn48–49
Agip, Inc., 93n12
Aijmer, Göran, 166f
Akfadou, 252, 261n46
Akpan, Monday B., 271, 276–278, 286n15, 286nn17–18, 286n20
Al Qaeda, 104, 190
aldeia comunal, 219, 231, 235n20, 236n33
aldeamento, 230f
Alden, Chris, 234n11, 235n28
Alexander, Jocelyn, 235n17
Alfe Menashe, 296. *See also* Israel
Algeria
    creation of colonial state in, 256
    European settlers in, 242f, 248f, 251, 253f, 256, 258

French colonial state in, 242f
harkis in, 246, 253f, 257f, 262nn52–53
Nationalism in colonial A., 244ff
War of national independence
(1954–1962), 245–258
Algerian Communist Party, 245
Ali, T., 85
al-isti'mār (colonialism), 245. *See also*
Algeria, colonialism
aliyah, 300. *See also* Israel
al-Kader, Abd, 244
al-muwâtin al-jazâ'irî (Algerian patriot), 244
Alleg, Henri, 258n4
Allen, Tim, 127, 267
Allied Democratic Forces (ADF), 97–99, 104–110, 114–119
Alnaes, Kirsten, 20, 100, 120n5, 121n9, 121n16
Alpers, Edward, 234n5
Althusser, L., 54, 59
Amin, Idi, 101f, 104, 121n7, 124, 126, 134, 149, 150
Amirouche, colonel, 252f
Amnesty International, 126, 189
Anderson, Benedict, 21n2, 56, 168
Anderson, Benjamin J. K., 286n18
Angola, 215
anthropology
　contemporary a., 267
　forensic a., 194
　of state terror, 211
anticolonialism. *See* colonialism
'Anti-Terrorist Fence'. *See* Israel
Appadurai, Arjun, 21n2, 233n3
Apter, D.E., 88f, 92n5
Arbore (Uganda), 145. *See also* Uganda, Karamojong
Arendt, Hanna, 8, 61, 84f, 88f, 91, 92n7
Aretxaga, Begoña, 212, 233n3
Armed Forces of Liberia (AFL), 268f, 278f, 281
armed struggle. *See* war, warfare
arms. *See also* disarmament,
　　pastoralism, Karamojong
　and hand weapons, 150, 152
　and pastoralism, 143–158
　dealings in Africa, 153
　global proliferation of a., 143

army. *See also* war, warfare
　Burundian a., 184n7
　colonial Liberian a., 276–279
　Colombian a., 188, 200, 203
　Congolese a., 113f
　French colonial a., 241–262
　Guatemalan a., 188, 192–197, 203f
　Israeli a., 11, 297f, 301
　Kenyan a., 152
　Liberian a., 269, 273, 280f, 283f, 286n24
　Mozambican a., 215–226, 234n15
　Nigerian a., 93n12
　Russian a., 54f, 66f, 70f, 73, 75f
　Rwandan a., 169, 175, 177
　Ugandan a., 105ff, 110, 112–115, 124–140, 151
　U.S. a., 33–37, 40–43, 48
Arrighi, Giovanni, 23n15, 59, 76, 214
Artur, Domingos do Rosario, 220, 236n34
Ashcroft, Bill, 235n29
Ashforth, Adam, 235n29
Ashkenazi, Michael, 303n12
assassinations. *See* extra-judicial
　villings, death squads, violence
Autodefensas Campesinas de Córdoba
　y Urabá (ACCU), 199, 201. *See
　also* paramilitarism, Colombia
Autodefensas Unidas de Colombia
　(AUC), 197, 201ff. *See also*
　paramilitarism, Colombia
Ateker, 146. *See also* Uganda, Nilotes, Cushitic
Atkinson, Philippa, 269
Austin, J.L., 7
Avilés, W., 191

BaAmba, 99f, 108, 120n2, 121n16
Badiou, Alain, 77
Bafuruki, 146. *See also* Uganda, Karamojong
Baker, Bruce, 233n2
Baker, W.G., 148f, 157
Bakonjo Life History Research Rwenzori, 100
BaKonzo, 99f, 108, 120n2, 120n5, 121n16
Balakrishnan, Gopal, 233n3

Banyamulenge, 105, 122n19
Banyoro, 146. *See also* Uganda, Karamojong
bare life, 60–61, 73, 75–77, 119, 127, 191–197, 212f, 225–232, 299. *See also homo sacer*, Agamben, Giorgio
Barth, Fredrik, 145
Basayev, Shamil, 54, 67–71, 75
Bates, R., 191
Bateson, Gregory, 172
Baudrillard, Jean, 62, 76, 85, 89, 92n5
Bauman, Zygmunt, 8, 266
Baxter, P., 145
beheading. *See also* violence and body
 in Chechnya, 54
 in Bundibugyo (Uganda), 106, 116
Beinart, William, 234n10
Beinin, Joel, 302n2
Beira, 222, 229f, 236n31
Beit Jala, 294, 302n3
Beit Sahour, 292–294
Bellman, Beryl, 270f, 274f
Beltrán, A., 192
Benyahia, Mohammed, 250, 252
Berkeley, Bill, 278, 283
Bertelsen, Bjørn Enge, 11, 21, 91, 216, 226, 235n22
Bethlehem, 292, 294–296, 302n3
Bhebe, Ngwabi, 234n9
Bienen, Henry, 286n25
'big men', 273, 284. *See also* warriors
Bigwood, J., 200
biological determinism, 168
bio-politics, 61, 267, 283f, 303n6. *See also* power, state, empire and bio-power
Blackwater, Inc., 18, 23nn16–17, 40, 44–46, 49. *See also* war, privatization of
Blamo, J. Bernard, 276, 286n17
Bledsoe, Caroline, 271
Bley, Helmuth, 122n25
Boal, Frederick, 302n6
Bøås, Morten, 278
body
 and violence. *See* violence and body
 politic, 278
 social b., 232, 295

metaphors of b., 118, 169–170, 176–181, 301
Bokora, 148. *See also* Karamojong, Uganda
Boltwood, E., 33
border. *See* state and border
Borkenau, F., 86
Bornstein, Avram, 302n5
Boro, Isaac, 93n11
Boserup, Rasmus, 21, 260n29
Bourdieu, Pierre, 7, 167, 258n3, 259n5, 259n11
Bowen, Merle, 226
Bowman, Glenn, 12, 21, 301
Boyer, Dominic, 56
Boyer, P., 85, 93n8
Branch, Adam, 127
Branche, Raphaëlle, 258n4
Breman, H., 149
Brenner, A.D., 205
Brenner, R., 76
Briggs, Charles, 56
Brown, L.H., 149
Brown, W., 206n2
Brubaker, Roger, 78n11
Bundibugyo, 20, 97, 99–101, 105–112, 114f
Bundu, 274. *See also* Poro
Burke, Anthony, 8
Burundi, 117f, 146, 172, 177f, 184n7
Bush, George, 41
Bush, George W., 29–32, 39f, 41, 43, 45–49, 189
Buur, Lars, 226, 236n34
Bwamba county, 98–100, 114
Bwambale, Bamusede, 100, 121nn6–7, 121n16

Cabral, Amilcar, 91
Cabrita, João M., 234n6
Cahen, Michel, 233n2, 234n7, 234n11
Cali cartel, the, 200, 202
Camacho, Á., 207n5
Campbell, B.B., 205
camp. *See also* naked life, Agamben, Giorgio
 and state, 61, 299
 and refugees, 102f, 106, 109–112, 117f, 138f, 301

concentration c., 61, 192, 299, 303n11
guerrilla/army c., 101, 104, 106, 108, 113, 132, 193, 224, 258n3
Caparini, Marina, 18, 23n16
capital. *See also* military-industrial complex, capitalism, neoliberalism
  crisis of global c., 2, 16
  crisis of U.S. c., 29, 46
  dominance of global c., 83, 214, 233n3, 266
  immanence of c., 12
  national control of c., 201
  state and reproduction of c., 62
  war and the restructuring of c., 76f, 83, 92, 130
  welfare c., 34
capitalism, 22n13, 23n17, 30, 32, 46. *See also* neoliberalism, corporate control, corporate state
  and accumulation, 31, 39. *See also* accumulation
  and bare life, 61, 77
  crisis of global c., 76f
  ontology of c., 163f
Carlier, Omar, 259n10
Carter, Angela, 76
Castaño, Carlos, 202f
Castells, M., 61, 76
Central Intelligence Agency (U.S.) (CIA), 199
Chad, postcolonial state in, 127f
chaotic mode of domination, 57–65, 68–72, 75f
Chauvin, Stéphanie, 260n22
Chechnya. *See* Russia
Cheikh, Slimane, 259n5, 260n32
Chel, 192–197
Chernomyrdin, Viktor, 67
Chevron Corp., 89
child soldiers, 134, 270, 285n8 . *See also* war and youth
Chimoio, 210f, 214, 217f, 220, 222f, 227–230, 233nn1–2
Chrétien, Jean-Pierre, 174, 176f
Christie, Iain, 234n6
circulation. *See* movement, Rwanda
civil war. *See* war

class. *See* globalization and c., neoliberalism, capital, capitalism
Clastres, Pierre, 6, 21n1, 22n5, 164f, 168f, 212
Coalition pour la Défense de la République (CDR) (Rwanda), 176f, 179f, 183n3. *See also* Rwanda
Coelho, João Borges, 230f, 234n4, 236nn32–33
Cold War, 30, 32, 35, 39f, 48, 83, 128, 212, 281. *See also* post-cold war era
collective violence. *See* violence, war
Colombia
  clandestine state violence in, 188, 197, 202, 206
  corruption in, 201. *See also* corruption
  decentralization reforms in, 188, 199
  economy of coca in, 198, 200–202, 205
  limpieza in, 201
  narco-bourgeoisie in, 200, 207n5
  'narco-guerrillas' in, 200
colonial state/administration, *see also* colonialism
  Algeria, 242–243, 246, 256
  and violence, 4f
  and bureaucratic coding (India and Sri Lanka), 9
  and ethnic categories (Rwanda), 168
  and indirect rule, 99, 259n12, 271, 279, 281
  and racial categories (Algeria), 256
  and *régulos* (chiefs) in Mozambique, 224, 231
  British Protectorate authorities (Uganda) and c. s., 99
  in Liberia, 271, 273, 276–279
  in Mozambique, 230f
  in Russia, 54f
  in Rwanda, 165
colonialism
  and anti-colonialism, 54, 99, 244
  as capture, 9f
  expansion in Southern Africa, 2
  in Algeria, 243–246
  in Colombia, 198
  in Mozambique, 214f

Colton, Timothy J., 69f, 75
commando. *See* warrior
Comaroff, Jean, 15, 60
Comaroff, John L., 15, 60
Communism, 39
Communist, 258n4
    elite in Russia, 57
    Party in Algeria, 245. *See also* Algeria
    Party in Chechnya, 64. *See also* Russia
    Party in Soviet Union and Russia, 57f, 70, 78n7. *See also* Russia
concentration camp. *See* camp
conflict. *See* violence, war
Congo. *See* Democratic Republic of Congo
Congos, 286n16
conspiracy, 53–55, 252
    and mode of domination, 57, 76
    and spectacle, 57, 76, 81n31
    c. narratives in Russia, 54–57, 75
    c. theory as form of knowledge, 56
    structural c., 77
Cook, Catherine, 293f, 297
corporate control, 4, 14–19, 30f, 33f, 38f, 41, 44f, 83, 87, 89, 91, 190f, 199. *See also* neoliberalism, corporate state, privatization
corporate state, 4, 15–19, 91
    and civil war, 18
    Iraq as an instance of a c. s., 18
    Mozambique as an instance of a c. s., 214, 232
corporate violence, 87
corporate warriors, 23n16. *See also* privatization, state relations to the military/army
Corrigan, Philip, 60
corruption
    and rhetoric of transparency, 187, 189, 191, 201, 206n3
    of military contractors to the U.S., 31, 49n1. *See also* military-industrial complex
    in Post-Soviet Russia, 65, 69f. *See also* Russia
    in Mozambique, 227, 230, 232, 236n30

rhetoric of c. as state discourse, 12
cosmology, 64, 213f, 216, 220, 226–228, 232, 280, 284
    and power, 22n6, 169, 179, 182f
    and war, 125
Coupez, André, 169, 172
Courrière, Yves, 260n31, 261n48
Crais, Clifton, 235n29
Cramer, Christopher, 191, 214
crime, 38f, 111, 143, 155, 210f, 229. *See also* accumulation
    and death squads, 211, 213, 232, 233n2. *See also* death squads, Mozambique
    and globalization, 2
    and Israeli state, 300
    and paramilitaries, 200f
    and war, 68
    organized c., 58, 64, 69
    war c., 241, 247f, 255, 258n4, 262n52
Cubides, F.C., 198, 202
Cushitic, 147. *See also* Uganda, Nilotes
cyberspace, 12–14, 22n13, 83f. *See also* warfare, digital
cyst, 292, 301, 303n6. *See also* encystation

Daghistan. *See* Russia and occupation of
Dalit movement, 9, 13
Das, Veena, 192
Dassanetch, 145. *See also* Uganda, Karamojong, Ethiopia
Davies, T.M., Jr., 196
Davis, D.D., 190
d'Azevedo, Warren, 274–276, 286n20
de Boeck, Filip, 133, 286n21
de Certeau, Michel, 282
de Heusch, Luc, 103, 121n14, 170
de Montoya, M. Lindh, 206n3
de Tocqueville, Alexis, 4
de Waal, Thomas, 55, 64–66, 78n13, 79n15
Dean, Mitchell, 284
death-event, 117
death-world, 117
death squads, 20. *See also* policing members of recruited to Blackwater, 23n16

in Guatemala, 192. *See also* Guatemala
in Mozambique, 210ff, 227f, 230, 232f, 233n2. *See also* Mozambique
Débord, Guy, 61, 79n19. *See also* spectacle
DeGrasse, Robert M., Jr., 49n5
d'Hertefelt, Marcel, 169, 172
Deleuze, Gilles, 3f, 11f, 14, 19, 22n3, 22n4, 59, 61, 212, 223f, 226, 230, 234n8, 235n26, 236n32. *See also* Guattari, Félix, state and war machine
Democratic Republic of Congo, 20, 99, 101, 103–106, 108, 112–114, 119, 120n1, 127, 129, 150
Denning, Dorothy, 14
depth barriers, 297. *See also* Israel, Palestine
Derluguian, Georgi M., 63
deterritorialization, 11f, 62, 218, 221, 224. *See also* state and territory
development
　agencies and agents, 92, 130, 157
　and authoritarian rule, 84, 87
　and empire, 265f. *See also* empire
　and structural adjustment, 128. *See also* World Bank, International Monetary Fund, neoliberalism
　and war, 18, 90, 128, 130
　literature, 235n23
　policy and pastoralists, 149f
　success of d. in Uganda, 125
developmental eutopianism, 124
Dimitrijevic, Vojin, 300
disarmament
　of guerrillas 194, 198
　of pastoralists, 144, 151f, 157
disarmament, demobilization, and reintegration (DDR), 113, 194, 198
discourse, 165, 189
　and Foucault, 164
　and violence, 89, 91, 165
　idealistic d., 5
　Israeli d., 297, 301. *See also* Israel, Palestine
　Neoliberal d., 213
　of corruption, 12. *See also* corruption
　of human rights, 17f
　of liberation, 254f
　of militarization and war, 83, 86f
　of community development, 84
　on retreating states, 199
　political d., 84, 86, 88, 194
　popular d., 145
discursive
　and the imaginary, 181f
　and violence, 166
　from pre-discursive to d., 167
　idiom, 166
　power, 205
　practice, 7, 16, 91
Dodoth, 146. *See also* Uganda, Karamojong
Doe, Samuel K., 268, 278f, 285n5, 286nn24–25
Dolan, Chris, 221
Donnan, Hastings, 302n6
Dorobo, 147. *See also* Uganda, Karamojong
Douglas, Mary, 302n6
Douglas, O., 89
Doukas, Dimitra, 39
Droz, Bernhard, 261n48
Drug Enforcement Administration (DEA) (U.S.), 200
Dudaev, Dzhokhar, 55, 64–67, 78n5
Dunlop, John B., 63,
Durkheim, Emile, 164f
Dynamising Groups, 215, 234n7
Dyson-Hudson, N., 145
dzindza, 235n18

ECOMOG, 268f
economies of deprivation, 164. *See also* capitalism, accumulation, corporate state
economism, 164f
Efrat, 294
Egerö, Bertil, 234n7
Egypt, 296
Ejercito Guerillero de los Pobres (EGP). *See* Guerilla Army of the Poor
Elin Saheb refugee camp, 301. *See also* Israel, Palestine, camp
Ellis, Stephen, 233n2, 268, 272, 274, 278f, 285n7

Elmolo, 147. *See also* Uganda, Karamojong, Kenya
empire, 14, 190, 214, 231, 233n3, 265–268, 279, 282, 284, 285n2, 285n4. *See also* Michael Hardt and Antonio Negri
and bio-power, 266–268, 279–285. *See also* bio-politics, power
Chinese e., 4
of disorder. *See* Joxe
Ottoman e., 4, 242, 262n55
Postmodern e., 61
Russian e., 74, 78n9, 78n11, 80n26
U.S. e., 20, 29, 31, 92
encystation. *See* Israel, Palestine
Englund, Harri, 18, 206n2
Espeland, R.H., 146
Ethiopia, 145f, 151
Jews in, 300, 303n12
ethnic cleansing, 293, 302n8
ethnic discrimination and war, 43. *See also* Iraq
ethnic violence, 9
ethnicity. *See also* sovereignty, ethnic formations of
and group formation in Uganda, 144f, 148, 150
and group formation in Liberia, 279, 281, 283
and critique of ethnic conflict argument, 127f, 156f, 266f, 283
and empire, 266. *See also* empire
and the Russian state, 58–60, 64, 70, 72, 77, 78n11, 80n30
and the Rwandan state, 10, 168ff
transnational assemblages of e., 2, 15
ethnification, of Liberian army, 283
ethological, the, 166f
Europe
and colonialism. *See* colonialism
and anti-Semitism, 301
press in, 296
state formation in E., 4–6, 16, 88, 198f, 277, 285n4
Evangelista, Mathew, 63–66, 70f, 78n9
extra-judicial killings, 87–89, 126, 154, 174, 193f, 201–203, 205, 210–212, 227f, 230, 232, 233n2, 241, 251–253, 257f, 260n26, 261n41, 278, 298, 301. *See also* death squads, violence

Fairbairn, Geoffrey, 261n37
Fanon, Frantz, 91, 119, 259n5
Fascism, 2, 5, 57, 215
Fauvelle-Aymar, François-Xavier, 235n29
fear
and distrust, 101, 103, 129
and power, 191–197, 229, 295
and symbols, 166
as integral to spectacle, 61f, 69ff. *See also* spectacle
collective f., 167, 222
political manipulation of f., 197, 201
of army/police, 132, 134, 191
of disarmament, 152
of rebels/guerrillas/paramilitaries, 191, 196, 203, 218
of violence/war, 97f, 107, 109–111, 115, 117, 124, 218, 226, 229f, 274
Feldman, Allen, 205, 235n25
Ferguson, R. Brian, 221
Ferme, Mariane, 277, 283f
Fernando, Domingos, 236n34
fertility
and Israeli appropriation of land, 296
and sorcery, 228. *See also* sorcery
the king's assurance of f., 169–171, 176f, 182
financial crisis, 16. *See also* corporate state
Finel, B.I., 189
Finnström, Sverker, 20, 127f, 138
Fitzpatrick, P., 192
Florêncio, Fernando, 236n34
Florini, A., 189
Ford, Martin, 271, 277, 286n20
Foucault, Michel, 7, 21n2, 22n8, 61, 163–165, 254, 266f, 283f
Franco, Jean, 205
Frente de Libertação de Moçambique (FRELIMO), 212–216, 218–227, 229, 231, 234nn5–8, 234n12, 234n16. *See also* Mozambique
Friedman, Jonathan, 22n11, 61, 267

Front de Libération Nationale (FLN) (Algeria), 242–264. *See also* Algeria
Fuerzas Armadas Revolucionarias de Colombia (FARC). *See* Revolutionary Armed Forces of Colombia.
Fulton, Richard, 272–275
Fung, A., 206n3

Gall, Carlotta, 55, 64–66, 78n13, 79n15
Garsten, C., 206n3
Gaza, 11, 292–294, 296, 298f, 302n2, 302n8
Geffray, Christian, 234n11, 234n16
gender, 35, 280
General Electric (U.S.), 29f, 32–35, 38f, 47
Geneva Convention, the, 31, 44, 189f, 295
genocide, 87, 90, 93n12, 266. *See also* Rwanda
  and Rwandan refugees to Uganda, 101f
  by Federal Nigerian Army, 93n12
  of OvaHerero, 122n25
Germany, 45, 122n25
gerontocracy, 276, 270, 279, 286n14
Gersony, Robert, 234n14
Geschiere, Peter, 235n29
Gibbs, James, 274
Giladi, Gideon, 303n12
Gill, L., 191, 201, 206n2
Girard, René, 84f, 88, 91
Gledhill, John, 6
globalization
  and class, 84, 92
  and global distribution of wealth, 233n3
  and global peripheries, 1, 83, 126, 128f, 140, 231f, 233n3
  and New World Order, 129
  power of, 22n11
Gluckman, Max, 1
Gorbachev, Mikhail, 57f, 64, 78n7
gotokoto, 235n21
governmentality, 133, 267. *See also* Foucault, Michel
Graham, M., 206n3

Gramsci, Antonio, 22n9, 57, 59. *See also* hegemony
Gray, John, 5
Gray, S., 148, 150f, 157
Grozny, 55, 65–67, 79n17. *See also* Russia and war in/with Chechnya
Gruffydd-Jones, Branwen, 214, 225
Grupos Dinamizadores. See Dynamizing Groups
Guatemala, 133, 187f, 192, 195, 199, 204
  Chel massacre in G. *See* Chel
  civil patrols in G., 194, 196, 203, 205
  mozo system in G., 203f
  mutuality in G., 203ff
  parallel powers in G., 192
  Truth Commission in G., 193f
  violence in G., 191f, 203
Guattari, Félix, 3f, 11f, 14, 19, 22n3, 22n4, 59, 61, 212, 223f, 226, 230, 234n8, 235n26, 236n32. *See also* Deleuze, Gilles, state and war machine
Guantánamo, 31, 303n11. *See also* torture
Gudeman, Stephen, 203
Guebuza, Armando, 210f, 232
Guerilla Army of the Poor, 193, 196. *See also* Colombia
'Guerrilla Promise', 116f
guerrillas. *See* warfare, paramilitarism
Guinea
  and war in Liberia, 269f, 274, 286n14, 286n18. *See also* Liberia
Guinea Bissau, 215, 282
Guizado, A. Camacho, 200
Gulliver, P.H., 145f
Gumilev, L. N., 80n30
Gunaratna, Rohan, 104
guns. *See* arms
Gwynne, M.D., 149, 157

habitus, 8, 167
Habyarimana, Juvénal, 121n13, 121n15, 172–177, 179–183
Hall, Margaret, 234n16, 226
Halper, Joel, 302n2
Hamar, 145. *See also* Uganda, Karamojong
Hamas, 76

Hamoumou, Mohand, 254
Handelman, Don, 8
handguns. *See* arms
Hanlon, Joseph, 214, 234n7
Hansen, Thomas Blom, 22n7, 212f, 266, 281, 287n28
Haram esh-Sharif, 294, 298
ḥarb al-isitqlāl, 245, 255. *See also* Algeria, war of independence
Harbi, Mohammed, 242, 245f, 249, 253, 259n5, 259n8, 260n16, 260nn18–19, 261n34, 261n48
Hardt, Michael, 12, 59, 61, 129, 214, 233n3, 265–267, 282, 284, 285nn2–3. *See also* Negri, Antonio, empire
Harley, George Way, 271–275, 286n9
Harris, David, 269
Harvey, David, 23n15, 31, 62, 77, 206n2
Healy, Shawn, 14
Hedges, Chris, 40
hegemony
 capitalist h., 233n3
 corporate h. (U.S.), 33f, 38f, 133n3
 crisis of h. in post-Soviet Russia, 57
 end of capitalist h., 76f
 of ruling classes, 3, 59
 of the state, 59, 181
 U.S. global h., 21
Herbst, Jeffrey, 129
Hersh, S.M., 189
Herzl, Theodor, 301
hizb Khaled. *See* Khaled's Party
Hlophe, Stephen, 276
Hobbes, Thomas, 6, 16, 18, 60, 68, 84, 118, 163, 283. *See also* Leviathan
Hoejbjerg, Christian Kordt, 274, 286nn13–14
Holocaust, 8
Holzner, B., 189
Holzner, L., 189
homo economicus, 165
homo politicus, 165
homo sacer, 73, 191, 299. *See also* bare life, Agamben, Giorgio
Hopkins, Elizabeth, 121n9
Horne, Alistar, 261n40
Human Rights Watch, 71, 79n21, 84, 92n5, 129, 189, 197f, 201

Humphrey, Caroline, 58
Hutchinson, Martha Crenshaw, 259n6, 261n40
Hutu power/a, 103, 121n13, 183n3
Hutu refugees, 101f
Hutu Tutsi relations, 103, 116f, 146, 168f, 174f, 178f. *See also* Rwanda

Ibrahim, Tarek, 303n9
ideology, 168f
 master/slave i., 164
 neoliberal i., 15f. *See also* neoliberalism
 of necessity of the state, 6f. *See also* state
 political i., 59, 174
 racial i., 243
Ifeka, Caroline, 18, 20, 86, 92n8
Ijaw National Congress (Nigeria), 89, 93n11
imaana, 169f, 172, 175, 179, 181–183
imaginary, the, 166f, 183
 and the cultural, 2
 and discourse, 181f
 and film in war, 280
 and violence, 169–181
 of state crisis, 6. *See also* state, crisis
imbuto, 177
impurity
 and kingship, 170f
 ritual i., 181
Independent National Patriotic Front of Liberia (INPFL), 268, 280
internal war. *See* war
International Monetary Fund (IMF), 128, 211, 214. *See also* World Bank, Structural Adjustment Programs
Interahamwe guerrillas, 103, 121n15, 180, 184n8
International Criminal Court (ICC), 127, 285n6
Iraq, 29, 31f, 37, 49, 183, 189f, 301
 American women as soldiers in I., 43
 as a corporate state, 18, 44
 Bush' strategy in I., 31
 Gulf War in I., 41
 Mexican citizens as American soldiers in I., 43

oil resources in I., 44
private military operators in I., 18, 23n16
privatization of war in I., 40–42, 45
privatization of the state in I., 43–47
recruitment to war in I., 48
secrecy of private military action in I., 45
utopian ideas of liberation of I., 5
war in I., 29
Irenge, 147. *See also* Uganda, Karamojong, Kenya
Israel, 11f, 14, 21, 35, 292–303
and cross-border violations, 297f, 300–302, 302n6, 303n10
and sovereign exception, 299
'Anti-Terrorist Fence' in I., 292–303
architecture of entombment in I., 293–295
checkpoints in I., 294, 296, 302n3
'Closed Military Areas' in I., 298
encystation in I., 292, 295–301, 302n6
ethnic cleansing in I., 292f
'frontierist' conception of borders in I., 298
Green Line in I., 296, 303n9
rescue missions organized by, 300
state in I., 292, 296–303
Israel Beitenu, 299f
ishyano, 170f, 181
Iteso, 131, 151. *See also* Uganda, Karamojong
Ituri forest, 114

jabha at-taḥrīr al-waṭanī, 245. *See also* Front de Libération Nationale (FLN)
Jacobs, A.H., 144
Jacoby, Russell, 5
James, Harold, 34
Jameson, Fredrick, 61
Jansen, Stef, 206n1
Jansson, O., 207
Jauffret, J-Ch., 260n23, 261n39
Jenin, 296
Jerusalem, 294f, 302n3
Jie, 146f, 152, 158. *See also* Uganda, Karamojong

Jihad, Abu, 301
Jiye, 146. *See also* Uganda, Karamojong, Sudan
Johnson, Chalmers, 41f, 49n3
Johnson, Prince Y., 268
Jordan, 296
and Israel/Palestine conflict, 295–298, 302n8. *See also* Israel, Palestine
Joxe, Alain, 5, 22n7, 22n11, 84, 92, 232, 233n3, 266, 285n3

Kabwegyere, Tarsis B., 130
Kagarlitsky, Boris, 70f, 75
Kaldor, Mary, 62
Kapferer, Bruce, 84, 91, 118f, 125, 128, 168, 179, 191, 199, 223, 285n3
Karamoja, 143, 146–149, 151–154, 156f
Karamojong, 144–152, 155f
Karatzogianni, Athina, 22n13
Karinga (drum of Burundi), 178
Karlström, Mikael, 124f, 130f
Kasese District, 97, 105, 121n7
Kasingien, 104
Kasozi, A.B.K., 134
Keen, David, 269
Keesing, Roger, 22n6
Kelly, Raymond C., 145, 153
Kemedi, D.V., 87
Kemp, Adriana, 297f, 300
Kenya, 144, 146, 153–155
colonial state's relocation of Pokot people from K. to Uganda, 148
state's disarmament of nomads in K., 149–152
Khaled's Party, 244
Khattab, Ibn al-, 68–71, 75, 79n17
Kibaale District, 146. *See also* Uganda
kidnapping. *See* abduction
killings. *See* extra-judicial killings, violence
Kilembe, 105, 112
Kimmerling, Baruch, 301f
King-Irani, Laurie, 299
kingship
sacred, 165, 168f, 171f, 174, 176–179, 182
Kirindi, 110
Klein, Naomi, 206n2

Kony, Joseph, 126, 133. *See also* Lord's Resistance Army/Movement (LRA/M)
Korean war, 30f, 34, 36
Kornberg, Jacques, 301
Korte, Werner, 286n25
Korvah, Paul M., 272
Koulakssis, Ahmed, 244
kufunga muiri, 228f
kufunga taiyao, 228f
Kyaminyawandi, Augustine, 100, 121nn6–7, 121n16
Kyed, Helene, 226, 233n2, 236n34

Lake Turkana, 147
Lamphear, J., 146f
Lamprey, H.F., 149
Lamwaka, Caroline, 126
Lango, 131, 151. *See also* Uganda, Karamojong
Last, Murray, 115
Latin America, 20, 187f, 198f, 203, 205
law, 202. *See also* state, sovereignty, *homo sacer*
　and order, 70f, 84, 88, 90, 92n7, 196, 201, 204
　and sovereignty, 60f, 192, 213, 299
　and transparency, 187
　and violence, 61, 187f, 201, 205, 206n1
　antiterrorist l. *See* war against terror
　international and national l., 44, 84, 205, 298
　martial l., 64
　Roman l., 191
'Law of Return', 300. *See also* Israel
Lazar, Sian, 17
Lebanon, 259n9, 298, 301. *See also* Israel, Palestine
Ledeneva, Alena, 57,
Legrand, Françoise, 222
Legrand, Jean-Claude, 234n11, 235n27
Leopold, Robert Selig, 271
Lever, Evelyne, 261n48
Leviathan, 6, 22n7. *See also* Hobbes, Thomas
Lewin, C., 195
Lewis, I.M., 145
Liauzu, Claude, 259n5

liberal
　democratization, 43, 130f, 174, 183n3, 187f, 191, 200, 204f, 206nn2–3, 225, 270
　peace, 187f, 202, 205
Liberia, 21, 265–287
　Americo-Liberians in L., 276, 278, 286n16, 286n23, 286n25
　and empire, 279–285
　civil war in L., 268–271
　colonization of L., 267f, 276–278
　contested sovereignty of state in L., 265, 281, 284, 285n4, 286n17
　exotification of violence in L., 272
　hinterland in L., 271, 276f, 281
　state-run violence in L., 271–276
Liberian Frontier Forces (LFF), 273, 277–279, 286n19
Liberian Peace Council (LPC), 269
Liberians United For Reconciliation and Democracy (LURD), 269f
Libya, 268
Liebenow, J. Gus, 270f, 278, 286n17, 286n23, 286n25
Lieberman, Avigdor, 299f
life-world, 117, 122n26
Lilley, Sasha, 92n2
Little, Kenneth, 274
Litvin, Daniel, 92n2
Livingstone, G., 198, 200, 202
Löfving, Staffan, 11, 20, 191, 193, 205
López Restrepo, A., 200
Lorcin, Patricia, 259n14
Lord, K.M., 189
Lord's Resistance Army/Movement (LRA/M), 110, 122n22, 126–129, 133, 135f, 141
Lotringer, Sylvére, 83, 89f, 92n5
Lourenço, Vitor, 236n34
Loveman, B., 196
Lundin, Irãe, 236n34
Lutz, Catherine, 31
Luzhkov, Yuri, 70, 73. *See also* Russia
Lyotard, Jean-François, 76

Macamo, Elísio S., 214
Machel, Samora, 215, 234n6
Machiavelli, Niccolò, 5
Mack, B., 84, 88, 89

Maclellan, Nic, 23n16
Malawi, 18
Mali, 149, 286n18
Malkki, Liisa, 117f, 235n17
Mamdani, Mahmood, 101–104, 116, 121nn9–10, 121nn12–14, 121n16, 168, 212, 277, 281
Mandel, Robert, 14
Martin, Terry, 78n11
Marx, Karl, 4, 60, 206n2
Marxist-Leninism, 215, 231
Maskhadov, Ashlan, 68, 71. *See also* Russia and war with/in Chechnya
Massing, Andreas, 271, 273, 277f, 286n20
Matheniko, 144f, 148, 150, 152. *See also* Karamojong, Uganda
Mateus, Dalila, 234n5
Mayi Mayi rebels, 110, 113, 121n16
Mazula, Brazão, 234n13
Mbembe, Achille, 22n6, 228, 266, 286n26
McCauley, Clark, 221
McFaul, Michael, 69f, 75
Meacher, M., 83
Médicins sans Frontières (MSF), 98, 107f
Meillassoux, Claude, 234n11
Mekhaled, Boucif, 260n17
Melman, Seymore, 49n1
memory. *See also* mythico-histories
 and violence/war, 48, 136, 195f, 224
 collective m., 179
 historical m., 63f
Merle, Renae, 23n16
Messali, Hadj, 244, 249f. *See also* Messalists
Messalists, 244, 249f, 256–258, 260n16
Meynier, Gilbert, 244, 250, 253f
Middle East, 31, 40, 44, 47, 69, 241, 256
 Israel in the M. E., 295f
Migdal Oz, 294
migration
 and cattle raiding, 146
 and corporate state, 17
 and pastoralism, 147, 149, 156
militarism, 31, 39. *See also* paramilitarism

military-industrial complex (U.S.), 33–49. *See also* state relations to the military/army
Mobutu, Sese Seko, 101, 103f, 120n1, 121n16
MONUC, 113, 114
Moore, David, 224
Moran, Mary, 225, 271f, 279f, 283, 286n10
Morozzo della Rocca, Roberto, 234n12
Morris, Benny, 295
Mouvement Revolutionnaire National pour le Dévelopement et la Démocratie (MRND), 121n15, 174ff, 179f, 183nn3–4, 184n8
movement
 and roadblocks, 135–137, 139f, 184n8, 296
 pastoralist m., 144–148
Movement for the Survival of the Ogoni Peoples (MOSOP), 93n11. *See also* Nigeria
Mozambique, 210–240. *See also* FRELIMO, RENAMO
 civil war in M., 212–225
 death squads in M., 210ff, 227f, 230, 232f, 233n2. *See also* death squads
 postcolonial state in M., 212–215, 226f
 sorcery in M., 226–232
 state and sovereignty in M., 211
 state and violence in M., 211, 216
 state and war machine in M., 221–225
 war against the colonial state in M., 230
mujāhidūn, 246, 252, 254. *See also* Algeria
Mukirania, Isaya, 100
Mukulu, Jamil, 104
Mukungwa, 176f
Multinational corporations. *See* corporate state, corporate control, neoliberalism
Mumbere, Charles Wesley, 100, 108
murder. *See* extra-judicial killings, violence
Murphy, William, 270
musābilūn, 246, 261n49

Museveni, Yoweri, 101f, 105f, 110, 114–116, 124–126, 129–132, 151
mythico-histories, 117f. *See also* Malkki, Liisa

Nahimana, Ferdnand, 168
naked life. *See* bare life
n'anga, 228, 235n21
Nangolo, Mvula ya, 122n24
narrative
    and the symbolic, 166f
    anticolonial n., 54. *See also anticolonialism*
    approach, 194f
    conspiracy n., 54, 56. *See also* conspiracy
    of transformation, 39
    of violence, 220. *See also* violence
narration, 56, 220
Nash, June, 14, 20, 29, 34, 36f, 49n1
National Army for the Liberation of Uganda (NALU), 108, 113, 119
National Islamic Front (Sudan), 104
National Patriotic Front of Liberia (NPFL), 268f, 279–281
National Resistance Movement/Army (NRA/M) (Uganda), 102f, 124, 126, 131
NATO, 56, 69
Nazism, 5, 303n11
Nazpary, Joma, 56–58, 61, 76f, 78n6, 78n11. *See also* Rigi, Jakob
Ndadaye, Melchior, 177–179, 184n7
Ndekezi, Bonaparte, 176
Negri, Antonio, 12, 59, 61, 129, 214, 233n3, 265–267, 282, 284, 285n2, 285n3. *See also* Hardt, Michael, empire
neoliberalism
    and bare/naked life, 61. *See also* naked life
    and bureaucracy, 15
    and commodification, 61, 77
    and corporate influence, 15
    and New Public Management, 15
    and reforms in Russia, 69f. *See also* Russia
    and transparency, 206n2
    and violence, 188, 201. *See also* Guatemala, Colombia
    and war, 128. *See also* Uganda
    global dominance of n., 214
    outsourcing of military recruitment/warfare as part of n., 35, 42. *See also* privatization
    poverty created by n., 61, 77
    statehood under n., 4, 18, 59, 213
network
    and empire. *See* empire
    and plunder, 58f, 62, 70. *See also* chaotic mode of domination
    and power over life and death, 75f
    and war, 67f, 71f, 75
    and war machine. *See* state and war machine
    economic n., 58–60, 63, 66, 83, 87, 198, 278
    elite n., 62
    of state officials, 63, 70
    paramilitary n., 199, 205f
    political n., 58–60, 62, 87, 224, 278
    social n., 144, 283
    urban terrorist n., 251, 253, 261n39. *See also* guerrilla, paramilitarism
network-based state, 75
Newcomer, P.J., 145
Newitt, Malyn, 230
Newman, Katherine S., 39
Ngoga, Pascal, 130
Niger Delta, 84, 86, 89, 92n6, 93nn11–12
Nigeria
    Agip and warfare in N., 93n12
    authoritarian rule in and multinational oil companies in N., 93n9, 93n11
    Chevron and violence/warfare in N., 88f, 90, 93n11
    Odi massacre in N., 93n12
    killing of the Twon Brass Three in N., 93n12
    oil-producing communities in N., 88–92
    oil wars in N., 85f, 89
    state's sacrificial killings in N., 88f
    Shell and violence/warfare in N., 88–90, 93n11
Nilotes, 131, 146f

Nimba County, 268, 270, 273, 279f, 284, 287n27
Nixon, Richard, 37
Nkayarwa, George, 122n20
Nonini, Donald, 31, 233n3
Nordstrom, Carolyn, 84, 137, 139, 223, 235n22
Norwegian Initiative on Small Arms Transfers (NISAT), 143
nostalgia, 55, 210
Ntalindwa, Raymond, 97
Ntoroko County, 99, 114
Nuer, 145, 153. *See also* Uganda, Karamojong, Sudan
Nwafor, Azinna, 234n4
Nyabarongo River, 176f
Nyabugogo River, 170
Nyamnjoh, Francis, 235n29
Nyiginya, 168, 170f
Nyamutswa, 120n5
Nyangatom, 146. *See also* Uganda, Karamojong, Sudan
Nzongola–Ntalaja, Georges, 120n1

Obama, Barack, 29f, 49
Obote, Milton, 121n8, 121n10, 124, 131, 134
Odi, Bayelsa state, 93n12. *See also* Nigeria
OECD anti-bribery convention, the, 189
Ogoniland, 89, 93n11. *See also* Movement for the Survival of the Ogoni Peoples (MOSOP)
oil. *See* Nigeria, sovereignty, Sudan
Okello, Tito, 124, 131
Okonta, I., 88f
Okuku, Juma, 132
Oldenbourg, Zoé, 86
Oloka-Onyango, J., 132
Olorode, 89, 93n11
Omara-Otunnu, Amii, 128, 131
Ong, Aihwa, 22n11
ontological uncertainty, 197, 203
ontology
  and ideology, 179
  and violence, 118f
  and power, 182f
  individualistic, 163, 181

Opello, Walter, 234n5
Organization of the American States (OAS), 198
Osiraq, 301
Oslo Accords, 292f, 297, 299
Osterhammel, Jürgen, 259n12
Ostheimer, Andrea, 234n13
Ottemoeller, Dan, 131
Owen, Roger, 259n13

Palestine, 292–303
  'Anti-Terrorist Fence' and P., 293f
  and loss of lands to Israel, 293f, 298ff
  as prison, 302n8
  bypass roads and trapping of people in P., 294
  cantons in P., 297
  emigration from P., 292, 295
  enclavement of communities in P., 295–297, 302
  encystation of communities in P., 295–297
  expulsion from P., 295
  Intifada in P., 13f, 294, 298
  loss of aquifiers to Israel in P., 296f
  settlements in P., 293, 296–298, 300
  state formation in P., 297
panda gari, 134–135, 140. *See also* Uganda
Pappe, Ilan, 302n8
paramilitarism, 11, 20f, 131, 187–192, 194, 196–203, 205f, 206n2, 207n5, 273. *See also* militarism, warfare
pastoralism, 144, 147f
  and arms, 143–158
  and raiding, 152–154, 156
  and state, 121n12, 148–152
Patrullas de Autodefensa Civil (PAC). *See* Guatemala, civil patrols in
Pax Americana, 83
peace. *See also* liberal p.
  activists, 67
  alternatives, 35–38
  and business, 86f
  and state, 4
  boundaries between p. and war, 49, 88, 93n9, 129, 187, 192, 211, 213, 233n3, 274

expectations of p., 203–205
utopian ideas of p., 5
peacekeeping. *See relevant missions*
  among pastoralists, 154f
Peacock, S.C., 192
Peluso, N.L., 92nn5–6
Pereira, A.W., 190
Perrot, Claude-Hélène, 235n29
Pervillé, Guy, 251, 253, 258n2, 259n5, 260n25, 261n36, 261n39
Pian, 148. *See also* Karamojong, Uganda
Pitcher, M. Anne, 214, 225
Pittsfield, Massachusetts, 29, 31–35, 38f
Planche, Jean-Louis, 250
Pokot, 148, 154. *See also* Kenya, Uganda, Karamojong
Polanyi, Karl, 5
policing
  and death squads, 210ff, 227f, 233n2. *See also* death squads, Mozambique
  and extortion/corruption, 80n23, 232
  and organized crime, 59, 72
  and paramilitarism, 202
  and pastoralism, 149
  and sovereignty, 211
  and violence, 72f, 93n9
  community p., 229f, 236n31
  French colonial p. in Algeria, 258n4
  Israeli border p., 298. *See also* Israel, state and border
  of the corporate state, 18f
political violence. *See* violence political
Politkovskaya, Anna, 72
Poole, D., 192
Poro, 274–276, 286n9, 286n13. *See also* war and secret societies
Porterfield, Todd, 259n14
postcolonial condition. *See also* state
  and necropolitics, 228
  and violence, 231–232
post-cold war era, 83, 128, 281. *See also* Cold war
Poulantzas, Nicos, 57, 59
power. *See also* state, sovereignty, corporate state
  and disposable people, 191–197. *See also* bare life, *homo sacer*
  and ideology, 169
  and individualism, 163f
  and knowledge, 164
  and transparency, 189–191
  and paramilitarism, 198. *See also* paramilitarism
  and violence, 84–87, 89, 91, 92n7. *See also* violence
  as a commodity, 60
  as all-encompassing, 163
  authoritarian p., 205
  bio-power, 61, 266–268, 279–285. *See also* bio-politics
  consensual p., 88–91
  conspiracy about p., 56f. *See also* conspiracy
  corporate p., 199. *See also* corporate state, corporate control
  crisis of p., 10, 12
  economic p., 14, 16, 83
  excess of p., 22n6
  imperial p., 31, 188, 302
  killing as expression of p., 119, 229. *See also* sovereignty
  military p., 83
  parallel p., 192
  practices of p., 212
  royal p., 170
  sovereign p., 6, 18, 60, 75f, 128, 130, 140, 213, 221, 299
  state p., 1–19, 57, 90, 125, 163, 181ff, 188, 199–203, 212
  transmuting p., 197
power-staging violence. *See* violence
Pratt, D.J., 149, 157
Priest, D., 189
privatization. *See also* neoliberalism, corporate state, corporate control
  and lack of political oversight, 48f
  as part of neoliberalism, 128, 189
  of military contracts, 41. *See also* military-industrial complex, state relations to the military/army
  of services, 29, 40
  of Iraqi state, 33, 44f, 48. *See also* Iraq
  of Mozambican state, 214. *See also* Mozambique

of Russian state, 59f. *See also* Russia
of war, 31, 43. *See also* war
Privatized Military Firms (PMFs), 23n16
profete, 228
Prunier, Gérard, 10, 115, 121n11, 121nn14–15, 129
Putin, Vladimir, 69–71, 75, 77n3, 79n18, 79n20

Qalqilyah, 295f
Quiwonkpa, Thomas, 278f, 287n26

Radcliffe-Brown, A.R., 163
Raduyev, Salman, 67f, 79n16. *See also* Russia and war with/in Chechnya
Rainey, Timothy A., 286n19
Ranger, Terence, 234n9
Raulff, Ulrich, 303n11
Reagan, Ronald, 29, 35f, 39
real, the, 9, 166f, 195, 212f, 228. *See also* ontology, imaginary, symbolism
reciprocity
  social r., 204f
  state and citizen r., 283. *See also* social contract
'refugee, the', 192
refugees, 109, 120n3, 145 *See also* camp
  and war, 13, 130
  Burundian r., 117f
  Chechen r., 55, 66
  Congolose r., 103, 106
  Liberian, 269
  Palestinian, 298, 301
  Rwandan r., 101–103, 116
régulos, 216, 220, 224f, 231
Reinhart, T., 302n2
religion
  and war, 85
Reno, William, 62f, 269, 281
Resistência Nacional de Moçambique (RENAMO), 212f, 215–222, 224–227, 229, 231, 234n12, 234nn15–16, 235n19, 235n27, 236n32. *See also* Mozambique
reterritorialization, 10–12, 21, 220f. *See also* state and territory
revolution, 76, 90
  American r., 33
  Central American r., 39
  Cuban r., 199
  English r., 6
  French r., 76, 243
  moments in r., 91, 270
  Rwandan r., 103, 167
Revolutionary Armed Forces of Colombia (FARC), 200
revolutionary movements, 184n4, 193, 195, 230
Reyna, Steve, 127, 129
Reyntjens, Felip, 173
rhizome, 3, 11–14, 19, 22n3, 223, 234n8, 285n2. *See also* state and war machine
Rhodesia, 215f, 219, 222, 225, 230. *See also* Zimbabwe
Richani, N., 200f
Richards, Paul, 267, 284
Rift Valley, 145f, 153f
Rigi, Jakob, 17f, 20, 55, 57, 78n6
ritual, 169–171, 177f
  destroyed by war, 220
  of war, 286n12
  killing in Rwanda, 118f
  political r., 166
  state r., 165, 182
  territorial r., 297
  violence in r., 274
Robbins, P., 84
Roesch, Otto, 234n10
Roitman, Janet, 277
Romero, Mauricio, 191, 198–202, 204f
Ron, J., 207n5
Rousseau, Jean-Jacques, 18
Rönson, Bent, 108, 112
Ruganzu Ndori, 167f
rumor, 97f, 151, 193, 195, 203, 218
Rumsfeld, Donald H., 23n17, 30, 40f, 43, 45, 189f
Russia. *See also* conspiracy, spectacle, chaotic mode of domination
  and occupation of Daghistan, 54, 69–71
  and war with/in Chechnya, 53–81
  bombings in R., 65, 70–72
  commodification of war in R., 67–68
  imperial nationalism in R., 54f, 72–75, 77

nostalgia for Soviet era in R., 55
post-Soviet politics of spectacle, 62, 65–71, 75–77, 79n19, 81n31
Rwanda. *See also* blocked beings, movement
  blocked beings in R., 118, 170, 173, 179, 182f. *See also* movement
  closed circuit in R., 171
  ethnogenic process in R., 168f. *See also* ethnicity
  genocide in R., 101, 103, 115, 172, 183, 184n6, 184n8, 267
  imaginary and violence in R., 169–181
  king's body as a conduit in R., 170, 179, 181f
  precolonial state in R., 167–172
  significance of rivers in R., 176f
Rwanda Patriotic Front (RPF), 102f, 172f, 176–179, 184n6. *See also* Rwanda
Rwenzori mountains, 97ff, 106, 120n4
Rwenzururu rebellion, 100f, 104, 108, 121n16

Saadi, Yacef, 261n41
sacred kingship. *See* kingship
sacrifice. *See also* violence and sacrifice, *homo sacer*
  and cattle raiding in Uganda, 156
  and kingship in Rwanda, 170–172, 174, 176f, 181–183, 183n1
  and warfare, 274, 286n12
  for national good in Guatemala and Colombia, 203–205
Sahlins, Marshall, 5, 140, 145, 164f, 169
Said, Edward, 117
Salafi Foundation, 104
sanctuary space, 205
Sande, 274f. *See also* Poro
Sanders, Todd, 56, 235n29, 236n34
Sassen, Saskia, 22n11
Saul, John, 234n4
Sawyer, Amos, 275
Sayer, Derek, 60
Schafer, Jessica, 221
Scahill, Jeremy, 18, 23n16, 30
Schirmer, J., 191, 196f, 204

Schmidt, Bettina, 221
Schrader, Charles R., 261n42
Schreier, Fred, 18, 23n16
Schröder, Günter, 271–274, 286n25
Schröder, Ingo, 221
Schwab, George, 271–273, 286n12
Scott, James C., 8, 21n2, 56
Seaton, Jean, 267
secret societies. *See* war and s. s.
Seibel, Dieter, 271–274
Seleti, Yonah, 233n2
Semliki, 106, 120n4
September 11, 2001, 30, 45, 71, 81n31, 117, 127. *See also* War against terror
Sharon, Ariel, 76, 294–298, 302n2
Shavit, Ari, 295
Shaw, Rosalind, 267, 284
Shell Corp., 89, 93n11
Shivji, Issa, 128
Shlaim, Avi, 295, 303n13
Shlapentokh, Vladmir, 62, 69
Sidaway, James, 215
Sieder, R., 192
Siegmann, William, 274
Sierra Leone, 268, 284
  and war in Liberia, 269f, 274, 277
  state in S. L., 283
Simons, Anna, 221
Singer, P.W., 23n16
Sklair, L., 84
Sluka, Jeffrey, 129, 197, 211
Smith, R.J., 189
Sobania, N., 145, 148
social contract, 7, 16, 18, 283. *See also* Hobbes, corporate state
social navigation, 282
social networks. *See* networks
Socialist
  state formation in Mozambique, 216, 231. *See also* Mozambique
  states in Europe in 20th Century, 4f. *See also* state
Sollenberg, Margreta, 136
Somalia, 129, 140
Sontag, Susan, 189f
Sopa, António, 234n6
South Africa
  apartheid period of, 10

326 | Index

as destabilising Southern Africa, 216, 222f
weapons from S. A., 153
sovereign
   bodies, 281, 287n28
   figure/body of the s., 167, 181f, 211, 228. *See also* Rwanda and king's body
sovereignty
   and borders/frontiers, 297f
   and donor dependency, 127f, 213f, 226
   and exception, 292, 298f
   and state power, 190–192, 220f, 224, 297–299, 301
   and territory, 59f
   and violence, 232, 233n3
   assertion of s. through performance, 211–213, 227f. *See also* sovereignty and violence
   chaotic form of s., 18, 59–62, 76
   contested s., 265, 281, 284
   ethnic formations of s., 84f, 87, 89, 91
   global formations of s., 85, 98, 226
   global oil s., 83, 84, 87–89
   imperial s., 301f
   internal and external s., 5f, 130, 140
   in Iraq, 30, 46
   multiple s., 188, 211f, 226, 230, 232f
   new forms of s., 1, 128, 229
   wild s., 18, 128
sovereignties, 20, 83, 85, 89, 91, 188, 226, 230
Soyinka, Wole, 134
space
   and body, 267
   and violence, 267
   global sociopolitical organization of s., 129
   living s. and warfare, 11
   sanctuary s., 205
   socioeconomic s., 277
   of death, 277
   of state interest, 3. *See also* state and space, empire
Spanish Civil War, 86
Spencer, P., 144f
spectacle, 57. *See also* conspiracy

society of s., 61–62. *See also* Debord, Guy
Sri Lanka
   and state violence, 10
   civil war in S. L., 9
state. *See also* sovereignty, corporate state, corporate control, neoliberalism
   accountability, 15, 49, 128, 187, 189–191, 206n2, 229. *See also* transparency
   African postcolonial s., 127–130
   and bio-power, 279–285. *See also* empire and bio-power, bio-politics
   and borders, 297–300
   and counter-state building, 241–258
   and production of society, 7
   and space, 3, 8, 11, 215, 223f, 234n8. *See also* space
   and subjectivities, 3, 21n2, 181
   and territory/territorialization, 3, 9–15, 21, 31, 54, 58, 62–64, 69, 73, 78n9, 78n11, 80nn26–27, 112, 127, 136, 168, 170f, 191f, 197–199, 215, 218, 220f, 223f, 226, 232, 234n8, 242f, 259nn9–10, 262n55, 267, 277, 283, 286n18, 294–302, 303, 303n10. *See also* deterritorialization, reterritorialization, space
   and violence. *See* violence
   and war machine, 3f, 11f, 14, 19, 22nn3–4, 91, 212f, 221–227, 230, 235n26, 235n32
   bifurcated s., 277. *See also* Mamdani, Mahmood
   colonial s. *See* colonial state/administration, colonialism
   erosion of s., 87, 128
   Fascist s., 2, 5, 57, 215
   shadow s., 281
   migration and confrontation with s., 148, 157
   of exception, 7, 57, 61, 76, 130
   of nature, 68, 84, 163
   precolonial s., 168–172, 272
   predatory s., 59f, 284

postcolonial s., 14, 84, 90, 211–214, 127–130. *See also* postcolonial condition
s. sovereignty. *See* sovereignty
s. power, 1–19
s. relations to the military/army, 4, 11, 14, 18, 20, 23n17, 29–33, 40. *See also* military-industrial complex
weak s., 265, 281
state bureaucracy
and war/conflict, 8–10, 21n2, 22n10
Stebbings, E.P., 149
Stein, Rebecca L., 302n2
Stepputat, Finn, 22n7, 133, 212f, 266, 281, 287n28
Stern, Nicholas, 225
Stiglitz, Joseph, 40, 92n5
Stora, Benjamin, 258n2, 260n20
Storaas, Frode, 20, 144, 150
Strange, Susan, 15, 22n11, 198, 233n3
Strathern, Marilyn, 15
stratification
and state, 9
social s., 168
Structural Adjustment Programs, 214, 128. *See also* International Monetary Fund, World Bank
subjectivities
and power, 164
and state, 3, 21n2, 181
subjects
and citizens, 212. *See also* Mamdani, Mahmood
and power, 164
and state, 62, 99
legal s., 303n11
postcolonial s., 232
violence as disciplining s., 4f, 267f, 275f, 277, 283
Sudan, 105, 144, 146, 149f
and war in Uganda, 125–127, 135–137, 151
oil resources in and state violence, 84, 86, 89, 92n6, 93n9, 93n12
Sudan People's Liberation Movement/Army (SPLM/A), 126, 135
Sudrez-Orozco, M., 93n10
summary executions. *See* extra-judicial killings, death squads, violence

Swirski, Shlomo, 303n12
symbolism
and violence, 254, 268, 286n11. *See also* violence
and state, 276, 279. *See also* state
body-symbolism, 118, 179. *See also* Rwanda
iconic s., 166f, 172, 183. *See also* Rwanda
Syria, 259n9, 298

Tabliqs, 104
Tanzania, 21n2, 167
refugees from Rwanda genocide in, 103, 117f
Taussig, Michael, 22n6, 201, 207n6, 277
Taylor, Charles, 268–270, 285n25
Taylor, Christopher, 10, 20, 118, 121nn14–15, 170f, 179, 267
Teguia, Mohammed, 259n5, 261n48
Tepes, 147, 150, 156, 158. *See also* Uganda, Karamojong
Tequ'a, 294
territorialisation. *See* state and territory
territory. *See* state and territory
terror, 20, 105, 107, 118, 217, 251, 255, 268, 270. *See also* violence, war, torture, war against t.
regimes of t., 84, 93n10
state t., 10f, 189, 205, 211, 281
terrorism, 67f, 117, 203
discourse and politics of t., 31, 56, 71, 127, 129, 140, 192, 201, 250, 293–295, 297. *See also* war against terror
wars to counter t., 31. *See also* war against terror
terrorizing violence. *See* violence
Thénault, Sylvie, 258n4
Tilly, Charles, 256, 258, 262n56
Tonkin, Elizabeth, 271, 273, 286n22, 286n24
Toposa, 146, 149. *See also* Sudan, Uganda, Karamojong
Toro, 99f, 120n2
Torture, 45, 47, 79n21, 179, 189, 241, 248, 252, 258n4m 261n46. *See also* Abu Ghraib, Guantánamo

transparency, 187, 189f, 206nn1–3. *See also* state accountability
and authoritarianism, 189
and state, 76, 192
and violence, 188, 191, 198, 200, 205
as global phenomenon, 15, 189, 197
Transparency International, 189
Trouillot, M-R., 163
Tuck, T., 84
Tulkarm, 294–296, 302n5
Turkana, 145–147, 149–155. *See also* Kenya, Uganda
Turner, Terence, 128
Turton D., 148
Tutsi Hutu relations. *See* Hutu Tutsi relations
Twa, 168f, 179

ubuhake, 175, 184n5
uburetwa, 168
umutabazi, 170f, 172–181
Uganda
amnesty bill in U., 129, 132
colonial politics in U., 147–149
donor dependency in U., 127f
humanitarian profiteering in U., 137–139
mass arrests (*panda gari*) in U., 134–135, 140
no-party Movement system in U., 125, 130f
Operation Iron Fist in U., 127
panda gari, 134–135, 140
poaching in U., 138
postcolonial state in U., 124f, 149–152
roadblock harassments in U., 135–137, 139f
Rwandans in U., 101–103
state policy in U., 148–152
uprising in 1919 in U., 99
Uganda People's Congress (UPC), 100f, 121n10
Uganda People's Defence Force (UPDF), 97, 104–106, 109, 111–113, 122n21
United Liberation Movement of Liberia (ULIMO, ULIMO-J, ULIMO-K), 268–270

United States of America (USA). *See also* war against terror, Iraq, empire, corporate state
crisis of capital in U., 29–50
economy and warfare by U., 39–46
fusion of corporate, Pentagon and government structures in U., 31f
industrial history in U., 39ff
repatriated slaves to Liberia in U., 276, 286n16
war in Iraq by U., 5, 46ff
Uribe, M.V., 198, 202
Utas, Mats, 21, 267, 269f, 282, 285n5, 285n8, 286n11

Vaïsse, M., 260n23, 261n39
Vansina, Jan, 167f, 183n1
Venâncio, Moisés, 235n28
Verschuur, Christine, 234n11
Vidal-Naquet, Pierre, 258n4
Vieira, C., 203
Vietnam War, 31, 47f
and general draft, 36
and growth of U.S. military-industrial complex, 30, 36. *See also* military-industrial complex
and war in Iraq, 48f
and militarization of U.S. society, 31
U.S. veterans of war in, 30, 37f, 40, 47f
Vigh, Henrik, 282
Vines, Alex, 222, 234n10
Violence. *See also* war, warfare
and body, 118f, 154, 166f, 176–182, 222f, 227f, 232, 235n25, 247, 267, 278
and liberation struggles, 87f, 91, 102, 116f, 119, 216, 245ff. *See also* Fanon, Frantz
and memory. *See* memory and violence/war
and migration, 2
and sacrifice, 85ff, 260n29. *See also* sacrifice
and state, 165–167
and state sovereignty, 17
as erasing culture, 217–221
as pure, 8, 85, 89, 91

of burning of victims, 105f, 108, 116–119
cohesive v., 252–253
disciplinary v., 247–248
environmental v., 92n6
intimidating v., 245–247
monopolizing v., 249f
polarizing v., 248f
political v., 83ff, 86–89, 91, 92n6, 135, 139, 197
power-staging v., 253f
spatializing v., 233n3. *See also* Joxe, Alain, empire
symbolic v., 7–9
terrorizing v., 250–252
victim-killer structure of v., 85, 87f, 91. *See also* Girard, René
Virilio, Paul, 22n14, 83, 89f, 92n5
Volkov, Vadim, 57, 60, 66

Wacquant, Loïc, 206n1
Wagaw, Teshome, 303n12
Wagner, Roy, 166
Wallensteen, Peter, 136
Wallerstein, Immanuel, 129
War. *See also* military-industrial complex, violence, warfare
and memory. *See* memory and violence/war
and authoritarian political systems, 84
and secret societies, 274f, 279f. *See also* Poro
and women, 32, 35f, 43, 66, 79n21, 103f, 107, 116, 134, 136, 148f, 152, 178, 192f, 217, 245, 268, 281. *See also* abduction, women
and youth, 86, 270, 273, 276, 279f, 285n8
civil w. *See* war, internal
imperial/imperialist w., 30f, 47, 53
internal w., 9, 18f, 21, 78n9, 80n27, 84–86, 109, 111, 124–141, 145, 150, 212–228, 231f, 233n3, 235n22, 242, 253, 255, 258, 265, 267–272, 274, 276, 279, 281f, 285n8
privatization of w., 30f. *See also* Privatized Military Firms
(PMFs), privatization, state relations to the military/army
regional w. complex, 126, 135f, 268–270, 277
scorched earth tactics in w., 86, 105, 108, 118, 193, 218, 219
War against terror, 8, 13f, 19, 29–33, 127, 129, 140, 188–190. *See also* terrorism
war machine. *See* state and war machine
War of 1812, 33
warfare, 211, 279. *See also* army, war, violence
and creation of European nation-states, 256
and death event, 117
and magic, 224, 232, 273, 279
and migration, 148, 282, 292, 295. *See also* migration, violence and m.
and ritual, 172
and state-run violence, 271–276
and U.S. domestic political economy, 31, 39f, 46, 49. *See also* military-industrial complex
conventional w., 197, 246
counterinsurgency w., 35, 203, 218, 224, 246f, 253, 276f
digital w., 14. *See also* cyberspace
'ethnic w.', 266f
guerrilla w., 20f, 86–89, 103, 125f, 130, 192–201, 212, 214–225, 230, 234n8, 236n32, 241–262. *See also* paramilitarism
high-technology w., 41, 46
proxy w., 136
regulation of w., 189f, 247f, 251, 255. *See also* Geneva Convention, the
'traditional w.', 151, 172, 212–214, 220f, 224f, 236n32, 267, 272, 280, 285n4, 286n10
warriors, 280f, 286n10
and gender, 280
traditional/modern. *See* warfare
warlords, 54, 67f, 70f, 207n6, 217, 269, 273, 279, 281f
Warschawski, Michel, 303n10
Watts, Michael, 92nn5–6
Weah, George, 284f

weapons. *See* arms
Weber, Max, 59, 202, 285n1
Weil, D., 206n3
Weiner, Jessica, 300
Weingrod, Alex, 303n12
Weizman, Eyal, 11, 297
Werbner, Richard, 223
West Bank, 292–299, 302n8
West, Harry, 56, 235nn29–30
Westermann, Diedrich, 272f
Wieviorka, Michel, 139
Wild sovereignty. *See* sovereignty
Williams, Andrew Paul, 14
Wilson, Andrew, 57
Wilson, Henry, 277, 286n20
Wilson, Ken, 234n14, 234n16
Wilson, Thomas M., 302n6
Wiwa, Ken Saro, 88f, 93n11
Wolf, Eric, 2
Wolpe, Harold, 17
Wood, Ellen M., 62
women, 170f, 215. *See also* war and women
World Bank, 40, 92n5, 128, 149, 189, 211, 214. *See also* International Monetary Fund

World Trade Organization (WTO), 19, 128
World War I, 30, 33
World War II, 30, 34, 36
   American workforce in defense industries during WWII, 40
Wyschogrod, Edith, 117, 122n6

Yeld, Rachel, 121nn10–11
Yeltsin, Boris, 55, 58f, 63–66, 70, 75, 77n3, 78n7, 79n16
Yeoman, Guy, 120n4
Young, Crawford, 128
Young, E., 234n15
Young, Tom, 226
youth. *See* war and youth

Zetterström, Kjell, 274
Zimbabwe, 150
   liberation war, 216, 222, 235n9
   movement across Z. border with Mozambique to, 217, 222, 224f
   soldiers from Z. in Mozambique, 219, 225
Žižek, Slavoj, 190, 192
Zubaida, Sami, 259n13, 260n15